The
Psychology
of Groups

Edited by Craig D. Parks
and Giorgio A. Tasca

The Psychology of Groups

AMERICAN PSYCHOLOGICAL ASSOCIATION
PUBLISHING

Published by
American Psychological Association
750 First Street, NE
Washington, DC 20002
https://www.apa.org

Order Department
https://www.apa.org/pubs/books
order@apa.org

In the U.K., Europe, Africa, and the Middle East, copies may be ordered from Eurospan
https://www.eurospanbookstore.com/apa
info@eurospangroup.com

Typeset in Meridien and Ortodoxa by Circle Graphics, Inc., Reisterstown, MD

Printer: Sheridan Books, Chelsea, MI
Cover Designer: Gwen J. Grafft, Minneapolis, MN

Library of Congress Cataloging-in-Publication Data

Names: Parks, Craig D., editor. | Tasca, Giorgio A., editor.
Title: The psychology of groups : the intersection of social psychology and
  psychotherapy research / edited by Craig D. Parks and Giorgio A. Tasca.
Description: Washington : American Psychological Association, 2021. |
  Includes bibliographical references and index.
Identifiers: LCCN 2020005886 (print) | LCCN 2020005887 (ebook) |
  ISBN 9781433831805 (paperback) | ISBN 9781433831898 (ebook)
Subjects: LCSH: Social groups. | Social groups–Psychological aspects. |
  Social psychology–Research. | Psychotherapy—Research.
Classification: LCC HM711 .P79 2020 (print) | LCC HM711 (ebook) |
  DDC 305—dc23
LC record available at https://lccn.loc.gov/2020005886
LC ebook record available at https://lccn.loc.gov/2020005887

http://dx.doi.org/10.1037/0000201-000

Printed in the United States of America

10 9 8 7 6 5 4 3 2 1

CONTENTS

CONTRIBUTORS

Michael R. Baumann, PhD, Department of Psychology, The University of Texas at San Antonio

Joanna Cheek, MD, Department of Psychiatry, The University of British Columbia, Vancouver, Canada

Tegan Cruwys, PhD, Research School of Psychology, The Australian National University, Canberra

James C. Deller, PhD, Department of Psychology, The University of Texas at San Antonio

Donelson R. Forsyth, PhD, Jepson School of Leadership Studies, University of Richmond, Richmond, VA

Diana M. Grace, PhD, Research School of Psychology, The Australian National University, Canberra

S. Alexander Haslam, PhD, School of Psychology, The University of Queensland, St. Lucia, Australia

David Kealy, PhD, Department of Psychiatry, The University of British Columbia, Vancouver, Canada

D. Martin Kivlighan, III, PhD, Department of Psychological and Quantitative Foundations, The University of Iowa, Iowa City

Cheri L. Marmarosh, PhD, Professional Psychology Program, The George Washington University, Washington, DC

Hilary Maxwell, PhD, Operational Stress Injury Clinic, Royal Ottawa Mental Health Centre, Ottawa, Ontario, Canada

Rayna C. Narvaez, MA, Department of Psychological and Quantitative Foundations, The University of Iowa, Iowa City

John S. Ogrodniczuk, PhD, Department of Psychiatry, The University of British Columbia, Vancouver, Canada

Craig D. Parks, PhD, Department of Psychology, Washington State University

Leandra Parris, PhD, School of Education, The College of William & Mary, Williamsburg, VA

Michael J. Platow, PhD, Research School of Psychology, The Australian National University, Canberra

Stephen D. Reicher, PhD, School of Psychology and Neuroscience, The University of St. Andrews, Fife, Scotland

Kevin S. Spink, PhD, College of Kinesiology, University of Saskatchewan, Saskatoon, Canada

Amy Sproul, MSc, Professional Psychology Program, The George Washington University, Washington, DC

Giorgio A. Tasca, PhD, School of Psychology, University of Ottawa, Ottawa, Ontario, Canada

Meredith V. Tittler, MS, Department of Psychology, Iowa State University, Ames

Nathaniel G. Wade, PhD, Department of Psychology, Iowa State University, Ames

Eric D. Wesselmann, PhD, Department of Psychology, Illinois State University, Normal

Martyn Whittingham, PhD, Counseling Psychology, Whittingham Psychological Services, West Chester, OH

The Psychology of Groups

Introduction

Groups as Vehicles for Change, Growth, and Productivity

Craig D. Parks and Giorgio A. Tasca

It is indisputable that the group is the core of social existence. Other than the rare person who chooses to live off the grid and in isolation, all of us depend on collectives for almost everything. Fundamental needs like security, commerce, education, and infrastructure; psychological needs like support, well-being, self-understanding, and propriety; and social needs like collaboration, task execution, and communal thriving are satisfied by interactions with others. Philosophers have consistently recognized the central role of the group in life quality. To take just two examples: Aristotle, in his discussion of *eudaimonia*, or objective life happiness, argued that it is impossible to achieve this state without being surrounded by others toward whom one can be virtuous, helpful, and supportive, and from whom one can receive virtue, help, and support. Adam Smith in his *Theory of Moral Sentiments* (1759/2002) suggested that achievement of self-interest, as discussed in his *Wealth of Nations* (1776/2000), merely satisfies a base need, and that once it is met, the person can turn his or her attention to the higher needs (or, to use Smith's term, "noble virtues") of approval and expression of sympathy, both of which he argued are innate. To express sympathy and win approval, the person performs good works for others in the community, which strengthens the community, allowing others to pursue their needs for approval and sympathetic expression, and ultimately results in a strong, tight, and happy society. Aristotle and Smith both ultimately argued that true happiness is not possible absent positive engagement with others.

http://dx.doi.org/10.1037/0000201-001
The Psychology of Groups: The Intersection of Social Psychology and Psychotherapy Research,
C. D. Parks and G. A. Tasca (Editors)

The group, then, can be a vehicle for personal flourishing. Indeed, Aristotle, Smith, and a host of other philosophers argued that the group is required for one to flourish. Generosity is a useless trait if there is no one to be generous toward. How to use groups to promote flourishing is a topic of considerable interest within psychology. Indeed, it is one of the oldest topics in the discipline with research stretching back to the late 19th and early 20th centuries (e.g., Triplett's, 1898, studies of physical performance alone versus in the presence of other actors; Pratt's, 1907, use of patient groups to provide support to tuberculosis sufferers). Researchers study groups as facilitators of workplace productivity, enhancers of health and mental health treatment, and promoters of (positive and negative) social experiences. They try to isolate the factors that distinguish a successful group from a dysfunctional group. They examine how the group experience impacts the individual members and how group dynamics change as a result of the particular combination of individual characteristics that the members bring to the group.

Clearly, group research spans a variety of types of groups and situations. The questions that arise are: To what extent are phenomena general across groups and situations? Does a factor that impacts the efficacy of a psychotherapy group also play a role in the performance of sport teams? Can a technique that encourages diligence among members of an exercise group produce similar results within a work group? One would expect to find hundreds of studies in the literature that test such questions and regular collaboration among experts who focus on different types of groups. Unfortunately, this is not so. Although in the early years of group research, this kind of collaborative cross-disciplinary research did happen to some degree, over at least the past 50 years, group research has largely been siloed. The primary goal of this book is to promote a reversal of this trend.

DEFINITIONS

What exactly do researchers mean by *group*? At first glance, this is an unusual question, not unlike asking what is meant by *tree* or *dog*. But, just as trees and dogs have scientifically determined definitional boundaries—a true tree, for example, has a trunk that thickens each year, which means that a palm "tree" is not a tree but a monocotyledon, which is in the same family as sugar cane and wheat—so does a "group" have a specific set of features that distinguishes it from a mere collection of people who happen to occupy the same physical space. For our purposes, a *group* is a set of people who have assembled for a common reason, whose activities are somehow combined into a single output, and who engage in some form of sustained interpersonal interaction. This definition distinguishes the group from other collections of people, such as audiences, crowds, queues, and coacting individuals. For example, people who are all in the same public park on a sunny Saturday afternoon are not a group because their actions are independent and directed toward different goals; any effect of one person's behavior on another person's outcomes is likely coincidental. From this, it follows that *group members* are those individuals who have a common interest, are engaged in interactions, and are contributing to the output. Groups are often characterized by fuzzy definitional boundaries that can make it hard to determine who belongs and who does not (Lamont & Molnár, 2002), so clarifying what we consider to be a group member is crucial. Some of the groups that our authors discuss have clear boundaries—there should be no confusion over whether someone is a member of a therapy group, for example—but others do not. Should we consider someone to be a member of a volunteer group if they regularly attend meetings but do not contribute effort toward projects? What are we to make of someone who signs up for a physical rehabilitation group but rarely comes to workout sessions? Should a worker from one department who consults for another department be considered a member of that second department? How these questions are answered affect the analyses of these groups.

A similar fuzzy concept is that of *group leader.* Once again, for certain groups, the leader is easily identified, but for many other groups, including some for which a person has been formally appointed as leader, it is not so clear. Leaderless groups rarely operate as a true democracy; one or a few members typically emerge as dominant forces in the group (e.g., Waldman, Atwater, & Davidson, 2004). Furthermore, if a group has an appointed leader who is weak or unsupported, members may look to a subordinate colleague to informally manage aspects of the group's daily functioning (e.g., Wickham & Walther, 2007). In their chapter on leadership in this volume (Chapter 6), Platow, Haslam, Reicher, Grace, and Cruwys carefully walk us through what a leader is and is not, and their framework is applicable to all discussions of group leadership in this book.

GROUP PSYCHOLOGY RESEARCH VERSUS GROUP PSYCHOTHERAPY RESEARCH

In 1980, Morton Deutsch, a social psychologist who was also a licensed therapist, suggested that the enterprise of studying groups had gone in two directions: (a) a theory-driven approach mostly interested in deriving broadly applicable models to explain one cause while ignoring the contributions of other causes and the question of why the model does not work in certain situations; and (b) a problem-driven approach that sought to identify the strongest solution for one specific situation, pulling in multiple causes but without regard for trying to understand why that particular combination of causes worked or how the approach might be modified to be of use in other situations. (See Chapter 1 in this volume for a detailed review of Deutsch's argument.) Deutsch felt that experimental group researchers were largely following the first path, and group psychotherapy researchers, the second. He was not saying that psychotherapy researchers were ignoring theory or that group psychologists were uninterested in solving real-world problems; rather, his argument was that each set of researchers had coalesced around one approach to research and were only rarely engaging in the other. Group psychologists suggested that their theories might be of value for real groups but never actually tested this hypothesis. Group psychotherapists noted consistent findings across studies and commented that the consistency might indicate the existence of a general theoretical principle; however, they often did not take the time to develop those principles.

Deutsch (1980) felt that the strongest approach to understanding groups was to unite the two perspectives specifically to identify variables that are influential across many types of groups and situations, to know the limitations of those variables by identifying groups and situations in which their influence is diminished, to know how the variables combine to impact groups and why those combinations are impactful, and ultimately to be able to enter into any group situation with a solid understanding of what variables to bring to bear so as to produce maximum benefit within the group. This idea is the guiding principle behind this book. We recruited as authors experts on some aspect of experimental groups or psychotherapeutic groups and asked them to think broadly about their topic and to discuss how the major findings in their area are pertinent and important for other forms of groups. We were especially interested in identifying and revealing common themes across the two domains of experimental group psychology and of group psychotherapy. A key goal was to reveal that considerable overlap exists between group psychology and group psychotherapy research, and that collaboration across the domains is not difficult.

INTERGROUP VERSUS INTRAGROUP RESEARCH

Floating underneath Deutsch's (1980) distinction between theory-driven and problem-driven research is the distinction between *intergroup research*, which examines how groups compare with each other on various dynamics, and *intragroup research*, which focuses on how individual members impact, and are impacted by, the group environment. Although it is not difficult to find examples of both types of studies in the group psychology and group psychotherapy literatures, it has generally been the case that laboratory-based researchers have focused on intergroup dynamics and field-based researchers, on intragroup dynamics. At one level, this is not surprising. Intragroup phenomena typically develop over time and cannot be simulated in ad hoc groups that exist for a single experimental session, and intergroup analyses generally require an ability to control confounding variables to make the groups as comparable as possible. However, it is these very limitations that underscore the need for collaboration. Research that focuses only on within-group phenomena ignores the possibility that those phenomena may ultimately have little bearing on group performance, and strictly intergroup comparisons provides no insight into how group members generated their final product. The literature offers excellent examples of what can be learned when intergroup and intragroup approaches are combined—for example, the research on how group member conflict impacts the quality of group decisions (de Wit, Greer, & Jehn, 2012)—but such work is the exception rather than the rule.

RESEARCH VERSUS PRACTICE

A primary focus of Parks's historical review in Chapter 1 of how the groups field got to where it is today is the drifting apart of researchers and practitioners: why it happened, how it happened, why it persists today. Key to the review is that the separation did not always exist. Indeed, for the first few decades of inquiry into group dynamics, researchers and practitioners worked regularly together and often wore both hats. Recall that Morton Deutsch was both an academic researcher and a practicing group psychotherapist. There was widespread recognition that research on groups needed to be (in modern terms) translational, and there was no reason to believe that findings generated from study of a decision-making group would by definition be irrelevant for understanding the dynamics of a T-group, or a workplace assembly line, or an athletic team. Indeed, early writers often emphasized that their results needed to be tested on intact groups whose procedures had real consequences for its members. Practitioners in turn were hungry for tools and knowledge that would help them more effectively manage the groups that they oversaw, and organizations often asked university-based researchers to conduct research on-site. Practitioners and researchers have thus historically worked side by side toward the goal of better understanding how groups operate and how to use them.

We use the term *practitioner* in the broad sense to mean anyone who works with any type of real group on a regular basis. Thus, group psychotherapists are practitioners but so are athletic coaches, work shift supervisors, youth group counselors, and military unit officers. In this book, we focus primarily on practitioner psychotherapists, but we believe that all of the chapters are of value and potential interest to anyone who works with real groups or who hopes to someday work with such groups. Indeed, we would be pleased to receive feedback that topics discussed by our authors are applicable to groups that the authors did not mention. Our primary goal is to stimulate this kind of thinking.

ORGANIZATION OF THE BOOK

The book opens with a review by Parks (Chapter 1) of the original collaborative efforts between group psychologists and group psychotherapists, and a discussion of how and why those groups diverged over time. We then have six chapters on aspects of group psychology, reviews of relevant research findings, and discussion of how those findings can inform the practice of group psychotherapy. First, Wesselmann and Parris (Chapter 2) discuss the negative experiences of ostracism and exclusion, and propose a group trauma therapy approach to help people deal with and overcome those experiences. Next, Baumann and Deller (Chapter 3) take up the issue of group composition, in particular, how compositional variables (positively and negatively) impact group performance. They note that group composition is an understudied aspect of group psychotherapy and that such research could not only help refine aspects of the provision of therapy but would also fill critical gaps in our understanding of composition and group performance. Parks (Chapter 4) follows this discussion with a chapter on the dynamics of cooperation among group members, focusing on how cooperation is impacted by norms, group identification, morality, and individual traits, and then showing how these variables can be fruitfully used to improve participation among members of psychotherapy groups. Next, Forsyth (Chapter 5) discusses how group members are impacted (again, positively and negatively) by various forms of social influence and how these influence strategies can be used to promote success in psychotherapy groups. Platow, Haslam, Reicher, Grace, and Cruwys (Chapter 6) then present a new model of leadership and show how it can inform and expand our understanding of the therapeutic alliance between the therapist and his or her clients. The section closes with Spink (Chapter 7), who reviews research on sport and exercise groups, and demonstrates a close connection between the aims and principles underlying physical activity groups and those associated with psychotherapy groups.

The next part of the book features six chapters written by researchers of group psychotherapy who discuss key findings in their topic areas and how those findings can help us better understand the dynamics of group psychology. Tasca and Maxwell (Chapter 8) open with a review of attachment theory as a key influence on the efficacy of group psychotherapy and then connect this research to work and organizational group performance. Marmarosh and Sproul (Chapter 9) discuss at length the central role of cohesion in the success of group psychotherapy. Because cohesion is a concept that is much discussed but poorly understood in group psychology, the authors are able to draw numerous connections between the group psychotherapy research and questions of interest for group psychology researchers. Next, Kivlighan and Narvaez (Chapter 10) review the research on mutual influence in group psychotherapy under which the group and the individual produce change in each other; they then show how this research can help us better understand dynamics of long-term performance groups like military teams, work groups, and sport teams. Wade and Tittler (Chapter 11) follow with a discussion of group psychotherapy interventions to promote forgiveness and suggest that this research can inform strategies to address intergroup conflict, especially among individuals and groups with different social identities. Ogrodniczuk, Cheek, and Kealy (Chapter 12) discuss processes of development within psychotherapy groups, showing how this research can be used to better understand the evolution of intact or long-term performance and social groups. Closing out this section is Whittingham (Chapter 13) with a presentation on how the individual who is struggling with interpersonal problems undergoes positive change as a result of the group psychotherapy experience. He argues that these principles can help us understand how members of task and performance groups in which improvement is desired (e.g., sport teams, military groups) might benefit from the experience of being a group member and how the group can assist the person with such improvement.

A number of themes emerge across these chapters, including the importance of leadership; the central role of a sense of connectedness to the group and its members; the ability of a group to promote harmony; the need to study groups as dynamic entities that evolve over time and impact their members through this evolution; and the large impact of background variables like demographics, norms, and the age and stage of development of the group. Indeed, the consistency of these themes across the chapters provides excellent evidence of our thesis that the various types of groups are more similar than they are different.

Aristotle and Smith emphasized the centrality of the group for personal well-being and life quality, and we all may benefit from our membership in social and spiritual communities, sports teams, work units, and therapy groups. Our intent is for the chapters in this book to inspire the reader to begin studying the similarities across these varying group contexts, to promote synergies across areas of group, and to guide the field of group research and practice back to its roots of collaborative cross-disciplinary scholarship.

REFERENCES

Deutsch, M. (1980). Socially relevant research: Comments on "applied" versus "basic" research. In R. F. Kidd & M. J. Saks (Eds.), *Advances in applied social psychology* (Vol. 1, pp. 97–112). New York, NY: Taylor & Francis.

de Wit, F. R. C., Greer, L. L., & Jehn, K. A. (2012). The paradox of intragroup conflict: A meta-analysis. *Journal of Applied Psychology, 97*, 360–390. http://dx.doi.org/10.1037/a0024844

Lamont, M., & Molnár, V. (2002). The study of boundaries in the social sciences. *Annual Review of Sociology, 28*, 167–195. http://dx.doi.org/10.1146/annurev.soc.28.110601.141107

Pratt, J. H. (1907). The class method of treating consumption in the homes of the poor. *JAMA, 49*, 755–759.

Smith, A. (2000). *An inquiry into the nature and causes of the wealth of nations.* New York, NY: The Modern Library. (Original work published 1776)

Smith, A. (2002). *The theory of moral sentiments* (K. Haakonssen, Ed.). Cambridge, England: Cambridge University Press. (Original work published 1759)

Triplett, N. E. (1898). The dynamogenic factors in pacemaking and competition. *American Journal of Psychology, 9*, 507–533. http://dx.doi.org/10.2307/1412188

Waldman, D. A., Atwater, L. E., & Davidson, R. A. (2004). The role of individualism and the five-factor model in the prediction of performance in a leaderless group discussion. *Journal of Personality, 72*, 1–28. http://dx.doi.org/10.1111/j.0022-3506.2004.00254.x

Wickham, K. R., & Walther, J. B. (2007). Perceived behaviors of emergent and assigned leaders in virtual groups. *International Journal of e-Collaboration, 3*, 1–17. http://dx.doi.org/10.4018/jec.2007010101

1

A Review of Research Synergies (and Lack Thereof) Between Group Psychology and Group Psychotherapy

Craig D. Parks

Few areas of inquiry within psychology seem to fit together more naturally than the dynamics of real-world groups and the dynamics of therapy groups. Knowing whether a process that occurs within a task group or social group also occurs in a therapy group would provide important insight into the nature of the phenomenon and valuable guidance for practitioners who work with and oversee groups of all forms.

At one time, this outlook was predominant among those who had an interest in group dynamics. Lewin (1939, 1944), for example, argued that groups can be used to study both the dynamics of personality and to induce changes to an individual's personality. In his review of Moreno's book *Who Shall Survive?*, which served as the foundation for one form of group psychotherapy, social psychologist Murphy (1935) lauded the work for providing a methodological bridge between those who were interested in social processes within groups and those who treated psychiatric disorders. Sullivan (1940), a psychiatrist, considered troubled individuals to ultimately be struggling with social relations, and Newcomb (1947), a social psychologist, expanded on this idea to argue that researchers of social groups and practitioners of group psychotherapy are ultimately interested in the same basic issue, namely, how to foster positive interpersonal relations. Cartwright (1951) laid out eight principles establishing the group as a medium and target of change, and took as a given that techniques identified through basic experimentation on groups would then be migrated into a group therapeutic setting, and the techniques refined after application.

http://dx.doi.org/10.1037/0000201-002
The Psychology of Groups: The Intersection of Social Psychology and Psychotherapy Research,
C. D. Parks and G. A. Tasca (Editors)

Bach (1954), a student of Lewin's, devoted one third of the chapters in his book on group psychotherapy to the question of how group dynamics might impact the therapeutic process and based his argument on Cartwright's principles. Bach then identified a number of topics that he saw as ripe for collaborative focus: management of interpersonal conflict, group leader behavior, cohesion, status differences, treatment of norm deviants and nonconformists, integration of newcomers, formation and impact of subgroups and coalitions, same- versus mixed-sex group composition, and achievement of consensus.

Unfortunately, this promise largely went unrealized. In 1977, Parloff and Dies, both therapists, published a review of group psychotherapy outcome research that began with the pointed comment that they had assembled the paper because they perceived that practitioners were finally ready to consume research results after a long period of resistance. A broader critique was published by Deutsch (1980), also a Lewin student, who bemoaned the bifurcation of the groups area into theory-centered and problem-centered work. Although he took graduate programs to task for not easily—or at all—providing students with the opportunity to experience both realms, Deutsch perceptively identified differences between the two lines of inquiry that he felt could certainly cause suspicion and antagonism between those primarily interested in developing theories and those more interested in solving problems. Specifically, he argued that problem-oriented experts start with outcomes and seek to induce the multiple causes of those outcomes; develop interventions that draw from multiple theoretical perspectives to address those multiple causes at once; may not know—or care—why that specific set of theories is applicable to this particular situation; consider a model to have value if it applies to the particular problem they are trying to solve, even when it is applicable in no other situations; place greatest value on repetition of results; seek to be actively engaged with the groups that they study; and must confront potentially difficult ethical issues because of their interest in producing lasting, positive change in group members. By contrast, theorists begin with a cause and investigate what outcomes are associated with that cause; recognize that other phenomena contribute to the outcomes, but the theorists are usually not interested in identifying those other causes; consider a model to be valuable if it is broadly applicable, even if it does not have explanatory power in certain situations; place greatest value on surprising and unexpected results; seek to be disengaged from the groups that they study; and have ethical concerns only as they arise with mundane laboratory interventions intended to produce brief and temporary change. Deutsch was not arguing or implying that one perspective is more desirable than the other. Rather, he was explicit that each needs the other and that in the long run, the discipline as a whole will suffer because society will not long accept a discipline that produces results that cannot be applied to real problems or that advocates trendy interventions without an evidentiary basis.

Twenty years ago, Forsyth (2000) speculated that experimental group and group psychotherapy research could develop stronger collaborative connections in the future. Individual reliance on groups would need to increase, research on groups would need to become more sophisticated, and the theory–problem divide identified by Deutsch (1980) would have to be bridged. These changes have occurred: Groups are more prominent and central in society than ever, research on groups uses strong analytical tools unavailable at Forsyth's writing (Tasca, 2016), and funding agencies and journals increasingly demand that investigators address the translational or applied value of their research. However, the collaboration that Forsyth hoped for is not much in evidence. Greene (2017) suggests that the problem has gotten worse: Not only is there little dialogue between experimental group and group psychotherapy researchers, group psychotherapy researchers and practitioners also do not interact much. Similar observations have been made in the organizational psychology literature in which researchers and practitioners who once worked in close collaboration are growing apart and in which there is strong interest in the dynamics of work teams (Bartunek & Rynes, 2014).

My goal in this chapter is to provide a relatively broad and overarching review of how interest in groups diverged into experimental group research, therapy group research, and group practice. The phenomenon is not unique to the groups field or even to psychology. Many authors over the past 40-plus years have offered suggestions for how to rectify this situation; none has worked. Although I do not claim to have special insight into the problem, I nonetheless present at the end of the chapter some new (data-driven) ideas about how the field might reunify our various researchers and our practitioners.

EXPERIMENTAL GROUP RESEARCH VERSUS GROUP PRACTICE RESEARCH

A hallmark of early groups research was its execution in real settings. Consider just a few famous and influential examples:

- The studies of the employees of the Hawthorne Works: Elton Mayo and Fritz Roethlisberger, researchers from Harvard University, observed workers at the Western Electric plant in Hawthorne, Illinois, with a goal of trying to understand how individuals performing physical tasks come to coordinate their efforts to produce a single output (Roethlisberger & Dickson, 1939). The groups they observed improved their productivity as the study progressed. Mayo and Roethlisberger concluded that individuals will naturally cohere into teams given proper attitudes, leadership, and social dynamics. However, on revisiting the data, Roethlisberger and William Dickson (1939) reached a different conclusion: The workers improved merely because they knew they were being watched. The "Hawthorne effect" remains controversial today, but for our purposes, the original study is a nice example of early field work.

- Newcomb's (1943) research on friendship dynamics in student residence halls: In 1935, Theodore Newcomb, then a researcher at Bennington College (a women's college at the time), planned to track the attitudes and preferences of a group of incoming freshmen across their 4 years of study. He was given permission to randomly assign the women to two-person rooms in a dormitory, which meant that each woman likely had a roommate and immediate neighbors whom she did not know. Newcomb observed that most of the roommate pairs became friendly as the study progressed, and when the study ended in 1939, roommates tended to identify each other as close friends and to consider immediate neighbors as good friends. This finding demonstrated the central role of proximity as an influence on the formation of friendships.

- Pratt's (1907) conducting of support group–type sessions for tuberculosis sufferers: Joseph Pratt was a physician in the outpatient unit at Massachusetts General Hospital who brought together small groups of tuberculosis sufferers each week at a local church. Pratt's idea was to have the patients share their stories, experiences, and frustrations so that the physician leading the group could dispense advice that would benefit multiple people at once, but also so that the patients could learn from each other and develop a sense of camaraderie. (In a wonderful example of Pratt's insight, he took pains to make sure the physician was as similar as possible to the patients. For example, groups of Jewish patients were led by a Jewish physician and were encouraged to conduct sessions in Yiddish.) Pratt reported an astounding 75% recovery rate for his group participants. Pratt did not attribute the success solely to the weekly meetings—he considered fresh air, regular physical treatment by the nursing staff, and careful daily record-keeping to be important—but his observations of the groups clearly demonstrate the positive impact that they had on the patients.

Kurt Lewin was a primary agent of the naturalistic group approach. A German Jew who had to leave his home country in the 1930s because of the rise of fascism, Lewin's professional motivation was the instigation of social change, which he believed could only be accomplished by applying interventions in natural habitats (Burnes, 2007). Because Lewin also believed that the groups to which one belongs are the primal influences on one's thoughts and behaviors, it followed that one could bring about positive change by acting on the groups to which the target individuals belonged. The Research Center for Group Dynamics, founded by Lewin at the Massachusetts Institute of Technology in 1945 and moved to the University of Michigan by Cartwright after Lewin's death in 1946, emphasized the study of groups in their natural settings.

A challenge—recognized early on—with such naturalistic research was the difficulty in developing clear explanations for the observed effects. For example, Moreno (1947) took issue with many of the conclusions reached in the Hawthorne research on the grounds that the researchers made deep inferences using shallow observational data that did not consider external influences or human variation. Contemporary examinations of these early studies have led to similar concerns about the viability of their conclusions given their data (e.g., Billig's, 2015, critique of Lewin's, 1939, research on styles of leadership). More generally, application of the naturalistic approach to studying groups was haphazard: "Real" groups were sometimes just ad hoc groups assembled outside of the lab rather than inside, groups that had existed for a short time were equated with groups that had existed for a long time, control groups were often just untreated groups that happened to be handy and not necessarily comparable with the treatment group, and groups assigned to complete the same general task might nonetheless end up using very different processes to execute the task (Barlow, Burlingame, & Fuhriman, 2000; Parks, 2018). And indeed, it did not take long for the Research Center to turn away from naturalistic research and toward tightly controlled laboratory experimentation on groups; other key research venues followed suit (McGrath, 1997).

This shift meant that researchers interested in understanding the dynamics of therapeutic groups were going to have to devise ways to import laboratory tools into the therapy setting. Some tried and achieved a modicum of success. To take just one example, Heckel, Holmes, and Rosecrans (1971) conducted a factor-analytic interaction process analysis of the development of long-term therapy groups to document the changing nature of interaction among members as time goes on. However, the methodological challenges to conducting careful research on therapy groups served as a major inhibitor of empirical inquiry into the 1970s (Dies, 1979). In addition, division within the group dynamics area persisted over what should be the key focus of the research: understanding when and why group outputs differ from individual outputs for the same task or charting the process by which group members move from inputs to output (McGrath, 1997). Notably absent from this debate was the question of how the group experience impacts the members, a line of inquiry that would provide clear connection to the interests of group psychotherapy researchers. This topic would eventually arise with the full flowering of European group dynamics research in the 1970s (Hogg, 2008), but at that point, the divide between the study of empirical groups and of therapy groups had become a chasm. (Indeed, that the two areas were drifting apart was recognized quite early on; see Bennis, 1960.)

A complicating factor for the methodology dilemma is the need for group therapy researchers to be able to isolate the effect of the group setting itself on individual member improvement. That the group setting offers benefits that cannot be realized when performing as an isolated individual is only implied in group dynamics research, but researchers rarely need to confirm this implication. Presumably no one would be compelled to provide evidence for the assertion that a decision-making group can discuss the issue and share relevant information with each other, but a decision-making individual cannot. This is not the case for therapy research, however, because group therapy researchers often seek to establish that the group setting itself has a facilitative effect and thus provides advantages over individual therapy (e.g., McDermut, Miller, & Brown, 2001; Tucker & Oei, 2007). Other treatment-oriented fields have the same interest, for example, a current school of thought within pharmacy is that context can enhance the performance of active drugs in that certain situations can activate biochemical and cellular mechanisms that, in turn, make the ingested drug more effective (Benedetti, 2008). Unlike physiological outcomes, however, statistically documenting and measuring the impact of context on psychological or behavioral outcomes is difficult.

Consequently, the group dynamics researchers and group psychotherapy researchers quickly came to exist in different methodological worlds. Experimental groups were artificial and tightly controlled, and had no consequences associated with their actions. Researchers cared only about the collective outcome produced by the group and began with the assumption that the group product would be at least as good as anything an individual working on the same task would produce. On the other hand, psychotherapeutic groups were real, existed in largely uncontrolled settings, and had potentially quite profound consequences associated with their actions. Group therapy researchers were interested in the impact of the group on the individual members and began with no assumption that the group environment would be advantageous relative to an individual-based approach. It is not surprising that the two sets of scholars would perceive little common ground.

HUMAN POTENTIAL MOVEMENT

Adding to the perceived divide was the rise of the "human potential movement." Although this movement eventually came to encompass many aspects of social change that encouraged open expression, the key activity of this movement for this discussion is the *encounter group*. Encounter groups have their origins in the mid-1940s and were originally based on Lewin's (1944) ideas about the group as a vehicle for social change. The original goal was to train community leaders in a group setting how to address and defuse intergroup tensions within their communities. However, the potential therapeutic value of Lewin's group was quickly realized, and group leaders began to integrate Freudian and Rogerian ideas into the sessions. The training groups, now referred to as *sensitivity training groups* or *T-groups*, thus became less of a tool for improving social conditions and primarily a tool for self-analysis and self-improvement (see Highhouse, 2002, for an outstanding review of the T-group). An early application of T-groups was to executive leadership training, and by the late 1950s, such training was extremely popular; indeed, Highhouse (2002) estimated that in 1966 alone, more than 20,000 people participated in an executive training T-group. The basic idea underlying the T-group was that participants could be made sensitive to group process dynamics and their own approach and contribution to these dynamics; be taught how to deal with these dynamics across many types of groups and contexts; and then integrate these lessons into their work lives, thus becoming more effective group members as a result. Importantly, despite the psychoanalytic/Rogerian philosophy underlying the T-group, it was nonetheless implied that sessions were for educational training of healthy adults and were inappropriate for individuals with psychological problems (Weigel, 2002). Eventually, offshoots began to develop that deemphasized the group functioning aspect in favor of personal exploration, growth, and release of inhibitions. These groups became popular and publicized. As Spence (2007) noted, given the turbulent time that was the late 1960s into the early 1970s, personal growth groups undoubtedly provided a measure of comfort to many people.

The problem was that the basis for these groups was heavily, and often entirely, atheoretical, and the groups were not being subjected to empirical study. Data collection was conducted in the early days of the T-group, but by the 1960s, systematic research was hard to find. Although this decline was, to some extent, the result of dwindling resources, both Highhouse (2002) and Weigel (2002) cited as a key issue the proliferation of group leaders who were oriented purely toward practice and had no need to test the efficacy of the group milieu. Concerns about the lack of empirical support for the presumed impact of T-groups were first raised by Campbell and Dunnette (1968), and Yalom (1970) and Frank (1971) offered devastating critiques of the faddish and atheoretical nature of the various forms of encounter groups. A number of authors then began to document what were termed *encounter group casualties,* that is, people who were damaged as a result of participating in such groups (e.g., Hartley, Roback, & Arbramowitz, 1976; Kaplan, 1983; Smokowski, Rose, & Bacallao, 2001). The damage resulted partly from people's being placed into an intense situation for which they were unprepared and partly because of incompetent group leaders who failed to structure and execute the sessions according to T-group principles. Ultimately, lack of grounding in theory and research opened the door for zealotry, grandiose assertions, and interventions that seemed to come out of nowhere. Consider, for example, Bindrim's (1968) study supposedly documenting that nudity improves the effectiveness of encounter groups. The motivations for the study were Bindrim's observation that encounter group participants tended to strip naked to swim or sit in a hot tub after conclusion of a session and his perception that interactions between swimmers/bathers were transparent, open, and inclusive, and promoted feelings of belongingness. It is hard to identify—even then—a theoretical perspective that would suggest sitting naked with strangers as a method for promoting psychological growth as opposed to instigating body image concerns, embarrassment, anxiety, distracted attention, and physiological arousal.

Thus, besides having apparently little methodological common ground with group dynamics research, group psychotherapy research produced some vivid, theory-free studies that ran the risk of doing harm to participants; over-shadowed much good, careful research on therapy groups; and gave an appearance to those outside of the specialty area that group psychotherapists were following unappealing research strategies. An interesting parallel to personality research of the 1940s and 1950s is that this work was characterized by attribution of virtually any behavior to a personality trait; rampant use of unvalidated personality assessments to classify people, particularly in the workplace;

life-impacting decisions being made on the basis of these assessment results; and the eventual collapse of this approach when systematic evaluation identified almost all of the proposed traits as atheoretical and unsupported by evidence. All of these factors contributed to researchers' discounting personality traits as predictive factors in group process and performance research, a trend that began in the 1960s and is only just now starting to recede (Parks, 2018).

GROUP PRACTICE RESEARCH VERSUS THE PRACTICE OF GROUPS

The value of a group setting for the improvement of health conditions has long been recognized. I have already noted Pratt's (1907) work with patients with tuberculosis. Other early examples include group treatment of people with peptic ulcers as a means of providing social support for altered dietary regimens (Chappell, Stefano, Rogerson, & Pike, 1936), use of groups to reduce negative arousal in hypertensive patients (Buck, 1937), and group therapy as a means of helping people cope with neurologic diseases (e.g., multiple sclerosis: Long, 1954; Parkinson's disease: Chafetz, Bernstein, Sharpe, & Schwab, 1955). These practitioners saw the group as an effective tool for reducing negative psychological states that were thought to impact certain physiological systems in such a way as to make the condition worse. For example, Chafetz et al. (1955), understanding that negative emotional arousal is associated with increased severity of Parkinson's tremors, reasoned that groups of those with Parkinson's disease would be able to teach emotion-regulation strategies more effectively than would a single therapist who had not experienced the disease. In all of these cases, the theorists based their ideas on existing work, executed careful (for the time) studies of their ideas, and reported appropriately tempered conclusions.

Over the past several decades, however, a separation has been growing between those who study the practice of groups and those who lead group practice (e.g., Norcross & Wampold, 2011; Proctor et al., 2009). Indeed, it is characteristic of a general schism across many disciplines that has developed between those who study how to intervene and those who conduct interventions (e.g., management science: Ghoshal, 2005; Gulati, 2007; Kieser & Leiner, 2009; McKelvey, 2006; pharmacy: Rothwell, 2005; medicine: Berwick & Hackbarth, 2012; Fletcher-Lartey, Yee, Gaarslev, & Khan, 2016; Westfall, Mold, & Fagnan, 2007). Practitioners in these areas feel that researchers collect data in artificial settings that ignore variables and hence have no relevance to the real group environment (Pagoto et al., 2007). Although a work-team researcher may control group member ability to reduce statistical variability, the work-team manager needs to know what to do when ability levels cannot be held constant. Health researchers may advocate for a new tool for fighting a chronic condition without considering how difficult or unpleasant it will be for patients to integrate that new tool into their treatment regimen. Even the push for evidence-based medicine, which on its face seems impossible to criticize, is running into increasing skepticism from the practitioner community as researchers overpower their studies with huge samples and tout statistically significant treatment-driven outcomes that are, in practice, trivial (Greenhalgh, Howick, & Maskrey, 2014). Researchers, in turn, criticize practitioners for placing too much faith in intuition over hard data, believing that their professional experience alone endows them with the ability to determine what the problem is and how to fix it. Practitioner overconfidence is well documented and misplaced; many studies have revealed the flaws and biases in intuitive diagnosis, even among highly experienced professionals (Arkes, 2013; Beutler, 2009; Braude, 2009; Cascio & Aguinis, 2008; Djulbegovic et al., 2014; Giluk & Rynes-Weller, 2012; Highhouse, 2008; Lilienfeld, 2007).

How pharmacy and medicine arrived at this point is beyond the scope of this chapter, but the roots of the schism in group psychology and psychotherapy can generally be traced to the encounter group movement discussed earlier. At the peak of the movement, moderation was set aside in favor of fervent advocacy for the group intervention. Group leaders were sure that they could see group members changing for the better, and leaders wanted to believe they were positively impacting people. Indeed, the very notion of "living in the moment" that encounter groups promoted ran counter to the deliberative process of collecting data, analyzing it, comparing it, theorizing about it, and conducting follow-up tests. As Parloff and Dies (1977) documented, a substantial amount of important research was being conducted on therapy groups, but it was not being integrated into encounter groups and likely not even being attended to. The trend continues to persist; modern surveys of practicing psychotherapists have consistently revealed a tendency to favor intuition and colloquial advice from colleagues over evidence-based research (Cook, Schnurr, Biyanova, & Coyne, 2009; Lucock, Hall, & Noble, 2006; Stewart & Chambless, 2007).

CONCLUSION

It is worth reminding the reader of Newcomb's (1947) thesis that, fundamentally, all of us are interested in the same basic question: How can we help people function and thrive in social situations? This thesis is true regardless of whether one wants to use a group therapy setting to help people better manage mental health issues, or develop interventions for a decision-making group so that its members make better use of the information available to them, or help athletes on a struggling sports team refine their skill coordination, or improve the rehabilitation group climate so that postcardiac surgery patients feel supported by others and stay committed to their recovery program. We all see the group as a vehicle for improvement, we use the same terms, we know the same concepts, and we have at least some methodological skills in common. Furthermore, there are many potentially exciting avenues for collaboration.

As noted earlier, the rise of European-based groups research with its focus on how the group impacts the individual offers much opportunity for linkage between group dynamics and group psychotherapy, and connections are indeed beginning to develop. For example, many theorists have suggested that a sense of social identification with the therapy group, its members, and the therapist can promote success and positive change in group members because high identification induces a sense of trust among group members (Aviram & Rosenfeld, 2002; Cruwys, Haslam, Dingle, Haslam, & Jetten, 2014; Hornsey, Dwyer, & Oei, 2007). However, high identification can also lead to conformity to perceived norms that in therapy groups could discourage genuine responding (Hornsey et al., 2007). Similarly, Hornsey et al. (2007) proposed that ingroup homogeneity and perceived interdependence, phenomena known to impact experimental groups, may also be relevant to therapy groups, although in complex ways. Ingroup homogeneity may strengthen emotional harmony within the therapy group but also may blind group members to alternative viewpoints on a problem. A sense of interdependence may encourage self-disclosure but also may encourage free-riding and decreased rates of participation in the therapy sessions. All are promising lines of inquiry that offer much for both the psychotherapy researcher and experimental researcher to learn. Along these lines, Vickery, Gontkovsky, Wallace, and Caroselli (2006) provided evidence to suggest that group psychotherapy can improve self-concept in people with acquired brain injury (ABI). For an experimental psychologist, this evidence identifies an opportunity to study self-perception and group membership in a population that, to date, has received no systematic attention yet often needs assistance reintegrating into social life. Do the interpersonal phenomena that are well documented in healthy individuals replicate in people with ABI, and if not, how do they deviate? Are deviations predictable from the location of the brain injury? If deviation exists, what can the therapist do to help the person with an ABI adapt socially?

Another potential line of inquiry takes up the question of group influences on health outcomes. For example, some work has looked into the influence of group-induced motivation gains and losses on participation in exercise groups (e.g., Irwin, Scorniaenchi, Kerr, Eisenmann, & Feltz, 2012), and a recent review has called for a substantial increase in research into the conditions under which group-based physical activity will be more effective or less effective (Harden et al., 2015). Might, for example, a heart bypass recipient who is new to a physical rehabilitation group feel embarrassed because he or she cannot last as long on a treadmill as fellow patients, even though the person's relative lack of stamina is completely understandable? If so, does this imply that physical rehabilitation in a group could be counterproductive relative to individual therapy? Decades ago, there was interest in using the group to promote management of chronic health conditions. There is still much to learn about this idea, and some recent work has suggested promising findings (e.g., Type 2 diabetes: Arigo, Smyth, Haggerty, & Raggio, 2015; certain forms of cancer: Burke, West, Grocott, Brunet, & Jack, 2015; Kissane et al., 2007; weight management by those with mental illness: Aschbrenner et al., 2016).

An emerging area of focus addresses how group dynamics impact the health and mental health of soldiers. For example, strong ingroup identification is a key component of military service. We have identified ingroup identification as a possible key factor in the success, or lack of success, of group psychotherapy, and it may also play a similarly complex role in soldier mental health. Although group identification can help establish a support network for the struggling soldier, it also may inhibit help-seeking for a variety of mental health issues, including suicide (Bryan, Jennings, Jobes, & Bradley, 2012). Next, unit cohesion may be a factor in helping lesbian, gay, and bisexual soldiers deal with the stress and anxiety, and corresponding mental health issues, associated with being a sexual minority in the military (Cochran, Balsam, Flentje, Malte, & Simpson, 2013), and also may be critical to reducing the likelihood and severity of mental health issues in the wake of combat exposure (Jones et al., 2012). Furthermore, group-based prenatal care may have important advantages over individual-level care for active female soldiers (Kennedy et al., 2011). These examples and numerous others show how intellectually and practically vital collaborations among experimental group researchers, group practice researchers, and group practitioners can be.

The question then becomes how to bring these three sets of individuals together. This question goes back at least to Parloff and Dies (1977). Proposed solutions have usually oriented around the notion that circumstances will lead research professionals to see the errors of their ways and set aside their biases, and that practitioners need only be better educated on what the data are telling us (Lilienfeld, Ritschel, Lynn, Cautin, & Latzman, 2013). Fortunately, some new data-driven ideas suggest a path forward. Studies have shown that practitioners are more willing to consider use of empirically supported intervention techniques if researchers address implementation barriers and offer realistic suggestions for overcoming those barriers (Gallo & Barlow, 2012; Gaudiano, Brown, & Miller, 2011; Varra, Hayes, Roget, & Fisher, 2008). It is critical to also note that practitioners who work within some type of managed-care system or hierarchical corporation may face significant structural barriers to the adoption of new techniques, particularly managerial unwillingness to absorb the financial, time, and human resources costs of integrating a new procedure (see Lilienfeld et al., 2013, for an excellent discussion of structural barriers). Thus, although individual practitioners may resist the integration of empirical findings, researchers must recognize that integration may often be out of the practitioner's hands; indeed, some have argued that this factor rather than personal resistance is the primary cause of the research-practice gap (Chinman et al., 2005). Structural barriers aside, groups researchers would do well to consider and discuss the practical challenges associated with implementation of the interventions they propose.

Promoting collaboration between group psychology and group practice researchers is a task for which conditions are ripe. Anderson and colleagues (2019) argue that groups research is disappearing from prominence because of psychology's current emphasis on quickly produced multistudy papers.

They further suggest that this ethos effectively rules out study of many social problems for which data cannot be collected through an online crowdsourcing tool and that psychology needs to pause and reflect on how to promote and support research that is time-consuming and conducted in a variety of venues. As well, a growing recognition is that the world's most difficult problems are not solvable within one discipline but rather require collaboration across many disciplines (e.g., Brown, Harris, & Russell, 2010). Simply put, groups researchers need to go on the offensive, and it is clear that no one subset of those researchers can alone devise interventions that will make real groups function more effectively. Collaboration is mandated. Although some may be skeptical that this state of affairs is sufficient to bring group psychology and group psychotherapy researchers together, in the not-too-distant past, it was unthinkable that social scientists and earth scientists would work together on projects. Yet, the Future Earth initiative is just such a collaboration: a large multinational group that is tackling climate change issues (Future Earth, n.d.).

This brief review suggests an obvious need to understand the interplay between group identification, which is a universal occurrence, and one's experiences within a therapy group as well as potential value in studying interdependence, social comparison, group member homogeneity, and social processes in people with disordered thinking. A more exhaustive review would undoubtedly uncover more variables. Such collaborations would produce insights into how to refine therapeutic procedures and help identify the limits and breadth of group phenomena. This type of work ultimately represents nothing more than a return to the ideas of Lewin, Moreno, Cartwright, and others who saw the group as a unique vehicle for social improvement.

SUGGESTED READINGS

Bargal, D. (2008). Group processes to reduce intergroup conflict: An additional example of a workshop for Arab and Jewish youth. *Small Group Research*, *39*, 42–59. http://dx.doi.org/10.1177/1046496407313414

This article is a wonderful example of how group psychology and group psychotherapeutic processes can be combined to develop and implement a real-world intervention for an immediate social problem, in this case, conflict between Arab and Jewish youths in Israel.

Forsyth, D. R. (2010). Group processes and group psychotherapy: Social psychological foundations of change in therapeutic groups. In J. E. Maddux & J. P. Tangney (Eds.), *Social psychological foundations of clinical psychology* (pp. 497–513). New York, NY: Guilford Press.

This chapter reviews the manifestation of many different social psychological phenomena within the context of a therapy group and discusses how these phenomena interact with the therapeutic process to produce positive change in participants.

McLeod, P. L., & Kettner-Polley, R. B. (2004). Contributions of psychodynamic theories to understanding small groups. *Small Group Research, 35,* 333–361. http://dx.doi.org/10.1177/1046496404264973

In this article, the authors conduct a relatively uncommon examination of how group psychology researchers have drawn from and integrated psychodynamic theory into work on experimental group dynamics.

REFERENCES

Anderson, C. A., Allen, J. J., Plante, C., Quigley-McBride, A., Lovett, A., & Rokkum, J. N. (2019). The MTurkification of social and personality psychology. *Personality and Social Psychology Bulletin, 45,* 842–850. http://dx.doi.org/10.1177/0146167218798821

Arigo, D., Smyth, J. M., Haggerty, K., & Raggio, G. A. (2015). The social context of the relationship between glycemic control and depressive symptoms in Type 2 diabetes. *Chronic Illness, 11,* 33–43. http://dx.doi.org/10.1177/1742395314531990

Arkes, H. R. (2013). The consequences of hindsight bias in medical decision making. *Current Directions in Psychological Science, 22,* 356–360. http://dx.doi.org/10.1177/0963721413489988

Aschbrenner, K. A., Mueser, K. T., Naslund, J. A., Gorin, A. A., Kinney, A., Daniels, L., & Bartels, S. J. (2016). Feasibility study of increasing social support to enhance a healthy lifestyle intervention for individuals with serious mental illness. *Journal of the Society for Social Work and Research, 7,* 289–313. http://dx.doi.org/10.1086/686486

Aviram, R. B., & Rosenfeld, S. (2002). Application of social identity theory in group therapy with stigmatized adults. *International Journal of Group Psychotherapy, 52,* 121–130. http://dx.doi.org/10.1521/ijgp.52.1.121.45468

Bach, G. R. (1954). *Intensive group psychotherapy.* New York, NY: Ronald Press. http://dx.doi.org/10.1037/14491-000

Barlow, S. H., Burlingame, G. M., & Fuhriman, A. (2000). Therapeutic application of groups: From Pratt's "thought control classes" to modern group psychotherapy. *Group Dynamics, 4,* 115–134. http://dx.doi.org/10.1037/1089-2699.4.1.115

Bartunek, J. M., & Rynes, S. L. (2014). Academics and practitioners are alike and unlike: The paradoxes of academic-practitioner relationships. *Journal of Management, 40,* 1181–1201. http://dx.doi.org/10.1177/0149206314529160

Benedetti, F. (2008). Mechanisms of placebo and placebo-related effects across diseases and treatments. *Annual Review of Pharmacology and Toxicology, 48,* 33–60. http://dx.doi.org/10.1146/annurev.pharmtox.48.113006.094711

Bennis, W. G. (1960). A critique of group therapy research. *International Journal of Group Psychotherapy, 10,* 63–77. http://dx.doi.org/10.1080/00207284.1960.11507978

Berwick, D. M., & Hackbarth, A. D. (2012). Eliminating waste in US health care. *JAMA, 307,* 1513–1516. http://dx.doi.org/10.1001/jama.2012.362

Beutler, L. E. (2009). Making science matter in clinical practice: Redefining psychotherapy. *Clinical Psychology: Science and Practice, 16,* 301–317. http://dx.doi.org/10.1111/j.1468-2850.2009.01168.x

Billig, M. (2015). Kurt Lewin's leadership studies and his legacy to social psychology: Is there nothing as practical as a good theory? *Journal for the Theory of Social Behaviour, 45,* 440–460. http://dx.doi.org/10.1111/jtsb.12074

Bindrim, P. (1968). A report on a nude marathon: The effect of physical nudity upon the practice of interaction in the marathon group. *Psychotherapy: Theory, Research & Practice, 5,* 180–188. http://dx.doi.org/10.1037/h0088684

Braude, H. D. (2009). Clinical intuition versus statistics: Different modes of tacit knowledge in clinical epidemiology and evidence-based medicine. *Theoretical Medicine and Bioethics, 30,* 181–198. http://dx.doi.org/10.1007/s11017-009-9106-4

Brown, V. A., Harris, J. A., & Russell, J. Y. (2010). *Tackling wicked problems through the transdisciplinary imagination*. Washington, DC: Earthscan.

Bryan, C. J., Jennings, K. W., Jobes, D. A., & Bradley, J. C. (2012). Understanding and preventing military suicide. *Archives of Suicide Research, 16*, 95–110. http://dx.doi.org/10.1080/13811118.2012.667321

Buck, R. W. (1937). An article contributed to an anniversary volume in honor of Doctor Joseph Hersey Pratt: The class method in the treatment of essential hypertension. *Annals of Internal Medicine, 11*, 514–518. http://dx.doi.org/10.7326/0003-4819-11-3-514

Burke, S. M., West, M. A., Grocott, M. P. W., Brunet, J., & Jack, S. (2015). Exploring the experience of adhering to a prescribed pre-surgical exercise program for patients with advanced rectal cancer: A phenomenological study. *Psychology of Sport and Exercise, 16*(3), 88–95. http://dx.doi.org/10.1016/j.psychsport.2014.09.005

Burnes, B. (2007). Kurt Lewin and the Harwood studies: The foundations of OD. *Journal of Applied Behavioral Science, 43*, 213–231. http://dx.doi.org/10.1177/0021886306297004

Campbell, J. P., & Dunnette, M. D. (1968). Effectiveness of T-group experiences in managerial training and development. *Psychological Bulletin, 70*, 73–104. http://dx.doi.org/10.1037/h0026031

Cartwright, D. (1951). Achieving change in people: Some applications of group dynamics theory. *Human Relations, 4*, 381–392. http://dx.doi.org/10.1177/001872675100400404

Cascio, W. F., & Aguinis, H. (2008). Research in industrial and organizational psychology from 1963 to 2007: Changes, choices, and trends. *Journal of Applied Psychology, 93*, 1062–1081. http://dx.doi.org/10.1037/0021-9010.93.5.1062

Chafetz, M. E., Bernstein, N., Sharpe, W., & Schwab, R. S. (1955). Short-term group therapy of patients with Parkinson's disease. *The New England Journal of Medicine, 253*, 961–964. http://dx.doi.org/10.1056/NEJM195512012532204

Chappell, M. N., Stefano, J. J., Rogerson, J. S., & Pike, F. H. (1936). The value of group psychological procedures in the treatment of peptic ulcer. *American Journal of Digestive Diseases and Nutrition, 3*, 813–817. http://dx.doi.org/10.1007/BF02999273

Chinman, M., Hannah, G., Wandersman, A., Ebener, P., Hunter, S. B., Imm, P., & Sheldon, J. (2005). Developing a community science research agenda for building community capacity for effective preventive interventions. *American Journal of Community Psychology, 35*, 143–157. http://dx.doi.org/10.1007/s10464-005-3390-6

Cochran, B. N., Balsam, K., Flentje, A., Malte, C. A., & Simpson, T. (2013). Mental health characteristics of sexual minority veterans. *Journal of Homosexuality, 60*, 419–435. http://dx.doi.org/10.1080/00918369.2013.744932

Cook, J. M., Schnurr, P. P., Biyanova, T., & Coyne, J. C. (2009). Apples don't fall far from the tree: Influences on psychotherapists' adoption and sustained use of new therapies. *Psychiatric Services, 60*, 671–676. http://dx.doi.org/10.1176/ps.2009.60.5.671

Cruwys, T., Haslam, S. A., Dingle, G. A., Haslam, C., & Jetten, J. (2014). Depression and social identity: An integrative review. *Personality and Social Psychology Review, 18*, 215–238. http://dx.doi.org/10.1177/1088868314523839

Deutsch, M. (1980). Socially relevant research: Comments on "applied" versus "basic" research. In R. F. Kidd & M. J. Saks (Eds.), *Advances in applied social psychology* (Vol. 1, pp. 97–112). New York, NY: Taylor & Francis.

Dies, R. R. (1979). Group psychotherapy: Reflections on three decades of research. *Journal of Applied Behavioral Science, 15*, 361–373. http://dx.doi.org/10.1177/002188637901500310

Djulbegovic, B., Beckstead, J. W., Elqayam, S., Reljic, T., Hozo, I., Kumar, A., . . . Paidas, C. (2014). Evaluation of physicians' cognitive styles. *Medical Decision Making, 34*, 627–637. http://dx.doi.org/10.1177/0272989X14525855

Fletcher-Lartey, S., Yee, M., Gaarslev, C., & Khan, R. (2016). Why do general practitioners prescribe antibiotics for upper respiratory tract infections to meet patient expectations: A mixed methods study. *BMJ Open, 6,* e012244. http://dx.doi.org/10.1136/bmjopen-2016-012244

Forsyth, D. R. (2000). The social psychology of groups and group psychotherapy: One view of the next century. *Group, 24,* 147–155. http://dx.doi.org/10.1023/A:1007527831138

Frank, J. D. (1971). Therapeutic factors in psychotherapy. *American Journal of Psychotherapy, 25,* 350–361. http://dx.doi.org/10.1176/appi.psychotherapy.1971.25.3.350

Future Earth. (n.d.). *Who we are.* Retrieved from https://futureearth.org/about/who-we-are/

Gallo, K. P., & Barlow, D. H. (2012). Factors involved in clinician adoption and nonadoption of evidence-based interventions in mental health. *Clinical Psychology: Science and Practice, 19,* 93–106. http://dx.doi.org/10.1111/j.1468-2850.2012.01276.x

Gaudiano, B. A., Brown, L. A., & Miller, I. W. (2011). Let your intuition be your guide? Individual differences in the evidence-based practice attitudes of psychotherapists. *Journal of Evaluation in Clinical Practice, 17,* 628–634. http://dx.doi.org/10.1111/j.1365-2753.2010.01508.x

Ghoshal, S. (2005). Bad management theories are destroying good management practices. *Academy of Management Learning & Education, 4,* 75–91. http://dx.doi.org/10.5465/amle.2005.16132558

Giluk, T. L., & Rynes-Weller, S. L. (2012). Research findings practitioners resist: Lessons for management academics from evidence-based medicine. In D. M. Rousseau (Ed.), *Handbook of evidence-based management* (pp. 130–164). New York, NY: Oxford University Press. http://dx.doi.org/10.1093/oxfordhb/9780199763986.013.0008

Greene, L. R. (2017). Group psychotherapy research studies that therapists might actually read: My top 10 list. *International Journal of Group Psychotherapy, 67,* 1–26. http://dx.doi.org/10.1080/00207284.2016.1202678

Greenhalgh, T., Howick, J., & Maskrey, N. (2014). Evidence based medicine: A movement in crisis? *British Medical Journal, 348,* g3725. http://dx.doi.org/10.1136/bmj.g3725

Gulati, R. (2007). Tent poles, tribalism, and boundary spanning: The rigor-relevance debate in management research. *Academy of Management Journal, 50,* 775–782. http://dx.doi.org/10.5465/amj.2007.26279170

Harden, S. M., McEwan, D., Sylvester, B. D., Kaulius, M., Ruissen, G., Burke, S. M., . . . Beauchamp, M. R. (2015). Understanding for whom, under what conditions, and how group-based physical activity interventions are successful: A realist review. *BMC Public Health, 15,* 958. http://dx.doi.org/10.1186/s12889-015-2270-8

Hartley, D., Roback, H. B., & Arbramowitz, S. I. (1976). Deterioration effects in encounter groups. *American Psychologist, 31,* 247–255. http://dx.doi.org/10.1037/0003-066X.31.3.247

Heckel, R. V., Holmes, G. R., & Rosecrans, C. J. (1971). A factor analytic study of process variables in group therapy. *Journal of Clinical Psychology, 27,* 146–150. http://dx.doi.org/10.1002/1097-4679(197101)27:1<146::AID-JCLP2270270137>3.0.CO;2-0

Highhouse, S. (2002). A history of the T-group and its early applications in management development. *Group Dynamics, 6,* 277–290. http://dx.doi.org/10.1037/1089-2699.6.4.277

Highhouse, S. (2008). Stubborn reliance on intuition and subjectivity in employee selection. *Industrial and Organizational Psychology, 1,* 333–342. http://dx.doi.org/10.1111/j.1754-9434.2008.00058.x

Hogg, M. A. (2008). Personality, individuality, and social identity. In F. Rhodewalt (Ed.), *Personality and social behavior* (pp. 177–196). New York, NY: Psychology Press.

Hornsey, M. J., Dwyer, L., & Oei, T. P. S. (2007). Beyond cohesiveness: Reconceptualizing the link between group processes and outcomes in group psychotherapy. *Small Group Research, 38,* 567–592. http://dx.doi.org/10.1177/1046496407304336

Irwin, B. C., Scorniaenchi, J., Kerr, N. L., Eisenmann, J. C., & Feltz, D. L. (2012). Aerobic exercise is promoted when individual performance affects the group: A test of the Kohler motivation gain effect. *Annals of Behavioral Medicine, 44,* 151–159. http://dx.doi.org/10.1007/s12160-012-9367-4

Jones, N., Seddon, R., Fear, N. T., McAllister, P., Wessely, S., & Greenberg, N. (2012). Leadership, cohesion, morale, and the mental health of UK Armed Forces in Afghanistan. *Psychiatry, 75,* 49–59. http://dx.doi.org/10.1521/psyc.2012.75.1.49

Kaplan, R. E. (1983). The perils of intensive management training and how to avoid them. *Professional Psychology: Research and Practice, 14,* 756–770. http://dx.doi.org/10.1037/0735-7028.14.6.756

Kennedy, H. P., Farrell, T., Paden, R., Hill, S., Jolivet, R. R., Cooper, B. A., & Rising, S. S. (2011). A randomized clinical trial of group prenatal care in two military settings. *Military Medicine, 176,* 1169–1177. http://dx.doi.org/10.7205/MILMED-D-10-00394

Kieser, A., & Leiner, L. (2009). Why the rigor-relevance gap in management research is unbridgeable. *Journal of Management Studies, 46,* 516–533. http://dx.doi.org/10.1111/j.1467-6486.2009.00831.x

Kissane, D. W., Grabsch, B., Clarke, D. M., Smith, G. C., Love, A. W., Bloch, S., . . . Li, Y. (2007). Supportive-expressive group therapy for women with metastatic breast cancer: Survival and psychosocial outcome from a randomized controlled trial. *Psycho-Oncology, 16,* 277–286. http://dx.doi.org/10.1002/pon.1185

Lewin, K. (1939). Field theory and experiment in social psychology: Concepts and methods. *American Journal of Sociology, 44,* 868–896. http://dx.doi.org/10.1086/218177

Lewin, K. (1944). Constructs in psychology and psychological ecology. *University of Iowa Studies of Child Welfare, 20,* 23–27.

Lilienfeld, S. O. (2007). Psychological treatments that cause harm. *Perspectives on Psychological Science, 2,* 53–70. http://dx.doi.org/10.1111/j.1745-6916.2007.00029.x

Lilienfeld, S. O., Ritschel, L. A., Lynn, S. J., Cautin, R. L., & Latzman, R. D. (2013). Why many clinical psychologists are resistant to evidence-based practice: Root causes and constructive remedies. *Clinical Psychology Review, 33,* 883–900. http://dx.doi.org/10.1016/j.cpr.2012.09.008

Long, R. T. (1954). Insights gained through group therapy with multiple sclerosis patients. *Journal of Nervous and Mental Disease, 119,* 366.

Lucock, M. P., Hall, P., & Noble, R. (2006). A survey of influences on the practice of psychotherapists and clinical psychologists in training in the UK. *Clinical Psychology & Psychotherapy, 13,* 123–130. http://dx.doi.org/10.1002/cpp.483

McDermut, W., Miller, I. W., & Brown, R. A. (2001). The efficacy of group psychotherapy for depression: A meta-analysis and review of the empirical research. *Clinical Psychology: Science and Practice, 8,* 98–116. http://dx.doi.org/10.1093/clipsy.8.1.98

McGrath, J. E. (1997). Small group research, that once and future field: An interpretation of the past with an eye to the future. *Group Dynamics, 1,* 7–27. http://dx.doi.org/10.1037/1089-2699.1.1.7

McKelvey, B. (2006). Van de Ven and Johnson's "engaged scholarship": Nice try, but . . . *Academy of Management Review, 31,* 822–829. http://dx.doi.org/10.5465/amr.2006.22527451

Moreno, J. L. (1947). Progress and pitfalls in sociometric theory. *Sociometry, 10,* 268–272. http://dx.doi.org/10.2307/2785077

Murphy, G. (1935). J. L. Moreno. *Who shall survive? A new approach to the problem of human interrelations* [Book review]. *Journal of Social Psychology, 6,* 388–393.

Newcomb, T. M. (1943). *Personality and social change: Attitude formation in a student community.* New York, NY: Holt, Rinehart and Winston.

Newcomb, T. M. (1947). Autistic hostility and social reality. *Human Relations, 1*, 69–86. http://dx.doi.org/10.1177/001872674700100105

Norcross, J. C., & Wampold, B. E. (2011). Evidence-based therapy relationships: Research conclusions and clinical practices. *Psychotherapy, 48*, 98–102. http://dx.doi.org/10.1037/a0022161

Pagoto, S. L., Spring, B., Coups, E. J., Mulvaney, S., Coutu, M. F., & Ozakinci, G. (2007). Barriers and facilitators of evidence-based practice perceived by behavioral science health professionals. *Journal of Clinical Psychology, 63*, 695–705. http://dx.doi.org/10.1002/jclp.20376

Parks, C. D. (2018). Personality influences on group processes: The past, present, and future. In K. Deaux & M. Snyder (Eds.), *Handbook of personality and social psychology* (2nd ed., pp. 593–620). New York, NY: Oxford University Press.

Parloff, M. B., & Dies, R. R. (1977). Group psychotherapy outcome research 1966–1975. *International Journal of Group Psychotherapy, 27*, 281–319. http://dx.doi.org/10.1080/00207284.1977.11492304

Pratt, J. H. (1907). The organization of tuberculosis classes. *Boston Medical and Surgical Journal, 20*, 475–492.

Proctor, E. K., Landsverk, J., Aarons, G., Chambers, D., Glisson, C., & Mittman, B. (2009). Implementation research in mental health services: An emerging science with conceptual, methodological, and training challenges. *Administration and Policy in Mental Health and Mental Health Services Research, 36*, 24–34. http://dx.doi.org/10.1007/s10488-008-0197-4

Roethlisberger, F. J., & Dickson, W. J. (1939). *Management and the worker*. Cambridge, MA: Harvard University Press.

Rothwell, P. M. (2005). External validity of randomised controlled trials: "To whom do the results of this trial apply?" *The Lancet, 365*, 82–93. http://dx.doi.org/10.1016/S0140-6736(04)17670-8

Smokowski, P. R., Rose, S. D., & Bacallao, M. L. (2001). Damaging experience in therapeutic groups: How vulnerable consumers become group casualties. *Small Group Research, 32*, 223–251. http://dx.doi.org/10.1177/104649640103200205

Spence, G. B. (2007). Further development of evidence-based coaching: Lessons from the rise and fall of the human potential movement. *Australian Psychologist, 42*, 255–265. http://dx.doi.org/10.1080/00050060701648142

Stewart, R. E., & Chambless, D. L. (2007). Does psychotherapy research inform treatment decisions in private practice? *Journal of Clinical Psychology, 63*, 267–281. http://dx.doi.org/10.1002/jclp.20347

Sullivan, H. S. (1940). Conceptions of modern psychiatry [The First William Alanson White Memorial Lectures]. *Psychiatry, 3*, 1–117. http://dx.doi.org/10.1080/00332747.1940.11022272

Tasca, G. A. (2016). Statistical methods in group psychology and group psychotherapy: Introduction to the special issue. *Group Dynamics, 20*, 121–125. http://dx.doi.org/10.1037/gdn0000054

Tucker, M., & Oei, T. P. S. (2007). Is group more cost effective than individual cognitive behavior therapy? The evidence is not solid yet. *Behavioural and Cognitive Psychotherapy, 35*, 77–91. http://dx.doi.org/10.1017/S1352465806003134

Varra, A. A., Hayes, S. C., Roget, N., & Fisher, G. (2008). A randomized control trial examining the effect of acceptance and commitment training on clinician willingness to use evidence-based pharmacotherapy. *Journal of Consulting and Clinical Psychology, 76*, 449–458. http://dx.doi.org/10.1037/0022-006X.76.3.449

Vickery, C. D., Gontkovsky, S. T., Wallace, J. J., & Caroselli, J. S. (2006). Group psychotherapy focusing on self-concept change following acquired brain injury: A pilot investigation. *Rehabilitation Psychology, 51*, 30–35. http://dx.doi.org/10.1037/0090-5550.51.1.30

Weigel, R. G. (2002). The marathon encounter group—Vision and reality: Exhuming the body for a last look. *Consulting Psychology Journal: Practice and Research, 54,* 186–198. http://dx.doi.org/10.1037/1061-4087.54.3.186

Westfall, J. M., Mold, J., & Fagnan, L. (2007). Practice-based research—"Blue Highways" on the NIH roadmap. *JAMA, 297,* 403–406. http://dx.doi.org/10.1001/jama.297.4.403

Yalom, I. D. (1970). *The theory and practice of group psychotherapy.* New York, NY: Basic Books.

GROUP PSYCHOLOGY RESEARCH: IMPLICATIONS FOR GROUP PSYCHOTHERAPY

2

Inclusion, Exclusion, and Group Psychotherapy

The Importance of a Trauma-Informed Approach

Eric D. Wesselmann and Leandra Parris

Love and belonging might seem like a convenience we can live without, but our biology is built to thirst for connection because it is linked to our most basic survival needs.
—MATTHEW D. LIEBERMAN (2013, p. 43)

We are not only gregarious animals, liking to be in sight of our fellows, but we have an innate propensity to get ourselves noticed, and noticed favorably, by our kind. No more fiendish punishment could be devised, were such a thing physically possible, than that one should be turned loose in society and remain absolutely unnoticed by all the members thereof . . . sunk to such a depth as to be unworthy of attention at all.
—WILLIAM JAMES (1890/1950, pp. 293–294)

Humans have a strong need for reliable social relationships, both in terms of quantity and quality. Social relationships provide physical and psychological benefits in many ways, including social support during times of stress, a sense of identity, and an overall boost to self-esteem (Baumeister & Leary, 1995; Ellemers, Spears, & Doosje, 2002; Leary, 1999; Leary, Haupt, Strausser, & Chokel, 1998; Lieberman, 2013). Unfortunately, social interactions are not always positive. Humans' need for others also means that they become vulnerable to various aversive interpersonal experiences, such as being treated unfairly, exploited, or even expelled from their social groups.

Many psychologists have focused on understanding how various aversive interpersonal experiences affect people overall as well as how they relate to

http://dx.doi.org/10.1037/0000201-003
The Psychology of Groups: The Intersection of Social Psychology and Psychotherapy Research,
C. D. Parks and G. A. Tasca (Editors)

each other conceptually and empirically. One approach focuses on the broad category called *social exclusion:* any interpersonal experience that makes someone feel physically or emotionally separated from others (Riva & Eck, 2016). Individuals react to these interpersonal threats by experiencing pain (both on self-report and neurological measures; Eisenberger & Lieberman, 2004; MacDonald & Leary, 2005) and generally feeling relationally devalued by others (Smart Richman & Leary, 2009). In this chapter, we first summarize the research on types of social exclusion. Then we discuss current theoretical and empirical debates in the field as well as areas in need of future research. We end with a discussion on how to merge social exclusion research with the clinical literature and highlight ways in which therapists may treat individuals who suffer from chronic exclusion in both individual and group therapy sessions.

A BRIEF TOUR OF SOCIAL EXCLUSION RESEARCH

When people are made to feel socially excluded either at the interpersonal or societal level, they typically feel relationally devalued in some way (Smart Richman & Leary, 2009). Social exclusion can communicate the idea that someone (or their group) is not considered important or a worthwhile contributor to social life. People can be socially excluded in various ways, which can be broadly categorized into rejection-based and ostracism-based methods (Wesselmann et al., 2016).

Rejection-Based Exclusion

Rejection-based exclusion involves experiences in which people are given explicit information that they are unwanted by others (Blackhart, Nelson, Knowles, & Baumeister, 2009). This information can be delivered in a many ways and can vary in extremity. For example, direct forms of discrimination and stigmatization can be considered a form of rejection (Smart Richman & Leary, 2009). Furthermore, language used to demean or dehumanize social groups (e.g., racial slurs; Sue et al., 2007) suggests that those groups are not worthy of full respect, moral consideration, or even inclusion in society broadly (e.g., Crimston, Hornsey, Bain, & Bastian, 2018; Demoulin et al., 2004; Goff, Eberhardt, Williams, & Jackson, 2008). Even subtle, often unintentional forms of discrimination—often called *microaggressions*—communicate a form of social rejection by making the person feel invalidated or otherwise *othered* from mainstream society (Nadal, 2011; Sue, 2010). These types of discrimination are frequently insensitive comments or questions but can sometimes take the form of offensive jokes that disparage one's social group. Preliminary research suggests that individuals can experience disparaging humor similarly to other forms of interpersonal rejection (Wesselmann, Schneider, Ford, & DeSouza, 2018). One may not need to hear an explicit joke to feel rejected;

simply being laughed at in a hurtful or mean-spirited manner can serve as a rejection cue (Klages & Wirth, 2014).

Ostracism-Based Exclusion

Ostracism-based exclusion involves experiences characterized predominately by being ignored. Early empirical research on ostracism used multimethod approaches, both qualitative and quantitative, to understand the intrapsychic experience of feeling ignored in the presence of others. This research found that people typically associated these feelings with being given the silent treatment by one's relationship partners, whether they be romantic partners, friends, family, or coworkers (Sommer, Williams, Ciarocco, & Baumeister, 2001; Williams, Cheung, & Choi, 2000; Williams, Shore, & Grahe, 1998; Williams & Sommer, 1997). Even though this experience is common, people experience being ostracized as aversive even when it occurs among strangers (Nezlek, Wesselmann, Wheeler, & Williams, 2012). One theme consistently emerged across studies: Participants indicated the experience of being ostracized was aversive predominately because being ignored made them feel invisible and meaningless, as if they were not even worth receiving negative attention (Williams, 2001).

Many of these early studies involved research methods explicitly training confederates to ignore participants completely by refusing to respond to them or even look in their direction (see Wesselmann & Williams, 2017, and Wirth, 2016, for reviews). However, people can be made to *feel* ignored in many ways without someone physically ignoring them and refusing to acknowledge their presence. Early self-report research found that people indicated one of the most common ways they feel ignored is when someone does not give them eye contact (Williams et al., 1998), and subsequent experimental data support this finding (Böckler, Hömke, & Sebanz, 2014; Wesselmann, Cardoso, Slater, & Williams, 2012; Wirth, Sacco, Hugenberg, & Williams, 2010). Interestingly, awkward silences during group discussions can also make people feel ignored subtly (Koudenburg, Postmes, & Gordijn, 2011). The lack of eye contact and uncomfortable pauses may serve as two exclusionary cues that contribute to why people report feeling ignored when interaction partners check their cell phone in the midst of a conversation (Hales, Dvir, Wesselmann, Kruger, & Finkenauer, 2018).

People may make someone feel ignored, often unintentionally, in other subtle ways. For example, when someone is left out of the loop on information that others have, that person reports feeling ignored (e.g., Jones, Carter-Sowell, Kelly, & Williams, 2009). Most research on feeling out of the loop focuses on task-relevant information, but it likely extends to other types of social information (e.g., unfamiliar pop culture references; Iannone, Kelly, & Williams, 2018). Furthermore, someone likely feels ignored if most people in their social network have specific information (e.g., "Person X is pregnant" or "is engaged") and that person was one of the few people who did not know, especially if her or she interpreted lacking that information as representing their perceived social value in their network.

Another way that people can feel ignored involves the language others use around them. Experimental studies demonstrate that people can feel ignored or otherwise excluded when others are having a conversation in front of them in a foreign language (Dotan-Eliaz, Sommer, & Rubin, 2009; Hitlan, Kelly, Schepman, Schneider, & Zárate, 2006). People in this situation feel ignored presumably because they neither can understand nor contribute to the conversation; for all intents and purposes, they may as well not even be there! People may also feel ignored when others use language that does not include them. One program of studies found that androcentric language in job descriptions can make women feel more ignored than if the description used gender-neutral language (Stout & Dasgupta, 2011). This language effect may extend to other domains as well, such as when people use gender-binary language to describe nonbinary individuals (Galupo, Henise, & Davis, 2014; Nadal, Davidoff, Davis, & Wong, 2014; Nadal, Skolnik, & Wong, 2012). Regardless of whether these linguistic behaviors are intentional or unintentional, they each communicate a lack of acknowledgment toward certain groups of individuals, perhaps leading to a general feeling of invisibility.

Damage Done by Exclusion

Whether or not the exclusion is rejection- or ostracism based, extreme or subtle, purposeful or unintentional, it leads to a host of negative outcomes. These outcomes occur over a time course from immediately after the exclusion occurs to the time in which people reflect on the exclusion and try to make sense of it (Bernstein, 2016; Williams, 2009). Excluded individuals immediately experience feelings of pain; functional magnetic resonance imaging research demonstrates that areas of the brain activated by physical pain are also activated by laboratory manipulations of social exclusion (e.g., Eisenberger, Lieberman, & Williams, 2003). Furthermore, exclusion manipulations can cause increased cardiovascular activity and heightened cortisol levels, which, if they occur over prolonged periods, can lead to health problems (Dickerson & Kemeny, 2004; Iffland, Sansen, Catani, & Neuner, 2014; Reiter-Scheidl et al., 2018). Excluded individuals also experience an increase in negative emotions (e.g., anger, sadness) and threats to basic psychological needs (i.e., belonging, control, self-esteem, and meaningful existence; Williams, 2009). These outcomes occur whether the exclusion happens in face-to-face or cyber-based social interactions (Wirth, 2016), and they have been investigated in various social contexts outside the traditional laboratory setting, such as schools and the workplace (Ferris, Brown, Berry, & Lian, 2008; Gilman, Carter-Sowell, DeWall, Adams, & Carboni, 2013; Robinson, O'Reilly, & Wang, 2013; Saylor et al., 2012).

One of the most common experimental paradigms for studying exclusion is an ostracism-based paradigm called Cyberball (Williams et al., 2000). In *Cyberball* participants typically are told they are playing an online ball-tossing game with two other players (in reality, the other players are computer-controlled confederates). Researchers instruct the participants to use the task as a *mental visualization* exercise: to imagine what various aspects of the game would be like if this were a face-to-face interaction, such as who they think the other players are and what they think the weather is like. During the game, participants either receive an equal number of ball tosses (inclusion condition) or they receive one toss each from each confederate and then are ignored for the remainder of the game (ostracism condition). Researchers have used this paradigm in at least 120 published studies in various countries and across multiple age groups (Hartgerink, van Beest, Wicherts, & Williams, 2015).

After people have been excluded, they are motivated to engage in behaviors that help them recover from their experiences. Excluded participants often engage in prosocial behaviors, typically in the hope of obtaining reinclusion. For example, excluded participants may work harder on a collective task (Williams & Sommer, 1997), and they are more susceptible to social influence (e.g., conformity, compliance; Carter-Sowell, Chen, & Williams, 2008; DeWall, 2010; Williams et al., 2000). Paradoxically, participants are also likely to respond to exclusion with aggression (Leary, Twenge, & Quinlivan, 2006; Warburton, Williams, & Cairns, 2006; Wesselmann, Butler, Williams, & Pickett, 2010). Williams (2009) argued that these conflicting behavioral responses can be explained by which basic psychological needs participants are most focused on fortifying. If participants are focused on fortifying belonging or self-esteem, they should respond prosocially in service of reinclusion; participants who are focused on fortifying control or meaningful existence should respond antisocially as a way of obtaining attention.

KEY UNRESOLVED QUESTIONS IN SOCIAL EXCLUSION RESEARCH

Even though considerable research has been published on social exclusion over the past few decades, contentious areas still need further investigation. Some of these contentious areas have implications that extend beyond basic research questions and have implications for clinical applications as well.

Is It All About Exclusion or Inclusion?

Some researchers have argued about the effect social exclusion has on people's affect. A considerable portion of studies suggest that exclusion has ubiquitously negative effects on participants' emotions (Gerber & Wheeler, 2009); however, researchers also argue that any effects on emotions are driven by social inclusion and that exclusion instead makes people emotionally numb (Blackhart et al., 2009). At first blush, these two patterns seem contradictory. However, subsequent studies suggest ways to resolve the controversy. Some research suggests that the specific paradigms used to manipulate exclusion can influence participants' affective responses in opposite ways. Manipulations that focus on short-term exclusion experiences typically have negative effects on participants' emotions and basic need satisfaction, and manipulations that focus on making participants anticipate long-term future exclusion lead to emotional numbness and flattened responses to need satisfaction measures (Bernstein & Claypool, 2012a, 2012b). Researchers should also consider whether participants may be motivated to claim that they were not bothered by exclusion simply as a way to save face publicly, when they may privately still be bothered (Bernstein et al., 2013). Such face-saving may mask any effects an exclusion condition has when compared with a control condition.

Is Bad Attention Better Than No Attention?

Williams (2009) argued a key aspect that makes ostracism uniquely painful among other types of social exclusion: Individuals are ignored by others rather than just told explicitly they are unwanted. Early qualitative research on ostracism supports this assertion. Many ostracized individuals expressed feelings of being invisible, as if they were unworthy of even receiving negative or hostile attention. Some individuals explicitly noted they would have preferred negative attention because at least then, they would know they mattered (Williams, 2001). Other researchers have suggested being ostracized may be more negative than experiencing other direct forms of bullying predominantly because of the effect that being ignored has on one's feelings of meaningful existence (Williams & Nida, 2009). These ideas are intriguing theoretically but are supported by little direct empirical evidence. However, a recent study (Rudert, Hales, Greifeneder, & Williams, 2017) directly examined being ignored with being explicitly rejected via negative comments during a group interaction. The data suggest that even though both experiences are aversive, participants experienced less negative outcomes when they were given negative attention compared with being ubiquitously ignored. We must be clear that both this study and previous studies suggest that neither rejection-based nor ostracism-based exclusion experiences are positive for the target individuals. This is simply a matter of degree of negative outcomes.

TREATMENT OF SOCIAL EXCLUSION AS A FORM OF TRAUMA

Studies reveal that the pain of social exclusion can be reexperienced on reflection (Chen, Williams, Fitness, & Newton, 2008) and can have downstream consequences on individuals' thoughts, feelings, and behaviors similar to effects from real-time exclusion manipulations (Godwin et al., 2014; Wirth, 2016). These studies typically have focused on short-term recall effects in laboratory studies in which participants randomly recall an autobiographical memory in which they were socially excluded (compared with other conditions of interest, e.g., physical pain, social inclusion, a neutral control condition) and examine the immediate effects on downstream outcomes. The data suggest, however, that these reliving effects may also occur outside the laboratory when individuals organically recall exclusion episodes. Thus, individuals who experience triggers relevant to exclusion in their daily lives likely reexperience their emotional distress, and if this happens chronically, they may find themselves in a continual state of social pain.

As such, the influence of exclusion, even from one discrete incident, can have long-term, recursive effects. When the incident is not discrete but rather ongoing and chronic, these negative outcomes are even more salient. For example, victims of neglect demonstrate more severe symptoms of psychosocial dysfunction (e.g., depression, social withdrawal) than victims of direct abuse, regardless of whether that abuse is physical, sexual, or verbal (e.g., McElroy & Hevey, 2014). These data add further support that being ignored may be more hurtful than direct, negative attention. In addition, ongoing exclusion among peers can constitute *relational bullying,* a form of peer aggression often associated with greater rates of psychosocial difficulty (van der Wal, de Wit, & Hirasing, 2003). Furthermore, others are less likely to intervene when relational bullying is occurring, which further isolates the victim (Bauman & Del Rio, 2006). Thus, targets of relational bullying may feel doubly excluded, both by the perpetrators and by the bystanders.

Individuals who are chronically excluded often develop feelings of alienation, depression, learned helplessness, and a feeling of overall meaninglessness (Riva, Montali, Wirth, Curioni, & Williams, 2017). These individuals may ultimately withdraw from social relationships entirely and develop suicidal ideation (Williams, 2009). Thus, chronically excluded individuals face dire outcomes. In the clinical literature, *trauma* is a psychological experience resulting from a set of circumstances or event(s) that involve intense physical or emotional harm for an individual, and the individual experiences lasting adverse effects on their physical or psychological well-being (Substance Abuse and Mental Health Services Administration [SAMHSA], 2014, p. 7). Chronic peer exclusion and bullying, as well as neglect (i.e., being ignored), have been associated with symptoms of trauma (Blitz & Lee, 2015; Vidourek, King, & Merianos, 2016). Thus, even though chronic social exclusion may not typically be thought of in the same domain as other types of trauma (e.g., physical abuse, extreme neglect), it seems similar to them in terms of many of the negative psychological outcomes. In addition, one of the first strategies clinicians and crisis teams implement following traumatic events (e.g., school shooting, natural disaster) involves fortifying victims' feelings of inclusion via social support resources, second only to basic physiological and safety needs (Brock et al., 2016). Therefore, it behooves researchers from both the "social exclusion" and the "trauma" literatures to consider how their theoretical models and empirical findings overlap to forge new directions for basic research and intervention development.

TRAUMA-INFORMED GROUP PSYCHOTHERAPY

We now provide an example in which the literatures of social exclusion and trauma may be merged in the hope of both providing initial suggestions for future research and of inspiring other potential connections between these two literatures. First, we first provide a general approach many practitioners use when treating clients dealing with trauma, and then we describe a specific application of this general approach.

Regardless of the type of trauma, practitioners generally focus on four pillars for implementing trauma-informed care (TIC): (a) realize the impact of trauma, (b) recognize the symptoms of trauma, (c) respond to distress, and (d) resist revictimization (SAMHSA, 2014). These stages are not linear but rather represent a recursive process through which practitioners deliver services either by individual therapists or as an agency as a whole. These four pillars are beneficial for addressing social exclusion as well as isolation with the group setting because they help validate and normalize symptoms (realize), link group members who experience similar symptomology (recognize), and provide concrete ways to address feelings related to, and incidents of, social exclusion (respond and resist revictimization).

Permeating all four pillars are six guiding principles: (a) physical and psychological safety; (b) trustworthiness and transparency; (c) peer support; (d) collaboration and mutuality; (e) empowerment, voice, and choice; and (f) cultural, historical, or gender issues (SAMHSA, 2014). Given the focus on social connection among practitioner, client, and peers, TIC is a useful approach in treating clients who are experiencing distress related to exclusion (e.g., peer victimization; Blitz & Lee, 2015). Indeed, survivors of trauma often experience exclusion and general feelings of isolation both within their peer group and by the larger society; these feelings of exclusion and isolation can compound the already negative effects of their experience (Nietlisbach & Maercker, 2009). Furthermore, social support and connectedness have been found to be some of the most crucial components of effective coping with trauma and stressful situations (Brock et al., 2016). As such, TIC is designed specifically to validate and increase feelings of connectedness among individuals receiving services. Multiple guiding principles are aimed at increasing feelings of support and belonging. Regarding trustworthiness and transparency, increasing social connectedness and feelings of inclusion would be hard to accomplish if group leaders or members were excluding, even unintentionally, other members. Organizations and group leaders following a TIC model must assure that trust is present through inclusive practice.

Furthermore, TIC promotes peer support between group members as a means to increase social connectedness and reduce feelings of isolation that hinder healing. Just as it is hard to build trust without inclusion, it is also difficult to feel supported by one's peers if they are not supportive during group meetings. Thus, groups following a TIC model build into their programming ways to provide opportunities for building and maintaining positive, inclusive support among group members. This type of support can also be seen through the principle of mutuality and collaboration. TIC does not require that all group members like each other; any professional who has led a therapy or intervention group knows that would be impossible to guarantee. However, TIC does promote and support the sense of collaboration and mutual self-respect and support. In this way, even if certain members are unable to engage with the principle of peer support, they are at least supported through collaborative group efforts and mutual understanding among group members.

Furthermore, the emphasis on cultural considerations with the TIC model can help provide a responsive and inclusive environment to reduce the risk that marginalized or less represented groups will feel excluded because of cultural factors. By taking into account the ways in which social systems may isolate members of a given population, group leaders can help address those concerns within their groups. Doing so is extremely important because one finds it hard to feel connected to other group members if that person feels other members do not support or recognize his or her culture, identity, and the historical background of his or her culture. Group therapy that is grounded in a TIC framework can help ameliorate the effects of exclusion and isolation experienced by persons struggling with traumatic events, mental health deficits, or other stressors. By promoting social inclusion, connectedness, cultural acceptance, and mutual respect, TIC can offer the support that clients may be lacking as a result of their presenting concern. In addition, a TIC approach can help to not only address social exclusion experienced by group members outside of group but within the group, too. TIC is an approach to providing services that does not necessarily require that all group members have experienced a traumatic event. The six principles of TIC are beneficial for all groups regardless of the stressor or presenting concern being addressed by group therapy.

We now discuss the Trauma-Informed Program for Promoting Success (TIPPS; Parris & Foley, 2017) as a concrete example of how a trauma-informed approach to group psychotherapy can increase intervention effectiveness and also address clients' own experiences of exclusion. TIPPS is an adaptation of the Peer Victimization Intervention (Varjas et al., 2006), a group-based intervention curriculum for helping victims of bullying cope with the stress of peer victimization. Research using this original intervention model showed decreased posttraumatic stress symptoms and increased adaptive coping among middle school students who were coping with trauma (Varjas et al., 2006). Given these data and evidence that peer victimization can lead to traumatic symptoms (Vidourek et al., 2016), TIPPS used the original model and included additional sessions as well as an intentional TIC framework for group intervention implementation. The additional sessions specifically helped group members recognize, realize, and respond to signs of traumatic stress (e.g., their stomach hurting, indicating they are feeling anxious) and integrated narrative therapy techniques associated with trauma-informed practice (Black, Woodworth, Tremblay, & Carpenter, 2012). Preliminary data suggest TIPPS can increase participants' feelings of social support within schools, reduce reported stress related to peer victimization and social exclusion, and increase confidence in regulating emotions to better engage in social relationships (Foley, Charczuk, & Parris, 2019).

Currently, TIPPS is provided to middle school students who have experienced peer victimization. Beyond this presenting concern, many student participants also have experienced economic marginalization, exposure to foster care, and substance abuse as a way to cope with their stress. Per TIC principles, TIPPS emphasizes promoting inclusion, mutual self-help, and peer support to increase students' capacity for overcoming chronic stress through school connectedness and a sense of belonging among peers. In the following sections, we outline the specific ways that TIPPS uses TIC principles to address exclusion within and outside of the group therapy setting.

Pillars of TIC

The four pillars of TIC are important for addressing feelings of exclusion and social isolation among group members. To reiterate, it is important that group facilitators reduce exclusion within the group setting while simultaneously build clients' awareness of, and skill in using, strategies for coping with and addressing exclusion within their personal lives.

The first pillar, *realize the impact of trauma*, focuses on the client's knowledge of why trauma or, in this case, social exclusion, has such a negative impact on one's functioning. TIPPS is designed to first teach students why the stress of exclusion is harmful to their body (e.g., changes in eating and sleeping resulting from the physiological stress response) and mind (e.g., cognitive distortions that can develop from repeated exclusion). This first pillar of the TIC approach helps clients become more aware that although "sticks and stones" (i.e., physical aggression) certainly hurt, words (or a lack thereof) can also hurt them.

The second pillar, *recognize the symptoms of trauma*, can serve to help clients recognize when they are experiencing exclusion and the impact that this experience is currently having on their overall functioning. For example, the TIPPS curriculum specifically teaches students to recognize not only their own emotions and thoughts related to loneliness and exclusion but the emotions and stressors of others. Doing so helps them to become fully aware their own feelings of exclusion while also improve their ability to recognize the signs of similar distress in others.

This leads to the third pillar, which is to *respond to the stressor* (i.e., exclusion). It is important that clients be able to realize the overall negative impact that exclusion can have on their functioning and learn how to respond when they recognize those feelings or thoughts. Using TIPPS as an example, students are taught that once they recognize their distress or the distress of others that is resulting from exclusion, they should consult their Coping Bag. The Coping Bag is designed as part of the curriculum to include positive thoughts, solutions, and emotion regulation techniques that students can use to cope. Students develop these strategies across lessons and build on their own strengths and experiences with effective coping. Doing so helps them respond in the moment and provides them an opportunity to explore prevention strategies.

Such prevention strategies compose the fourth pillar: *resist revictimization*. The TIPPS program helps students design strategies they can use independently or as a group to create spaces within their schools and lives in which the risk of social exclusion is reduced. From a systematic approach, TIPPS also supports this pillar by giving the students the tools they need to address their own experiences of exclusion (e.g., social support seeking) and reduce their own engagement in exclusionary behaviors toward others. TIPPS also resists revictimization of students who experience exclusion by not allowing such incidents to occur within the group without consequence (e.g., group expectations, consequences).

Principles of TIC

Across the TIPPS curriculum, all six principles are emphasized through group expectations and activities. First, *physical and psychological safety* is promoted through the use of group rules that maintain that members will strive to maintain confidentiality, actively listen to others, and include each other in conversations without engaging in exclusionary behaviors. Indeed, social exclusion may threaten a person's general sense of safety (e.g., MacDonald & Leary, 2005; Wesselmann, Hales, Ren, & Williams, 2015). TIPPS uses student-led discussions so participants can process how and why they feel safe, identify the people they feel are safe, and learn ways to enhance these feelings of safety for each other by promoting a shared positive space. These discussions can help participants develop cognitive skills in how they understand exclusion experiences so they can avoid harmful internal attributions or rumination on those events that may intensify or prolong psychological distress (e.g., Williams, 2009; Zadro, Boland, & Richardson, 2006). Ultimately, by including participants in setting group expectations for acceptance, all members should feel included in the process and develop a shared understanding of the group's climate—one of social safety. In addition, TIPPS emphasizes rules related to including others—not excluding or isolating group members—and maintaining a safe climate.

Following the second principle, TIPPS facilitators promote *trustworthiness and transparency* through group expectations and modeling throughout each lesson. Trust and clarity can be disrupted by feelings of exclusion, which creates tensions both within and outside of the group. The facilitators work to maintain a transparent approach to the group process, always explaining the group purpose and reviewing the group expectations at the beginning of each lesson. Furthermore, facilitators are trained to build a trusting space through consistency in behavior management and clear maintenance of confidentiality between them and the students. Trust and transparency can be harder to build between group members, particularly if group members have excluded each other within the group or are currently being excluded outside the group in their daily lives. In either case, group members may begin to withdraw socially as a way of avoiding future exclusion; this response has also been observed in basic research on social exclusion (Ren, Wesselmann, & Williams, 2016; Wesselmann, Williams, Ren, & Hales, 2014). Therefore, a reliance on group expectations that clearly outline that these behaviors are unacceptable is necessary.

The third and fourth principles, *peer support* and *collaboration and mutual self-help*, are considered the cornerstones of this program. TIPPS facilitators focus on increasing inclusive behaviors among group members and encouraging group members to remind each other of coping strategies and shared narratives to reorients students' focus away from reliance on adult intervention and more toward collaboration and support among peers. This approach is more helpful in reducing feelings of exclusion and peer aggression than adult intervention (Bauman & Del Rio, 2006; Tenenbaum, Varjas, Meyers, & Parris, 2011). By increasing students' recognition of their peers as a source of support and collaboration, the program seeks to reduce their engagement in exclusionary behaviors and increase their openness to including other students, even those outside of the group. In general, socially excluded individuals seek affiliation as a way to fortify their thwarted psychological needs (e.g., belonging; see Wesselmann, Ren, & Williams, 2015, for a review). Thus, having a therapy group that highlights inclusion is a source of belonging that they are not receiving elsewhere. In addition to gaining skills in eliciting and giving social support, the experience of shared narratives helps students recognize their common feelings, thoughts, and experiences, further reducing their feelings of isolation. They learn that they are not alone.

The fifth principle of TIC is *empowerment, voice, and choice*. The connection between this principle and exclusion may not be readily apparent. However, TIPPS's authors explicitly recognize the importance of providing students who experience exclusion with choice and strengths-based resources (i.e., empowerment). When experiencing exclusion, the victim can be left with a feeling that he or she is not in control or has no voice in the situation (Williams, 2009). Indeed, a lack of say, input, or perceived control into the world around a person, a by-product of exclusion, can be disorienting and stressful. This lack of power is important to address with group members. As such, strategies that promote decision making among members regarding group activities, the order of topics, and so forth can be beneficial in promoting feelings of inclusion within the group setting. Furthermore, empowerment can be promoted through activities that focus on identifying personal strengths and values within the group setting. Laboratory research on ways to recover from social exclusion demonstrate that self-affirmation activities—those encouraging people to identify and reflect on values that are important to their lives—can help people recover their thwarted psychological need satisfaction (Hales, Wesselmann, & Williams, 2016; Knowles, Lucas, Molden, Gardner, & Dean, 2010). Thus, it is likely that these types of activities would be useful in a group therapy context as well, especially if the group works to identify shared values that will define the group climate (e.g., inclusion). By promoting choice, decision making, the inclusion of different voices within group, and the identification of personal skill sets and strengths, group members are better able to offset and respond to exclusion outside of the group.

The sixth principle suggests that practitioners need to take cultural diversity into consideration when designing the format, organization, structure, and activity choices for each group. For example, discrimination based on sexual orientation and race are often presenting concerns for clients, and lessons specifically designed to address these issues are included as options for group facilitators of TIPPS. Learning how to respond to types of discrimination is important given both outright discrimination and subtle insensitive disparaging remarks and behaviors regarding one's minority status (i.e., microaggressions), which a person can experience as forms of social exclusion (Wesselmann et al., 2016). As such, these lessons are crucial for inclusion in group psychotherapy to address feelings of exclusion. Simply having these aspects of a person's identity acknowledged will likely increase their feelings of inclusion. Furthermore, the overall effectiveness of group psychotherapy in these contexts is improved when group members' cultural needs and uniqueness are identified and addressed in a responsive way (e.g., Robinson-Wood, 2017). The recognition and celebration of one's cultural identity is one of the most salient forms of social inclusion.

Evidence supports that TIC approaches (e.g., TIPPS) can be beneficial to trauma-focused group therapy (Nietlisbach & Maercker, 2009; SAMHSA, 2014; Varjas et al., 2006). This area of research would benefit from directly merging with social exclusion research to investigate ways that TIC approaches could directly address clients' social exclusion concerns outside of and within group therapy settings, especially from a systems-level service delivery perspective (e.g., Blitz & Lee, 2015). As we have reviewed, the connections are there implicitly and are supported by preliminary data (Foley et al., 2019; Varjas et al., 2006); however, direct testing is needed to assess the effectiveness of these approaches on outcomes relevant to social exclusion (e.g., feelings of social isolation, basic need satisfaction). Research designs that include a control or comparison group are crucial for identifying the ways in which a TIC framework for psychotherapeutic group therapy can be used with any given population. We make a call for researchers to consider the ways TIC approaches may be integrated into the group therapy process through investigations that are multiple method and span across multiple populations and presenting concerns. We have suggested TIPPS as one option but encourage research to consider how the principles of TIC may be integrated into their own preferred programs.

CONCLUSION

It is clear that social exclusion can have a negative impact on the lives of people, and clients who are dealing with trauma may be particularly vulnerable. Indeed, chronic exclusion also may be considered a type of trauma. Both literatures thus should build off each other to develop a more nuanced understanding of social exclusion in its various forms and to develop appropriate ways in which psychotherapeutic group setting can better handle clients' experiences with, and engagement in, exclusionary behaviors. Ultimately, group therapy could be used to help individuals effectively cope with social exclusion, whether it is their primary trauma or co-occurring with (and intensifying) other traumas. We recommend that group therapists consider using a

TIC approach because it has aspects uniquely designed to address areas of concern related to social exclusion.

In this chapter, we described TIPPS, an example program grounded in TIC research (Parris & Foley, 2017). We then highlighted the key aspects of this program and how they are relevant to exclusion research, especially research on coping with exclusion. TIPPS promotes peer support and collaboration, a focus on physical and psychological safety, adaptive coping, and teachings that enable clients to prevent exclusion for themselves as well as others. By following a trauma-informed group therapy approach, clinicians can ensure a safe, inclusive environment that increases the effectiveness of addressing various forms of social exclusion. Furthermore, this approach can help clients build the necessary awareness and skills for addressing these experiences and subsequent negative outcomes in their life.

SUGGESTED READINGS

Blitz, L. V., & Lee, Y. (2015). Trauma-informed methods to enhance school-based bullying prevention initiatives: An emerging model. *Journal of Aggression, Maltreatment & Trauma, 24,* 20–40. http://dx.doi.org/10.1080/10926771.2015.982238

In this article, Blitz and Lee describe a model for integrating trauma-informed care within the school context. The authors recount school-university partnerships designed to determine the effectiveness of trauma-informed services in reducing peer aggression among students. They outlined specific components of trauma-informed care that are necessary for such a model, systems-level approaches to implementation, and preliminary findings from the implementation of this model within school districts. This article clearly outlines the ways in which trauma-informed services are important to addressing exclusion-related stress among students. Furthermore, it lays the foundation for understanding the importance of trauma-informed approaches in group settings.

Substance Abuse and Mental Health Services Administration. (2014). *Trauma-informed care in behavioral health services* (Treatment Improvement Protocol Series 57; HHS Publication No. [SMA] 14-4816). Rockville, MD: Author. Retrieved from https://www.integration.samhsa.gov/clinical-practice/SAMSA_TIP_Trauma.pdf

This book outlines the need for and effective use of trauma-informed care. It includes an outline of protocol improvements for providing treatment within the trauma-informed care model. Furthermore, it offers specific information for group-based psychotherapeutic services. The authors provide a comprehensive, practical outline of how to integrate a trauma-informed approach throughout various modes of service delivery.

Wesselmann, E. D., Grzybowski, M. R., Steakley-Freeman, D. M., DeSouza, E. R., Nezlek, J. B., & Williams, K. D. (2016). Social exclusion in everyday life. In P. Riva & J. Eck (Eds.) *Social exclusion: Psychological approaches to understanding and reducing its impact* (pp. 3–23). Cham, Switzerland: Springer. http://dx.doi.org/10.1007/978-3-319-33033-4_1

This chapter provides an overview of diverse types of negative interpersonal interactions that can be considered forms of social exclusion. The authors organize these various forms within a taxonomy and then discuss the conceptual and empirical overlaps among the forms. The authors then close with suggestions for future directions that would advance a comprehensive literature focused on social exclusion.

Williams, K. D. (2009). Ostracism: A temporal need-threat model. In M. P. Zanna (Ed.), *Advances in experimental social psychology* (Vol. 41, pp. 275–314). San Diego, CA: Academic Press. http://dx.doi.org/10.1016/S0065-2601(08)00406-1

This article provides an in-depth review of the psychological research on ostracism, a specific type of social exclusion characterized by being ignored. The author extensively reviews the history of studying ostracism (and other forms of social exclusion) within psychology and provides a theoretical model of studying ostracism experimentally. He then reviews the various methods and findings used to study the immediate effects of ostracism and the way in which ostracized individuals focus on recovery. The author suggests avenues for future research on studying the effects of chronic ostracism on individuals' physical and psychological well-being.

REFERENCES

Bauman, S., & Del Rio, A. (2006). Preservice teachers' responses to bullying scenarios: Comparing physical, verbal, and relational bullying. *Journal of Educational Psychology, 98*, 219–231. http://dx.doi.org/10.1037/0022-0663.98.1.219

Baumeister, R. F., & Leary, M. R. (1995). The need to belong: Desire for interpersonal attachments as a fundamental human motivation. *Psychological Bulletin, 117*, 497–529. http://dx.doi.org/10.1037/0033-2909.117.3.497

Bernstein, M. J. (2016). Research in social psychology: Consequences of short- and long-term social exclusion. In P. Riva & J. Eck (Eds.), *Social exclusion: Psychological approaches to understanding and reducing its impact* (pp. 51–72). Cham, Switzerland: Springer International Publishing. http://dx.doi.org/10.1007/978-3-319-33033-4_3

Bernstein, M. J., & Claypool, H. M. (2012a). Not all social exclusions are created equal: Emotional distress following social exclusion is moderated by exclusion paradigm. *Social Influence, 7*, 113–130. http://dx.doi.org/10.1080/15534510.2012.664326

Bernstein, M. J., & Claypool, H. M. (2012b). Social exclusion and pain sensitivity: Why exclusion sometimes hurts and sometimes numbs. *Personality and Social Psychology Bulletin, 38*, 185–196. http://dx.doi.org/10.1177/0146167211422449

Bernstein, M. J., Claypool, H. M., Young, S. G., Tuscherer, T., Sacco, D. F., & Brown, C. M. (2013). Never let them see you cry: Self-presentation as a moderator of the relationship between exclusion and self-esteem. *Personality and Social Psychology Bulletin, 39*, 1293–1305. http://dx.doi.org/10.1177/0146167213495281

Black, P. J., Woodworth, M., Tremblay, M., & Carpenter, T. (2012). A review of trauma-informed treatment for adolescents. *Canadian Psychology, 53*, 192–203. http://dx.doi.org/10.1037/a0028441

Blackhart, G. C., Nelson, B. C., Knowles, M. L., & Baumeister, R. F. (2009). Rejection elicits emotional reactions but neither causes immediate distress nor lowers self-esteem: A meta-analytic review of 192 studies on social exclusion. *Personality and Social Psychology Review, 13*, 269–309. http://dx.doi.org/10.1177/1088868309346065

Blitz, L. V., & Lee, Y. (2015). Trauma-informed methods to enhance school-based bullying prevention initiatives: An emerging model. *Journal of Aggression, Maltreatment & Trauma, 24*, 20–40. http://dx.doi.org/10.1080/10926771.2015.982238

Böckler, A., Hömke, P., & Sebanz, N. (2014). Invisible man: Exclusion from shared attention affects gaze behavior and self-reports. *Social Psychological and Personality Science, 5*, 140–148. http://dx.doi.org/10.1177/1948550613488951

Brock, S., Nickerson, A., Reeves, M., Conolly, C., Jimerson, S., Pesce, R., & Lazzaro, B. (2016). *School crisis prevention and intervention: The PREPaRE model.* Bethesda, MD: National Association of School Psychologists.

Carter-Sowell, A. R., Chen, Z., & Williams, K. D. (2008). Ostracism increases social susceptibility. *Social Influence, 3*, 143–153. http://dx.doi.org/10.1080/15534510802204868

Chen, Z., Williams, K. D., Fitness, J., & Newton, N. C. (2008). When hurt will not heal: Exploring the capacity to relive social and physical pain. *Psychological Science, 19*, 789–795. http://dx.doi.org/10.1111/j.1467-9280.2008.02158.x

Crimston, D., Hornsey, M. J., Bain, P. G., & Bastian, B. (2018). Toward a psychology of moral expansiveness. *Current Directions in Psychological Science, 27*, 14–19. http://dx.doi.org/10.1177/0963721417730888

Demoulin, S., Leyens, J. P., Paladino, M. P., Rodriguez-Torres, R., Rodriguez-Perez, A., & Dovidio, J. F. (2004). Dimensions of "uniquely" and "non-uniquely" human emotions. *Cognition and Emotion, 18*, 71–96. http://dx.doi.org/10.1080/02699930244000444

DeWall, C. N. (2010). Forming a basis for acceptance: Excluded people form attitudes to agree with potential affiliates. *Social Influence, 5*, 245–260. http://dx.doi.org/10.1080/15534511003783536

Dickerson, S. S., & Kemeny, M. E. (2004). Acute stressors and cortisol responses: A theoretical integration and synthesis of laboratory research. *Psychological Bulletin, 130*, 355–391. http://dx.doi.org/10.1037/0033-2909.130.3.355

Dotan-Eliaz, O., Sommer, K. L., & Rubin, Y. S. (2009). Multilingual groups: Effects of linguistic ostracism on felt rejection and anger, coworker attraction, perceived team potency, and creative performance. *Basic and Applied Social Psychology, 31*, 363–375. http://dx.doi.org/10.1080/01973530903317177

Eisenberger, N. I., & Lieberman, M. D. (2004). Why rejection hurts: A common neural alarm system for physical and social pain. *Trends in Cognitive Sciences, 8*, 294–300. http://dx.doi.org/10.1016/j.tics.2004.05.010

Eisenberger, N. I., Lieberman, M. D., & Williams, K. D. (2003). Does rejection hurt? An fMRI study of social exclusion. *Science, 302*, 290–292. http://dx.doi.org/10.1126/science.1089134

Ellemers, N., Spears, R., & Doosje, B. (2002). Self and social identity. *Annual Review of Psychology, 53*, 161–186. http://dx.doi.org/10.1146/annurev.psych.53.100901.135228

Ferris, D. L., Brown, D. J., Berry, J. W., & Lian, H. (2008). The development and validation of the Workplace Ostracism Scale. *Journal of Applied Psychology, 93*, 1348–1366. http://dx.doi.org/10.1037/a0012743

Foley, J., Charczuk, P., & Parris, L. (2019, February–March). *Evaluating the trauma-informed program for promoting success: Implications for practice.* Paper presented at the National Association of School Psychologists Annual Convention, Atlanta, GA.

Galupo, M. P., Henise, S. B., & Davis, K. S. (2014). Transgender microaggressions in the context of friendship: Patterns of experience across friends' sexual orientation and gender identity. *Psychology of Sexual Orientation and Gender Diversity, 1*, 461–470. http://dx.doi.org/10.1037/sgd0000075

Gerber, J., & Wheeler, L. (2009). On being rejected: A meta-analysis of experimental research on rejection. *Perspectives on Psychological Science, 4*, 468–488. http://dx.doi.org/10.1111/j.1745-6924.2009.01158.x

Gilman, R., Carter-Sowell, A., DeWall, C. N., Adams, R. E., & Carboni, I. (2013). Validation of the Ostracism Experience Scale for Adolescents. *Psychological Assessment, 25*, 319–330. http://dx.doi.org/10.1037/a0030913

Godwin, A., MacNevin, G., Zadro, L., Iannuzzelli, R., Weston, S., Gonsalkorale, K., & Devine, P. (2014). Are all ostracism experiences equal? A comparison of the autobiographical recall, Cyberball, and O-Cam paradigms. *Behavior Research Methods, 46,* 660–667. http://dx.doi.org/10.3758/s13428-013-0408-0

Goff, P. A., Eberhardt, J. L., Williams, M. J., & Jackson, M. C. (2008). Not yet human: Implicit knowledge, historical dehumanization, and contemporary consequences. *Journal of Personality and Social Psychology, 94,* 292–306. http://dx.doi.org/10.1037/0022-3514.94.2.292

Hales, A. H., Dvir, M., Wesselmann, E. D., Kruger, D. J., & Finkenauer, C. (2018). Cell phone-induced ostracism threatens fundamental needs. *Journal of Social Psychology, 158,* 460–473. http://dx.doi.org/10.1080/00224545.2018.1439877 (Correction published 2019, *Journal of Social Psychology, 160,* 264–266. http://dx.doi.org/10.1080/00224545.2019.1599547)

Hales, A. H., Wesselmann, E. D., & Williams, K. D. (2016). Prayer, self-affirmation, and distraction improve recovery from short-term ostracism. *Journal of Experimental Social Psychology, 64,* 8–20. http://dx.doi.org/10.1016/j.jesp.2016.01.002

Hartgerink, C. H., van Beest, I., Wicherts, J. M., & Williams, K. D. (2015). The ordinal effects of ostracism: A meta-analysis of 120 Cyberball studies. *PLoS ONE, 10,* e0127002. http://dx.doi.org/10.1371/journal.pone.0127002

Hitlan, R. T., Kelly, K. M., Schepman, S., Schneider, K. T., & Zárate, M. A. (2006). Language exclusion and the consequences of perceived ostracism in the workplace. *Group Dynamics: Theory, Research, and Practice, 10,* 56–70. http://dx.doi.org/10.1037/1089-2699.10.1.56

Iannone, N. E., Kelly, J. R., & Williams, K. D. (2018). "Who's that?": The negative consequences of being out of the loop on pop culture. *Psychology of Popular Media Culture, 7,* 113–129. http://dx.doi.org/10.1037/ppm0000120

Iffland, B., Sansen, L. M., Catani, C., & Neuner, F. (2014). Rapid heartbeat, but dry palms: Reactions of heart rate and skin conductance levels to social rejection. *Frontiers in Psychology, 5,* 956. http://dx.doi.org/10.3389/fpsyg.2014.00956

James, W. (1950). *Principles of psychology* (Vol. 1). New York, NY: Dover. (Original work published 1890)

Jones, E. E., Carter-Sowell, A. R., Kelly, J. R., & Williams, K. D. (2009). "I'm out of the loop": Ostracism through information exclusion. *Group Processes & Intergroup Relations, 12,* 157–174. http://dx.doi.org/10.1177/1368430208101054

Klages, S. V., & Wirth, J. H. (2014). Excluded by laughter: Laughing until it hurts someone else. *Journal of Social Psychology, 154,* 8–13. http://dx.doi.org/10.1080/00224545.2013.843502

Knowles, M. L., Lucas, G. M., Molden, D. C., Gardner, W. L., & Dean, K. K. (2010). There's no substitute for belonging: Self-affirmation following social and nonsocial threats. *Personality and Social Psychology Bulletin, 36,* 173–186. http://dx.doi.org/10.1177/0146167209346860

Koudenburg, N., Postmes, T., & Gordijn, E. H. (2011). Disrupting the flow: How brief silences in group conversations affect social needs. *Journal of Experimental Social Psychology, 47,* 512–515. http://dx.doi.org/10.1016/j.jesp.2010.12.006

Leary, M. R. (1999). Making sense of self-esteem. *Current Directions in Psychological Science, 8,* 32–35. http://dx.doi.org/10.1111/1467-8721.00008

Leary, M. R., Haupt, A. L., Strausser, K. S., & Chokel, J. T. (1998). Calibrating the sociometer: The relationship between interpersonal appraisals and state self-esteem. *Journal of Personality and Social Psychology, 74,* 1290–1299. http://dx.doi.org/10.1037/0022-3514.74.5.1290

Leary, M. R., Twenge, J. M., & Quinlivan, E. (2006). Interpersonal rejection as a determinant of anger and aggression. *Personality and Social Psychology Review, 10,* 111–132. http://dx.doi.org/10.1207/s15327957pspr1002_2

Lieberman, M. D. (2013). *Social: Why our brains are wired to connect*. New York, NY: Crown.

MacDonald, G., & Leary, M. R. (2005). Why does social exclusion hurt? The relationship between social and physical pain. *Psychological Bulletin, 131*, 202–223. http://dx.doi.org/10.1037/0033-2909.131.2.202

McElroy, S., & Hevey, D. (2014). Relationship between adverse early experiences, stressors, psychosocial resources and wellbeing. *Child Abuse & Neglect, 38*, 65–75. http://dx.doi.org/10.1016/j.chiabu.2013.07.017

Nadal, K. L. (2011). The Racial and Ethnic Microaggressions Scale (REMS): Construction, reliability, and validity. *Journal of Counseling Psychology, 58*, 470–480. http://dx.doi.org/10.1037/a0025193

Nadal, K. L., Davidoff, K. C., Davis, L. S., & Wong, Y. (2014). Emotional, behavioral, and cognitive reactions to microaggressions: Transgender perspectives. *Psychology of Sexual Orientation and Gender Diversity, 1*, 72–81. http://dx.doi.org/10.1037/sgd0000011

Nadal, K. L., Skolnik, A., & Wong, Y. (2012). Interpersonal and systemic microaggressions toward transgender people: Implications for counseling. *Journal of LGBT Issues in Counseling, 6*, 55–82. http://dx.doi.org/10.1080/15538605.2012.648583

Nezlek, J. B., Wesselmann, E. D., Wheeler, L., & Williams, K. D. (2012). Ostracism in everyday life. *Group Dynamics: Theory, Research, and Practice, 16*, 91–104. http://dx.doi.org/10.1037/a0028029

Nietlisbach, G., & Maercker, A. (2009). Effects of social exclusion in trauma survivors with posttraumatic stress disorder. *Psychological Trauma: Theory, Research, Practice, and Policy, 1*, 323–331. http://dx.doi.org/10.1037/a0017832

Parris, L., & Foley, J. (2017). *The Trauma-Informed Program for Promoting Success* (TIPPS). Normal, IL: The Center for Climate, Affective Education, and Mental Health in Schools, Illinois State University.

Reiter-Scheidl, K., Papousek, I., Lackner, H. K., Paechter, M., Weiss, E. M., & Aydin, N. (2018). Aggressive behavior after social exclusion is linked with the spontaneous initiation of more action-oriented coping immediately following the exclusion episode. *Physiology & Behavior, 195*, 142–150. http://dx.doi.org/10.1016/j.physbeh.2018.08.001

Ren, D., Wesselmann, E. D., & Williams, K. D. (2016). Evidence for another response to ostracism: Solitude seeking. *Social Psychological and Personality Science, 7*, 204–212. http://dx.doi.org/10.1177/1948550615616169

Riva, P., & Eck, J. (2016). The many faces of social exclusion. In P. Riva & J. Eck (Eds.), *Social exclusion: Psychological approaches to understanding and reducing its impact* (pp. ix–xv). Cham, Switzerland: Springer. http://dx.doi.org/10.1007/978-3-319-33033-4

Riva, P., Montali, L., Wirth, J. H., Curioni, S., & Williams, K. D. (2017). Chronic social exclusion and evidence for the resignation stage: An empirical investigation. *Journal of Social and Personal Relationships, 34*, 541–564. http://dx.doi.org/0265407516644348

Robinson, S. L., O'Reilly, J., & Wang, W. (2013). Invisible at work: An integrated model of workplace ostracism. *Journal of Management, 39*, 203–231. http://dx.doi.org/10.1177/0149206312466141

Robinson-Wood, T. (2017). *The convergence of race, ethnicity, and gender: Multiple identities in counseling* (5th ed.). Los Angeles, CA: Sage.

Rudert, S. C., Hales, A. H., Greifeneder, R., & Williams, K. D. (2017). When silence is not golden: Why acknowledgment matters even when being excluded. *Personality and Social Psychology Bulletin, 43*, 678–692. http://dx.doi.org/10.1177/0146167217695554

Saylor, C. F., Nida, S. A., Williams, K. D., Taylor, L. A., Smyth, W., Twyman, K. A., . . . Spratt, E. G. (2012). Bullying and Ostracism Screening Scales (BOSS): Development and applications. *Children's Health Care, 41*, 322–343. http://dx.doi.org/10.1080/02739615.2012.720962

Smart Richman, L., & Leary, M. R. (2009). Reactions to discrimination, stigmatization, ostracism, and other forms of interpersonal rejection: A multimotive model. *Psychological Review, 116*, 365–383. http://dx.doi.org/10.1037/a0015250

Sommer, K. L., Williams, K. D., Ciarocco, N. J., & Baumeister, R. F. (2001). When silence speaks louder than words: Explorations into the intrapsychic and interpersonal consequences of social ostracism. *Basic and Applied Social Psychology, 23*, 225–243. http://dx.doi.org/10.1207/S15324834BASP2304_1

Stout, J. G., & Dasgupta, N. (2011). When he doesn't mean you: Gender-exclusive language as ostracism. *Personality and Social Psychology Bulletin, 37*, 757–769. http://dx.doi.org/10.1177/0146167211406434

Substance Abuse and Mental Health Services Administration. (2014). *Trauma-informed care in behavioral health services* (Treatment Improvement Protocol Series 57; HHS Publication No. [SMA] 14-4816). Rockville, MD: Author. Retrieved from https://www.integration.samhsa.gov/clinical-practice/SAMSA_TIP_Trauma.pdf

Sue, D. W. (Ed.). (2010). *Microaggressions and marginality: Manifestation, dynamics, and impact.* Hoboken, NJ: Wiley.

Sue, D. W., Capodilupo, C. M., Torino, G. C., Bucceri, J. M., Holder, A. M. B., Nadal, K. L., & Esquilin, M. (2007). Racial microaggressions in everyday life: Implications for clinical practice. *American Psychologist, 62*, 271–286. http://dx.doi.org/10.1037/0003-066X.62.4.271

Tenenbaum, L., Varjas, J., Meyers, J., & Parris, L. (2011). Coping strategies and perceived effectiveness in fourth through eighth grade victims of bullying. *School Psychology International, 32*, 263–287. http://dx.doi.org/10.1177/0143034311402309

van der Wal, M. F., de Wit, C. A., & Hirasing, R. A. (2003). Psychosocial health among young victims and offenders of direct and indirect bullying. *Pediatrics, 111*, 1312–1317. http://dx.doi.org/10.1542/peds.111.6.1312

Varjas, K., Meyers, J., Henrich, C. C., Graybill, E. C., Dew, B. J., Marshall, M. L., . . . Avant, M. (2006). Using a participatory culture-specific intervention model to develop a peer victimization intervention. *Journal of Applied School Psychology, 22*, 35–57. http://dx.doi.org/10.1300/J370v22n02_03

Vidourek, R. A., King, K. A., & Merianos, A. L. (2016). School bullying and student trauma: Fear and avoidance associated with victimization. *Journal of Prevention & Intervention in the Community, 44*, 121–129. http://dx.doi.org/10.1080/10852352.2016.1132869

Warburton, W. A., Williams, K. D., & Cairns, D. R. (2006). When ostracism leads to aggression: The moderating effects of control deprivation. *Journal of Experimental Social Psychology, 42*, 213–220. http://dx.doi.org/10.1016/j.jesp.2005.03.005

Wesselmann, E. D., Butler, F. A., Williams, K. D., & Pickett, C. L. (2010). Adding injury to insult: Unexpected rejection leads to more aggressive responses. *Aggressive Behavior, 36*, 232–237. http://dx.doi.org/10.1002/ab.20347

Wesselmann, E. D., Cardoso, F. D., Slater, S., & Williams, K. D. (2012). To be looked at as though air: Civil attention matters. *Psychological Science, 23*, 166–168. http://dx.doi.org/10.1177/0956797611427921

Wesselmann, E. D., Grzybowski, M. R., Steakley-Freeman, D. M., DeSouza, E. R., Nezlek, J. B., & Williams, K. D. (2016). Social exclusion in everyday life. In P. Riva & J. Eck (Eds.), *Social exclusion: Psychological approaches to understanding and reducing its impact* (pp. 3–23). Cham, Switzerland: Springer. http://dx.doi.org/10.1007/978-3-319-33033-4_1

Wesselmann, E. D., Hales, A. H., Ren, D., & Williams, K. D. (2015). Ostracism threatens personal security: A temporal need threat framework. In P. J. Carroll, R. M. Arkin, & A. L. Wichman (Eds.), *Handbook of personal security* (pp. 191–206). New York, NY: Psychology Press.

Wesselmann, E. D., Ren, D., & Williams, K. D. (2015). Motivations for responses to ostracism. *Frontiers in Psychology, 6*, 40. http://dx.doi.org/10.3389/fpsyg.2015.00040

Wesselmann, E. D., Schneider, K. T., Ford, T. E., & DeSouza, E. R. (2018, April). Disparaging humor as a form of social exclusion. In C. Liu (Chair), *Are you ostracized at work? Investigating different forms of ostracism.* Symposium conducted at the meeting for the Society for Industrial and Organizational Psychology, Chicago, IL.

Wesselmann, E. D., & Williams, K. D. (2017). Social life and social death: Inclusion, ostracism, and rejection in groups. *Group Processes & Intergroup Relations, 20,* 693–706. http://dx.doi.org/10.1177/1368430217708861

Wesselmann, E. D., Williams, K. D., Ren, D., & Hales, A. H. (2014). Ostracism and solitude. In R. J. Coplan & J. C. Bowker (Eds.), *A handbook of solitude: Psychological perspectives on social isolation, social withdrawal, and being alone* (pp. 224–241). Hoboken, NJ: Wiley-Blackwell.

Williams, K. D. (2001). *Ostracism: The power of silence.* New York, NY: Guilford Press.

Williams, K. D. (2009). Ostracism: A temporal need-threat model. In M. P. Zanna (Ed.), *Advances in experimental social psychology* (Vol. 41, pp. 275–314). San Diego, CA: Academic Press. http://dx.doi.org/10.1016/S0065-2601(08)00406-1

Williams, K. D., Cheung, C. K. T., & Choi, W. (2000). Cyberostracism: Effects of being ignored over the Internet. *Journal of Personality and Social Psychology, 79,* 748–762. http://dx.doi.org/10.1037/0022-3514.79.5.748

Williams, K. D., & Nida, S. A. (2009). Is ostracism worse than bullying? In M. J. Harris (Ed.), *Bullying, rejection, & peer victimization: A social cognitive neuroscience perspective* (pp. 279–296). New York, NY: Springer.

Williams, K. D., Shore, W. J., & Grahe, J. E. (1998). The silent treatment: Perceptions of its behaviors and associated feelings. *Group Processes & Intergroup Relations, 1,* 117–141. http://dx.doi.org/10.1177/1368430298012002

Williams, K. D., & Sommer, K. L. (1997). Social ostracism by coworkers: Does rejection lead to loafing or compensation? *Personality and Social Psychology Bulletin, 23,* 693–706. http://dx.doi.org/10.1177/0146167297237003

Wirth, J. H. (2016). Methods for investigating social exclusion. In P. Riva & J. Eck (Eds.), *Social exclusion: Psychological approaches to understanding and reducing its impact* (pp. 25–47). Cham, Switzerland: Springer. http://dx.doi.org/10.1007/978-3-319-33033-4_2

Wirth, J. H., Sacco, D. F., Hugenberg, K., & Williams, K. D. (2010). Eye gaze as relational evaluation: Averted eye gaze leads to feelings of ostracism and relational devaluation. *Personality and Social Psychology Bulletin, 36,* 869–882. http://dx.doi.org/10.1177/0146167210370032

Zadro, L., Boland, C., & Richardson, R. (2006). How long does it last? The persistence of the effects of ostracism in the socially anxious. *Journal of Experimental Social Psychology, 42,* 692–697. http://dx.doi.org/10.1016/j.jesp.2005.10.007

3

Composition and Compilation

A Selective Review and Applications to Therapy Groups

Michael R. Baumann and James C. Deller

Group behavior is a product of many factors, including the characteristics the group's members possess (Bell, Brown, Colaneri, & Outland, 2018; Hackman & Morris, 1975; McGrath, 1984), the nature of the group's task (Laughlin, 2011), and how these factors combine (Prewett, Walvoord, Stilson, Rossi, & Brannick, 2009). The role of member characteristics and how they interact with the group task has been studied across a range of literatures under several labels, including group composition, diversity, and social combination. Combined across these various labels, the literature is sufficiently developed to have supported recent meta-analyses on a range of member characteristics, including member personality (e.g., Bell, 2007; Prewett et al., 2009) as well as demographic characteristics and task-related knowledge or expertise (e.g., van Dijk, van Engen, & van Knippenberg, 2012). For convenience, we refer to these member characteristics collectively as *group composition.*

Although group composition has been heavily studied in group decision making and related contexts in social and organizational psychology, it has also been called one of the least studied factors in group therapy (Burlingame, Fuhriman, & Mosier, 2003). In keeping with the theme of this volume, the goals of the current chapter are (a) to examine the social and organizational psychology literature on group composition for insights that may be of use to practitioners of group therapy and (b) to identify ways in which research with therapy groups may further inform research on group composition in other settings. We first provide background on composition and its operationalization. Second,

http://dx.doi.org/10.1037/0000201-004
The Psychology of Groups: The Intersection of Social Psychology and Psychotherapy Research,
C. D. Parks and G. A. Tasca (Editors)

we compare group therapy to the contexts typically used in the study of composition to identify areas of the composition literature that are likely to be relevant to therapeutic success. Then we review what is known about composition for these variables. We end the chapter by drawing insights regarding likely effects of composition on group therapy and suggest ways in which composition researchers may benefit from the study of groups in therapeutic settings.

OVERVIEW OF COMPOSITION AND COMPILATION PROCESSES

The term *composition* has multiple meanings in the groups literature. The older and more common use of the term refers to the mix of characteristics possessed by members of a given group, for example, the mixture of member personalities, demographics, knowledge, and abilities. However, the term can also refer to the process by which those characteristics combine to influence group outcomes. Kozlowski and Klein (2000) proposed a range of combination processes anchored by *composition* processes on one end and *compilation* processes on the other. In processes toward the compositional end, each member's standing on the relevant characteristic(s) has equal impact on the group outcome of interest. For processes toward the compilation end, different members' characteristics have different impact on the outcome of interest. Any one characteristic may impact multiple outcomes through multiple processes. Therefore, when predicting how various combinations or configurations of member characteristics may impact group outcomes, it is important to think carefully about the process(es) through which those characteristics combine (Kozlowski & Klein, 2000). To date, much of the research on group composition has relied on models of combination drawn from a typology developed by Steiner (1966).

Steiner (1966) proposed several models of how member inputs might combine to influence group outcomes. In what Steiner called an *additive model*, the group outcome is the sum of member inputs. A classic application of this model is a game of tug-of-war. The total force exerted by each group is the vector sum of the forces exerted by each member of the group. When assuming an additive model, it is reasonable to operationalize group composition in terms of the average of members' scores on the characteristic of interest (i.e., strength). That is, additive models are consistent with compositional processes in that each member's contribution has equal influence on the group outcome.

Moving slightly away from composition toward compilation, Steiner (1966) also discussed two models in which a key individual, rather than all members, determines the group's performance. For one of these, the *disjunctive model*, performance is a function of the resources of the most able member, for example, when the first member of a team to cross the finish line defines which team wins a race. In contrast, in the *conjunctive model*, performance is a function of the resources of the least able member. An example is a team of mountain climbers tethered to one another; the team can climb no faster than its slowest member. Because each of these models gives more weight to one member than others, each is more compilational in nature relative to additive models. Outcomes are not predicted by the average of member characteristic but rather by the "best" or "worst" member, respectively, regardless of other members' characteristics.

Moving yet further in the direction of what is now called compilation, Steiner (1966) also discussed *complementary models*. In these models, the outcome is determined by how members' inputs fit together. For example, if the outcome is determining which of two pharmaceuticals to develop and market, a group may need to consider legal issues, research and development issues, and manufacturing issues. As long as some member understands the legal issues, some member understands the research and development, and some member understands the manufacturing issues, the group can succeed. No one member need understand it all. The quality of group's solution is not determined by their total knowledge (additive) or most knowledgeable member (disjunctive) but by how well members' knowledge fits together. In a similar vein, how well members get along may be determined by how each member's personality fits (or does not fit) with others' rather than the average, highest, or lowest member's scores.

In addition to each of the preceding models, there is often theoretical reason to expect group outcomes to vary as a function of differences between members (heterogeneity). Operationalizations based on heterogeneity are common in the diversity literature and include separation, variety, and disparity (Harrison & Klein, 2007). These three differ from each other in important ways. *Separation* involves variability along a continuous dimension (e.g., conscientiousness) and is assessed with familiar statistics, such as standard deviations. In contrast, *variety* involves differences in kind (e.g., demographic category) and is assessed in terms of the proportion of group members' falling into each possible category (e.g., Blau's index; Blau, 1977). The more equally each category is represented, the greater the variety. *Disparity* maps differences to differences in power or resources (e.g., coefficient of variation, Gini coefficient; see Allison, 1978). A group with relatively low separation could have relatively high disparity. For example, a group with a relatively small standard deviation in member age but in which power is concentrated among the oldest members would have low separation but high disparity. Thus, even looking at the same groups, one may obtain very different results depending on the operationalization used (Harrison & Klein, 2007).

As demonstrated by the earlier examples, there are many ways in which member characteristics can combine to influence group outcomes. These examples are common in one or more of the areas contained in this review but are by no means exhaustive.

GROUP THERAPY

The models by which member inputs combine often vary by task type (Laughlin, 2011; Prewett et al., 2009). As such, to apply the composition literature to group therapy requires careful consideration of the nature of group therapy, the processes and states one wants to create in group therapy, and what parts of the composition literature speak to those states in similar contexts. Most composition research has been conducted in the context of members' working to jointly create some product (e.g., make a decision, generate a plan, assemble a device). The amount and nature of interaction between members varies from study to study. In group therapy, the group is a vehicle for helping members gain insights into themselves and into managing the challenges that led them to seek therapy. The process involves extensive direct interaction between group members over time. In exploring curative factors in group therapy (e.g., Butler & Fuhriman, 1983; Yalom, 2005), we noted three involving processes or states that have been often studied in the social and organizational literature on composition: (a) members' sharing and use of information, (b) group cohesion, and (c) intragroup conflict.

The extent to which members volunteer their information to the group and learn from information others provide can be key to successful outcomes (Yalom, 2005). Sharing experiences with others facing similar challenges can provide perspective on thoughts and feelings related to those challenges (VanDeusen & Carr, 2003). Group members can also aid each other by disclosing coping strategies they have used that others might not know (e.g., Classen et al., 2001). Feedback from other members can also provide individuals with insight into the causes and effects of their own behaviors and feelings (Butler & Fuhriman, 1983).

Meta-analyses on group therapy have repeatedly identified group cohesion as an important contributor to therapeutic success (Burlingame et al., 2003; Burlingame, McClendon, & Yang, 2018). In the social and organizational literature, including on composition, cohesion is typically treated as having two components: task cohesion and social cohesion (Salas, Grossman, Hughes, & Coultas, 2015). That is, these literatures treat it as a combination of unity of purpose and social attraction to group members rather than either alone. As discussed in more depth by Marmarosh and Sproul (Chapter 9, this volume) and others (e.g., Burlingame & Jensen, 2017), the definition most often used in group therapy focuses on feelings of connection, social bonds, and emotional safety. Meta-analyses in the social and organizational literature have found that the strength of the relation of cohesion to outcomes and antecedents thereof varies with the definition of cohesion used (e.g., Beal, Cohen, Burke, & McLendon, 2003; Grossman, 2014). As such, although findings from the social and organizational literature on composition may inform effects of composition on cohesion in the sense meant in group therapy, caution should be taken when doing so.

In the social and organizational literatures, intragroup conflict often interferes with information sharing and use, and with group cohesion. For the purposes of the current chapter, we limit our use of the term *conflict* to what the group decision-making literature calls *affective* (Amason, 1996) or *relationship conflict* (Jehn, 1995). These terms refer to forms of conflict in which the disagreement is "taken personally" by at least one member of the group and results in negative feelings toward another. This is the antithesis of social cohesion and emotional safety.

It is important to note that there are many plausible process models for how composition may relate to information sharing and use, cohesion, and conflict. For example, consistent with an additive model (i.e., compositional process), it is plausible that the more each member adds his or her unique, relevant information, the greater the opportunities for others to gain insights into and strategies for addressing the issues for which they sought treatment. However, it is also likely that members who differ from each other in experience, perspective, or both, can achieve insights none had before by integrating their disparate information (e.g., Fraidin, 2004; van Ginkel & van Knippenberg, 2008). That is, complementary processes (i.e., compilation) may take place alongside of or instead of additive ones. One can imagine a single member engaging in sufficiently negative behavior to sabotage information sharing and cohesion in a conjunctive fashion (i.e., compilation). In short, more than one model may be relevant to any outcome, and the best model for predicting one outcome may not work for predicting others.

COMPOSITION AND COMPILATION IN INFORMATION SHARING AND GROUP PERFORMANCE

Much of the research on group composition focuses on tasks involving coordination or discussion between group members and its impact on group performance. This literature can be loosely organized based on the member characteristics examined: personality, demographics, and information or expertise.

Personality

Much of the composition literature on personality examines either the five-factor model personality model (McCrae & Costa, 1987) or emotional intelligence (Salovey & Mayer, 1990). Composition in this literature is often operationalized as the mean of group members' scores on the variable in question, although conjunctive, disjunctive, and heterogeneity models (primarily separation) are also used (see Bell, 2007, or Prewett et al., 2009, for tallies). A meta-analysis by Bell (2007) found significant positive associations of mean agreeableness, conscientiousness, openness to experience, extraversion, emotional stability, and emotional intelligence to performance. However, when using a conjunctive (lowest member's score) operationalization, only agreeableness and conscientiousness remained significant. When using a disjunctive operationalization, only openness did. No significant relations were found for heterogeneity.

Building on Bell (2007), Prewett et al. (2009) conducted a meta-analysis testing the amount and nature of interactions between members as a possible moderator of the association between composition and performance. Collapsing across tasks, Prewett et al. found, much like Bell (2007), that the mean of members' scores significantly predicted performance for each personality variable tested. In addition, several associations that did not achieve significance in Bell (2007) did so in Prewett et al., specifically, the associations of performance to heterogeneity (separation) in extroversion (positive) and agreeableness (negative), and disjunctive (highest members' score) operationalizations of conscientiousness, extraversion, and emotional stability (all positive). As predicted, several of these associations were moderated by the task. For tasks involving greater and more complex interactions between members, both mean and lowest member scores for agreeableness and conscientiousness had significant associations with performance. Of these associations, only mean conscientiousness was significant when complexity was low. Presumably, when the task requires members to interact often and in complex ways, high levels of agreeableness and conscientiousness on average *and* of the least agreeable or conscientious member facilitate task-performance behaviors like attention to detail, open communication, and willingness to consider alternate points of view. These findings highlight the importance of the task when examining group composition as well as the potential damage a single bad member can do when the task requires extensive interaction between members.

Overall, the literature suggests that for those personality variables examined, information sharing and use were often significantly associated with additive operationalizations of composition and on occasion with other operationalizations. However, for some characteristics, more than one operationalization yielded a significant association. Caution is required when interpreting such patterns because they could mean two processes are at work or indicate overlap between models. For example, when mean and lowest member score each predict an outcome, each could do so separately through its own mechanism. However, because the lowest member score is part of calculating the mean, the two operationalizations overlap.

Demographics

Much of the research on demographic composition comes from the diversity literature. In this literature, composition is operationalized as heterogeneity, often as separation for continuous variables (e.g., age) and variety for discrete variables (e.g., sex). As pointed out in the categorization-elaboration model (CEM; van Knippenberg, De Dreu, & Homan, 2004), to the extent demographic heterogeneity reflects heterogeneity in experiences and perspectives, it creates an opportunity for combination and the processing of more information. However, heterogeneity also creates a risk of social categorization and intergroup biases that may interfere with capitalizing on that opportunity. For example, a three-person research team consisting of one cognitive, one social, and one clinical psychologist has a broader knowledge base than one consisting of three people from any one subfield. However, subfields may have differences in methodology, terminology, and philosophy, or may even have stereotypes about each other. Such differences make it more difficult to reach across sub-fields than to work with others from one's own subfield. The benefits of a broader knowledge base only manifest when these obstacles are absent or can be overcome.

Several meta-analyses have assessed the relation between demographic heterogeneity and performance. One of these (van Dijk et al., 2012) also tested possible moderators suggested by the CEM. Consistent with other meta-analyses (e.g., Horwitz & Horwitz, 2007), no significant overall associations were found of performance with heterogeneity in age, ethnicity, gender, nationality, or education level. Interestingly, each of these variables had a significant negative association on rating-based measures of performance but not on objective measures. In addition, the relations were more likely to be negative for external ratings than for ratings provided by members of the groups themselves. Furthermore, heterogeneity in age, ethnicity, gender, and education level each had significant negative relations to performance of routine tasks (e.g., an assembly line). In contrast, performance on tasks requiring innovation (e.g., development of a novel manufacturing process) had a significant positive association with heterogeneity in educational level and no relation to heterogeneity in the other demographic variables. This pattern of findings is consistent with the notion that the potential value of informational differences associated with demographic heterogeneity is higher for tasks that benefit from members' sharing and integrating that information.

Meta-analyses such as van Dijk et al. (2012) are consistent with the notion that, overall, heterogeneity in age, ethnicity, gender, nationality, and education level is not significantly related to information sharing and use in and of themselves. As the CEM (van Knippenberg et al., 2004) points out, demographic heterogeneity may act as a proxy for heterogeneity in other characteristics, including knowledge, training, or personality, that directly impacts group outcomes. This would be consistent with the finding that the longer a group is together, the weaker the effects of demographic composition and the stronger the effects of other composition variables (e.g., perspectives, personality) become (Harrison, Price, Gavin, & Florey, 2002). It is important to think carefully about how each of these factors may influence possible effects of demographic composition on each outcome of interest.

Information and Expertise

One of a group's biggest strengths is its potential to integrate the differing knowledge, perspectives, and abilities of its members (Hackman & Morris, 1975; McGrath, 1984). As summarized by Laughlin (2011), decades of research have examined group choices and the extent to which groups choose the best answer proposed, the answer supported by a particular number of members before discussion (e.g., a majority), or some other function of member preferences. Research in this tradition has generally found that the extent to and manner in which members combine their information vary with a construct known as *demonstrability*.

Laughlin and Ellis (1986) defined demonstrability in terms of four conditions. These four conditions are: (1) members have a shared conceptual system allowing understanding and communication about the task; (2) members, collectively, have sufficient information to solve the task; (3) members who lack the solution are able to recognize it if it is provided to them; and (4) members who have the solution are willing and able to demonstrate it to the group. Several decades of research by Laughlin and others treated demonstrability as a continuum, and recent research has treated each of the conditions as continua as well (e.g., the extent to which members share an appropriate conceptual system, the extent to which the information available can narrow potential solutions; cf. Bonner & Baumann, 2012). Demonstrability is high when each of the conditions is largely fulfilled. Consider the task of evaluating the profitability of a product a company makes. If group members have a shared set of rules for what to count as revenues and costs, and how to count them, they have a shared conceptual system. If they have access to all of the files needed to fully tally those revenues and costs, they have sufficient information. Given enough time, each member could examine and demonstrate errors in any member's calculations (including their own). Demonstrability would be high in this case. In contrast, if members disagree on how to weigh revenues and costs, lack data on revenues or costs, or lack the time or motivation to examine and correct calculations, demonstrability would be low. Although some tasks (e.g., issues of objective fact) are more likely to be demonstrable than others (e.g., issues of aesthetics), the conditions under which the group performs the task are also important.

Members volunteer more information (Stasser & Stewart, 1992) and are more influenced by the accuracy of the answers offered (Laughlin, 2011) when demonstrability is higher rather than lower. The increase in influence is presumed to result from members attending more to the information given when demonstrability is higher (Levine & Smith, 2013). Under lower demonstrability, more extroverted members (Bonner, Sillito, & Baumann, 2007) and those with more extreme opinions (Bonner & Baumann, 2012; Kaplan & Miller, 1987) often have disproportionately high influence.

In the context of informational or expertise composition, which information is discussed is at least as important as how much is discussed. This is particularly true when members have different but equally relevant information or expertise. The diversity literature has studied this primarily in terms of variety in members' operational or disciplinary background, which the literature calls *functional diversity*. A research team consisting of one cognitive, one social, and one clinical psychologist would be more diverse than one consisting of three people from the same subfield. A design team of one computer engineer, one human factors psychologist, and one management professional would be even more so.

Meta-analyses have shown functional diversity to have a positive relation with performance, particularly when the cognitive and member interaction requirements of the task are high (van Dijk et al., 2012). This relation likely results from members discussing and integrating their unique information and perspectives. For example, laboratory experiments manipulating informational diversity have found information use and integration to mediate performance differences between diverse and homogeneous groups (e.g., Homan, van Knippenberg, Van Kleef, & De Dreu, 2007). A meta-analysis of laboratory studies in which researchers used fictional cases (e.g., choosing which of two fictional products to market) and manipulated which information was unique and which information members held in common (Mesmer-Magnus & DeChurch, 2009) yielded results consistent with that interpretation. Furthermore, the findings of that meta-analysis were also consistent with the notion that demonstrability played a role in the extent to which members discussed and integrated their unique information.

Although functional diversity is operationalized in terms of variety, in practice, the areas of expertise represented are typically complementary in the context of the task. For example, in Homan et al. (2007) and Mesmer-Magnus and DeChurch (2009), it was not merely that members mentioned more information but that each had different information relevant to the task. Several studies have examined the importance of complementarity directly (e.g., Fraidin, 2004; van Ginkel & van Knippenberg, 2008). Complementary models of group outcomes are common in the literature on informational and expertise composition. The literature on transactive memory is one prominent example.

Briefly, *transactive memory* (Wegner, 1986; Wegner, Giuliano, & Hertel, 1985) is a system by which members of a group divide the task of learning and retrieving information among members of the group. Each member is primarily responsible for a unique subset of the relevant information (the *differentiated aspect* of transactive memory) and holds some information in common with other members (an *integrative aspect* of transactive memory). The division of responsibility partly follows differences in skills and interests that members bring with them, but members may also take responsibility for areas to make the division more complementary (cf. Baumann & Bonner, 2017; Bonner, Baumann, & Netchaeva, 2016). Members have a shared understanding of how information is divided as well as processes for transferring knowledge between members and updating their understanding of each other's responsibilities (Brandon & Hollingshead, 2004). Transactive memory appears to facilitate combining unique information (Stasser, Stewart, & Wittenbaum, 1995) and performance on a range of collaborative tasks (see Lewis & Herndon, 2011, for a review).

COMPOSITION AND COMPILATION IN COHESION AND INTRAGROUP CONFLICT

Although performance on tasks requiring integration of members' informational input is arguably the most studied outcome in the composition literature, outcomes relating to group cohesion and intragroup conflict have been studied, too. As in the previous section, we organize these findings based on the member characteristics examined: personality, demographics, and information or expertise.

Personality

The composition literature on personality and its relations to group cohesion and intragroup conflict has used both mean-based and heterogeneity operationalizations of composition. The mean of members' agreeableness has been found to have a positive relation to later group cohesion and communication (Bradley, Baur, Banford, & Postlethwaite, 2013). Similarly, mean agreeableness, extroversion, and emotional stability have each been found to have positive associations with cohesion and negative associations with conflict in studies with cross-sectional designs (Barrick, Stewart, Neubert, & Mount, 1998). When composition is operationalized as heterogeneity (separation), agreeableness has a negative association with cohesion (Barrick et al., 1998), and agreeableness, conscientiousness, and emotional stability each has positive associations with conflict (Trimmer, Domino, & Blanton, 2002).

Demographics

The literature relating demographic composition to cohesion and conflict has focused mainly on heterogeneity, most often conceptualized as variety. As for information sharing and performance, the associations of demographic composition with group cohesion and conflict tend to be complex. For example, a meta-analysis (Guillaume, Brodbeck, & Riketta, 2012) examined the relationship of heterogeneity in easily observable demographic variables (e.g., sex, age, race/ethnicity) to identification and satisfaction with the group. Paralleling the findings of van Dijk et al. (2012) regarding demographic composition and performance, no main effects of heterogeneity were found, but a significant interaction of heterogeneity with level and quality of interaction was. Heterogeneity was negatively associated with identification and satisfaction for tasks in which minimal interaction was required, but the association disappeared when member interaction was more frequent. This finding is consistent with other findings showing the effects of demographic diversity diminish over a group's life span (e.g., Harrison et al., 2002). Member interaction, like time, may provide an opportunity to see past surface characteristics. This possibility would be consistent with findings that perceived heterogeneity may contribute to conflict even when objective heterogeneity does not (e.g., Hentschel, Shemla, Wegge, & Kearney, 2013).

There are indications that demographic heterogeneity may also moderate comfort volunteering information. For example, in a laboratory experiment in which demographic composition was manipulated to be homogenous or heterogenous, dissenting members reported more comfort expressing their opinion in demographically heterogeneous groups (Phillips & Loyd, 2006). Similar findings were obtained for integrating information in a field study with members of product development teams (Harvey, 2015). Seeing differences may help people be willing to risk showing differences (e.g., voicing dissent).

Information and Expertise

Studies of cohesion and conflict are less common for informational composition than for personality or demographic composition. However, sufficient work on the relation of task-related diversity (which is conceptually related to informational heterogeneity) to cohesion and closely related constructs have been done to support two meta-analyses (Horwitz & Horwitz, 2007; Webber & Donahue, 2001). Neither found a significant relation of task-related diversity to cohesion.

One of the few studies to directly examine the relation of functional diversity to cohesion found no overall relation. Rather, the authors found an interaction between the square of functional diversity and how members worked together between measurement waves (Tekleab, Karaca, Quigley, & Tsang, 2016). When member interaction between waves was poor, cohesion steeply decreased with functional diversity and then leveled off. When interaction was of a higher quality, cohesion slowly increased with diversity and then leveled off. Earlier in this chapter, we noted that functional diversity creates a potential for good performance that is only fulfilled if members work together. Tekleab et al.'s (2016) findings could be interpreted as functional diversity creating a potential threat to cohesion that members overcome by working together. This may be part of why earlier meta-analyses using concepts similar to functional diversity (e.g., Horwitz & Horwitz, 2007; Webber & Donahue, 2001) found no significant relations to cohesion.

EMPIRICAL GAPS AND EMERGING TRENDS

The preceding brief overview of the composition literature covered a specific subset of topics studied to date. Although the absence of some topics follows from space constraints and our choice of focus, other absences represent true gaps in the literature. For example, as with many topics in groups and teams, research on composition has predominantly been from a static rather than dynamic perspective (Kozlowski, 2015). As such, the literature provides little information on how the effects of composition change over the life span of a group or the processes by which composition affects emergent states and mediators of group outcomes. Also, relatively little work has been done on how change in membership (and thus composition) influences group outcomes. In a similar vein, the literature says far more about the relation of composition to performance and information sharing and use than it does about the relation of composition to cohesion and conflict. Efforts to better understand how composition impacts other group states and outcomes are ongoing (see Bell & Outland, 2017; Mathieu, Tannenbaum, Donsbach, & Alliger, 2014), but much still needs to be done.

COMPOSITION, COMPILATION, AND GROUP THERAPY

Practitioners of group therapy face many challenges assembling therapy groups that social and organizational psychologists assembling laboratory groups and work teams do not. Therapists do not select who seeks treatment, have limited pools of treatment seekers at any given time, and may experience both patient dropout and rolling enrollment. In addition, any one treatment seeker may manifest multiple diagnoses, and symptoms may overlap with their other characteristics (e.g., demographics, experiences). Combined, these factors create significant constraints to the study of composition on group therapy. It is no wonder Burlingame et al. (2003) referred to composition as one of the least studied issues in group therapy or that most work on composition in therapy groups has relied on comparisons across other treatment effectiveness studies with groups naturally varying in composition.

The composition literature suggests there is value to having informational diversity in groups, particularly on complex, information-heavy tasks. Group therapy involves members' combining information in complex ways to gain new insight. Therefore, we would expect therapy to be more effective when members are seeking treatment for similar issues but can each contribute unique experiences and perspectives during group. That is, group therapy should be more effective when groups are diagnostically homogenous but informationally diverse. This expectation is consistent with Burlingame et al. (2003), which found greater therapeutic value in studies in which therapy groups were homogeneous in diagnoses but heterogenous in terms of member sex. Having similar diagnoses increases the likelihood that members' unique experiences and strategies are relevant to each other. In U.S. culture, the sexes are socialized differently (Eccles, Jacobs, & Harold, 1990) and thus likely differ in their individual experiences and perspectives. This would increase the likelihood members would be exposed to new perspectives in group, thereby providing more opportunity to integrate across perspectives to form new insights.

The social and organizational literatures also suggest the value of informational diversity in group therapy may increase if groups are demographically diverse (e.g., Harvey, 2015; Phillips & Loyd, 2006). As noted in our review, the overall effects of demographic diversity on information sharing and use, cohesion, and conflict are neither consistently positive nor negative. Rather, they are heavily moderated. Three of those moderators were depth of interaction (van Dijk et al., 2012), length of interaction (Harrison et al., 2002) and task complexity (Guillaume et al., 2012). Group therapy involves members' interacting with each other face-to-face multiple times over multiple weeks and combining information to gain new insight. These conditions appear analogous to those in which the associations of demographic diversity were either nonsignificant or desirable. If obstacles to cohesion do occur, the practitioner can manage them (see Chapter 9, this volume).

The literatures on informational and demographic composition suggest potential opportunities practitioners might capitalize on. The literature on personality composition suggests both opportunities and hazards, many of which involve the five-factor personality model. In those rare circumstances in which practitioners have the luxury of assembling groups with higher average scores in each of the five domains, there is likely value to doing so. When that is not possible (likely the more common case), practitioners may benefit from selecting for heterogeneity in extroversion and against it in agreeableness. Each has been linked to information sharing and use (Prewett et al., 2009), intragroup conflict (Barrick et al., 1998; Trimmer et al., 2002), or both. Practitioners should be wary of including members scoring particularly low in agreeableness or conscientiousness. Each of these influences information sharing and use in a conjunctive fashion (Bell, 2007), particularly in groups involving the complexity and amount of interaction in group therapy (Prewett et al., 2009). Due to the popularity of the five-factor personality model, several validated short forms exist, including one that is only 10 items (Gosling, Rentfrow, & Swann, 2003). Such measures could potentially be added to existing group therapy suitability screening (cf. Burlingame, Cox, Davies, Layne, & Gleave, 2011).

In addition to the ways in which findings on composition might have useful applications to group therapy, the multiwave nature of therapy groups, deep interaction between members, and richness of interaction occurring in group therapy create potential opportunities for group therapy researchers to address gaps in the social and organizational literatures on composition. The groups literature often relies on single-meeting experiments or cross-sectional correlational designs, thus minimizing opportunities for in-depth study of dynamic effects. In contrast, the multiwave nature of group therapy makes it possible to examine the predictive value of initial composition for outcomes at multiple downstream time points (e.g., each week of therapy). Most experiments and correlational studies in the existing composition literature have limited access to the content of group discussion. In contrast, group therapy session leaders observe these conversations directly, allowing for qualitative analyses of process typically lacking in the composition literature. Furthermore, patient dropout provides a naturally occurring source of change in composition. As such, the study of naturally occurring change in therapy groups could be a benefit to research on dynamic effects of membership as called for by a number of groups researchers (e.g., Kozlowski, 2015; Mathieu et al., 2014).

In light of findings in the social and organizational literature on composition, we encourage practitioners of group therapy to consider screening group members to assess personality and demographic composition, and assess informational diversity either directly via discussions or by proxies to support future analyses of composition. The value to researchers and practitioners both in social and organizational psychology as well as in group therapy is potentially substantial. For example, they could use this information for prospective analysis of patient dropout or membership change; optimal and toxic combinations of personalities, diagnoses, and demographics for therapeutic success; and ways in which therapy group leader behaviors might moderate those effects. This information would be fruitful for both the practice of group therapy and improvement of our understanding of the dynamic process in groups.

CONCLUSION

To date, few studies have examined the role of group composition on thera-peutic effectiveness. However, many have examined processes and states important to therapeutic effectiveness, and thus provide potential guidance for composing therapy groups. No one operationalization of composition is appropriate to all characteristics (i.e., the processes and models for personal-ity may differ from those for demographics), and any given characteristic may combine to impact outcomes through more than one operationalization (i.e., both additive and heterogeneity operationalizations of agreeableness impact information sharing and cohesion). In a similar vein, one must pay close attention to the operationalization used when interpreting results and inferring underlying processes or intervention opportunities. Whereas the social and organizational literature has primarily examined composition effects in single-session laboratory experiments and other cross-sectional designs, examining composition effects in therapy groups provides an oppor-tunity to study changes in the predictive value of composition over time as well as the effects of changes in composition over time. As such, the study of composition in therapy groups could potentially help address gaps in the existing literature, thereby benefiting both groups and group therapy research and practice.

SUGGESTED READINGS

Bell, S. T., Brown, S. G., Colaneri, A., & Outland, N. (2018). Team composition and the ABCs of teamwork. *American Psychologist, 73*, 349–362. http://dx.doi.org/10.1037/amp0000305

Readers interested in the relation of group composition to the processes collectively referred to as teamwork may wish to read this.

Mathieu, J. E., Tannenbaum, S. I., Donsbach, J. S., & Alliger, G. M. (2014). A review and integration of team composition models: Moving toward a dynamic and temporal framework. *Journal of Management, 40*, 130–160. http://dx.doi.org/10.1177/0149206313503014

Readers interested in knowing more about composition and compilation, including models combining member characteristics and group characteristics, may wish to read this review of the topic.

van Knippenberg, D., & Mell, J. N. (2016). Past, present, and potential future of team diversity research: From compositional diversity to emergent diversity. *Organizational Behavior and Human Decision Processes, 136*, 135–145. http://dx.doi.org/10.1016/j.obhdp.2016.05.007

Readers interested in gaps in the existing literature and what is being done to address them, or interested specifically in composition in the context of diversity, may wish to read this.

REFERENCES

Allison, P. D. (1978). Measures of inequality. *American Sociological Review, 43*, 865–880. http://dx.doi.org/10.2307/2094626

Amason, A. C. (1996). Distinguishing the effect of functional and dysfunctional conflict on strategic decision making: Resolving a paradox for top management teams. *Academy of Management Journal, 39*, 123–148.

Barrick, M. R., Stewart, G. L., Neubert, M. J., & Mount, M. K. (1998). Relating member ability and personality to work-team processes and team effectiveness. *Journal of Applied Psychology, 83*, 377–391. http://dx.doi.org/10.1037/0021-9010.83.3.377

Baumann, M. R., & Bonner, B. L. (2017). An expectancy theory approach to group coordination: Expertise, task features, and member behavior. *Journal of Behavioral Decision Making, 30*, 407–419. http://dx.doi.org/10.1002/bdm.1954

Beal, D. J., Cohen, R. R., Burke, M. J., & McLendon, C. L. (2003). Cohesion and performance in groups: A meta-analytic clarification of construct relations. *Journal of Applied Psychology, 88*, 989–1004. http://dx.doi.org/10.1037/0021-9010.88.6.989

Bell, S. T. (2007). Deep-level composition variables as predictors of team performance: A meta-analysis. *Journal of Applied Psychology, 92*, 595–615. http://dx.doi.org/10.1037/0021-9010.92.3.595

Bell, S. T., Brown, S. G., Colaneri, A., & Outland, N. (2018). Team composition and the ABCs of teamwork. *American Psychologist, 73*, 349–362. http://dx.doi.org/10.1037/amp0000305

Bell, S. T., & Outland, N. (2017). Team composition over time. In E. Salas, W. B. Vessey, & L. B. Landon (Eds.), *Team dynamics over time: Advances in psychological theory, methods and practice* (Vol. 18, pp. 3–27). Bingley, England: Emerald Group. http://dx.doi.org/10.1108/S1534-085620160000018001

Blau, P. M. (1977). *Inequality and heterogeneity*. New York, NY: Free Press.

Bonner, B. L., & Baumann, M. R. (2012). Leveraging member expertise to improve knowledge transfer and demonstrability in groups. *Journal of Personality and Social Psychology, 102*, 337–350. http://dx.doi.org/10.1037/a0025566

Bonner, B. L., Baumann, M. R., & Netchaeva, E. (2016). Adapting to fill the void: Dynamic group coordination as a function of differing domain roles and instrumentality. *European Journal of Social Psychology, 46*, 63–76. http://dx.doi.org/10.1002/ejsp.2133

Bonner, B. L., Sillito, S., & Baumann, M. R. (2007). Collective estimation: Accuracy, expertise, and extroversion as sources of intra-group influence. *Organizational Behavior and Human Decision Processes, 103*, 121–133. http://dx.doi.org/10.1016/j.obhdp.2006.05.001

Bradley, B. H., Baur, J. E., Banford, C. G., & Postlethwaite, B. E. (2013). Team players and collective performance: How agreeableness affects performance over time. *Small Group Research, 44*, 680–711. http://dx.doi.org/10.1177/1046496413507609

Brandon, D. P., & Hollingshead, A. B. (2004). Transactive memory systems in organizations: Matching tasks, expertise, and people. *Organization Science, 15*, 633–644. http://dx.doi.org/10.1287/orsc.1040.0069

Burlingame, G. M., Cox, J. C., Davies, D. R., Layne, C. M., & Gleave, R. (2011). The Group Selection Questionnaire: Further refinements in group member selection. *Group Dynamics: Theory, Research, and Practice, 15*, 60–74. http://dx.doi.org/10.1037/a0020220

Burlingame, G. M., Fuhriman, A., & Mosier, J. (2003). The differential effectiveness of group psychotherapy: A meta-analytic perspective. *Group Dynamics: Theory, Research, and Practice, 7*, 3–12. http://dx.doi.org/10.1037/1089-2699.7.1.3

Burlingame, G. M., & Jensen, J. L. (2017). Small group process and outcome research highlights: A 25-year perspective. *International Journal of Group Psychotherapy, 67*(Suppl. 1), S194–S218. http://dx.doi.org/10.1080/00207284.2016.1218287

Burlingame, G. M., McClendon, D. T., & Yang, C. (2018). Cohesion in group therapy: A meta-analysis. *Psychotherapy, 55,* 384–398. http://dx.doi.org/10.1037/pst0000173

Butler, T., & Fuhriman, A. (1983). Curative factors in group therapy: A recent review of the literature. *Small Group Behavior, 14,* 131–142. http://dx.doi.org/10.1177/104649648301400201

Classen, C., Butler, L. D., Koopman, C., Miller, E., DiMiceli, S., Giese-Davis, J., . . . Spiegel, D. (2001). Supportive-expressive group therapy and distress in patients with metastatic breast cancer: A randomized clinical intervention trial. *Archives of General Psychiatry, 58,* 494–501. http://dx.doi.org/10.1001/archpsyc.58.5.494

Eccles, J. S., Jacobs, J. E., & Harold, R. D. (1990). Gender role stereotypes, expectancy effects, and parents' socialization of gender differences. *Journal of Social Issues, 46,* 183–201. http://dx.doi.org/10.1111/j.1540-4560.1990.tb01929.x

Fraidin, S. N. (2004). When is one head better than two? Interdependent information in group decision making. *Organizational Behavior and Human Decision Processes, 93,* 102–113. http://dx.doi.org/10.1016/j.obhdp.2003.12.003

Gosling, S. D., Rentfrow, P. J., & Swann, W. B., Jr. (2003). A very brief measure of the Big-Five personality domains. *Journal of Research in Personality, 37,* 504–528. http://dx.doi.org/10.1016/S0092-6566(03)00046-1

Grossman, R. (2014). *How do teams become cohesive? A meta-analysis of cohesion's antecedents* (Doctoral dissertation). Retrieved from http://stars.library.ucf.edu/etd/4609

Guillaume, Y. R. F., Brodbeck, F. C., & Riketta, M. (2012). Surface- and deep-level dissimilarity effects on social integration and individual effectiveness related outcomes in work groups: A meta-analytic integration. *Journal of Occupational and Organizational Psychology, 85,* 80–115. http://dx.doi.org/10.1111/j.2044-8325.2010.02005.x

Hackman, J. R., & Morris, C. G. (1975). Group tasks, group interaction process, and group performance effectiveness: A review and proposed integration. In L. Berkowitz (Ed.), *Advances in experimental social psychology* (Vol. 8, pp. 45–99). New York, NY: Academic Press. http://dx.doi.org/10.1016/S0065-2601(08)60248-8

Harrison, D. A., & Klein, K. J. (2007). What's the difference? Diversity constructs as separation, variety, or disparity in organizations. *Academy of Management Review, 32,* 1199–1228. http://dx.doi.org/10.5465/amr.2007.26586096

Harrison, D. A., Price, K. H., Gavin, J. H., & Florey, A. T. (2002). Time, teams, and task performance: Changing effects of surface- and deep-level diversity on group functioning. *Academy of Management Journal, 45,* 1029–1045. http://dx.doi.org/10.5465/3069328

Harvey, S. (2015). When accuracy isn't everything: The value of demographic differences to information elaboration in teams. *Group & Organization Management, 40,* 35–61. http://dx.doi.org/10.1177/1059601114561786

Hentschel, T., Shemla, M., Wegge, J., & Kearney, E. (2013). Perceived diversity and team functioning: The role of diversity beliefs and affect. *Small Group Research, 44,* 33–61. http://dx.doi.org/10.1177/1046496412470725

Homan, A. C., van Knippenberg, D., Van Kleef, G. A., & De Dreu, C. K. W. (2007). Bridging faultlines by valuing diversity: Diversity beliefs, information elaboration, and performance in diverse work groups. *Journal of Applied Psychology, 92,* 1189–1199. http://dx.doi.org/10.1037/0021-9010.92.5.1189

Horwitz, S. K., & Horwitz, I. B. (2007). The effects of team diversity on team outcomes: A meta-analytic review of team demography. *Journal of Management, 33,* 987–1015. http://dx.doi.org/10.1177/0149206307308587

Jehn, K. A. (1995). A multimethod examination of the benefit and detriments of intragroup conflict. *Administrative Science Quarterly, 40,* 256–282. http://dx.doi.org/10.2307/2393638

Kaplan, M. F., & Miller, C. E. (1987). Group decision making and normative vs informational influence: Effects of type of issue and assigned decision rule. *Journal of*

Personality and Social Psychology, 53, 306–313. http://dx.doi.org/10.1037/0022-3514.53.2.306

Kozlowski, S. W. J. (2015). Advancing research on team process dynamics: Theoretical, methodological, and measurement considerations. *Organizational Psychology Review, 5*, 270–299. http://dx.doi.org/10.1177/2041386614533586

Kozlowski, S. W. J., & Klein, K. J. (2000). A multilevel approach to theory and research in organizations: Contextual, temporal, and emergent processes. In K. J. Klein & S. W. J. Kozlowski (Eds.), *Multilevel theory, research, and methods in organizations: Foundations, extensions, and new directions* (pp. 3–90). San Francisco, CA: Jossey-Bass.

Laughlin, P. R. (2011). *Group problem solving.* Princeton, NJ: Princeton University Press.

Laughlin, P. R., & Ellis, A. L. (1986). Demonstrability and social combination processes on mathematical intellective tasks. *Journal of Experimental Social Psychology, 22*, 177–189. http://dx.doi.org/10.1016/0022-1031(86)90022-3

Levine, J. M., & Smith, E. R. (2013). Group cognition: Collective information search and distribution. In D. Carlston (Ed.), *The Oxford handbook of social cognition* (pp. 616–636). New York, NY: Oxford University Press.

Lewis, K., & Herndon, B. (2011). Transactive memory systems: Current issues and future research directions. *Organization Science, 22*, 1254–1265. http://dx.doi.org/10.1287/orsc.1110.0647

Mathieu, J. E., Tannenbaum, S. I., Donsbach, J. S., & Alliger, G. M. (2014). A review and integration of team composition models: Moving toward a dynamic and temporal framework. *Journal of Management, 40*, 130–160. http://dx.doi.org/10.1177/0149206313503014

McCrae, R. R., & Costa, P. T. (1987). Validation of the five-factor model of personality across instruments and observers. *Journal of Personality and Social Psychology, 52*, 81–90. http://dx.doi.org/10.1037/0022-3514.52.1.81

McGrath, J. E. (1984). *Groups: Interaction and performance.* Englewood Cliffs, NJ: Prentice Hall.

Mesmer-Magnus, J. R., & DeChurch, L. A. (2009). Information sharing and team performance: A meta-analysis. *Journal of Applied Psychology, 94*, 535–546. http://dx.doi.org/10.1037/a0013773

Phillips, K. W., & Loyd, D. L. (2006). When surface and deep-level diversity collide: The effects on dissenting group members. *Organizational Behavior and Human Decision Processes, 99*, 143–160. http://dx.doi.org/10.1016/j.obhdp.2005.12.001

Prewett, M. S., Walvoord, A. A. G., Stilson, F. R. B., Rossi, M. E., & Brannick, M. T. (2009). The team personality—team performance relationship revisited: The impact of criterion choice, pattern of workflow, and method of aggregation. *Human Performance, 22*, 273–296. http://dx.doi.org/10.1080/08959280903120253

Salas, E., Grossman, R., Hughes, A. M., & Coultas, C. W. (2015). Measuring team cohesion: Observations from the science. *Human Factors, 57*, 365–374. http://dx.doi.org/10.1177/0018720815578267

Salovey, P., & Mayer, J. D. (1990). Emotional intelligence. *Imagination, Cognition and Personality, 9*, 185–211. http://dx.doi.org/10.2190/DUGG-P24E-52WK-6CDG

Stasser, G., & Stewart, D. D. (1992). Discovery of hidden profiles by decision-making groups: Solving a problem versus making a judgment. *Journal of Personality and Social Psychology, 63*, 426–434. http://dx.doi.org/10.1037/0022-3514.63.3.426

Stasser, G., Stewart, D. D., & Wittenbaum, G. M. (1995). Expert roles and information exchange during discussion: The importance of knowing who knows what. *Journal of Experimental Social Psychology, 31*, 244–265. http://dx.doi.org/10.1006/jesp.1995.1012

Steiner, I. D. (1966). Models for inferring relationships between group size and potential group productivity. *Behavioral Science, 11*, 273–283. http://dx.doi.org/10.1002/bs.3830110404

Tekleab, A. G., Karaca, A., Quigley, N. R., & Tsang, E. W. K. (2016). Re-examining the functional diversity-performance relationships: The roles of behavioral integration, team cohesion, and team learning. *Journal of Business Research, 69*, 3500–3507. http://dx.doi.org/10.1016/j.jbusres.2016.01.036

Trimmer, K. J., Domino, M. A., & Blanton, J. E. (2002). The impact of personality diversity on conflict in ISD teams. *Journal of Computer Information Systems, 42*, 4–14.

VanDeusen, K. M., & Carr, J. L. (2003). Recovery from sexual assault: An innovative two-stage group therapy model. *International Journal of Group Psychotherapy, 53*, 201–223. http://dx.doi.org/10.1521/ijgp.53.2.201.42815

van Dijk, H., van Engen, M. L., & van Knippenberg, D. (2012). Defying conventional wisdom: A meta-analytic examination of the differences between demographic and job-related diversity relationships with performance. *Organizational Behavior and Human Decision Processes, 119*, 38–53. http://dx.doi.org/10.1016/j.obhdp.2012.06.003

van Ginkel, W. P., & van Knippenberg, D. (2008). Group information elaboration and group decision making: The role of shared task representations. *Organizational Behavior and Human Decision Processes, 105*, 82–97. http://dx.doi.org/10.1016/j.obhdp.2007.08.005

van Knippenberg, D., De Dreu, C. K. W., & Homan, A. C. (2004). Work group diversity and group performance: An integrative model and research agenda. *Journal of Applied Psychology, 89*, 1008–1022. http://dx.doi.org/10.1037/0021-9010.89.6.1008

Webber, S. S., & Donahue, L. M. (2001). Impact of highly and less job-related diversity on work group cohesion and performance: A meta-analysis. *Journal of Management, 27*, 141–162. http://dx.doi.org/10.1177/014920630102700202

Wegner, D. M. (1986). Transactive memory: A contemporary analysis of the group mind. In B. Mullen & G. R. Goethals (Eds.), *Theories of group behavior* (pp. 185–208). New York, NY: Springer-Verlag.

Wegner, D. M., Giuliano, T., & Hertel, P. T. (1985). Cognitive interdependence in close relationships. In W. Ickes (Ed.), *Compatible and incompatible relationships* (pp. 253–276). New York, NY: Springer-Verlag. http://dx.doi.org/10.1007/978-1-4612-5044-9_12

Yalom, I. D. (with Leszcz, M.). (2005). *The theory and practice of group psychotherapy* (5th ed.). New York, NY: Basic Books.

4

Principles of Cooperation

Implications for Group Psychotherapy

Craig D. Parks

One of the most fundamental issues across the social and behavioral sciences is how to induce people to work together for the common good, especially when the temptation is strong to let others do the work or the entity in question does not have direct benefit to the individual, or both. Consider, for example, a public playground that needs volunteers to assemble and maintain it. Why would a retiree whose grandchildren do not live in town want to take part in this project? Why not instead let local parents do the work? Yes, the grandchildren will enjoy the playground when they visit, but that only happens once or twice a year, whereas the local children can use the playground whenever they like. Why should the retiree expend effort to help maintain the playground when its benefit to him or her is so small? Similarly, all members of a student group working on a class project will receive the same grade regardless of how much individual effort a student contributed, and all members of a therapy group will benefit from the therapist's expertise regardless of their level of participation in the session. In such situations, a rationality or economic analysis prescribes that one should not contribute; rather, one should let others expend effort and then benefit from their efforts. Widespread application of this logic, though, is ruinous for the collective because it implies that no one should work for the common good. The continued existence of entities like charities and volunteer organizations, along with ample anecdotal experiences of group members working hard for the greater good, demonstrates that the rational approach is often ignored. What

http://dx.doi.org/10.1037/0000201-005
The Psychology of Groups: The Intersection of Social Psychology and Psychotherapy Research,
C. D. Parks and G. A. Tasca (Editors)

encourages people to forgo their personal interests and instead work for the good of the group?

Scenarios like those just described unfortunately occur with regularity and provide a challenge to the provision of a variety of goods and services that benefit the group as a whole. Somehow, we need to encourage some—often many and once in a great while, all—people to forgo personal interests and instead work for the good of the group. Furthermore, the issue arises not only with groups striving to provide socially beneficial entities but also within work groups, student groups, military groups, therapy groups, and sports teams. For each, one can find influences on the decision to cooperate that are unique to that type of group. For example, the degree of cooperation among players on a sports team is affected by the importance of the specific game: Teammates more likely to coordinate actions in a critical game and more likely to act selfishly in a relatively meaningless game (Duarte, Araújo, Correia, & Davids, 2012). It is unlikely that soldiers in a military unit would try to win a small firefight by themselves or that a member of a work team would offer to handle all of the tasks associated with the assembly of one of his or her company's less prominent products. However, some factors consistently emerge across many different forms of groups as important for the development of cooperation.

This chapter reviews these common causes. In many cases, research on these causes has been conducted in parallel across the different group types. A goal of this chapter is to highlight these similarities and encourage researchers who are interested in cooperation within one form of group to look to other forms for ideas on cooperative choice. A complete review of all the influences on cooperative behavior requires a book in its own right (the reader is referred to Van Lange, Balliet, Parks, & Van Vugt, 2014, for an introduction). For this chapter, let us focus on four influences that exist within therapy groups and thus make sense to examine as possible impacts on cooperation among therapy group members: behavioral norms, member identification with the group, a power versus morality perspective on the group's task, and individual difference qualities.

NORMS OF COOPERATION

Most cultures prescribe that certain situations, defined by the culture, demand that one act for the group; such expectations are referred to as *norms of cooperation* (Fehr & Fischbacher, 2004). To not offer assistance to a family whose house has been devastated by a fire or to stand by and watch as an elderly person struggles to carry a package is to incur social punishment for inaction at a time of clear need. The norms for obvious-need situations can then get generalized to more ambiguous situations (Peysakhovich & Rand, 2016; Tabellini, 2008; Zefferman, 2014). Thus, a person who sees some children selling baked goods as part of a fundraiser may define this as a "need" situation that requires response. This generalization can be quite broad. For example, good-sportsmanship norms within sports teams are a variant of the basic norm of cooperation (Shields, LaVoi, Bredemeier, & Power, 2007), and willingness to engage in organizational citizenship behavior can be positively impacted if a norm of cooperation is invoked (Bachrach, Powell, Bendoly, & Richey, 2006). Although this tendency to generalize may seem beneficial, it is a double-edged sword because a person who does not consider the situation to be need driven must be convinced otherwise, which is a very difficult task (Rand et al., 2014). Furthermore, there can be within-group variation in individual willingness to adhere to norms, meaning that alteration of the group norm, which would generally be easier than individual redefinition of a situation, would not necessarily lead to increased rates of cooperation (Chen, Wasti, & Triandis, 2007).

Norms of cooperation are enforced through social sanctions. As noted in the previous paragraph, the person who just watches as an elderly individual tries to manage a bulky package will likely receive scorn, anger, and ridicule from others who observe the event. Although those affected by the lack of cooperation often deliver these sanctions, *third-party sanctioning*, that is, social punishment from people with no vested interest in the situation, can also occur. Observers castigating someone who does not help an elderly person is an example of a third-party sanction as is a negative performance evaluation applied by a supervisor to an employee who is not a good organizational citizen in a company in which cooperation is normative (Bachrach et al., 2006). Third-party sanctions can be a powerful enforcer of norms (they form the basis of most modern legal systems; see Buckholtz & Marois, 2012) and are efficient because their effects linger much longer than do the effects of financial punishments (Nelissen & Mulder, 2013). They are typically motivated by guilt or anger that arises as a result of thinking about how the affected person is suffering (Nelissen & Zeelenberg, 2009), and those who detect a need to sanction a noncooperator but fail to do so are themselves vulnerable to social punishment (Kerr et al., 2009). Furthermore, expected third-party sanctions that do not arrive (e.g., spectators who fail to criticize an athlete who engages in poor sportsmanship) can reinforce failure to adhere to the norm (Shields et al., 2007).

Thus, mere awareness of social sanctions and that they can be imposed by nonparticipants in the dilemma should be sufficient to induce most people to cooperate when society, or even a subset of society, expects them to. Ironically, though, universal compliance with a norm of cooperation may not always be a desirable goal. Although complete cooperation may benefit a specific situation, even a small change to the dynamics of the situation can cause significant problems if everyone is participating at exactly the same level with no variability in degree of cooperative action (Schlüter, Tavoni, & Levin, 2016). Consider, for example, the Liberty Fund that the American Red Cross established in the wake of the 9/11 attacks to aid those who lost family members in the attacks. The fund reached its endowment target in a matter of days, and within 2 weeks, it had received close to $550 billion in donations. The Red Cross decided to shift much of the excess money to a fund held for preparation for future terrorist attacks and to use the remaining money for other disasters. The negative reaction to this plan was so strong that the director of the Red Cross resigned, and the United States House of Representatives launched an investigation of the charity. (See Meisenbach, 2006, for an excellent review of the Liberty Fund incident.) This was a situation in which it was not necessary for everyone to donate to the fund, but people clearly felt compelled to do so. Once the situation had changed in that the organization had reached its funding target, the continued cooperation led to an extraordinary level of surplus resources that the entity was not allowed to repurpose. It would have been more efficient for American society to recognize it was not necessary for everyone to contribute to the Liberty Fund and to accordingly withhold judgment of anyone who opted not to donate.

Norms of cooperation, then, are powerful and universal tools for inducing cooperation in others. They can, however, be too rigidly enforced, leading to long-run disruptions of a cooperative ethic.

GROUP IDENTIFICATION

Another factor that induces cooperation is identification with the group. We want groups that are important to us to be successful, and a key part of helping them achieve that success is to merge one's personal goals with group goals; that is, we come to believe that what is good for the group is good for us (De Cremer & van Dijk, 2002). Indeed, this belief is so important for group success that researchers of performance-oriented groups (e.g., work groups, sports teams) distinguish between *teams of experts*, which are mere collections of talented people, and *expert teams*, which are sets of skilled people who coordinate effort, support each other, and emphasize group performance over individual performance (Eccles & Tenenbaum, 2004). People are thus generally willing to contribute effort toward the success of their favored groups. But how does a person come to ascribe sufficient importance to a group such that he or she is willing to forgo personal interests in favor of the group's needs?

A key requirement is perceived similarity between self and group members (Krueger, Ullrich, & Chen, 2016); the basis for the perception is a combination of self-knowledge and the stereotypes one holds about the group (Cho & Knowles, 2013). In making the decision to cooperate, people maintain a *similarity threshold*, whereby any group that surpasses the threshold is deemed worthy of cooperation, and a group that falls short of the threshold is not (Fischer, 2009). While perception of deep similarity (e.g., social values) is best, even surface similarity (e.g., age, hobbies) can induce a certain level of cooperativeness (Dunlop & Beauchamp, 2011). Besides member similarity, the group's *agentic ability*, or capacity to achieve an outcome that the individual desires but cannot reach alone, can elevate its importance to an individual

(Stollberg, Fritsche, & Bäcker, 2015). A group's perceived integrity can also win cooperation because people are more willing to associate with, and contribute effort toward, a group whose moral standards are high (Brambilla & Leach, 2014; van Prooijen & Ellemers, 2015).

A corollary to the desire to help a favored group is reaction to a needy group that is unattractive. It will likely not surprise the reader to learn that people have little interest in supporting outgroups. This disinterest is most often driven by a singular focus on one's own groups; that is, rather than actively wishing for an outgroup to fail, people prefer to assign all of their resources to ingroups and leave outgroups to stand or fall however they can (Halevy, Weisel, & Bornstein, 2012; Parks, Joireman, & Van Lange, 2013). A nice example of this principle can be found in Anderson and Mellor (2009), who showed a negative correlation between frequency of church attendance and amount donated toward a publicly beneficial good. Regular attenders of church would likely have a strong attraction toward their denomination as an ingroup and would equally likely assume that most others who stand to benefit from the good have different faiths, that is, are members of outgroups. It follows that the strongly religious would want to conserve their resources for provision to their ingroup, and thus would not contribute much, if anything, to a good that will benefit outgroup members. It is important to emphasize that the potential contributors do not necessarily bear ill will toward the outgroup; rather, they are simply uninterested in helping the outgroup. This is an important distinction.

An aspect of group identification is *group cohesion*, or the sense of "we-ness" that exists within the group. One would expect members of a cohesive group to demonstrate high levels of cooperativeness, and many models of group performance assume such a connection (e.g., Milton & Westphal, 2005), but evidence for the connection is scant. Cooperation and cohesion do both increase when the group is under threat (Bornstein, 2003), although, even here, group members often demonstrate varying levels of cooperative action (Benard, 2012). Two fascinating field studies of groups in extreme conflict highlight group cohesion. In a study of military units, Ben-Shalom, Lehrer, and Ben-Ari (2005) observed that when under duress, soldiers tended to form "instant units" consisting of whatever military personnel were in the immediate area. These ad hoc groups showed high levels of cooperation despite having no opportunity to develop cohesion. Gilligan, Pasquale, and Samii (2014) visited communities in post-civil war Nepal and found a similar phenomenon: Those who could not or would not escape a town caught in the fighting banded together to provide each other with what was needed to survive. Gilligan et al. (2014) argued that cohesion developed as a result of this banding. They did not actually measure cohesion, so whether it occurred is debatable, but even if it did, it is still the case that cohesion followed cooperation, not the other way around. This is hardly to say that cohesion is an insignificant aspect of the group experience; rather, the point is that the assumption that cohesion leads to cooperation is an open issue.

MORALITY

Interest in the role of morality as a promoter of cooperation is rapidly developing. We have already seen that groups with a reputation for integrity are likely to attract cooperative actions. But to what extent does one's own moral outlook influence one's cooperative choice?

Viewing the situation through a morality lens does encourage people to be more cooperative (Aquino, Freeman, Reed, Lim, & Felps, 2009; Simpson, Harrell, & Willer, 2013). It has been argued that morality itself is a form of cooperation in that behaving morally requires suppression of selfish tendencies (Tomasello & Vaish, 2013). The research on leadership provides good evidence that a group leader who sees himself of herself as having a moral responsibility to empower and develop subordinates, promote a positive group climate, and ensure that the group considers the larger impact of its decisions before acting (this type of leader is termed a *servant leader*) can induce high rates of cooperation among group members (see van Dierendonck, 2011). As well, organizations that undertake a corporate social responsibility initiative under which the organization seeks to perform community good works are more likely to have buy-in and participation from employees if the motivation for the activities is moral ("It is our responsibility to help the community in which we exist") rather than strategic ("These actions will improve our image and attract customers"; Graafland & van de Ven, 2006). Morality also seems to be related to good sportsmanship and athlete commitment to team goals (Kavussanu, 2008).

Considering the issue of cooperation from a moral standpoint, then, is an effective means of inducing people to cooperate. Getting people to see the situation as a moral task is another issue, however. As discussed in more detail later in the chapter, a fundamental finding in the research on personality-based influences on cooperation is that people who have a competitive social value orientation view interpersonal situations not as morally driven but in terms of power: to cooperate is to be weak, and to act selfishly is to be strong (Balliet, Parks, & Joireman, 2009). It is thus likely that we will have to prompt group members to consider the moral implications of cooperating or not. Successfully doing so is difficult, a few interventions can work. Some evidence indicates that belief in supernatural punishment is an effective inducer of cooperation in that "God is watching" serves as a type of moral policing and, hence, social sanctioning (Atkinson & Bourrat, 2011; Norenzayan & Shariff, 2008; Preston & Ritter, 2013). There is, however, controversy over the impact of the effect. The aggregate evidence suggests that, although awareness of being watched does seem to prompt cooperative action, the degree of cooperation is low and does not last long (Nettle et al., 2013; Sparks & Barclay, 2013). Moral behavior can also be induced by encouraging people to predict their emotional reaction to a potential outcome from an action. Anticipating that one could feel a self-conscious emotion (e.g., shame, guilt, embarrassment) as a result of a choice can be sufficient to deter the person from making that choice (Tangney, Stuewig, & Mashek, 2007).

PERSONALITY AND INDIVIDUAL DIFFERENCE TRAITS

In addition to the previously described cognitive factors, some traits also influence the choice to cooperate. A number of individual qualities have been tentatively connected to cooperation, and some traits have been studied exclusively within one type of group. We focus here on just those traits that have strong empirical support and have been examined across a number of different group forms. The reader who is interested in a more complete review is referred to Parks (2018).

Personality Traits and Disorders

Much work has tried to connect the Big Five personality traits of extraversion, agreeableness, conscientiousness, anxiousness, and openness to cooperation. The bulk of the research has focused on agreeableness, and most studies find a connection to cooperation in that high-agreeable people are more cooperative than low-agreeable people (Graziano & Habashi, 2015; Zhao & Smillie, 2015). Agreeableness has also been shown to facilitate success in group psychotherapy (e.g., Ogrodniczuk, Piper, Joyce, McCallum, & Rosie, 2003; Spek, Nyklíček, Cuijpers, & Pop, 2008). Occasional studies have found support for other Big Five traits (e.g., Hirsh & Peterson, 2009, on extraversion and low neuroticism; Al-Ubaydli, Jones, & Weel, 2016, on openness), but to date, not enough systematic evidence exists to confidently advocate for these traits as influencers of cooperation. It is especially surprising that conscientiousness has not been tested because a dimension of the conscientiousness trait is the extent to which one is "responsible." Given that one's actions in an interdependence situation have impact on others' outcomes, it would seem that one's sense of responsibility, or lack thereof, would affect the decision to cooperate.

Another personality trait studied heavily is *social value orientation*, or one's predisposition to respond in a particular way in situations of interdependence. Many potential orientations exist, but in most studies, three have emerged: *cooperation*, or a desire to maximize the joint outcome to all group members and minimize differences in outcomes across group members; *competition*, or a desire to maximize the difference between own outcomes and others' outcomes; and *individualism*, or a desire to maximize own outcomes without concern for how well or poorly others do. Most people have a detectable orientation, and these orientations are clearly predictive of behavior in most situations of interdependence (Balliet et al., 2009; Bogaert, Boone, & van Witteloostuijn, 2012; De Dreu, 2010).

An intriguing, yet understudied, topic is cooperation by individuals with borderline personality disorder (BPD). People with high levels of BPD are characterized by an inability to trust others, difficulty with impulse control, and unstable relationships (Fonagy & Bateman, 2006). All of these phenomena should decrease both the likelihood that a high-BPD person will cooperate and that he or she will sustain cooperation over the period of interaction. King-Casas and colleagues (2008) indeed found BPD individuals to deviate quickly from cooperation and demonstrate an inability to return to cooperative actions, but follow-up research has been sparse. Occasional studies have found people with BPD to be more attuned to the objective fairness of others' behaviors (i.e., less influenced by emotional distractors) than non-BPD individuals (Franzen et al., 2011; Miano, Fertuck, Arntz, & Stanley, 2013), but, on the whole, we know little about how BPD impacts cooperative social functioning.

Individual Difference Traits

Researchers have long tried—but with little success—to establish a link between sex and cooperation. At various points in the literature, females were argued to be more cooperative than males, males were argued to be more cooperative than females, and yet others claimed no difference between the two. A meta-analysis by Balliet and colleagues (Balliet, Li, Macfarlan, & Van Vugt, 2011) has brought some order to the findings. They showed that, overall, there is no difference in frequency of cooperation between males and females, but differences do show up depending on situational factors. Social interactions between males are more cooperative than are interactions between females, although if the members of all-male therapy groups have high levels of competitiveness, that can hinder the efficacy of those groups for at least some problems (Nahon & Lander, 2010). In mixed-sex social groups, females are more cooperative than males quite likely because of perceived pressure to follow gender-role expectations. Gender-role expectations have been shown to impact the efficacy of therapy when applied to mixed-sex treatment groups, and females benefit from the treatment more than males do (Wade & Goldman, 2006). Males are also more cooperative than females in repeated social interactions.

Further research into sex-driven cooperation has focused on the role of physical attractiveness in cooperation. This work has shown that physical symmetry, which increases attractiveness, is associated with noncooperation in both all-male (Sanchez-Pages & Turiegano, 2010) and all-female (Muñoz-Reyes, Pita, Arjona, Sanchez-Pages, & Turiegano, 2014) groups. This finding is presumably because symmetrically attractive people are better able to obtain resources on their own and so are disinclined to join with others. However, a low waist-to-hip ratio in females, which also increases attractiveness, is associated with increased rate of cooperation in all-female groups. This is a function of expected behavior of other members in that females with a high waist-to-hip ratio do not expect other females to cooperate with them (Muñoz-Reyes et al., 2014). Surprisingly, though, physical attractiveness does not seem to play a role in mixed-sex cooperative interaction (Bhogal, Galbraith, & Manktelow, 2017).

Intelligence is another individual difference proposed as an influence on cooperation, but results have been inconsistent. To cite just a few examples, Jones (2008) examined mean rates of cooperation in 36 social dilemma studies conducted between 1959 and 2003, and noted at which school the data were collected for each study. He found a 5% to 8% increase in frequency of cooperation for every 100-point increase in the school's average SAT® score. Lohse (2016) reported experimental evidence consistent with this pattern. However, Kanazawa and Fontaine (2013) found intelligence to be inversely related to cooperation—at least in one-time interactions. A possible explanation for these inconsistencies may be provided by Rand (2016), who argued that deliberation-based decision making (as opposed to intuitive decision making) will produce different rates of cooperation depending on whether future consequences are associated with one's actions: Deliberation will enhance cooperation if there are indeed consequences and suppress it when there are no consequences. It may thus be that higher intellect is associated with a deliberative decision making style, which, in turn, encourages attention to the consequential nature of the situation. If so, it follows that a prediction that higher intellect leads to more or less cooperation is too simplistic.

EXTENSIONS TO THERAPY GROUPS

We have seen that norms of cooperation, the extent to which one identifies with the group, one's moral outlook on cooperation, one's degree of agreeableness and form of social value orientation, one's sex, and possibly one's level of intellect are factors that influence willingness to cooperate across many different group settings. With the notable exception of agreeableness, these effects have been established on experimental groups or productivity groups and not in therapy groups. This situation is unfortunate because a good many of these variables can be studied fruitfully within therapy groups. And indeed, understanding of cooperative processes within therapy groups is important given that perceived cooperativeness among members is a factor in the development of cohesion within the group (Strauss, Burlingame, & Bormann, 2008).

Two immediately important lines of inquiry are to what extent a therapy group is part of a member's self-concept and whether a norm of cooperation or propriety prevails in the typical therapy session. We have seen that identification with a group is an important contributor to cooperation. Unfortunately, although there are well-known exceptions (e.g., Alcoholics Anonymous), participation in therapy tends to confer a stigma, and as such, members often keep their involvement private. It is important to know whether a therapy group member includes group membership as part of his or her self-concept. This knowledge could do much to help predict the degree of the person's commitment to the group. Furthermore, even if the person does indeed self-identify as a member of the therapy group, it is possible that, as the person improves through therapy, improvement will lead that person to diminish the role of the group in his or her self-concept. As an example, consider a member of a grief counseling group. In the early stages, the person may place great value on the group and be wholly committed to its success, but as the person recovers, he or she may start to disidentify with the group ("This group is for people in the depths of grief, which is not me anymore") and be less willing to cooperate with other members. By way of comparison, consider the level of identification and lasting commitment often shown by members of support groups for people with permanent conditions (e.g., breast cancer survivor groups).

Regarding norms, although a therapy group is defined as a helping group, which should encourage members to use the norm of cooperation to guide their behaviors, it is also a situation in which one is expected to reveal personal details to strangers, which could invoke a norm of appropriate sharing and hence reticence to say too much. (A useful analogue from the medical world is the normative conflict faced by a female who is expected to disrobe for a male doctor but whose culture prescribes being covered in the presence of males; see Padela & Rodriguez del Pozo, 2011). If norms of propriety tend to govern behavior in therapy groups, altering those norms to induce one of cooperation is not necessarily the right strategy, however. It can be argued that a therapy group is a situation in which the collective best outcome— improvement by each participant—is congruent with personal best interests. Thus, emphasizing that all members should cooperate might, for example, inhibit a member from challenging another person's point of view, expressing unhappiness with the direction in which the group is moving, or even speaking up at all, all of which might be important for that person's healing process (Hornsey, Dwyer, Oei, & Dingle, 2009).

It might instead be better to reframe the therapy setting to downplay perceived conflict between individual and collective experience (e.g., "Sharing personal details might lead others to feel their situations are not so bad, but it will be embarrassing for me") and emphasize congruence between own and collective goals ("Sharing personal details will help us all want to support each other"). An excellent example of the efficacy of such reframing can be found in the research on cooperation in the service of proenvironmental behaviors. Acting in an environmentally responsible manner is often seen in sharp conflict with personal convenience and comfort: "I can drive to work when it suits me, or I can stand outside and wait for the bus, which only arrives on the half-hour." Performance of proenvironmental behaviors increases, however, when such behaviors are reframed to be congruent with actor values: "I could sit in my car and focus only on driving, or I could do work on the bus and arrive at my office with a head start on the day's tasks" (Schultz & Zelezny, 2003). Some work on reframing in therapy sessions exists in the work on group psychotherapy for terminal cancer patients, who often struggle with the questions of why this illness has happened to them and whether they have lived a good-quality life. It has been shown that the group can be framed as a vehicle for discovering meaning in one's life by talking others through their life accomplishments, which will bring one's own accomplishments into focus; in this way, helping others helps oneself (Breitbart, Gibson, Poppito, & Berg, 2004). There is, then, much potential in studying how group therapy members frame the group task and how it might be framed, particularly to emphasize goal congruence.

Interestingly, it may be that within therapy groups, there is an incentive to encourage fellow group members to be selfish. Reticence by some group members means that more floor time is available to conversant group members. Put another way, a therapy group member who wants to spend extended time verbalizing his or her issues benefits from the presence of group members who are happy to just sit and listen to a dialogue between that person and the therapist. While it may seem counterintuitive that a therapy group member would tolerate others who do not participate in a discussion, and might even encourage it, some research supports the idea. Specifically, the "lone wolf" phenomenon has identified individuals who do not like to divide work among colleagues and prefer to complete all tasks themselves, even though others will share in the reward for successful completion (Barr, Dixon, & Gassenheimer, 2005). The phenomenon works against the promotion of cooperation, and a lone wolf will sometimes actively sabotage attempts to instill a norm of cooperation. It is possible that a therapy group member may prefer to be a lone wolf and focus fully on his or her problems, even though doing so is effortful and emotional, and others will benefit from the dialogue without having had to share their own details.

Extension of the research on whether cooperation is viewed through a moral or power lens to therapy groups may also have value. Domestic violence offenders in group-based treatment programs can experience profound moral confusion from being required to acknowledge guilt and shame in front of strangers, and this confusion can seriously inhibit the efficacy of the program (Loeffler, Prelog, Prabha Unnithan, & Pogrebin, 2010). As such, offenders tend to view situations in terms of power and control (Babcock, Green, & Robie, 2004), and it is quite likely that they see any form of personal revelation as a weakness that others will exploit. If so, this perception would be a major inhibitor of group success. which, in turn, would suggest that group therapy may be less effective for individuals who see cooperation as a power issue than for those who see it as a moral issue. Knowing how the person frames cooperation could thus help the therapist decide whether individual or group therapy is most appropriate for the person. It may also be possible to change the person's frame from power to morality, although research has not yet investigated whether such a change can be executed.

CONCLUSION

Research on cooperative behavior is at once inclusive and exclusive. It is inclusive in that psychology researchers do a better job of drawing on research in other disciplines than do psychologists who study other topics. It is exclusive in that much of the research silos around one particular type of group. It is hard to find systematic empirical comparisons of cooperation across different forms of groups.

At the start of the chapter, we noted that the focus would be only on phenomena documented in a number of different types of group. Many other variables have been shown to influence cooperation in one type of group, yet they have not been tested in any other type of group. A review of those variables would require a separate and much longer chapter. It is hoped that readers interested in the general phenomenon of cooperative behavior will use this chapter as inspiration to seek out those variables and begin such testing. We still have much to learn about a behavior that is fundamental to a successful therapy group and society.

SUGGESTED READINGS

Cruwys, T., Haslam, S. A., Dingle, G. A., Jetten, J., Hornsey, M. J., Desdemona Chong, E. M., & Oei, T. P. S. (2014). Feeling connected again: Interventions that increase social identification reduce depression symptoms in community and clinical settings. *Journal of Affective Disorders, 159*, 139–146. http://dx.doi.org/10.1016/j.jad.2014.02.019

This article is an excellent example of the use of a cooperative naturalistic group to deliver a therapeutic intervention designed to heighten social identification among people with depression.

Ogrodniczuk, J. S., & Piper, W. E. (2003). The effect of group climate on outcome in two forms of short-term group therapy. *Group Dynamics: Theory, Research, and Practice, 7*, 64–76. http://dx.doi.org/10.1037/1089-2699.7.1.64

The authors demonstrate the impact of normative orientation within a therapy group on member participation. Relevant to our discussion, they document the problems that can arise when group members feel overly bound by perceived group norms and the benefits that occur when group members equate personal interests with group interests.

Wade, N. G., Post, B. C., Cornish, M. A., Vogel, D. L., & Tucker, J. R. (2011). Predictors of the change in self-stigma following a single session of group counseling. *Journal of Counseling Psychology, 58*, 170–182. http://dx.doi.org/10.1037/a0022630

The dynamic and impact of the stigma of participation in group psychotherapy is reviewed, and the authors test some factors that might reduce felt stigma and increase willingness to take part in the group.

REFERENCES

Al-Ubaydli, O., Jones, G., & Weel, J. (2016). Average player traits as predictors of cooperation in a repeated prisoner's dilemma. *Journal of Behavioral and Experimental Economics, 64*, 50–60. http://dx.doi.org/10.1016/j.socec.2015.10.005

Anderson, L. R., & Mellor, J. M. (2009). Religion and cooperation in a public goods experiment. *Economics Letters, 105*, 58–60. http://dx.doi.org/10.1016/j.econlet.2009.05.016

Aquino, K., Freeman, D., Reed, A., II, Lim, V. K. G., & Felps, W. (2009). Testing a social-cognitive model of moral behavior: The interactive influence of situations and moral identity centrality. *Journal of Personality and Social Psychology, 97*, 123–141. http://dx.doi.org/10.1037/a0015406

Atkinson, Q. D., & Bourrat, P. (2011). Beliefs about God, the afterlife and morality support the role of supernatural policing in human cooperation. *Evolution and Human Behavior, 32,* 41–49. http://dx.doi.org/10.1016/j.evolhumbehav.2010.07.008

Babcock, J. C., Green, C. E., & Robie, C. (2004). Does batterers' treatment work? A meta-analytic review of domestic violence treatment. *Clinical Psychology Review, 23,* 1023–1053. http://dx.doi.org/10.1016/j.cpr.2002.07.001

Bachrach, D. G., Powell, B. C., Bendoly, E., & Richey, R. G. (2006). Organizational citizenship behavior and performance evaluations: Exploring the impact of task interdependence. *Journal of Applied Psychology, 91,* 193–201. http://dx.doi.org/10.1037/0021-9010.91.1.193

Balliet, D., Li, N. P., Macfarlan, S. J., & Van Vugt, M. (2011). Sex differences in cooperation: A meta-analytic review of social dilemmas. *Psychological Bulletin, 137,* 881–909. http://dx.doi.org/10.1037/a0025354

Balliet, D., Parks, C., & Joireman, J. (2009). Social value orientation and cooperation in social dilemmas: A meta-analysis. *Group Processes & Intergroup Relations, 12,* 533–547. http://dx.doi.org/10.1177/1368430209105040

Barr, T. F., Dixon, A. L., & Gassenheimer, J. B. (2005). Exploring the "lone wolf" phenomenon in student teams. *Journal of Marketing Education, 27,* 81–90. http://dx.doi.org/10.1177/0273475304273459

Benard, S. (2012). Cohesion from conflict: Does intergroup conflict motivate intragroup norm enforcement and support for centralized leadership? *Social Psychology Quarterly, 75,* 107–130. http://dx.doi.org/10.1177/0190272512442397

Ben-Shalom, U., Lehrer, Z., & Ben-Ari, E. (2005). Cohesion during military operations: A field study on combat units in the Al-Aqsa Intifada. *Armed Forces & Society, 32,* 63–79. http://dx.doi.org/10.1177/0095327X05277888

Bhogal, M. S., Galbraith, N., & Manktelow, K. (2017). Physical attractiveness, altruism and cooperation in an Ultimatum Game. *Current Psychology, 36,* 549–555. http://dx.doi.org/10.1007/s12144-016-9443-1

Bogaert, S., Boone, C., & van Witteloostuijn, A. (2012). Social value orientation and climate strength as moderators of the impact of work group cooperative climate on affective commitment. *Journal of Management Studies, 49,* 918–944. http://dx.doi.org/10.1111/j.1467-6486.2011.01029.x

Bornstein, G. (2003). Intergroup conflict: Individual, group, and collective interests. *Personality and Social Psychology Review, 7,* 129–145. http://dx.doi.org/10.1207/S15327957PSPR0702_129-145

Brambilla, M., & Leach, C. W. (2014). On the importance of being moral: The distinctive role of morality in social judgment. *Social Cognition, 32,* 397–408. http://dx.doi.org/10.1521/soco.2014.32.4.397

Breitbart, W., Gibson, C., Poppito, S. R., & Berg, A. (2004). Psychotherapeutic interventions at the end of life: A focus on meaning and spirituality. *Canadian Journal of Psychiatry, 49,* 366–372. http://dx.doi.org/10.1177/070674370404900605

Buckholtz, J. W., & Marois, R. (2012). The roots of modern justice: Cognitive and neural foundations of social norms and their enforcement. *Nature Neuroscience, 15,* 655–661. http://dx.doi.org/10.1038/nn.3087

Chen, X.-P., Wasti, S. A., & Triandis, H. C. (2007). When does group norm or group identity predict cooperation in a public goods dilemma? The moderating effects of idiocentrism and allocentrism. *International Journal of Intercultural Relations, 31,* 259–276. http://dx.doi.org/10.1016/j.ijintrel.2006.02.004

Cho, J. C., & Knowles, E. D. (2013). I'm like you and you're like me: Social projection and self-stereotyping both help explain self-other correspondence. *Journal of Personality and Social Psychology, 104,* 444–456. http://dx.doi.org/10.1037/a0031017

De Cremer, D., & van Dijk, E. (2002). Reactions to group success and failure as a function of identification level: A test of the goal-transformation hypothesis in social dilemmas. *Journal of Experimental Social Psychology, 38,* 435–442. http://dx.doi.org/10.1016/S0022-1031(02)00009-4

De Dreu, C. K. W. (2010). Social conflict: The emergence and consequences of struggle and negotiation. In S. T. Fiske, D. T. Gilbert, & G. Lindzey (Eds.), *Handbook of social psychology* (Vol. 2, pp. 983–1023). New York, NY: Wiley. http://dx.doi.org/10.1002/9780470561119.socpsy002027

Duarte, R., Araújo, D., Correia, V., & Davids, K. (2012). Sports teams as superorganisms: Implications of sociobiological models of behaviour for research and practice in team sports performance analysis. *Sports Medicine, 42,* 633–642. http://dx.doi.org/10.1007/BF03262285

Dunlop, W. L., & Beauchamp, M. R. (2011). Does similarity make a difference? Predicting cohesion and attendance behaviors within exercise group settings. *Group Dynamics: Theory, Research, and Practice, 15,* 258–266. http://dx.doi.org/10.1037/a0023642

Eccles, D. W., & Tenenbaum, G. (2004). Why an expert team is more than a team of experts: A social-cognitive conceptualization of team coordination and communication in sport. *Journal of Sport and Exercise Psychology, 26,* 542–560. http://dx.doi.org/10.1123/jsep.26.4.542

Fehr, E., & Fischbacher, U. (2004). Social norms and human cooperation. *Trends in Cognitive Sciences, 8,* 185–190. http://dx.doi.org/10.1016/j.tics.2004.02.007

Fischer, I. (2009). Friend or foe: Subjective expected relative similarity as a determinant of cooperation. *Journal of Experimental Psychology: General, 138,* 341–350. http://dx.doi.org/10.1037/a0016073

Fonagy, P., & Bateman, A. W. (2006). Mechanisms of change in mentalization-based treatment of BPD. *Journal of Clinical Psychology, 62,* 411–430. http://dx.doi.org/10.1002/jclp.20241

Franzen, N., Hagenhoff, M., Baer, N., Schmidt, A., Mier, D., Sammer, G., . . . Lis, S. (2011). Superior "theory of mind" in borderline personality disorder: An analysis of interaction behavior in a virtual trust game. *Psychiatry Research, 187,* 224–233. http://dx.doi.org/10.1016/j.psychres.2010.11.012

Gilligan, M. J., Pasquale, B. J., & Samii, C. (2014). Civil war and social cohesion: Lab-in-the-field evidence from Nepal. *American Journal of Political Science, 58,* 604–619. http://dx.doi.org/10.1111/ajps.12067

Graafland, J., & van de Ven, B. (2006). Strategic and moral motivation for corporate social responsibility. *Journal of Corporate Citizenship, 2006,* 111–123. http://dx.doi.org/10.9774/GLEAF.4700.2006.su.00012

Graziano, W. G., & Habashi, M. M. (2015). Searching for the prosocial personality. In D. A. Schroeder & W. G. Graziano (Eds.), *Handbook of prosocial behavior* (pp. 231–255). New York, NY: Oxford University Press.

Halevy, N., Weisel, O., & Bornstein, G. (2012). "In-group love" and "out-group hate" in repeated interaction between groups. *Journal of Behavioral Decision Making, 25,* 188–195. http://dx.doi.org/10.1002/bdm.726

Hirsh, J. B., & Peterson, J. B. (2009). Extraversion, neuroticism, and the prisoner's dilemma. *Personality and Individual Differences, 46,* 254–256. http://dx.doi.org/10.1016/j.paid.2008.10.006

Hornsey, M. J., Dwyer, L., Oei, T. P. S., & Dingle, G. A. (2009). Group processes and outcomes in group psychotherapy: Is it time to let go of "cohesiveness"? *International Journal of Group Psychotherapy, 59,* 267–278. http://dx.doi.org/10.1521/ijgp.2009.59.2.267

Jones, G. (2008). Are smarter groups more cooperative? Evidence from prisoner's dilemma experiments, 1959–2003. *Journal of Economic Behavior & Organization, 68,* 489–497. http://dx.doi.org/10.1016/j.jebo.2008.06.010

Kanazawa, S., & Fontaine, L. (2013). Intelligent people defect more in a one-shot prisoner's dilemma game. *Journal of Neuroscience, Psychology, and Economics, 6,* 201–213. http://dx.doi.org/10.1037/npe0000010

Kavussanu, M. (2008). Moral behavior in sport: A critical review of the literature. *International Review of Sport and Exercise Psychology, 1*, 124–138. http://dx.doi.org/10.1080/17509840802277417

Kerr, N. L., Rumble, A. C., Park, E. S., Ouwerkerk, J. W., Parks, C. D., Gallucci, M., & Van Lange, P. A. M. (2009). "How many bad apples does it take to spoil the whole barrel?": Social exclusion and toleration for bad apples. *Journal of Experimental Social Psychology, 45*, 603–613. http://dx.doi.org/10.1016/j.jesp.2009.02.017

King-Casas, B., Sharp, C., Lomax-Bream, L., Lohrenz, T., Fonagy, P., & Montague, P. R. (2008). The rupture and repair of cooperation in borderline personality disorder. *Science, 321*, 806–810. http://dx.doi.org/10.1126/science.1156902

Krueger, J. I., Ullrich, J., & Chen, L. J. (2016). Expectations and decisions in the volunteer's dilemma: Effects of social distance and social projection. *Frontiers in Psychology, 7*, 1909. http://dx.doi.org/10.3389/fpsyg.2016.01909

Loeffler, C. H., Prelog, A. J., Prabha Unnithan, N. P., & Pogrebin, M. R. (2010). Evaluating shame transformation in group treatment of domestic violence offenders. *International Journal of Offender Therapy and Comparative Criminology, 54*, 517–536. http://dx.doi.org/10.1177/0306624X09337592

Lohse, J. (2016). Smart or selfish: When smart guys finish nice. *Journal of Behavioral and Experimental Economics, 64*, 28–40. http://dx.doi.org/10.1016/j.socec.2016.04.002

Meisenbach, R. J. (2006). Habermas's discourse ethics and principle of universalization as a moral framework for organizational communication. *Management Communication Quarterly, 20*, 39–62. http://dx.doi.org/10.1177/0893318906288277

Miano, A., Fertuck, E. A., Arntz, A., & Stanley, B. (2013). Rejection sensitivity is a mediator between borderline personality disorder features and facial trust appraisal. *Journal of Personality Disorders, 27*, 442–456. http://dx.doi.org/10.1521/pedi_2013_27_096

Milton, L. P., & Westphal, J. D. (2005). Identity confirmation networks and cooperation in work groups. *Academy of Management Journal, 48*, 191–212. http://dx.doi.org/10.5465/amj.2005.16928393

Muñoz-Reyes, J. A., Pita, M., Arjona, M., Sanchez-Pages, S., & Turiegano, E. (2014). Who is the fairest of them all? The independent effect of attractive features and self-perceived attractiveness on cooperation among women. *Evolution and Human Behavior, 35*, 118–125. http://dx.doi.org/10.1016/j.evolhumbehav.2013.11.005

Nahon, D., & Lander, N. R. (2010). The effectiveness of gender role re-evaluation and non-gender-focused group psychotherapy in the treatment of recently separated men. *International Journal of Men's Health, 9*, 102–125. http://dx.doi.org/10.3149/jmh.0902.102

Nelissen, R. M. A., & Mulder, L. B. (2013). What makes a sanction "stick"? The effects of financial and social sanctions on norm compliance. *Social Influence, 8*, 70–80. http://dx.doi.org/10.1080/15534510.2012.729493

Nelissen, R. M. A., & Zeelenberg, M. (2009). Moral emotions as determinants of third-party punishment: Anger, guilt, and the functions of altruistic sanctions. *Judgment and Decision Making, 4*, 543–553.

Nettle, D., Harper, Z., Kidson, A., Stone, R., Penton-Voak, I. S., & Bateson, M. (2013). The watching eyes effect in the Dictator Game: It's not how much you give, it's being seen to give something. *Evolution and Human Behavior, 34*, 35–40. http://dx.doi.org/10.1016/j.evolhumbehav.2012.08.004

Norenzayan, A., & Shariff, A. F. (2008). The origin and evolution of religious prosociality. *Science, 322*, 58–62. http://dx.doi.org/10.1126/science.1158757

Ogrodniczuk, J. S., Piper, W. E., Joyce, A. S., McCallum, M., & Rosie, J. S. (2003). NEO-five factor personality traits as predictors of response to two forms of group psychotherapy. *International Journal of Group Psychotherapy, 53*, 417–442. http://dx.doi.org/10.1521/ijgp.53.4.417.42832

Padela, A. I., & Rodriguez del Pozo, P. (2011). Muslim patients and cross-gender interactions in medicine: An Islamic bioethical perspective. *Journal of Medical Ethics, 37*, 40–44. http://dx.doi.org/10.1136/jme.2010.037614

Parks, C. D. (2018). Personality influences on group processes: The past, present, and future. In K. Deaux & M. Snyder (Eds.), *The Oxford handbook of personality and social psychology* (2nd ed., pp. 593–620). New York, NY: Oxford University Press.

Parks, C. D., Joireman, J., & Van Lange, P. A. M. (2013). Cooperation, trust, and antagonism: How public goods are promoted. *Psychological Science in the Public Interest, 14*, 119–165. http://dx.doi.org/10.1177/1529100612474436

Peysakhovich, A., & Rand, D. G. (2016). Habits of virtue: Creating norms of cooperation and defection in the laboratory. *Management Science, 62*, 631–647. http://dx.doi.org/10.1287/mnsc.2015.2168

Preston, J. L., & Ritter, R. S. (2013). Different effects of religion and God on prosociality with the ingroup and outgroup. *Personality and Social Psychology Bulletin, 39*, 1471–1483. http://dx.doi.org/10.1177/0146167213499937

Rand, D. G. (2016). Cooperation, fast and slow: Meta-analytic evidence for a theory of social heuristics and self-interested deliberation. *Psychological Science, 27*, 1192–1206. http://dx.doi.org/10.1177/0956797616654455

Rand, D. G., Peysakhovich, A., Kraft-Todd, G. T., Newman, G. E., Wurzbacher, O., Nowak, M. A., & Greene, J. D. (2014). Social heuristics shape intuitive cooperation. *Nature Communications, 5*, 3677. http://dx.doi.org/10.1038/ncomms4677

Sanchez-Pages, S., & Turiegano, E. (2010). Testosterone, facial symmetry and cooperation in the prisoners' dilemma. *Physiology & Behavior, 99*, 355–361. http://dx.doi.org/10.1016/j.physbeh.2009.11.013

Schlüter, M., Tavoni, A., & Levin, S. (2016). Robustness of norm-driven cooperation in the commons. *Proceedings of the Royal Society B: Biological Sciences, 283*, 20152431. http://dx.doi.org/10.1098/rspb.2015.2431

Schultz, P. W., & Zelezny, L. (2003). Reframing environmental messages to be congruent with American values. *Human Ecology Review, 10*, 126–136.

Shields, D. L., LaVoi, N. M., Bredemeier, B. L., & Power, F. C. (2007). Predictors of poor sportspersonship in youth sports: Personal attitudes and social influences. *Journal of Sport and Exercise Psychology, 29*, 747–762. http://dx.doi.org/10.1123/jsep.29.6.747

Simpson, B., Harrell, A., & Willer, R. (2013). Hidden paths from morality to cooperation: Moral judgments promote trust and trustworthiness. *Social Forces, 91*, 1529–1548. http://dx.doi.org/10.1093/sf/sot015

Sparks, A., & Barclay, P. (2013). Eye images increase generosity, but not for long: The limited effect of a false cue. *Evolution and Human Behavior, 34*, 317–322. http://dx.doi.org/10.1016/j.evolhumbehav.2013.05.001

Spek, V., Nyklíček, I., Cuijpers, P., & Pop, V. (2008). Predictors of outcome of group and internet-based cognitive behavior therapy. *Journal of Affective Disorders, 105*, 137–145. http://dx.doi.org/10.1016/j.jad.2007.05.001

Stollberg, J., Fritsche, I., & Bäcker, A. (2015). Striving for group agency: Threat to personal control increases the attractiveness of agentic groups. *Frontiers in Psychology, 6*, 649. http://dx.doi.org/10.3389/fpsyg.2015.00649

Strauss, B., Burlingame, G. M., & Bormann, B. (2008). Using the CORE-R battery in group psychotherapy. *Journal of Clinical Psychology, 64*, 1225–1237. http://dx.doi.org/10.1002/jclp.20535

Tabellini, G. (2008). The scope of cooperation: Values and incentives. *Quarterly Journal of Economics, 123*, 905–950. http://dx.doi.org/10.1162/qjec.2008.123.3.905

Tangney, J. P., Stuewig, J., & Mashek, D. J. (2007). Moral emotions and moral behavior. *Annual Review of Psychology, 58*, 345–372. http://dx.doi.org/10.1146/annurev.psych.56.091103.070145

Tomasello, M., & Vaish, A. (2013). Origins of human cooperation and morality. *Annual Review of Psychology, 64,* 231–255. http://dx.doi.org/10.1146/annurev-psych-113011-143812

van Dierendonck, D. (2011). Servant leadership: A review and synthesis. *Journal of Management, 37,* 1228–1261. http://dx.doi.org/10.1177/0149206310380462

Van Lange, P. A. M., Balliet, D., Parks, C. D., & Van Vugt, M. (2014). *Social dilemmas: The psychology of human cooperation.* New York, NY: Oxford University Press.

van Prooijen, A.-M., & Ellemers, N. (2015). Does it pay to be moral? How indicators of morality and competence enhance organizational and work team attractiveness. *British Journal of Management, 26,* 225–236. http://dx.doi.org/10.1111/1467-8551.12055

Wade, N. G., & Goldman, D. G. (2006). Sex, group composition, and the efficacy of group interventions to promote forgiveness. *Group Dynamics: Theory, Research, and Practice, 10,* 297–308. http://dx.doi.org/10.1037/1089-2699.10.4.297

Zefferman, M. R. (2014). Direct reciprocity under uncertainty does not explain one-shot cooperation, but demonstrates the benefits of a norm psychology. *Evolution and Human Behavior, 35,* 358–367. http://dx.doi.org/10.1016/j.evolhumbehav.2014.04.003 (New results published 2014, *Evolution and Human Behavior,* http://dx.doi.org/10.1101/004135)

Zhao, K., & Smillie, L. D. (2015). The role of interpersonal traits in social decision making: Exploring sources of behavioral heterogeneity in economic games. *Personality and Social Psychology Review, 19,* 277–302. http://dx.doi.org/10.1177/1088868314553709

5

Social Influence Theory and Research

Implications for Group Psychotherapy

Donelson R. Forsyth

The capacity to change—to modify one's thoughts, actions, and emotions appropriately over time and across situations—is an essential element of mental health, but achieving a desired change can be a difficult and daunting task. Individuals who are depressed may want to face each day with vitality and optimism, yet they continue to experience negative affect and self-blame. Failing students may wish to study more diligently, but they are drawn to more immediately pleasurable experiences. People with social phobia hope each of their social encounters will be positive and productive, but when their anxiety reappears when they join with other people, they are disappointed in the results and in themselves.

What can be done to help people make positive, health-promoting changes in themselves and in others? Psychologist Kurt Lewin (1943), many years ago, suggested an answer: Rather than changing individuals, change their groups instead. Lewin conducted one of his most convincing studies of the use of groups as change agents during a period of beef shortages caused by the Second World War. The National Research Council, to ease the crisis, was searching for ways to convince homemakers to serve readily available but less desirable meat products (e.g., beef hearts, brains, kidneys) to their families. Lewin developed two approaches and tested them experimentally. One group of women met with a well-informed nutrition expert who lectured them on the patriotic importance of serving these meats, ways to prepare the foods, and their nutritional value. A second group of homemakers discussed the same information covered by the lecturer, but these women were also urged

http://dx.doi.org/10.1037/0000201-006
The Psychology of Groups: The Intersection of Social Psychology and Psychotherapy Research,
C. D. Parks and G. A. Tasca (Editors)

to reach a group consensus on the issue. Thus, the first approach sought to change individuals' opinions, whereas the second approach focused on changing the group.

Follow-up interviews revealed differences between the two approaches. Only four of the women who heard the lecture served the unique meats (10%), but 23 of the women who discussed the meats in their group served at least one dish containing the less desirable foods (52%). Of the 14 women in the group condition who had never before served these foods, 29% tried them within the next week. In contrast, none of the women in the lecture conditions who had never served the food tried the foods the following week. On the basis of these findings and studies conducted in other contexts, Lewin (1951) concluded that "it is easier to change individuals formed into a group than to change any of them separately" (p. 228).

But what was the source of the group's impact on its members? The study of social influence provides insights into the reasons why more of the home-makers Lewin (1943) studied changed when they were part of an intact group. People live out their lives with other people and continually adjust their actions, thoughts, and emotions in response to those around them. This process, *social influence*, includes "the myriad ways that people impact one another, including changes in attitudes, beliefs, feelings, and behavior that result from the comments, actions, or even the mere presence of others" (Gilovich, Keltner, & Nisbett, 2011).

Researchers in a variety of fields and specializations study this influence process—developmental psychologists examine parenting, clinical and counseling psychologists explore how therapists achieve change in their clients, organization scientists examine management and teamwork, and so on—but this chapter draws first on theory and research in social psychology before examining the implications of this work in therapeutic groups.

SOCIAL INFLUENCE IN GROUPS

Researchers have been studying social influence since the time of the field's founding. Le Bon's (1895/1960) classic study of crowds and mobs, for example, suggested emotions could be passed from one person to another though a contagionlike influence process. Ross (1908), in the first text with the title *Social Psychology*, included chapters dealing with suggestibility, conventionality, and the "laws" of imitation. But it was Asch (1955), using his well-known line-judgment task, and Milgram (1963), in his equally famous (or infamous) obedience studies, who conducted the seminal investigations into influence. They demonstrated empirically that people conform to the judgments of others and obey another person's commands, even when they should disagree and disobey.

These early studies made one point clearly: People influence and are influenced by others in ways that range from the quotidian to the extraordinary.

That work also generated the search for the psychological and interpersonal processes that explain why individuals are so often influenced by those around them and the conditions that limit their response to that influence. Some of that work is reviewed in the following sections, which focus on insights that may prove useful to individuals who rely on groups in therapeutic contexts.

Informational Influence

Conformity occurs when "individuals' opinions, judgments, or actions change to become more consistent with those manifested by other people" (Forsyth, 2013, p. 305). The members of a self-help group reciting the Serenity Prayer, students wearing the same kinds of clothing as their peers, and the homemakers in Lewin's (1943) National Research Council study agreeing to serve kidney pie to their families are all conforming to the observed actions of others. In some cases, people deliberately modify their actions and attitudes to align better with those around them, but more often than not, individuals, without conscious awareness, gradually change how they think and how they act.

When people conform, they are not necessarily abandoning their own beliefs and changing their actions just to go along with the rest of the group. They are, instead, revising their own response based on the information they have gained by observing others' responses. This *informational influence* becomes increasingly likely when individuals are uncertain or inexperienced and when the others in the group are exhibiting a relatively high level of consensus. If everyone in the group publicly endorses serving unusual meats to their families, and you have no opinion on the issue, it is rational to let the group guide your choice. As the principle of social proof suggests, we "view behavior as correct in a given situation to the degree that we see others performing it" (Cialdini, 2009, p. 100).

In his theory of social comparison, Festinger (1954) went so far as to suggest that we have a fundamental need for accuracy and cognitive clarity, which we satisfy through comparison with others:

> The "social reality" upon which an opinion or attitude rests for its justification is the degree to which the individual perceives that this opinion or attitude is shared by others. An opinion or attitude that is not reinforced by others of the same opinion will become unstable generally. (Festinger, Schachter, & Back, 1950, pp. 168–169)

This comparison process is not an entirely objective one, however. If too selective when sampling others' positions, group members may mistakenly conclude that their own beliefs, emotions, and actions are consistent with others (the *false consensus effect*). When calibrating their ranking in the group on qualities that are socially evaluable, people may prefer to compare themselves with others who are relatively unsuccessful (*downward social comparison*). When they need to bolster their optimism and enthusiasm, they compare themselves with others who have succeeded rather than foundered (*upward social comparison*).

Normative Influence

Conformity results from not only informational influence but also *normative influence:* Individuals tailor their actions to fit the social norms that describe what behaviors should and should not be performed in a given context. *Norms*, by definition, describe what is "normal" or "appropriate," and in so doing also identify the sorts of action one should avoid if at all possible. People conform to their group's standards rather than risk the social consequences that counternormative tendencies can bring, such as ostracism, ridicule, or criticism. But they also conform to the group's standards because these standards are consensual. Norms are not necessarily a group's mandated rules and regulations that members grudgingly accept but patterns of thought, affect, and action that members accept as their own. In some circumstances, people internalize their group's norms, and when they do, the group's standards become their personal standards.

Cialdini (2011), in his focus theory of normative conduct, explained the relationship between informational and normative influence, and two different types of social norms: descriptive and injunctive. A *descriptive norm* defines what people typically do in any given situation, whereas *injunctive norms* describe what people should do. Both descriptive norms (informational influence) and injunctive norms (normative influence) are powerful, but Cialdini's focus theory suggests these two forms of influence work in different ways. Informational influence requires individuals to notice what most others do in a situation. Normative influence, in contrast, requires more cognitive resources; only when members can focus on the injunctive norm and its implications will individuals change to comply with the norm's standard.

Normative influence pulls group members together because it reduces uncertainty, increases coordination, and unifies the members in the pursuit of group-level goals. Normative influence can also be harnessed to sustain members' motivation as they struggle to reach challenging individual-level goals, such as exercising regularly and eating healthy foods (see Chapter 7, this volume). But norms can be a negative influence. They may silence dissent and promote the mistreatment of members who are less than prototypical. Some norms, too, are ones that are harmful rather than healthy, and as normative influence increases, so does the group's threat to its members' health and well-being. Sports teams and military units, for example, may demand excessive levels of physical sacrifice from their members. Some groups, such as fraternities, adopt norms that define hazing to be an acceptable group tradition. The norms of some groups, such as cheerleading squads, dance troupes, and sororities, define binging and purging as a normal means of controlling one's weight, and the levels of eating disorders in such groups tend to be elevated (Crandall, 1988).

Direct Influence

Informational and normative influences in groups are relatively indirect forms of influence. The pressure they exert on members is relatively subtle—so subtle that group members often do not recognize their influence at all. When they explain why they changed, they usually cite personal reasons for their choices and reject as inaccurate the very idea that they were influenced by what the others in the group were doing (Cialdini, 2005). But in other cases, groups influence their members in ways that are far more direct—and, in some cases, far more coercive. The group may give another member the silent treatment until that individual changes to agree with the group's standards. One member may insult other members or use threats against them to force them to change. A leader may issue an order to another member of the group, which, if disobeyed, will result in punishment of some kind. Harassment, threats, punishment, bribery, and bullying are examples of direct, hard influence tactics because they limit the "freedom an influence recipient is allowed in choosing whether or not to comply with a request or a demand" (Pierro, Kruglanski, & Raven, 2012, p. 41).

Social psychological studies of power and influence have repeatedly confirmed the surprising extent to which people will comply with the demands of those in positions of authority in their groups. Milgram's (1963) well-known behavioral study of obedience, for example, provided suggestive evidence of the power of direct social influence. He invited volunteers to take part in what they thought was a study of learning. Some participants were assigned the role of the teacher and so were required to deliver shocks of increasing intensity to another participant—the learner—if the learner made mistakes when their memory was tested. What the participants did not know, however, was that the learner received no shocks because he was member of the research team, and his mistakes were all prearranged. Given the magnitude of the shocks and the learner's apparent pain when receiving them, Milgram expected very few participants would obey the authority's orders. However, all of the participants agreed to the give shocks to the learner, and a substantial percentage (65%) gave the maximum level of shock possible.

Milgram's (1963) research remains controversial, both ethically and procedurally. Follow-up studies, however, have repeatedly confirmed that people, when ordered by an authority do something they would prefer not do, tend to obey (e.g., Burger, 2009). However, those studies also have suggested that study participants did not display blind obedience but instead responded to the combined effects of information, normative, and direct influence. In groups, members are willing to sacrifice their own autonomy to help the group, and its leader, reach its goals, particularly if they considered the group and its leader to be legitimate. Hence, in Milgram's (1963) study, some participants obeyed only because the experimenter forced them to do so, but many continued because they trusted the experimenter, respected his authority, and wanted to help the researchers achieve what they thought were scientifically laudable goals (Haslam, Reicher, & Birney, 2014). In many group situations, a variety of social forces—some direct and some more indirect—combined to create a situation in which obedience is probable and disobedience, improbable.

Minority Influence

Groups tend to favor the status quo and choose the path endorsed by the majority of the members. As consensus on an issue builds, informational, normative, and direct influence processes push any dissenters to join the majority either openly or at least implicitly by remaining silent. A jury's decision, for example, often follows the majority-rules heuristic: The verdict favored by a majority of the jurors initially—even before deliberation—is the usually the group's decision when a final poll is taken. Groups are generally quick to adopt the decision favored by a clear majority of the members.

But groups do not ignore entirely novel ideas, new directions, or untried opportunities. As Moscovici (1994) and his colleagues argue in their conversion theory of influence, a dissenting individual or subgroup of individuals within the group—those holding the minority position rather than the majority position—can influence the group's discussion and decision. When the group listens only to the ideas, information, and opinions expressed by the majority of the members, they may fail to consider alternatives, identify novel solutions, or recognize mistaken interpretations of events and experiences. In some cases, too, people do not think very much about an issue once they discover where most people stand; they just adopt that position as their own without considering alternatives. When that happens, they may change their position after the group disbands because they have not actually thought through the justification for the majority's position.

Those who disagree with the group, in contrast, shake the confidence of the majority and force the group to work harder to reach consensus and clarity on the issue. Those who express an unusual idea or opinion are often the target of strong and direct influence by the other group members, but their dissent prompts the group members to consider the accuracy of their position. When majorities find that someone in their midst disagrees with the dominant view, they spend time critically examining the evidence and, in consequence, process the issue more fully, causing group members to reinterpret or cognitively restructure key aspects of the issue. Moreover, if the minority is able to withstand the pressure of the majority and continue to advocate for an alternative, they may eventually succeed in converting some or all of the group members to their position. Because this conversion process takes longer than the compliance process, the effects of a minority on the majority sometimes do not emerge until the group has completed its session and adjourned.

IMPLICATIONS FOR PRACTICE

Those who study groups, including social and organizational psychologists, and those who make use of groups to achieve therapeutic outcomes, including clinical and counseling psychologists, share a similar goal: to explain and promote positive change in others. Both basic and applied researchers and practitioners recognize that change often occurs spontaneously as a result of some life experience, but in other cases, change can be achieved through explicit, intentionally designed interventions. Social influence is one of the means by which those who work in groups with therapeutic purposes help the members of those groups achieve the changes they are seeking. Following the tradition of Goldstein, Heller, and Sechrest (1966), the ideas presented in this chapter represent only a sample of the possible applications of findings obtained in group dynamics research to therapeutic contexts; many other extrapolations are possible.

Universalism

When individuals join with one another in groups, they usually reveal personal information about themselves, share details about their experiences, and offer their opinions on issues. This pooling of information often results in the building of consensus on issues, concerns, and problems as interpretations that are voiced by more members of the group are accepted by majority of the members and as alternative views gradually lose favor. The most immediate effect of this process is a positive one: The members come to realize that the problems they are experiencing are shared by others in the group. Yalom (2005) termed this experience *universalism*: "After hearing other members disclose concerns similar to their own, clients report feeling more in touch with the world and describe the process as a 'welcome to the human race' experience" (p. 6), or "we're all in the same boat."

This informational influence process can, however, result in the group's settling on decisions and interpretations that are not necessarily adaptive or desirable. Studies of groups that are making decisions suggest these groups are too often biased in their sharing of information; they spend much more time discussing information that members hold in common before discussion (the *shared information bias*; Stasser, 1992). This bias is a result of the tendency for groups to seek reassuring consensus on issues rather than the most accurate interpretation of those issues. Group sessions help individuals marshal the evidence and information they need to understand their problems and identify ways to achieve their therapeutic goals, but groups facing highly ambiguous, upsetting issues often seek consensus and closure rather than accuracy. The bias is attenuated if groups work slowly, if experienced members (e.g., the leaders) push for individuals who are reticent to express their views, and if the group is a diverse one (Reimer, Reimer, & Czienskowski, 2010).

Social Comparison

Therapeutic groups provide members with not only useful information and support in dealing with their difficulties but also information about their relative standing on skills, competencies, and outcomes. Downward social comparison—comparing oneself with others in the group who are experiencing even more severe hardships or are failing to cope well with their problems—is usually salubrious because it serves to bolster one's confidence and sense of well-being. Upward social comparison, in contrast, involves comparing oneself with people who are coping effectively with their problems. This type of comparison can also be beneficial given that it helps members identify ways to improve their own situation and promotes their feelings of hope.

These benefits of social comparison are more likely when individuals are selective in the framing of the social comparison data. If engaged in upward comparison, focusing on the fact that one is performing worse than others can be disheartening, so individuals who focus on the positive aspects of the data—that it is possible to improve—should respond more positively. Conversely, downward comparison, if framed negatively, suggests that one might get even worse and so, in time, will experience the same declines and setbacks as those who are not coping well with the problem. Thus, those group members who engage in downward social comparison but use that data as an indicator that they themselves are coping relatively well should respond more positively than those who frame the comparison data more negatively.

One's subjective beliefs regarding the likelihood of change is one of the key factors that determines how individuals will frame the data gained by social comparison: Those who are confident they will improve respond more positively to upward comparison data, but those who know their condition may worsen respond more negatively to downward social comparison data (Wood & VanderZee, 1997). Upward comparison can also be threatening when comparisons involve attributes or skills central to individuals' self-definitions. In such cases, individuals may deliberately avoid interacting in the group, and members may exacerbate this reaction by frequently exposing them, during the group's sessions, to esteem-threatening upward social comparison information. Even well-meaning comembers may tell their fellow group members, "The same thing happened to me, but I'm doing fine now" rather than downward social comparison information, such as "You are doing so much better than I am."

Localized Comparison

Persuasive communicators often seek to influence listeners by providing them with statistical, aggregated information. A health professional may explain that, for most people, the depression that follows the loss of a loved one diminishes after approximately 6 months. A professor may warn her students that the average grade in her class is a C. The lecturer in Lewin's (1943) study of food preparation practices could explain that 30% of all patriotic American homemakers serve their families braised beef heart once a week. But members of small, intact groups can make more localized comparisons. The members of a grief counseling group can learn from one of their own members that the sadness and despair he experienced when his wife passed lifted over time. Students in classes compare their grades immediately after receiving exam feedback. The homemakers in Lewin's food-use study could learn that one of their member's family raved about her beef heart entrees.

Studies of this local dominance effect confirm the "tendency for comparisons with a few, discrete individuals to have a greater influence on self-assessments than comparisons with larger aggregates" (Zell & Alicke, 2010, p. 268). When individuals were exposed to information about their performance relative to a large aggregate of 1,500 people or to their performance compared with other members of their five-person group, the local comparison data proved more influential than the more diffuse, general data. Individuals are not, however, aware of their sensitivity to more local data; they reported they prefer to learn about their performance relative to the group of 1,500 rather than their performance relative to their group members, and they thought the general information would be more useful (Zell & Alicke, 2009). These findings confirm the informational value of small, face-to-face groups but also suggest the leaders of such groups should monitor the members' statements for accuracy. A lone group member who make claims based on his or her personal experiences that are inconsistent with empirically supported recommendations pertaining to health and adjustment may substantially influence the beliefs of the other group members.

Creation of Group Norms

Therapeutic groups, as groups, will rapidly develop a set of norms that will become powerful determinants of members' actions. These group-level standards emerge naturally over time, but those that grow organically might not be the most conducive for helping the members reach their therapeutic goals. In consequence, one of the primary responsibilities of the leaders of therapeutic groups is the creation and maintenance of a "work group culture" that facilitates change (Bion, 1959). Skilled group therapists must organize each session so that each group member becomes part of the collective experience; no one should feel excluded or isolated from the group as a whole. Therapists must also be sensitive to the personal needs, vulnerabilities, and readiness of each group member, and take steps to make certain each member's experiences in the session are positive and productive. Therapists should also take advantage of the group's resources, so they should rely on other members of the group to act in ways that help the group achieve its goals. But, among these myriad responsibilities, the one most crucial to group influence is the capacity to put in place, and continually maintain, normative structures that guide the group and its members' interactions in positive, health-promoting ways.

An interpersonal approach to group psychotherapy suggests that certain group-level processes facilitate change in groups, and so the group's norms should be congruent with these facilitating factors. Yalom's (2005) process approach to group treatment, for example, favors a normative structure that focuses members' attention on each other and the processes that sustain or detract from their relationships within the group itself (a so-called here-and-now focus). The group's norms should also be consistent with those factors that Yalom identified that increase the group's therapeutic, or curative, influence on its members. These curative factors include processes that facilitate change, such as opportunities to learn from other members of the group (social learning) as well as conditions that will increase members' commitment to the group itself (group cohesion). Yalom's list includes the installation of hope, universality, the imparting of information, altruism, the corrective recapitulation of the primary family group, the development of socializing techniques, imitative behavior, interpersonal learning, group cohesiveness, catharsis, and existential factors. Yalom found that members also report they gain a great deal when the group offers them insight into the source of their personal and interpersonal difficulties, but he remained unconvinced that this factor is a significant mediator of change (Yalom, 2005).

Models such as Yalom's (2005) describe the normative content that should be built into a highly effective group. But beyond that content are the processes that will increase the impact of these norms on the group members. Findings from research conducted on performance-focused groups, such as work groups and teams in organizations, suggest that the degree of clarity and group consensus regarding norms is as important as the content of norms themselves. One study of high-performance teams, for example, initially focused on multiple factors when seeking to explain why some teams outproduced others, including the composition of the teams in terms of diversity, the level of skills of the members, and type of work norms that the group adopted. But what mattered most was not group composition, members' skills, or the content of the norms but the clarity of the norms. When all agreed on the norms of the group, these norms sustained the group's workflow, creativity, and commitment, and the teams tended to prosper (Duhigg, 2016).

Cohesion and Normative Influence

Yalom's (2005) list of curative factors includes cohesion, which has been variously defined as the attraction of the members to the group, the group's esprit de corps or "we-ness," the strength of the interpersonal bonds acting to keep members in the group, and members' commitment to the group and its goals. By including cohesion on his list, Yalom joined a long line of researchers who have concluded that cohesive groups exert more influence over their members than do noncohesive ones. Cartwright (1951), for example, suggested that if groups are used as change agents, then the members should have a strong sense of group identity and belonging. Bach (1954) noted that the "cotherapeutic influence of peers" in the therapy group requires group cohesion (p. 348). Goldstein et al. (1966), in their attempt to extrapolate from basic, theory driven research in psychology to clinical practice, devoted an entire chapter to the topic, presenting a series of suggestions for increasing cohesiveness by structuring clients' expectancies, promoting intergroup conflict, and including one or more individuals in the group who disagree with the other members' views.

Marmarosh and Sproul's (see Chapter 9, this volume) review of empirical investigations of group cohesion affirms this predicted relationship between cohesion and therapeutic gain. Cohesive groups are associated with increases in members' sense of psychological safety and continuity of membership. Members of cohesive groups are willing to engage, at a more personal level, in the group process. They share more personal, intimate information about themselves with the group and so signal their commitment to the therapeutic process. Members of cohesive groups rarely miss meetings, they take part in the planning of the group's topics and activities, and they may even explicitly mention the group's esprit de corps and sense of camaraderie. Cohesive groups tend to be more supportive of their members, and they deal more effectively with conflict when such conflicts arise. Members find membership in cohesive groups to be more satisfying than membership in less socially unified groups.

But increases in cohesion also go hand in hand with increases in normative social influence. As Lewin's (1951) field theory of group behavior suggests, people in cohesive groups tend to more readily accept the group's goals, decisions, and norms. Furthermore, conformity pressures are greater in cohesive groups, and individuals' resistance to these pressures is weaker. For example, Back (1951), in study of communication patterns in cohesive dyads, directly manipulated cohesiveness by telling group members that they would either enjoy being in the group (because care had been taken in assembling highly compatible teams) or that the group would not be cohesive because the members were incompatible. During the subsequent group session, when the members of cohesive groups discovered that they disagreed with their comember's interpretations of ambiguous stimuli, they were more diligent in efforts to influence their partner, relative to the members of noncohesive groups. In addition, conformity to the partner's influence attempt was also greater in cohesive dyads.

Applied to therapeutic groups, these findings suggest that cohesiveness leads to greater compliance with change-producing norms but that cohesion is not all benefit without cost. Membership in a cohesive group is more satisfying, in general, for members, and such groups are more psychologically influential. However, when group members are motivated more by a desire to maintain group cohesion, they may sacrifice opportunities for therapeutic gains simply to maintain harmony in the group (see Chapter 8, this volume). A group must, however, achieve at least a modicum of cohesion if it is to retain its members and influence its members. Therefore, leaders of therapeutic groups must be mindful of the strength of the interpersonal relations that bond members to one another and to the group. Steps to take to ensure that the group is a cohesive one include using pretraining interventions to prepare members for the group experience, screening potential members to identify those who will not benefit from a group approach to change, dealing directly and effectively with threats to cohesion (e.g., continuance of an unproductive conflict among the members; late-arriving members; members who too frequently act in idiosyncratic, self-promoting ways; challenges to the leader unrelated to the group's analysis of authority relations), matching interventions to the developmental stage of the group, and sustaining a high level of empathy and emotional responsiveness (Marmarosh & Van Horn, 2010).

Indirect and Direct Social Influence

Unlike support or self-help groups, psychotherapy groups have a designated leader: the therapist who is charged with guiding the others in their pursuit of improved mental health. Even though most would agree that the therapist–leader strives to stimulate a change in the client's behavior, no one technique has emerged as clearly superior to other techniques (Forsyth, 2019). Many group therapists, for example, prefer a nondirective style of leadership in which all group members communicate with one another. These group-oriented approaches encourage the analysis of the group's processes, and the therapist-leader sometimes facilitates process but at other times provides no direction whatsoever. The therapist-leader guides the flow of the session through questioning, summarizing, and rephrasing members' statements; provides information; suggests solutions; questions the members' interpretations of problems; and offers his or her own interpretations (Forsyth, 2019; Solomonov, Kuprian, Zilcha-Mano, Gorman, & Barber, 2016).

Other therapists use more directive methods of influence. In such groups, the leader controls the course of the interaction, assigns various tasks to the group members, occupies the center of a centralized communication network, and offers interpretations of the causes of the clients' problems (Forsyth, 2019). Strong (1968), for example, considers therapeutic change to be a form of persuasive social influence. He maintains that clients seek help when they are dissatisfied or frustrated with their current behaviors but do not feel that they can resolve these problems without assistance. The therapist, therefore, takes the role of the psychological expert who suggests interpretations of the client's experiences and ways to deal with current problems. *Interpretations*, in the social influence framework, are statements, suggestions, summaries, or questions that offer new ways of viewing the client's problems (Strong & Claiborn, 1982). As a result, therapists who possess certain characteristics that enhance their expertness, attractiveness, legitimacy, and trustworthiness influence their clients more than therapists who are less credible, attractive, and so on. For example, professional-looking facilities, displays of credentials, and even manner of dress influence clients' perceptions of the therapist and may enhance her or his impact on the group and its members. Group therapists can also increase their expertness by using appropriate (and abstract) psychological terminology; by asking appropriate, thought-provoking questions; and by remaining confident and assertive. Moreover, because trust tends to augment influence, Strong (1968) recommended that therapists deliberately act to increase their perceived trustworthiness, including maintaining "a reputation for honesty," adopting a role that is associated with trust (e.g., physician or clergy), and emphasizing one's "sincerity and openness," and "lack of motivation for personal gain" (p. 217).

These direct methods of influence are not necessarily more powerful than more indirect ones. Lewin (1943), when he studied ways to achieve change in groups, contrasted an indirect approach—the women discussed the issue together and publicly expressed commitment to making the change—and a persuasion approach involving a communicator who discussed the reasons why the homemakers should change. This second approach was not subtle at all: The women knew the speaker was an expert who was trying to change their minds about the foods they served their family. And this method was not as successful as the more indirect, group-centered approach. Therapists who are directive will be as effective as therapists who are more nondirective provided they succeed in building and sustaining an inclusive, change-promoting group experience for their clients (Bauman, 2010; Forsyth, 2019; Lieberman & Golant, 2002; Lieberman, Yalom, & Miles, 1973). Moreover, just as leaders in organizational settings sometimes vary their interventions to fit the situation, so effective leaders in therapeutic settings shift their methods over time. During the early stages of treatment, members may respond better to a more directive leader, whereas in the later stages, a less directive approach may yield more positive results (Kivlighan, 1997).

IMPLICATIONS FOR RESEARCH

Why did more of the homemakers in Lewin's (1943) classic study of food preparation practices in American homes during World War II change when they were part of a group? This chapter explained that change, and change in therapeutic groups in general, by considering theory and research examining sources of social influence in groups, including informational, normative, direct, and minority influence.

The research–practice relationship is a mutual one, however. Meta-analytic reviews have confirmed the effectiveness of group-level approaches to treatment: "When identical treatments, patients, and doses are compared, individual and group formats produce statistically indistinguishable outcomes" (Burlingame et al., 2016, p. 457). However, additional research is needed to identify ways to further improve group approaches, particularly with regard to the social influence processes in such groups. Researchers have made substantial progress in investigating the nature of groups, but the extrapolations offered in this chapter are based more on speculation than on compelling empirical evidence. Informational and normative influence have been studied in many different types of group settings, such as work teams, decision-making groups, and ad hoc groups working in controlled experimental studies, but caution is required before extending these findings to therapeutic groups. The features of therapeutic groups, including degree of psychological challenge, continuity over time, levels of conflict, and shifting focus on individual- and group-level goals, will likely substantially influence members' reliance on the others as information sources (informational influence) and their willingness to conform to the group's formal and emergent norms (normative influence). Individuals who consistently disagree with their group's emerging position on some significant issue pertaining to adjustment and mental health may, in time, influence the majority of the other group members, as conversion theory suggests, but unique features of therapeutic groups may substantially moderate the likelihood and the level of harm that results from this change process.

Researchers, then, must be prepared to test general theories of social influence in contexts that are as psychologically complex and multifaceted as the therapeutic experience. Groups of any type are notoriously difficult to study, and the study of therapeutic groups is no exception. Because individuals are nested in groups, researchers must differentiate between individual- and group-level effects. Although much can be gained from cross-sectional data because therapeutic groups change over times as the group matures, as norms and roles evolve, and as the group's focus of attention shifts from one issue to another, researchers should consider relying more frequently on longitudinal designs. Because group processes, such as leadership, communication, and social influence, are difficult to document with such traditional measurement tools as surveys and observations, researchers should consider using alternative assessment methods, such as unobtrusive measures, natural language analysis, and qualitative methods. This perspective suggests that more work is needed that directly tests the hypotheses offered here in studies of groups that more closely approximate the dynamics of ongoing therapeutic groups. As Goldstein and his colleagues explained in their treatise on translational research, "the ultimate incorporation or rejection of a given extrapolated research finding . . . will be a function of later formal or clinical research" (Goldstein et al., 1966, p. 7).

CONCLUSION

Influence in groups is often painted as socially suspect. Those who yield to others' influence are viewed as weak willed or easily fooled. Those who influence others are characterized as bullies or Machiavellian manipulators of their hapless targets. But social influence is part of the reason why groups help members achieve therapeutic goals that they cannot reach on their own as individuals. Such groups not only provide members with social support, role models to emulate, and opportunities to practice their interpersonal skills, but they also pull and push members along as they pursue personal change. Change often requires abandoning long-held but unhealthy self-conceptions, dealing with setbacks and environmental threats, and gaining mastery of one's emotions and motivations: Many people benefit from being part of a group that provides a helpful push in the direction of that change.

SUGGESTED READINGS

Harkins, S. G., Williams, K. D., & Burger, J. (Eds.). (2017). *The Oxford handbook of social influence*. New York, NY: Oxford University Press.

Harkins, Williams, and Burger offer a carefully curated set of 26 chapters dealing with all aspects of social influence in groups. Specific chapters pertain to conformity, compliance, obedience, power, and norms.

Levine, J. M., & Tindale, R. S. (2015). Social influence. In M. Mikulincer & P. R. Shaver (Eds.), *APA handbook of personality and social psychology* (Vol. 2, pp. 3–34). Washington, DC: American Psychological Association.

Levine and Tindale provide a general overview of empirical studies of social processes that influence groups. They discuss choices and decisions, and give particular attention to the many theoretical analyses proposed to account for minority and majority influence.

Marmarosh, C. L., & Van Horn, S. M. (2010). Cohesion in counseling and psychotherapy groups. In R. K. Conyne (Ed.), *The Oxford handbook of group counseling* (pp. 137–163). New York, NY: Oxford University Press.

Marmarosh and Van Horn thoroughly review theory and empirical findings pertaining to cohesion in therapeutic groups. They offer a number of practical suggestions to follow to increase the level of cohesion in groups with therapeutic purposes.

REFERENCES

Asch, S. E. (1955). Opinions and social pressures. *Scientific American, 193*, 31–35. http://dx.doi.org/10.1038/scientificamerican1155-31

Bach, G. R. (1954). *Intensive group psychotherapy*. Oxford, England: Ronald Press. http://dx.doi.org/10.1037/14491-000

Back, K. W. (1951). Influence through social communication. *Journal of Abnormal and Social Psychology, 46*(1), 9–23. http://dx.doi.org/10.1037/h0058629

Bauman, S. (2010). Group leader style and functions. In R. K. Conyne (Ed.), *The Oxford handbook of group counseling* (pp. 325–345). New York, NY: Oxford University Press.

Bion, W. R. (1959). *Experiences in groups and other papers*. London, England: Tavistock.

Burger, J. M. (2009). Replicating Milgram: Would people still obey today? *American Psychologist, 64*, 1–11. http://dx.doi.org/10.1037/a0010932

Burlingame, G. M., Seebeck, J. D., Janis, R. A., Whitcomb, K. E., Barkowski, S., Rosendahl, J., & Strauss, B. (2016). Outcome differences between individual and group formats when identical and nonidentical treatments, patients, and doses are compared: A 25-year meta-analytic perspective. *Psychotherapy, 53*, 446–461. http://dx.doi.org/10.1037/pst0000090

Cartwright, D. (1951). Achieving change in people: Some applications of group dynamics theory. *Human Relations, 4*, 381–392. http://dx.doi.org/10.1177/001872675100400404

Cialdini, R. B. (2005). Basic social influence is underestimated. *Psychological Inquiry, 16*, 158–161. http://dx.doi.org/10.1207/s15327965pli1604_03

Cialdini, R. B. (2009). *Influence: Science and practice* (6th ed.). Boston, MA: Allyn & Bacon.

Cialdini, R. B. (2011). The focus theory of normative conduct. In P. A. M. Van Lange, A. W. Kruglanski, & E. T. Higgins (Eds.), *Handbook of theories of social psychology* (pp. 295–312). Thousand Oaks, CA: Sage.

Crandall, C. S. (1988). Social contagion of binge eating. *Journal of Personality and Social Psychology, 55,* 588–598. http://dx.doi.org/10.1037/0022-3514.55.4.588

Duhigg, C. (2016). *Smarter faster better: The secrets of productivity in life and business.* New York, NY: Random House.

Festinger, L. (1954). A theory of social comparison processes. *Human Relations, 7,* 117–140. http://dx.doi.org/10.1177/001872675400700202

Festinger, L., Schachter, S., & Back, K. (1950). *Social pressures in informal groups.* New York, NY: Harper.

Forsyth, D. R. (2013). Social influence and group behavior. In H. Tennen, J. Suls, & I. B. Weiner (Eds.), *Handbook of psychology* (Vol. 5, pp. 305–328). New York, NY: Wiley.

Forsyth, D. R. (2019). *Group dynamics* (7th ed.). Boston, MA: Cengage Learning.

Gilovich, T., Keltner, D., & Nisbett, R. E. (2011). *Social psychology* (2nd ed.). New York, NY: Norton.

Goldstein, A. P., Heller, K., & Sechrest, L. B. (1966). *Psychotherapy and the psychology of behavior change.* New York, NY: Wiley.

Haslam, S. A., Reicher, S. D., & Birney, M. E. (2014). Nothing by mere authority: Evidence that in an experimental analogue of the Milgram paradigm participants are motivated not by orders but by appeals to science. *Journal of Social Issues, 70,* 473–488. http://dx.doi.org/10.1111/josi.12072

Kivlighan, D. M., Jr. (1997). Leader behavior and therapeutic gain: An application of situational leadership theory. *Group Dynamics: Theory, Research, and Practice, 1,* 32–38. http://dx.doi.org/10.1037/1089-2699.1.1.32

Le Bon, G. (1960). *The crowd: A study of the popular mind.* New York, NY: Viking Press. (Original work published 1895)

Lewin, K. (1943, October). Forces behind food habits and methods of change. In Committee on Food Habits, National Research Council, *The problem of changing food habits* (NRC Bulletin No. 108; pp. 35–65). Washington, DC: National Research Council, National Academy of Sciences.

Lewin, K. (1951). *Field theory in social science.* New York, NY: Harper.

Lieberman, M. A., & Golant, M. (2002). Leader behaviors as perceived by cancer patients in professionally directed support groups and outcomes. *Group Dynamics, 6,* 267–276. http://dx.doi.org/10.1037/1089-2699.6.4.267

Lieberman, M. A., Yalom, I., & Miles, M. (1973). *Encounter groups: First facts.* New York, NY: Basic Books.

Marmarosh, C. L., & Van Horn, S. M. (2010). Cohesion in counseling and psychotherapy groups. In R. K. Conyne (Ed.), *The Oxford handbook of group counseling* (pp. 137–163). New York, NY: Oxford University Press.

Milgram, S. (1963). Behavioral study of obedience. *Journal of Abnormal and Social Psychology, 67,* 371–378. http://dx.doi.org/10.1037/h0040525

Moscovici, S. (1994). Three concepts: Minority, conflict, and behavioral styles. In S. Moscovici, A. Mucchi-Faina, & A. Maass (Eds.), *Nelson-Hall series in psychology: Minority influence* (pp. 233–251). Chicago, IL: Nelson-Hall.

Pierro, A., Kruglanski, A. W., & Raven, B. H. (2012). Motivational underpinnings of social influence in work settings: Bases of social power and the need for cognitive closure. *European Journal of Social Psychology, 42,* 41–52. http://dx.doi.org/10.1002/ejsp.836

Reimer, T., Reimer, A., & Czienskowski, U. (2010). Decision-making groups attenuate the discussion bias in favor of shared information: A meta-analysis. *Communication Monographs, 77,* 121–142. http://dx.doi.org/10.1080/03637750903514318

Ross, E. A. (1908). *Social psychology.* New York, NY: Macmillan.

Solomonov, N., Kuprian, N., Zilcha-Mano, S., Gorman, B. S., & Barber, J. P. (2016). What do psychotherapy experts actually do in their sessions? An analysis of psychotherapy integration in prototypical demonstrations. *Journal of Psychotherapy Integration, 26,* 202–216. http://dx.doi.org/10.1037/int0000021

Stasser, G. (1992). Pooling of unshared information during group discussions. In S. Worchel, W. Wood, & J. A. Simpson (Eds.), *Group process and productivity* (pp. 48–67). Thousand Oaks, CA: Sage.

Strong, S. R. (1968). Counseling: An interpersonal influence process. *Journal of Counseling Psychology, 15,* 215–224. http://dx.doi.org/10.1037/h0020229

Strong, S. R., & Claiborn, C. D. (1982). *Change through interaction.* New York, NY: Wiley.

Wood, J. V., & VanderZee, K. (1997). Social comparisons among cancer patients: Under what conditions re comparisons upward and downward? In B. P. Buunk & F. X. Gibbons (Eds.), *Health, coping, and well-being* (pp. 299–328). Mahwah, NJ: Erlbaum.

Yalom, I. D. (with Leszcz, M.). (2005). *The theory and practice of group psychotherapy* (5th ed.). New York, NY: Basic Books.

Zell, E., & Alicke, M. D. (2009). Contextual neglect, self-evaluation, and the frog-pond effect. *Journal of Personality and Social Psychology, 97,* 467–482. http://dx.doi.org/10.1037/a0015453

Zell, E., & Alicke, M. D. (2010). The local dominance effect in self-evaluation: Evidence and explanations. *Personality and Social Psychology Review, 14,* 368–384. http://dx.doi.org/10.1177/1088868310366144

6

The New Psychology of Leadership

Informing Clinical Practice

Michael J. Platow, S. Alexander Haslam, Stephen D. Reicher, Diana M. Grace, and Tegan Cruwys

U nsurprisingly perhaps, many traditional analyses of leadership focus on the leaders per se. Leaders are identified and studied in an attempt to identify qualities shared by leaders but not by nonleaders. Although a seemingly rational approach, this individualistic approach (i.e., focusing on individuals per se and individuating leadership processes more broadly) contains fundamental flaws. In this chapter, we review and critique several individualistic approaches to leadership. We then offer an alternative approach in which leadership is understood as necessarily a group process. In doing so, we acknowledge the importance of both leaders and followers, focus on the processes that enable the emergence of leadership (and leaders), and help explain a number of features commonly associated with leadership. We begin by outlining several traditional approaches to leadership. We then provide arguments and evidence for our new psychology of leadership and consider how our analysis can inform practice within the yet untested domain of clinical psychology.

TRADITIONAL UNDERSTANDINGS OF LEADERSHIP

Traditional analyses of leadership focus on attributes of leaders themselves, attributions of followers, and exchanges between the two. In this review, we highlight key findings of these analyses while identifying shortcomings and consider both when introducing our new psychology of leadership.

http://dx.doi.org/10.1037/0000201-007

The Psychology of Groups: The Intersection of Social Psychology and Psychotherapy Research,
C. D. Parks and G. A. Tasca (Editors)

Attributes of the Leader

Many analyses view leadership as a product of attributes of individuals as individuals or as an aspect of personality (e.g., Judge, Bono, Ilies, & Gerhardt, 2002). Meta-analyses examining personality attributes of people in leadership roles (e.g., sales managers, contractors, executives, human resources managers) suggest that certain aspects of personality are associated with relevant outcome variables. Bono and Judge (2004), Derue, Nahrgang, Wellman, and Humphrey (2011), and Fang et al. (2015) examined Big Five personality traits and other attributes conceptually associated with leadership (e.g., individual consideration of followers, use of contingent rewards, followers' job performance), whereas Miao, Humphrey, and Qian (2018) examined the relationship between individual differences in emotional intelligence and subordinate task performance (finding a positive relationship). Across studies, overall effect sizes were often modest; in some studies, they accounted for only 5% of the variance. Thus, although personality may be relevant, a substantial proportion of variability in leadership appears to reside beyond individual attributes.

Moreover, considerable variability is found in the relationships between specific personality predictors and specific outcome variables. For example, although narcissism (a focus on one's self more than others) positively predicts leader emergence, this effect is really accounted for by extraversion; in the end, narcissism is unrelated to leader effectiveness (Grijalva, Harms, Newman, Gaddis, & Fraley, 2015). Yet, when specifically examining extraversion, Derue et al. (2011) found no relationship between extraversion and group performance, whereas Bono and Judge (2004) found extraversion to be related to key aspects of inspirational ("transformational") leadership. In their analysis of leader conscientiousness, Derue et al.'s results suggested that 61.5% of the variance in group performance could be accounted for by this variable (a positive relationship) and Bono and Judge's results suggested it accounted for only 11% of the variance of inspirational leadership.

Of course, not all attributes of potential leaders emerge from stable individual differences. Specific behaviors can be intentionally chosen, learned, and enacted, as is seen most clearly in analyses of "transformational" leadership (Bass, 1985; Burns, 1978). Here, leadership is understood as being inspirational, and potential followers are motivated not simply to follow but to act to achieve and enact the leader's vision. This motivation can be achieved through leaders' promotion of the group's collective interests (e.g., via fairness and trust) and the framing of communications around collectively shared (normative) values. A key aspect of transformational leadership is the provision of *individual consideration* in which leaders respect fellow group members and allow them to voice their views via the leader's active listening. As we will see, this provision of voice is important in understanding leadership as a group process, and in applying leadership concepts to new domains, such as clinical practice.

Attributions of Followers

Rather than focusing on the leader per se, this view emphasizes how leaders are perceived by others. In this approach, it does not matter if would-be leaders possess specific attributes (or not) as long as the people they seek to lead attribute to them the appropriate leader qualities. This approach, explicated most fully in Lord, Foti, and Phillips's (1982) leader categorization theory, shifts the analysis from a focus on the leader to a focus on the followers. Thus, when potential followers attribute qualities associated with broader cultural stereotypes of leadership (e.g., fairness, intelligence, trustworthiness, charisma) to specific individuals, those target individuals will not only be attributed with leadership, they will be followed. This perspective represents a major step forward because it explicitly recognizes the role of followers in the creation of leaders.

Exchange

One classic approach to the study of leadership considers both leaders and followers, and the exchange between them. In these analyses, (potential) leaders offer some form of valued outcome to others in exchange for followership. In its simplest form, leadership extends only as far as leaders can effectively "buy" their followers. Although successful in gaining compliant followers (e.g., Podsakoff & Todor, 1985), it requires no special or independent psychological analysis beyond any other form of exchange.

In a more sophisticated analysis, leader–member exchange theory (Graen & Uhl-Bien, 1995; Scandura & Graen, 1984), simple exchange is not enough. Of importance is the quality of the relationship in which the exchange transpires. Meta-analyses show how high-quality exchange relationships predict positive outcomes, such as enhanced job commitment, performance, satisfaction, role clarity (Dulebohn, Bommer, Liden, Brouer, & Ferris, 2012; Gerstner & Day, 1997), and organizational citizenship behaviors (Ilies, Nahrgang, & Morgeson, 2007). Operationally, the relative quality of these relationships can be measured simply by asking potential follower questions such as, "How flexible do you believe your supervisor is about evolving change in your job?" and "To what extent can you count on your supervisor to 'bail you out' at his expense when you really need him?" (Liden & Graen, 1980) and "How would you characterize your working relationship with your leader?" and "How well does your leader recognize your potential?" (Graen & Uhl-Bien, 1995). Moreover, training in high-quality leader–member exchanges includes active listening, a form of individual consideration and voice provision. Critically for our current analysis, high-quality exchange relationships are considered in leader–member exchange theory as intragroup relationships and partnerships (Graen & Uhl-Bien, 1995; Scandura & Graen, 1984) and are characterized by a "high degree of mutual trust, respect, and obligation" (Graen & Uhl-Bien, 1995, p. 227).

Competence and Conformity

Two key components of leader emergence first discovered in the 1960s as part of exchange analyses were competence at achieving group goals and conformity to group norms (Hollander, 1964). Achievement of both allows one to establish leadership "credit" in the eyes of potential followers (known as *idiosyncrasy credit*) in part by establishing would-be leaders' ingroup credentials. Although focused on leaders' abilities to achieve these aims, this approach highlights the fundamental role of the group, including its goals and norms, and how the group cannot be divorced from leaders themselves (e.g., Abrams, Travaglino, Marques, Pinto, & Levine, 2018; Julian, Hollander, & Regula, 1969).

NEW PSYCHOLOGY OF LEADERSHIP AND THE PSYCHOLOGY OF GROUP MEMBERSHIPS

Diverging from these previous analyses, our new psychology of leadership begins with the proposition that leadership emerges only when others follow. Although this may read as a truism to some, the self-evidence of this statement is at odds with a view that people can be leaders even when not leading others. For our analysis, the concept of leadership is meaningless when abstracted and decontextualized from those to be led. This is because leadership is the process (not a person) of influencing others in a manner that enhances their contribution to the realization of group goals (S. A. Haslam, Reicher, & Platow, 2011).

Critically, the ability to lead—to influence others—emerges from shared group memberships (Turner, 1991). This relationship between potential leaders and potential followers is, thus, essential because shared group membership (a) sets the boundary conditions under which leadership will emerge and (b) is the psychological mediator through which other behaviors ensue. Understanding leadership processes from this relationship perspective underlies our analysis of the psychology of leadership. Eschewing decontextualized analyses of individuals, we move the analysis of relationships beyond interpersonal exchanges to broader psychological group memberships. At the heart of this analysis are groups, influence, and processes (not individuals or roles).

Central to this analysis is an understanding of psychological groups in contrast to sociological groups (e.g., Platow, Haslam, Reicher, & Steffens, 2015). With sociological groups, defining parameters can be identified, observed, and measured by independent observers irrespective of whether supposed group members see themselves as such. These parameters include interdependence; structure, roles, and norms; and consensually agreed on inclusionary criteria, such as sex, race, and ethnicity. Sociological groups are in a sense "real" groups in that they exist "out there" to be identified and studied (see Chapter 12, this volume). In contrast, psychological groups represent the subjective, self-defining inclusion of oneself in some collective and can vary independently of what others think or of other independent, definitional inclusionary criteria. Thus, it does not matter if someone is formally part of a sociological group. Building on social identity (Tajfel & Turner, 1986) and self-categorization analyses (Turner, Hogg, Oakes, Reicher, & Wetherell, 1987), what matters is that the person self-defines as a group member.

The distinction between sociological groups and psychological groups is critical. Those in leadership roles—who may be sociological leaders—may fail to garner a following if they ignore the importance of psychological group membership. Simply being employed by the same company as the CEO does not mean that workers see themselves sharing the same group membership as the CEO (Platow, Haslam, & Reicher, 2017); indeed, it may well be that the workers see "us workers" as quite distinct from "those managers." Knowing how to develop one's psychological ingroup credentials among those one seeks to lead is therefore one of the key practices that enables successful leadership. A successful leader needs to be an entrepreneur of identity (S. A. Haslam et al., 2011; Reicher, Haslam, & Hopkins, 2005).

Shared psychological group membership results from shared *self-categorizations* (Turner et al., 1987), subjective understandings of oneself as a group member that promote cooperation (de Cremer & van Vugt, 1999), trust (Platow, Foddy, Yamagishi, Lim, & Chow, 2012), helping (Levine, Prosser, Evans, & Reicher, 2005), and fairness (Opotow, 1990). They are also the basis through which social influence processes operate, including in advertising (e.g., Webb et al., 2017), educational (Mavor, Platow, & Bizumic, 2017), leadership (Hogg, 2001) and clinical (C. Haslam, Jetten, Cruwys, Dingle, & Haslam, 2018) settings. In our analysis of leadership, it is precisely through social influence processes that leaders are made. Other key leadership attributes are also outcomes of shared group membership, including attributions of charisma (Platow, van Knippenberg, Haslam, van Knippenberg, & Spears, 2006) and intelligence (Platow, McClintock, & Liebrand, 1990).

Two recent meta-analyses demonstrate how those categorized with self (fellow ingroup members) who best capture the attributes of "we" in context (i.e., those who are ingroup "prototypical") show the highest levels of leadership across a variety of outcome measures (Barreto & Hogg, 2017; Steffens, Munt, van Knippenberg, Platow, & Haslam, 2018). Assessing results from 117 independent samples, Steffens et al. (2018) observed that 15% of the outcome variance was accounted for by simply knowing the relative ingroup prototypicality of the leaders. This percentage was higher among formal (rather than informal) leaders and leaders in preexisting (rather than laboratory-created: e.g., private companies, day care centers, nonprofit organizations) groups. Echoing work just reviewed, group members with strong ingroup credentials emerge as leaders.

Engaging in behaviors that promote the collective can help establish one's ingroup credentials. This "doing it for us" has been shown in both laboratory and preexisting groups (e.g., students, nationality) to enhance social attraction (and group cohesion; Platow, O'Connell, Shave, & Hanning, 1995; cf. Spink, Chapter 7, this volume), and lead to increased leadership endorsement, influence (Platow, Hoar, Reid, Harley, & Morrison, 1997) and follower effort on behalf of the leader (S. A. Haslam & Platow, 2001). However, there are at least three additional ways to establish a shared collective identity with others: through practices of respect, fairness, and trust.

Respect is a powerful way to create a shared social identity. Often expressed in highly individualistic ways—by singling out individuals for the expression of respect—its consequences are highly collectivistic. In a laboratory context, for example, Platow, Huo, Lim, Tapper, and Tyler (2015) provided feedback to participants that was either highly respectful or disrespectful. These manipulations not only affected feelings of respect but, in turn, positively predicted participants' levels of collective identification and desire for continued group engagement. Ellemers, Sleebos, Stam, and de Gilder (2013) demonstrated a similar process outside the laboratory with military personnel in which feelings of being respected by others predicted enhanced collective identity with one's battalion. Respect also predicted soldiers' sense of their value to the group, which, in turn, predicted enhanced willingness for continued group engagement. One important component of respect is the provision of "voice," a key aspect of individual consideration. Here, people provide others with the opportunity to have their say on matters relevant to them. Both laboratory (Platow et al., 2013) and field research (Tyler & Degoey, 1995) have shown that the provision of voice leads to enhanced feelings of respect, enhancing collective identity.

Fairness as a behavior is conceptually and empirically related to respect, but fairness is also conceptually unique because it can be meted out in highly disrespectful ways and can take various forms. In their study of fairness, for example, Tyler and Degoey (1995) examined procedures followed by authorities (in this case, water authorities), including the provision of voice, the absence of bias in decision making, and the presence of trust. However, fairness can also emerge in the actual resource distributions between individuals and groups. Platow, Grace, Wilson, Burton, and Wilson (2008) found that people will infer shared group memberships (including national identity) from the nature of resource distributions. Normatively fair distributions between individuals lead to a sense of shared collective identity, whereas unfair distributions reduce social identification.

Placing one's trust in others is another way that shared social identification can develop (Tyler, 1994). In a recent study, trust was directly manipulated in an online investment game: Social identification with the partner was higher in the trust than in the no-trust condition (Cruwys, Platow, et al., 2019).

Of course, respect (through voice provision), fairness, and trust represent key aspects of transformational leadership (Bass, 1985). Our current leadership analysis, however, allows us to identify the important mediational process through which such individual consideration is translated into successful transformational leadership: shared ingroup membership. Traditional leadership analyses and the analysis offered by our new psychology of leadership are depicted in Figures 6.1 and 6.2, respectively. The key features of the new psychology of leadership are: (a) shared psychological group membership enables social influence and (b) social influence defines leadership. We have included other variables from Figure 6.1 and our review into Figure 6.2 to acknowledge their role in leadership processes. Importantly, we identify a single

FIGURE 6.1.   Traditional Analyses of Leadership

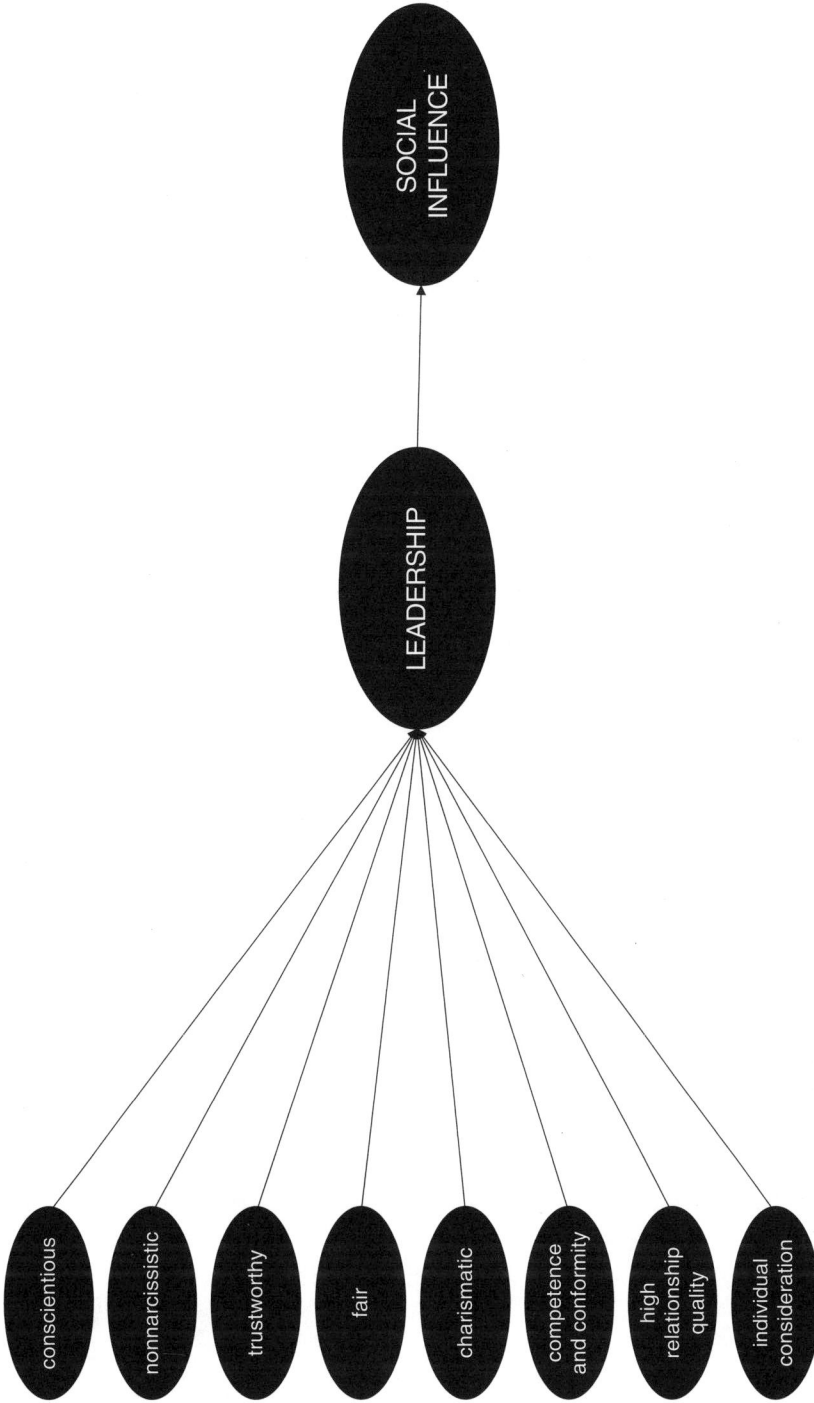

These analyses suggest that a variety of independent factors contributes to leadership that, in turn, allows one to influence others.

FIGURE 6.2. The New Psychology of Leadership

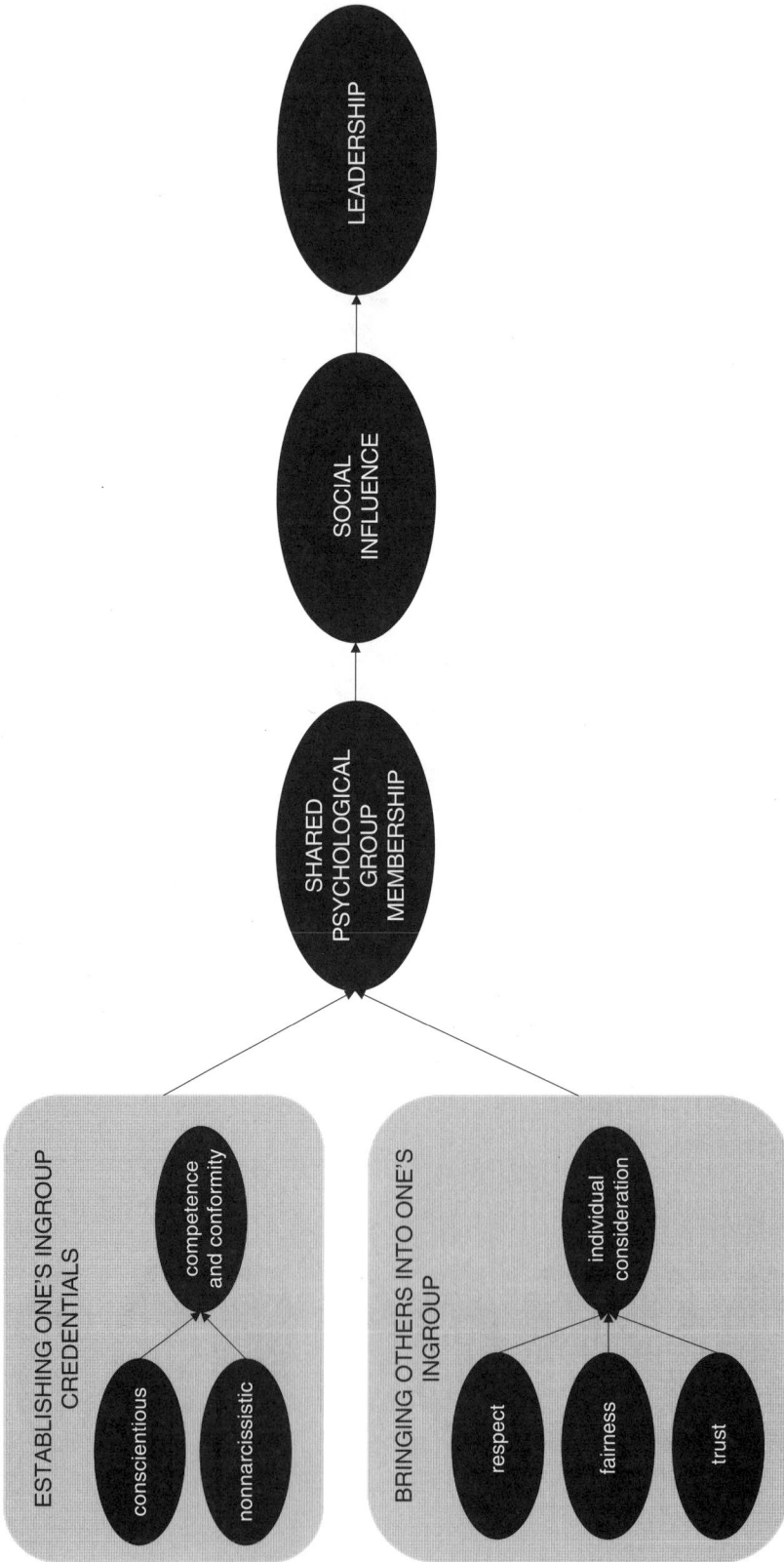

The single factor of shared psychological group membership allows one to influence others, enabling leadership to emerge. Of the many factors that can contribute to a sense of shared psychological group membership, we present two that are drawn specifically from traditional analyses of leadership.

psychological process by which leadership becomes operative while recognizing key variables that have known empirical relationships with leadership.

The full model presented in Figure 6.2 has never been tested, although many aspects of it have. Moreover, the Figure 6.2 model should not be read simplistically. If seen as a simple statistical mediation, the paths might suggest that people who score highly on a Big Five measure of conscientiousness would also report relatively high levels of social identification with a psychological group (in the abstract); this is not true. Instead, we simply note that being conscientious is likely to contribute positively to task competence. We are also aware that high-quality relationships as described in the conceptual analysis of Scandura and Graen (1984) are the outcome of a variety of factors not represented in Figure 6.2.

A second substantial point of difference between traditional leadership models and our new psychology of leadership is the causal order between social influence and leadership. Traditional models seek variables that lead to some conceptualization of leadership. Once people have these attributes, social influence is assumed to follow. That is, would-be leaders become influential after they become leaders. In our analysis, the process is reversed. Although several factors contribute to leadership in traditional models, only a single factor contributes to social influence in our analysis: shared psychological group membership (and the meanings associated with it). Nothing imbues individuals and group members with "leadership" beyond the ability to influence. Of course, how and why shared psychological group membership emerges still needs to be explained, and that is where additional variables are added to the model. Ultimately, however, it is shared psychological group membership that is the most proximal cause in creating the defining feature of leadership: social influence.

CLINICAL PRACTICE AND THE NEW PSYCHOLOGY OF LEADERSHIP

Understanding the centrality of social influence in the leadership process allows us to understand how and why analyses of leadership are relevant to other situations in which "leadership" might otherwise be seen as inapplicable. For example, what of contexts that might otherwise be seen as interpersonal in nature, such as between a clinical psychologist and a client? Here, the traditional concept of leadership, and even that of group membership, may seem irrelevant. However, if we accept that a key role of clinical practice is often one of social influence (e.g., Pentony, 1981), such as teaching clients new skills to manage thoughts, feelings, and behavior (Butler, Chapman, Forman, & Beck, 2006), then the analysis of leadership becomes critical, and all the processes that contribute to it can be brought to bear (see also Chapter 13, this volume).

Indeed, many of the leadership processes we have considered play out in clinical and therapeutic practice. For example, in an analysis of influence techniques used by clinical psychologists, Cooke and Kipnis (1986) observed that the most common technique was explicitly to provide voice to clients (e.g., "Well, what do you think?" and "Are you very upset by that?"; p. 23). Although such techniques have a variety of effects, they are traditionally conceptualized primarily as a tool for encouraging personal self-reflection. Yet they can also be seen through the lens of the leadership work we have reviewed: Respectful voice-giving is likely to lay the groundwork for developing a shared understanding of what "we" are doing in this context. Within the psychotherapy literature, this shared understanding has often been conceptualized in terms of the therapeutic alliance (e.g., Ardito & Rabellino, 2011).

Therapeutic alliance refers to the nature of the relationship between client and clinician or therapist, including the client's subjective sense of collaboration with the clinician, common goals, and a mutual bond (Hatcher & Barends, 1996). The therapeutic alliance is a frequent (if not the most frequent) common feature across different forms of therapy (Grencavage & Norcross, 1990) and can account for a substantial portion of variance in therapy outcomes (e.g., Joyce, Piper, & Ogrodniczuk, 2007). Indeed, this alliance meaningfully predicts positive outcomes in several meta-analyses (Flückiger, Del Re, Wampold, & Horvath, 2018; Horvath & Symonds, 1991; Karver, Handelsman, Fields, & Bickman, 2006; Martin, Garske, & Davis, 2000; Shirk & Karver, 2003). Again seen through the lens of our new psychology of leadership, this alliance can be understood as a shared psychological group membership (C. Haslam et al., 2018).

At least two questions arise at this point. First, are there social influence processes relevant to a clinical context that derive from shared psychological group memberships? For example, will understanding self-categorical-based social influence provide insight into which therapies or therapists achieve better outcomes in the domains of, say, psychological stress or physical pain? Second, can knowledge of leadership processes inform our understanding of the therapeutic alliance (and if so how)? We now consider two studies that bear on these questions.

S. A. Haslam, Jetten, O'Brien, and Jacobs (2004) demonstrated ingroup-based social influence in a domain particularly relevant to clinical practice. Higher state levels of stress were first induced among student participants by informing them they would complete a series of mathematical problems. Before completing the problems, however, participants viewed a video of an actor (portraying a previous participant) describing her experiences. The actor, identified either as an ingroup member (i.e., a student) or an outgroup member (i.e., a "stress disorder sufferer"), provided either a stress maintenance communication ("The experience was stressful . . .") or a stress inhibition communication ("It was a positive experience . . ."). The stress inhibition communication yielded lower stress levels than the stress maintenance communication but only when the communication was from a fellow student. The communications from the stress disorder sufferer had no impact.

A second experimental study measured stress reactions of participants experiencing temporary pain. Platow et al. (2007) found student participants' physiological arousal (as measured by galvanic skin response) was lower when reassured about a painful situation by a fellow ingroup member (someone enrolled in a similar area of study) than by an outgroup member (someone enrolled in a different area of study). Two important features of these data are: (a) participants had already experienced the pain situation, and (b) the measurement of galvanic skin response mitigates, in part, against potential concerns of the S. A. Haslam et al. (2004) study that students were simply verbally complying but internally remained stressed.

Together, these studies suggest that a shared group membership between psychologist and client in a clinical setting might potentially benefit therapy outcomes. To examine this hypothesis in a clinical setting one could consider, for example, the racial and ethnic backgrounds of both psychologist and client. Here, we might predict relatively favorable outcomes when the psychologist and client share racial or ethnic ingroup membership. A meta-analysis by Cabral and Smith (2011) did such an examination. They observed, on the one hand, significantly better outcomes when there was a racial or ethnic match between psychologist and client than when there was no such match. On the other hand, the overall effect was remarkably small ($d = .09$), leading the authors to conclude there was "almost no benefit" to this matching (see also, e.g., Behn, Davanzo, & Errázuriz, 2018).

How can we reconcile this finding with our current analysis? First, we note that the larger (albeit still small) effect sizes found by Cabral and Smith (2011) were among those racial or ethnic groups in which clients also reported more favorable perceptions of the ingroup psychologist. This finding serves as an important reminder of the distinction between psychological and sociological groups. In psychological groups, what is important is how people perceive others and how they self-categorize in context. In many circumstances, racial or ethnic groups are meaningful self-categorizations (e.g., Verkuyten & Nekuee, 2001), but they may not be relevant in the clinical setting. Here, other psychological groups may well come into play, including the psychological group characterized by the therapeutic alliance. In the studies reviewed by Cabral and Smith, leadership activities enacted by psychologists may have been unrelated to their racial or ethnic group membership. Again, a focus solely on sociological group memberships (e.g., racial or ethnic groups) can obfuscate observers' or practitioners' focus on the psychological groups that really matter to the client, leading them to "get it wrong."

So how can our analysis of leadership help practitioners "get it right"? By considering variables that contribute to the development of a shared psychological group membership, we see meaningful overlap between these variables and criteria often used in appropriate and successful therapeutic alliances. Horvath, Del Re, Flückiger, and Symonds's (2011) view that the "alliance is built by doing the work of therapy collaboratively" (p. 11) is particularly helpful here. This collaborative practice—this collective pursuit—is likely to be characterized by high relationship quality (cf., Graen & Uhl-Bien, 1995; Scandura & Graen, 1984) and can be developed by the psychologist through the pursuit of cooperation and engagement with the client (Tryon, Birch, & Verkuilen, 2018; Tryon & Winograd, 2011), and the expression of empathy (Elliott, Bohart, Watson, & Greenberg, 2011; Elliott, Bohart, Watson, & Murphy, 2018). Ackerman and Hilsenroth (2003) provided an extensive review of the variables that successfully predict a positive thera- peutic alliance, including competence, respect, support for the client, and listening and understanding.

Of course, these variables bear remarkable similarity to the very processes that lead to shared psychological group membership: (a) competence—to help establish one's ingroup credentials—and (b) individual consideration through respect and voice provision (in this case, listening for understanding). These components inform clients of their standing as valued ingroup members. Of course, other factors identified (e.g., warmth, friendliness, flexibility) may also help build a shared collective focus (C. Haslam, Cruwys, Haslam, Dingle, & Chang, 2016). The important point is that there is a role for leadership processes in clinical practice. The common feature that enables leadership and contributes strongly to successful clinical outcomes is a shared sense of common purpose developed through a sense of psychological group member- ship between client and psychologist or therapist.

THREE FACTORS INFORMING FUTURE RESEARCH

Our recognition that inherent leadership processes can be meaningful compo- nents of successful clinical practice helps link what may otherwise be seen as quite disparate domains of theory, research, and practice. Giving individual consideration through respect and voice provision, being conscientious and competent in pursuing the task at hand, recognizing that the task is about others and not oneself (i.e., not being narcissistic), and building a high-quality relationship with common purpose are factors shared by both domains. There remain, however, conceptual and empirical questions as we interrogate more fully the social and psychological processes enabling the success of these common factors. Next, we consider three of these questions.

Providing Voice

Providing opportunities for others to express their views is central to successful leadership and successful clinical practice. We have claimed that provision of voice is a means by which the voice provider symbolically embraces the other(s) into a common psychological ingroup. Yet voice provision is not isolated from voice expression and the social interaction that ensues. Thus, it remains unclear if our interpretation—that providing voice is a way of creating a high-quality relationship with common purpose—is truly the driving force. For example, clients may attend a clinical session—often having sought it out and paying for the service—with the precise intent of being able to voice the very problems troubling them. If viewed as paying for the opportunity to speak, denial would be seen as inappropriate and unfair. Of course, this remains both a conceptual and empirical question, and is further complicated if the voice provider (the therapist) is a priori recognized as an outgroup member (e.g., as someone with greater knowledge or as an authority) by the client. In addition, we need to consider the consequences if the voice provider ultimately fails to listen (or understand). The clinical psychology literature suggests that listening and understanding are essential (Ackerman & Hilsenroth, 2003), but this is an area of conceptual and empirical inquiry completely absent from traditional leadership work in which listening and understanding (if considered at all) are simply assumed.

Being One of Us While Being Separate

We have made a strong claim about the importance of psychological group memberships and, hence, psychological leadership, not sociological groups and sociological roles. Although we believe the psychological processes enabling successful leadership and clinical practice emerge from psychological group memberships, the reality is that much of our lives are lived in and through sociological groups. People are hired into organizations where others hold formal managerial and leadership roles, and where they are assumed to have specific skills and knowledge—often different from oneself—relevant to achieving successful organizational outcomes. Similarly, people seek psychological help explicitly from others known to be different from self, others who are known to have specific skills and knowledge relevant to achieving successful clinical outcomes. Thus, either by consequence (in an organizational context) or choice (in a clinical context), the reality of the world imposing itself on us is replete with cues and structures emphasizing differences between self and other, rather than the requisite similarities that come with shared ingroup membership.

Although these differences between self and other may challenge some of our analysis, it need not be fatal. It simply identifies need for further conceptual and empirical analyses. A key direction we recommend is to focus on the meaning of "us" in context. Psychological group memberships may be cognitively represented as social categories, but they are not empty categories. Groups have meanings and norms that influence identification and behavior. These meanings and norms can include how interpersonal relationships are to be played out within the group. It may even be that the meanings and norms of psychological group memberships need to include explicit sociological roles emphasizing difference and separateness, albeit with a common purpose (e.g., van Knippenberg, Haslam, & Platow, 2007).

Engaging in Group Psychotherapy

The analysis we have outlined has focused primarily on individual forms of clinical practice characterized by the dyadic relationship between the clinician or therapist and the client. In doing so, we have focused on the role of clinicians and therapists in guiding and influencing clients to achieve their personal goals. Of course, as considered in other chapters of this book, psychotherapy need not be limited to this dyadic relationship because group psychotherapy can offer clients an alternative that may well be equally suited, if not better suited, to their individual needs. In the context of group psychotherapy, then, we use our current social identity analysis to ask whom the leader might be. On the one hand, the clinician or therapist may well retain a type of leadership role. On the other hand, however, a critical feature of our analysis is that leadership is not tied to specific roles. Any group member can influence others and, hence, be a leader in the manner we have currently outlined. Critically, however, for any form of leadership to emerge, the socio-logical psychotherapy group still needs to be adopted and internalized as a psychological group. The group psychotherapy group members must still self-categorize with the others for any influence and leadership processes to emerge. As such, the processes previously outlined as contributing posi-tively to the therapeutic alliance—particularly respect, fairness, and trust—are likely to still be essential in the building of a broader sense of "we."

Critically, some initial work in the domain of group psychology has already been conducted from a social identity perspective. In two longitudinal studies, Cruwys, Steffens, et al. (2019) identified two factors that enhanced clients' social identification with their psychotherapy group: (a) the perceived similarity between oneself and the others in the group, and (b) the perceived match between their personal needs and the clinical focus (e.g., depression versus anxiety) of the group. A key lesson here is that clients need to see themselves as fitting into their psychotherapy group. If this perception can be achieved, then a shared social identity can be facilitated, and the processes we have outlined in this chapter are likely to become operative. We are confident that the social identity analysis we have put forward is ripe for expansion within the domain of group psychotherapy. Indeed, it has already been applied success-fully to other domains, such as work and organizations (S. A. Haslam, van Knippenberg, Platow, & Ellemers, 2003), education (Mavor et al., 2017), sports (S. A. Haslam, Fransen, & Boen, in press), and health (C. Haslam et al., 2018).

CONCLUSION

Our challenge was to cross subdisciplinary boundaries and explore how specific concepts and empirical findings from one area might inform another. We have endeavored to achieve this aim by considering how recent under-standings of leadership bear striking similarities to important aspects of clinical practice. In doing so, we made the case for the central role of shared psycholog-ical group membership. Shared psychological group membership enables social influence, the essential ingredient to leadership. Moreover, rather than disregard variables important in traditional analyses of leadership, we embraced many of them as contributing to this essential causal process, albeit in different ways from the original analyses. Critically, the new psychology of leadership turns our analysis away from decontextualized individuals and toward an analysis of psychological group processes.

Understanding leadership as an outcome of shared psychological group membership allows us to recognize important similarities in contexts not traditionally associated with leadership. Our focus on clinical psychological practices reminds us that clinical or therapeutic settings often entail crucial elements of social influence and that a high-quality therapeutic alliance between therapist and client yields positive clinical outcomes. By recasting the therapeutic alliance as shared psychological group membership, we have brought to bear many of the principles in our new psychology of leadership. Although currently propositional, we have noted at least three avenues for further empirical work. Overall, our analysis seeks to identify a single set of causal processes that can promote positive interactions and psychological well-being, including leadership and clinical practice.

SUGGESTED READINGS

Ackerman, S. J., & Hilsenroth, M. J. (2003). A review of therapist characteristics and techniques positively impacting the therapeutic alliance. *Clinical Psychology Review*, *23*, 1–33. http://dx.doi.org/10.1016/S0272-7358(02)00146-0

This comprehensive review of work examines the attributes and behaviors of therapists that contribute to the development of a successful therapeutic alliance. The authors identify key behaviors (e.g., warmth, respect, active listening and interest, competence and a collaborative focus) important to the current analysis because they share conceptual similarities with key behaviors that facilitate shared psychological group membership and enhanced leadership.

Haslam, C., Jetten, J., Cruwys, T., Dingle, G. A., & Haslam, S. A. (2018). *The new psychology of health: Unlocking the social cure*. London, England: Routledge. http://dx.doi.org/10.4324/9781315648569

This book explicates the contribution of psychological group memberships to physical and psychological well-being. Covering a range of health-related topics, it reviews traditional approaches before outlining the contribution of psychological group memberships. It views the therapeutic alliance as psychological group membership and presents an intervention to enhance people's engagement with a range of psychological groups in their lives.

Haslam, S. A., Reicher, S. D., & Platow, M. J. (2011). *The new psychology of leadership: Identity, influence and power*. New York, NY: Psychology Press.

This work is a comprehensive introduction of the analysis of leadership adopted in the current chapter. The authors review traditional analyses of leadership before detailing the formation and consequences of psychological group membership. They then explain why it is important for potential leaders to reflect the group's culture and represent that group to advance its goals and values so that it can ultimately realize those goals and values.

REFERENCES

Abrams, D., Travaglino, G. A., Marques, J. M., Pinto, I., & Levine, J. M. (2018). Deviance credit: Tolerance of deviant ingroup leaders is mediated by their accrual of proto-typicality and conferral of their right to be supported. *Journal of Social Issues, 74,* 36–55. http://dx.doi.org/10.1111/josi.12255

Ackerman, S. J., & Hilsenroth, M. J. (2003). A review of therapist characteristics and techniques positively impacting the therapeutic alliance. *Clinical Psychology Review, 23,* 1–33. http://dx.doi.org/10.1016/S0272-7358(02)00146-0

Ardito, R. B., & Rabellino, D. (2011). Therapeutic alliance and outcome of psycho-therapy: Historical excursus, measurements, and prospects for research. *Frontiers in Psychology, 2,* 270. http://dx.doi.org/10.3389/fpsyg.2011.00270

Barreto, N. B., & Hogg, M. A. (2017). Evaluation of and support for group prototypical leaders: A meta-analysis of twenty years of empirical research. *Social Influence, 12,* 41–55. http://dx.doi.org/10.1080/15534510.2017.1316771

Bass, B. M. (1985). *Leadership and performance beyond expectation.* New York, NY: Free Press.

Behn, A., Davanzo, A., & Errázuriz, P. (2018). Client and therapist match on gender, age, and income: Does match within the therapeutic dyad predict early growth in the therapeutic alliance? *Journal of Clinical Psychology, 74,* 1403–1421. http://dx.doi.org/10.1002/jclp.22616

Bono, J. E., & Judge, T. A. (2004). Personality and transformational and transactional leadership: A meta-analysis. *Journal of Applied Psychology, 89,* 901–910. http://dx.doi.org/10.1037/0021-9010.89.5.901

Burns, J. M. (1978). *Leadership.* New York, NY: Harper & Row.

Butler, A. C., Chapman, J. E., Forman, E. M., & Beck, A. T. (2006). The empirical status of cognitive-behavioral therapy: A review of meta-analyses. *Clinical Psychology Review, 26,* 17–31. http://dx.doi.org/10.1016/j.cpr.2005.07.003

Cabral, R. R., & Smith, T. B. (2011). Racial/ethnic matching of clients and therapists in mental health services: A meta-analytic review of preferences, perceptions, and outcomes. *Journal of Counseling Psychology, 58,* 537–554. http://dx.doi.org/10.1037/a0025266

Cooke, M., & Kipnis, D. (1986). Influence tactics in psychotherapy. *Journal of Consulting and Clinical Psychology, 54,* 22–26. http://dx.doi.org/10.1037/0022-006X.54.1.22

Cruwys, T., Platow, M. J., Drury, J., Williams, E., Kelly, A. J., & Weekes, M. (2019). *Risk-taking facilitates the development of shared social identity by enhancing trust.* Unpublished manuscript, Research School of Psychology, Australian National University, Canberra, Australian Capital Territory, Australia.

Cruwys, T., Steffens, N. K., & Haslam, S. A. Haslam, C., Hornsey, M. J., McGarty, C., & Skorich, D. P. (2019). Predictors of social identification in group therapy. *Psycho-therapy Research.* Advance online publication. http://dx.doi.org/10.1080/10503307.2019.1587193

de Cremer, D., & van Vugt, M. (1999). Social identification effects in social dilemmas: A transformation of motives. *European Journal of Social Psychology, 29,* 871–893. http://dx.doi.org/10.1002/(SICI)1099-0992(199911)29:7<871::AID-EJSP962>3.0.CO;2-I

Derue, D. S., Nahrgang, J. D., Wellman, N., & Humphrey, S. E. (2011). Trait and behavioral theories of leadership: An integration and meta-analytic test of their relative validity. *Personnel Psychology, 64,* 7–52. http://dx.doi.org/10.1111/j.1744-6570.2010.01201.x

Dulebohn, J. H., Bommer, W. H., Liden, R. C., Brouer, R. L., & Ferris, G. R. (2012). A meta-analysis of antecedents and consequences of leader-member exchange: Integrating the past with an eye toward the future. *Journal of Management, 38,* 1715–1759. http://dx.doi.org/10.1177/0149206311415280

Ellemers, N., Sleebos, E., Stam, D., & de Gilder, D. (2013). Feeling included and valued: How perceived respect affects positive team identity and willingness to invest in the team. *British Journal of Management, 24*, 21–37. http://dx.doi.org/10.1111/j.1467-8551.2011.00784.x

Elliott, R., Bohart, A. C., Watson, J. C., & Greenberg, L. S. (2011). Empathy. *Psychotherapy, 48*, 43–49. http://dx.doi.org/10.1037/a0022187

Elliott, R., Bohart, A. C., Watson, J. C., & Murphy, D. (2018). Therapist empathy and client outcome: An updated meta-analysis. *Psychotherapy, 55*, 399–410. http://dx.doi.org/10.1037/pst0000175

Fang, R., Landis, B., Zhang, Z., Anderson, M. H., Shaw, J. D., & Kilduff, M. (2015). Integrating personality and social networks: A meta-analysis of personality, network position, and work outcomes in organizations. *Organization Science, 26*, 1243–1260. http://dx.doi.org/10.1287/orsc.2015.0972

Flückiger, C., Del Re, A. C., Wampold, B. E., & Horvath, A. O. (2018). The alliance in adult psychotherapy: A meta-analytic synthesis. *Psychotherapy, 55*, 316–340. http://dx.doi.org/10.1037/pst0000172

Gerstner, C. R., & Day, D. V. (1997). Meta-analytic review of leader–member exchange theory: Correlates and construct issues. *Journal of Applied Psychology, 82*, 827–844. http://dx.doi.org/10.1037/0021-9010.82.6.827

Graen, G. B., & Uhl-Bien, M. (1995). Relationship-based approach to leadership: Development of leader-member exchange (LMX) theory of leadership over 25 years: Applying a multi-level multi-domain perspective. *Leadership Quarterly, 6*, 219–247. http://dx.doi.org/10.1016/1048-9843(95)90036-5

Grencavage, L. M., & Norcross, J. C. (1990). Where are the commonalities among the therapeutic common factors? *Professional Psychology: Research and Practice, 21*, 372–378. http://dx.doi.org/10.1037/0735-7028.21.5.372

Grijalva, E., Harms, P. D., Newman, D. A., Gaddis, B. H., & Fraley, R. C. (2015). Narcissism and leadership: A meta-analytic review of linear and nonlinear relationships. *Personnel Psychology, 68*, 1–47. http://dx.doi.org/10.1111/peps.12072

Haslam, C., Cruwys, T., Haslam, S. A., Dingle, G., & Chang, M. X.-L. (2016). Groups 4 Health: Evidence that a social-identity intervention that builds and strengthens social group membership improves mental health. *Journal of Affective Disorders, 194*, 188–195. http://dx.doi.org/10.1016/j.jad.2016.01.010

Haslam, C., Jetten, J., Cruwys, T., Dingle, G. A., & Haslam, S. A. (2018). *The new psychology of health: Unlocking the social cure*. London, England: Routledge. http://dx.doi.org/10.4324/9781315648569

Haslam, S. A., Fransen, K., & Boen, F. (Eds.). (in press). *Sport and exercise psychology: The social identity approach*. London, England: Sage.

Haslam, S. A., Jetten, J., O'Brien, A., & Jacobs, E. (2004). Social identity, social influence and reactions to potentially stressful tasks: Support for the self-categorization model of stress. *Stress and Health, 20*, 3–9. http://dx.doi.org/10.1002/smi.995

Haslam, S. A., & Platow, M. J. (2001). The link between leadership and followership: How affirming social identity translates vision into action. *Personality and Social Psychology Bulletin, 27*, 1469–1479. http://dx.doi.org/10.1177/01461672012711008

Haslam, S. A., Reicher, S. D., & Platow, M. J. (2011). *The new psychology of leadership: Identity, influence and power*. New York, NY: Psychology Press.

Haslam, S. A., van Knippenberg, D., Platow, M. J., & Ellemers, N. (Eds.). (2003). *Social identity at work: Developing theory for organizational practice*. New York, NY: Psychology Press.

Hatcher, R. L., & Barends, A. W. (1996). Patients' view of the alliance in psychotherapy: Exploratory factor analysis of three alliance measures. *Journal of Consulting and Clinical Psychology, 64*, 1326–1336. http://dx.doi.org/10.1037/0022-006X.64.6.1326

Hogg, M. A. (2001). A social identity theory of leadership. *Personality and Social Psychology Review, 5,* 184–200. http://dx.doi.org/10.1207/S15327957PSPR0503_1

Hollander, E. P. (1964). *Leaders, groups, and influence.* New York: Oxford University Press.

Horvath, A. O., Del Re, A. C., Flückiger, C., & Symonds, D. (2011). Alliance in individual psychotherapy. *Psychotherapy, 48,* 9–16. http://dx.doi.org/10.1037/a0022186

Horvath, A. O., & Symonds, B. D. (1991). Relation between working alliance and outcome in psychotherapy: A meta-analysis. *Journal of Counseling Psychology, 38,* 139–149. http://dx.doi.org/10.1037/0022-0167.38.2.139

Ilies, R., Nahrgang, J. D., & Morgeson, F. P. (2007). Leader-member exchange and citizenship behaviors: A meta-analysis. *Journal of Applied Psychology, 92,* 269–277. http://dx.doi.org/10.1037/0021-9010.92.1.269

Joyce, A. S., Piper, W. E., & Ogrodniczuk, J. S. (2007). Therapeutic alliance and cohesion variables as predictors of outcome in short-term group psychotherapy. *International Journal of Group Psychotherapy, 57,* 269–296. http://dx.doi.org/10.1521/ijgp.2007.57.3.269

Judge, T. A., Bono, J. E., Ilies, R., & Gerhardt, M. W. (2002). Personality and leadership: A qualitative and quantitative review. *Journal of Applied Psychology, 87,* 765–780. http://dx.doi.org/10.1037/0021-9010.87.4.765

Julian, J. W., Hollander, E. P., & Regula, C. R. (1969). Endorsement of the group spokesman as a function of his source of authority, competence, and success. *Journal of Personality and Social Psychology, 11,* 42–49. http://dx.doi.org/10.1037/h0027043

Karver, M. S., Handelsman, J. B., Fields, S., & Bickman, L. (2006). Meta-analysis of therapeutic relationship variables in youth and family therapy: The evidence for different relationship variables in the child and adolescent treatment outcome literature. *Clinical Psychology Review, 26,* 50–65. http://dx.doi.org/10.1016/j.cpr.2005.09.001

Levine, M., Prosser, A., Evans, D., & Reicher, S. (2005). Identity and emergency intervention: How social group membership and inclusiveness of group boundaries shape helping behavior. *Personality and Social Psychology Bulletin, 31,* 443–453. http://dx.doi.org/10.1177/0146167204271651

Liden, R. C., & Graen, G. (1980). Generalizability of the vertical dyad linkage model of leadership. *Academy of Management Journal, 23,* 451–465.

Lord, R., Foti, R., & Phillips, J. (1982). A theory of leadership categorization. In J. G. Hunt, U. Sekaran, & C. Schriesheim (Eds.), *Leadership: Beyond establishment views* (pp. 104–121). Carbondale: Southern Illinois University Press.

Martin, D. J., Garske, J. P., & Davis, M. K. (2000). Relation of the therapeutic alliance with outcome and other variables: A meta-analytic review. *Journal of Consulting and Clinical Psychology, 68,* 438–450. http://dx.doi.org/10.1037/0022-006X.68.3.438

Mavor, K. I., Platow, M. J., & Bizumic, B. (Eds.). (2017). *Self and social identity in educational contexts.* Abingdon, England: Routledge. http://dx.doi.org/10.4324/9781315746913

Miao, C., Humphrey, R. H., & Qian, S. (2018). A cross-cultural meta-analysis of how leader emotional intelligence influences subordinate task performance and organizational citizenship behavior. *Journal of World Business, 53,* 463–474. http://dx.doi.org/10.1016/j.jwb.2018.01.003

Opotow, S. (1990). Moral exclusion and injustice: An introduction. *Journal of Social Issues, 46,* 1–20. http://dx.doi.org/10.1111/j.1540-4560.1990.tb00268.x

Pentony, P. (1981). *Models of influence in psychotherapy.* New York, NY: Free Press.

Platow, M. J., Eggins, R. A., Chattopadhyay, R., Brewer, G., Hardwick, L., Milsom, L., . . . Welsh, J. (2013). Two experimental tests of relational models of procedural justice: Non-instrumental voice and authority group membership. *British Journal of Social Psychology, 52,* 361–376. http://dx.doi.org/10.1111/j.2044-8309.2011.02083.x

Platow, M. J., Foddy, M., Yamagishi, T., Lim, L., & Chow, A. (2012). Two experimental tests of trust in in-group strangers. The moderating role of common knowledge of group membership. *European Journal of Social Psychology, 42*, 30–35. http://dx.doi.org/10.1002/ejsp.852

Platow, M. J., Grace, D. M., Wilson, N., Burton, D., & Wilson, A. (2008). Psychological group memberships as outcomes of resource distributions. *European Journal of Social Psychology, 38*, 836–851. http://dx.doi.org/10.1002/ejsp.489

Platow, M. J., Haslam, S. A., & Reicher, S. D. (2017). Leadership and the essential role of psychological group memberships. In S. Harkins, K. D. Williams, & J. Burger (Eds.), *The Oxford handbook of social influence* (pp. 339–357). Oxford, England: Oxford University Press.

Platow, M. J., Haslam, S. A., Reicher, S. D., & Steffens, N. K. (2015). There is no leadership if no-one follows: Why leadership is necessarily a group process. *International Coaching Psychology Review, 10*, 20–37.

Platow, M. J., Hoar, S., Reid, S., Harley, K., & Morrison, D. (1997). Endorsement of distributively fair and unfair leaders in interpersonal and intergroup situations. *European Journal of Social Psychology, 27*, 465–494. http://dx.doi.org/10.1002/(SICI)1099-0992(199707)27:4<465::AID-EJSP817>3.0.CO;2-8

Platow, M. J., Huo, Y. J., Lim, L., Tapper, H., & Tyler, T. R. (2015). Social identification predicts desires and expectations for voice. *Social Justice Research, 28*, 526–549. http://dx.doi.org/10.1007/s11211-015-0254-6

Platow, M. J., McClintock, C. G., & Liebrand, W. B. G. (1990). Predicting intergroup fairness and in-group bias in the minimal group paradigm. *European Journal of Social Psychology, 20*, 221–239. http://dx.doi.org/10.1002/ejsp.2420200304

Platow, M. J., O'Connell, A., Shave, R., & Hanning, P. (1995). Social evaluations of fair and unfair allocators in interpersonal and intergroup situations. *British Journal of Social Psychology, 34*, 363–381. http://dx.doi.org/10.1111/j.2044-8309.1995.tb01071.x

Platow, M. J., van Knippenberg, D., Haslam, S. A., van Knippenberg, B., & Spears, R. (2006). A special gift we bestow on you for being representative of us: Considering leader charisma from a self-categorization perspective. *British Journal of Social Psychology, 45*, 303–320. http://dx.doi.org/10.1348/014466605X41986

Platow, M. J., Voudouris, N. J., Coulson, M., Gilford, N., Jamieson, R., Najdovski, L., . . . Terry, L. (2007). In-group reassurance in a pain setting produces lower levels of physiological arousal: Direct support for a self-categorization analysis of social influence. *European Journal of Social Psychology, 37*, 649–660. http://dx.doi.org/10.1002/ejsp.381

Podsakoff, P. M., & Todor, W. D. (1985). Relationship between leader reward and punishment behavior and group processes and productivity. *Journal of Management, 11*, 55–73. http://dx.doi.org/10.1177/014920638501100106

Reicher, S., Haslam, S. A., & Hopkins, N. (2005). Social identity and the dynamics of leadership: Leaders and followers as collaborative agents in the transformation of social reality. *Leadership Quarterly, 16*, 547–568. http://dx.doi.org/10.1016/j.leaqua.2005.06.007

Scandura, T. A., & Graen, G. B. (1984). Moderating effects of initial leader-member exchange status on the effects of leadership intervention. *Journal of Applied Psychology, 69*, 428–436. http://dx.doi.org/10.1037/0021-9010.69.3.428

Shirk, S. R., & Karver, M. (2003). Prediction of treatment outcome from relationship variables in child and adolescent therapy: A meta-analytic review. *Journal of Consulting and Clinical Psychology, 71*, 452–464. http://dx.doi.org/10.1037/0022-006X.71.3.452

Steffens, N. K., Munt, K. A., van Knippenberg, D., Platow, M. J., & Haslam, S. A. (2018). *A Meta-analytic review of leader group prototypicality and leadership effectiveness.* Unpublished manuscript, School of Psychology, University of Queensland, St. Lucia, Queensland, Australia.

Tajfel, H., & Turner, J. C. (1986). The social identity theory of intergroup behavior. In S. Worchel & W. G. Austin (Eds.), *Psychology of intergroup relations* (pp. 7–24). Chicago, IL: Nelson-Hall.

Tryon, G. S., Birch, S. E., & Verkuilen, J. (2018). Meta-analyses of the relation of goal consensus and collaboration to psychotherapy outcome. *Psychotherapy, 55,* 372–383. http://dx.doi.org/10.1037/pst0000170

Tryon, G. S., & Winograd, G. (2011). Goal consensus and collaboration. *Psychotherapy, 48,* 50–57. http://dx.doi.org/10.1037/a0022061

Turner, J. C. (1991). *Social influence.* Milton Keynes, England: Open University Press.

Turner, J. C., Hogg, M. A., Oakes, P. J., Reicher, S. D., & Wetherell, M. S. (1987). *Rediscovering the social group: A self-categorization theory.* Oxford, England: Blackwell.

Tyler, T. R. (1994). Psychological models of the justice motive: Antecedents of distributive and procedural justice. *Journal of Personality and Social Psychology, 67,* 850–863. http://dx.doi.org/10.1037/0022-3514.67.5.850

Tyler, T. R., & Degoey, P. (1995). Collective restraint in social dilemmas: Procedural justice and social identification effects on support for authorities. *Journal of Personality and Social Psychology, 69,* 482–497. http://dx.doi.org/10.1037/0022-3514.69.3.482

van Knippenberg, D., Haslam, S. A., & Platow, M. J. (2007). Unity through diversity: Value-in-diversity beliefs, work group diversity, and group identification. *Group Dynamics, 11,* 207–222. http://dx.doi.org/10.1037/1089-2699.11.3.207

Verkuyten, M., & Nekuee, S. (2001). Self-esteem, discrimination, and coping among refugees: The moderating role of self-categorization. *Journal of Applied Social Psychology, 31,* 1058–1075. http://dx.doi.org/10.1111/j.1559-1816.2001.tb02662.x

Webb, H., Jones, B. M., McNeill, K., Lim, L., Frain, A. J., O'Brien, K. J., . . . Cruwys, T. (2017). Smoke signals: The decline of brand identity predicts reduced smoking behaviour following the introduction of plain packaging. *Addictive Behaviors Reports, 5,* 49–55. http://dx.doi.org/10.1016/j.abrep.2017.02.003

7

Group Influences in Sports and Exercise Settings

Applications to Therapy Groups

Kevin S. Spink

While researchers studying groups typically stay within their own setting (e.g., work, school, health, psychotherapy), much can be learned by stepping outside our traditional silos. For instance, sports and exercise are settings where groups are pervasive and individual and group outcomes are important. Members of a sports team who perceive that the team lacks cohesiveness may exert less effort, which may compromise skill development and the ability to win games.

Researchers in sports and exercise settings have a history of examining group effects (Carron & Eys, 2012), and to be clear, some physical activity findings do migrate. The recognized tendency for individuals to exert less effort when working collectively versus individually (i.e., social loafing; Karau & Williams, 1993) originated with a sports task (tug-of-war). In addition, examination of the effect of present others on an individual's performance (social facilitation) came from the sports context of bike riding (Triplett, 1898). Yet, crossover of findings appears to be the exception rather than the rule.

The intent of this chapter is to (a) present representative research examining select group constructs in sports and exercise settings; (b) use the findings from these studies as a heuristic to suggest possible future research directions in areas both inside and outside of sports and exercise, including therapy groups; and (c) provide suggestions for practitioners. The framework outlined by Marvin Shaw (1981) in his celebrated text *Group Dynamics: The Psychology of Small Group Behavior* underpins the constructs selected for this chapter.

http://dx.doi.org/10.1037/0000201-008
The Psychology of Groups: The Intersection of Social Psychology and Psychotherapy Research,
C. D. Parks and G. A. Tasca (Editors)

According to Shaw (1981), a complex environmental context surrounds each group, and that context wields a powerful influence on almost every aspect of group process. To account for this complexity, he identified four different environments: the physical, personal, task, and social. The focus of the current chapter is on the social environment, which concerns the interpersonal relationships that occur once members have assembled and begin to interact. According to Shaw (1981), the social environment includes group composition, which concerns the relationships among the personal characteristics of the members and the consequences of these relationships for the functioning of the group. The social environment also includes understanding the pattern of relationships among positions in the group, termed *group structure*. The chapter focuses on select group constructs examined in physical activity that represent the composition (cohesion, Köhler effect) and structure (social norms, leadership) components of the social environment.

UNIQUE CHARACTERISTICS OF THE SPORTS AND EXERCISE SETTING

Although physical activity groups provide a Petri dish to examine group constructs generally, they have some inherent characteristics that should be considered when translating group findings to other settings. Consider the sports context. Carron and Eys (2012) provided a list of characteristics to define a sports team that included the following. They noted that the members of a sports team share a common identity. The Toronto Raptors are readily identifiable as a distinct professional basketball team by their members, opposing teams, and most people interested in professional basketball in North America. While other sports teams may not get as much press as the professionally based Raptors, members of other teams, even if only playing in a pickup game, will share a common identity as soon as they are matched against an opponent. Because members of psychotherapy groups do not have opponents, this common identity is not likely to emerge as easily. Given that a common group identity is tied to the development of group constructs such as cohesion (Spink, 2014) and group influence (Graupensperger, Benson, & Evans, 2018), development of identity may require more attention in psychotherapy groups.

Having an opponent provides two other characteristics serving to define sports teams (Carron & Eys, 2012). Members of a sports team share a common goal as well as a common fate. As noted in the rule book of all team sports, the goal is to score more points or more goals than your opponent. Thus, members of every sports team share at least one common goal: trying to win. Furthermore, given that each contest results in an outcome, members of each team also share a common fate: they win or they lose together. With these default positions in place owing to the inevitability of the win/loss outcome in the sports setting, it is clear how to intervene to positively impact group composition (e.g., using strategies to increase task cohesion) or group structure (e.g., promoting norms for member effort) components that would increase the probability of attaining a successful team outcome. With psychotherapy groups, these intervention paths to strengthening team composition or structure may not be as obvious because team winning/losing is not inherent in the therapy context, and the focus is on the individual.

Another defining characteristic of sports teams is that members hold a common perception about the psychological constructs that make up group structure, such as positions, roles, norms, and status (Carron & Eys, 2012). After joining and interacting with teammates on an ice hockey team for even a brief time, members will have a common understanding of the positions within the team (e.g., forward, defense, goaltender), the roles (e.g., goal scorer, playmaker), norms (e.g., everyone skates hard in practice and games), and status (e.g., leading scorer has more prestige than the player who scores less). Emergence and recognition of these elements by members of a psychotherapy group are less likely, and it might require that those leading such groups devote time and energy to solidifying group structure by making these elements clear to members.

Another physical activity setting is exercise done in a group. While exercise group settings typically do not possess the traditional structure and processes associated with sports teams (e.g., less likely to share a common goal, suffer a common fate, or have a common perception of the group structure) it has been argued (Spink & Carron, 1994) that exercise groups are more like minimal groups (Tajfel & Turner, 1979). Furthermore, within this understanding of them as minimal groups, differences exist. The setting can range from standard exercise classes in which members have little prior knowledge of each other and little interaction during the classes to groups in which group dynamic principles have been used to enhance group perceptions and cohesion (Burke, Carron, Eys, Ntoumanis, & Estabrooks, 2006). However, regardless of the nature of the exercise setting, group constructs appear to play an important role with respect to cohesion (Spink & Carron, 1994), Köhler effect (Samendinger et al., 2017), social norms (Priebe & Spink, 2015), leadership (Crozier & Spink, 2018), and groupness (Crozier, Martin, & Spink, in press) as they relate to group maintenance and member behavior. Given that psychotherapy groups are likely more similar to minimal than true groups, it could be posited that there might be a more direct transfer from findings in the exercise setting to psychotherapy groups.

GROUP COMPOSITION

As noted earlier, *group composition* refers to the relationships among the characteristics of members of the group (Shaw, 1981). Relationships capture the idea that it is not the specific member characteristics that are important but rather the differences in the characteristics of members. Furthermore, it is how these relationships play out that affect group process. In terms of relationships, interpersonal ones feature prominently.

Cohesion

Interpersonal relationships reflecting the degree to which members "hang together" is termed *cohesiveness,* which often is recognized as the most important small group variable (Lott & Lott, 1965). Although the importance of cohesiveness is long-standing (e.g., "United we stand, divided we fall"; Aesop's fables, which makes reference to group unity), its assessment has been checkered. In reviewing 50 years of empirical research, Mudrack (1989) noted the difficulty in defining the construct precisely or consistently. However, he did acknowledge one definition as noteworthy. In its updated iteration it reads, "The dynamic process which is reflected in the tendency for a group to stick together and remain united in the pursuit of its instrumental objectives and/or for the satisfaction of member affective needs" (Carron, Brawley, & Widmeyer, 1998, p. 213). Developed for a sports setting and extended to an exercise setting (Carron & Spink, 1992), it is presently the most accepted definition of group cohesion in physical activity settings.

One strength of cohesion research in the sports setting is that a standard measure exists to assess the construct: the Group Environment Questionnaire (GEQ; Carron, Widmeyer, & Brawley, 1985). Used extensively for more than 30 years and with only a few exceptions (e.g., Schutz, Eom, Smoll, & Smith, 1994), the GEQ has received psychometric support across many sports and situations (Carron et al., 1998; Whitton & Fletcher, 2014). Although many cohesion instruments both within and outside of sports have come and gone, the GEQ has lasted. Two reasons support its longevity. First, an accepted definition of cohesion (just presented) serves as its base (Carron et al., 1998). Second, an acknowledged conceptual framework of cohesion (presented next) guides the items assessed in the measure (Carron et al., 1985).

The conceptual model positions cohesion as a multidimensional construct including both individual and group aspects. The beliefs each member holds about the personal benefits of group membership compose the individual aspect, whereas the group aspect captures the beliefs each member holds about the group as a collective. These two aspects bifurcate into task and social considerations. Members' willingness to work collectively to achieve the team's objectives capture the *task* dimension, whereas *social considerations* refers to the orientation toward developing and maintaining social relationships within the group. This two-dimensional conceptual model (i.e., group/individual, task/social) results in four cohesion subscales in the GEQ (i.e., group/task, group/social, individual/task, and individual/social). These four subscales act together to create an integrated perception of cohesion, although this multidimensionality does not imply necessarily that all four subscales are equally present in all groups. For example, members might cohere for social reasons in some groups, whereas in others, for task reasons. Also, an original task/social orientation perception could change during the development of the group.

Having a standardized assessment with a 3-decade history allows for the generation of a valid and reliable body of knowledge. Four main conclusions emanate from the studies examining cohesion in sports and exercise settings.

First, true to its definition (i.e., sticking together), cohesion fosters group maintenance. Members who perceive greater cohesion (primarily task) attend more of their exercise classes whether in a structured setting in which sign up is required (Spink & Carron, 1994), an unstructured setting where no sign-up is required (Spink, Ulvick, Crozier, & Wilson, 2014) or maintain membership on a sports team (Carron, Widmeyer, & Brawley, 1988). Furthermore, this relationship between cohesion and adherence within the group extends to a longer term measure of intending to return to one's team the following season in both youth (Spink, McLaren, & Ulvick, 2018b) and adult soccer teams (Spink, Ulvick, McLaren, Crozier, & Fesser, 2015). Cohesion also relates to a member's actual return to his team in the following season (Spink, Wilson, & Odnokon, 2010).

Second, extant findings reveal that cohesion relates to team performance. Results from a meta-analysis revealed a positive relationship between cohesion and performance in sports (Filho, Dobersek, Gershgoren, Becker, & Tenenbaum, 2014). While this relationship appears solid, the direction is less clear. Results revealed no support for cohesion leading to success in elite youth soccer teams (Benson, Siska, Eys, Priklerova, & Slepicka, 2016). However, a qualitative analysis of English soccer teams revealed that members believed that strong team cohesion had a positive influence on performance (Pain & Harwood, 2007). Notwithstanding these mixed results about direction, enough evidence exists documenting a positive link between cohesion and outcome.

The third conclusion is that there are meaningful links between cohesion and a number of individual outcomes, many of which collectively could lead to stronger team performance. These include positive relationships between cohesion and important individual outcomes, such as effort (Spink, McLaren, & Ulvick, 2018a), sacrifice (Cronin, Arthur, Hardy, & Callow, 2015), role experiences (Benson, Eys, & Irving, 2016), coping (Wolf, Eys, Sadler, & Kleinert, 2015), and inverse relationships with social loafing (Høigaard, Säfvenbom, & Tønnessen, 2006) and self-handicapping (Carron, Prapavessis, & Grove, 1994).

Fourth, what leaders do relates to and influences cohesion levels within an activity group. These leadership/cohesion relationships are described in the subsequent Leadership section.

Although the cohesion literature in physical activity settings looms large, there are still issues that warrant examination. One concerns measurement. That may seem odd given that a long-standing cohesion measure exists. The GEQ is a self-report measure, so it brings with it inherent issues such as social desirability that could compromise validity (King & Bruner, 2000). To provide some measure of convergent validity requires other types of cohesion assessments. Some examples suggested in a review by Salas, Grossman, Hughes, and Coultas (2015) include using big data (i.e., a collection of cohesion indices via e-mail or texts), physiological metrics (i.e., brainwave data), or external observers (i.e., expert raters who estimate a team's cohesion).

Another measurement issue surrounds the conceptual model underpinning the GEQ. Although few dispute the multidimensional aspect of the model, the specific dimensions warrant further examination. Support for the task/social distinction appears strong even in nonphysical activity settings (Casey-Campbell & Martens, 2009). However, examination of cohesion in a youth sports (Eys, Loughead, Bray, & Carron, 2009) and the work setting (von Treuer, McLeod, Fuller-Tyszkiewicz, & Scott, 2018) provided no support for the individual versus group component of cohesion. This failure to find backing for the individual/group distinction could be an aberration given that a measure developed for the university classroom using the conceptual framework supported the original two-dimension model (Bosselut, Heuze, Castro, Fouquereau, & Chevalier, 2018). However, the mixed findings suggest more research is needed to examine the conceptual framework components both inside and outside of physical activity settings.

Of interest, although many studies exist examining relationships between cohesion and multiple variables, most reflect first-generation relationship questions (Zanna & Fazio, 1982). A review by Eys and Spink (2018) encouraged researchers to move to second-generation (i.e., examining moderators) and third-generation (i.e., examining mediators) research questions. In terms of possible moderators, examining task demands appears worthwhile. If one wants to understand group behavior, understanding the group task is essential (Kerr, 2017). Consider a sports team playing against a lesser skilled versus an equally skilled opponent. The task demands differ, likely requiring different group processes to achieve the group outcome. Is it possible that the relationship between team cohesion and team performance is stronger when the task demands are higher (i.e., playing an equally matched team requires members remaining united) than lower (i.e., playing a lesser team on which individual skill levels might win the day)? With respect to mediators, examining possible mechanisms identified as relating to both cohesion and team performance (e.g., communication, effort, social identity) would be informative.

In addition, physical activity researchers also could learn from studies done in group psychotherapy. One interesting approach could be the examination of individual-level predictors as possible moderators of cohesion/individual outcomes relationships. For example, the results of a group psychotherapy study revealed that attachment anxiety (i.e., preoccupation with relationships) moderated the relationship between cohesion and the frequency of binge eating (Gallagher, Tasca, Ritchie, Balfour, & Bissada, 2014). In terms of physical activity, one wonders whether the different individual needs for relationship approval expressed by members would moderate the association between cohesion and effort, with greater relationship needs equating with a stronger cohesion–effort link. By including individual-level predictors, the results would not only be informative but would also present a more complete picture of how group processes operate.

Implications for Group Psychotherapy Research

Of course, cohesion is not just important in physical activity settings. Students of group psychotherapy will know that Yalom and Leszcz (2005) identified cohesion as one of the key therapeutic agents in effective group therapy. In a 25-year review of small group processes, Burlingame and Jensen (2017) singled out cohesion for special mention. Although they recognized its moderate but consistent relationship with important group psychotherapy outcomes, they did note the inconsistency in measuring cohesion (e.g., as engagement, acceptance, identification). Given the importance of having a valid and reliable measure to build a solid research foundation, researchers outside of the physical activity setting may wish to devote time to developing and testing a multidimensional cohesion measure for their particular setting. This effort could involve adapting the well-tested GEQ to a new setting as done recently for the university classroom (Bosselut et al., 2018). Alternatively, the possibility exists of creating a different definition and conceptual model for cohesion as initially done by Carron and colleagues (1985) for sports, and then use these as guides to generate items for a new measure.

Implications for Group Psychotherapy Practice

Therapeutic treatments do not occur in a vacuum. As noted by others, it is impossible to separate the effects of psychological and social forces from the effect of a medical treatment itself (Crum, Leibowitz, & Verghese, 2017). When this suggestion is coupled with the observation that cohesion is one of the key therapeutic agents in effective group therapy (Yalom & Leszcz, 2005), practitioners may want to make assessing members' perceptions of the group's cohesiveness the standard of care regardless of treatment. If perceived cohesiveness is reported as low, the practitioner can introduce strategies for increasing cohesion (see the subsequent Leadership section for suggestions on how this might be done). As a field guideline, predictive perceptions of cohesion have emerged in minimal groups in as little as 3 weeks (Spink & Carron, 1994), so cohesion perceptions can be assessed relatively early in group development.

Köhler Effect

In terms of group composition, even when groups appear homogenous (e.g., professional sports team), differences exist. One difference often evident to members concerns skill level. Some members are simply better than others. While this difference perception can result in motivation losses, such as the *free rider effect* in which a less-skilled member reduces effort because of the belief that his or her effort will not influence the group outcome (Kerr & Bruun, 1983), such motivation losses are not a given. In 1926, Otto Köhler reported the results of a study indicating increases in member motivation resulting from member differences in which the discrepancy between members was moderate. He found that weaker members of a dyad in a team strength task increased their effort when paired with a stronger partner in a task in which the group's output was equal to the least capable member's output (i.e., conjunctive task [Steiner, 1972]).

The motivation gain resulting from this "productivity" differential is the *Köhler effect.* Although a number of different explanations exist, upward social comparison and perceived social indispensability typically surface as the two most plausible explanations for its effects (Kerr & Hertel, 2011). Upward social comparison captures the idea that a weaker partner may revise personal performance standards upward when confronted with a more capable partner. Indispensability flows from the suggestion that motivation is likely to increase when one sees one's effort as highly instrumental in achieving valued outcomes.

Results from a meta-analysis revealed weaker members exerted higher effort in groups tasks compared with when working alone (Weber & Hertel, 2007). This result generalized to physical persistence and cognitive maximizing tasks, to conjunctive and additive tasks (i.e., performance is the sum of each member's performance; Steiner, 1972), to coworkers present and absent, and to male and female participants. Furthermore, both upward social comparison and indispensability received support as explanatory mechanisms.

In physical activity, the Köhler effect emerges in both exercise and sports settings. A number of exercise studies involve exergames and virtual software-generated partners (SGPs). When participants were paired with a moderately more capable SGP and the task outcome was determined by the weaker partner's performance, the weaker partner demonstrated greater persistence than when exercising alone (Max, Feltz, Kerr, & Wittenbaum, 2018; Samendinger et al., 2017). These results provide support for the Köhler effect as well as SGPs as partners.

A few studies have examined the effect in the sports setting. As one example, weaker members of a swimming relay team swam significantly faster in the relay race (in which the individual times of four swimmers are combined for a total time) than they swam independently in their individual events (Osborn, Irwin, Skogsberg, & Feltz, 2012). In another, basketball players exerted more effort on defense if they perceived their teammates as more skilled (Emich, 2014). Both of these studies support motivation gains for weaker members in the presence of more skilled teammates when their performance affects the team outcome.

Given that variability around ability will be the norm, not the exception, in physical activity groups, harnessing the motivational effects of these ability differences becomes important. More research also is needed. Given that most of the existing studies are lab-based experiments, extending these findings to the real world of intact sports teams and exercise settings is vital (Irwin & Feltz, 2018). Within intact real-world sports teams, examination of other group processes, as potential moderators, emerges as worthwhile. For example, does the perceived cohesiveness of the team strengthen the Köhler effect? Weaker members on more cohesive teams might view their efforts as more indispensable for success because they perceive more unity with teammates in the pursuit of the team's instrumental objective of winning.

Other possible moderators to examine include members connecting a realistic chance to achieve positive outcomes for the team with a strong team performance, ensuring team outcomes are as attractive as individual work achievements (Hüffmeier, Filusch, Mazei, Hertel, Mojzisch, & Krumm, 2017) and a high member preference for teamwork (Hertel et al., 2018).

Examination of mechanisms also warrant examination. In line with other research (Hertel et al., 2018), would positive mood and meaningfulness of the game mediate the link between perceived indispensability to the team and member effort?

Implications for Group Psychotherapy Research

While sports teams represent an ideal setting for testing the Köhler effect (e.g., comparable individual and team performance measures often exist), examination in group therapy research is important. For instance, would the aforementioned factors also serve as mechanisms in mental health groups? Like physical activity groups, members of mental health therapy groups differ along different dimensions. For one, some members have a greater ability to contribute to group sessions than other members do, even if it relates simply to group tenure. Would new/weaker members of a psychotherapy group contribute more if the leader highlighted their indispensability to the group, which served to improve their mood?

Implications for Group Psychotherapy Practice

Given the knowledge that members within a psychotherapy group will differ and homogeneity is not the norm, leaders may wish to consider person–group fit. Results from a study examining trauma recovery and empowerment model therapy groups revealed an association between a stronger person–group fit for group conflict perceptions and group attendance (Paquin, Kivlighan, & Drogosz, 2013). Following from this observation, leaders of therapy groups might find it valuable to identify members with a weaker person–group fit early and highlight their fit with the group. Doing so might enhance their position with the group and increase their perceived indispensability to the group, which should result in a greater member contribution.

GROUP STRUCTURE

Another key component of the social environment is the group's structure. It refers to the pattern of relationships among positions in the group as noted previously (Shaw, 1981). Structure provides a coherent organizational pattern for the group that tends to remain relatively stable over time, even in the face of member turnover. The structure of a group also has a strong effect on individual members.

Social Norms

Rules understood and acted on by group members without the force of law are *social norms* (Cialdini & Trost, 1998). They provide structure in a group because they serve as a guide for member behavior and provide a prediction as to what other members will do. Furthermore, they result from the social interactions that occur in a group (Shaw, 1981).

A number of theories serve as frameworks for researchers to examine social norms, including social norms theory (Perkins & Berkowitz, 1986) deviance-regulation theory (Blanton, Stuart, & Van den Eijnden, 2001), social identity/self-categorization theory (Hogg & Terry, 2000), and the focus theory of normative conduct (Cialdini, Reno, & Kallgren, 1990). The focus theory of normative conduct (i.e., focus theory) has been used successfully to examine normative influence with a number of individual behaviors (e.g., recycling— Schultz, 1999; energy conservation—Nolan, Schultz, Cialdini, Goldstein, & Griskevicius, 2008). It also serves as the theoretical basis for numerous studies examining social norms in the physical activity setting.

Focus theory outlines how member perceptions of social norms may influence individual behavior (Cialdini et al., 1990). It has two main postulates. First, each of the two different kinds of normative influence, descriptive and injunctive, affects behavior differently. An individual's perception of the prevalence of others' behavior describes *descriptive norms*. If I observe most of my coworkers in my new job coming back early from lunch on most days, my lunch break also is likely to be short. These norms serve as a behavioral cue (Cialdini et al., 1990). They provide a measure of "social proof" (Cialdini, 2009). We view coming back early from lunch as more correct based on the degree that we see our coworkers returning early.

Evidence from physical activity groups supports the importance of descriptive norms. Positive relationships exist between descriptive norms and self-reported effort in sports (Crozier & Spink, 2018) and self-reported adherence in exercise settings (Priebe & Spink, 2011). These results extend to experimental studies in which changes in descriptive norms increased physical activity across behaviors and settings. These include increases in self-reported effort in volleyball players (Crozier & Spink, 2017b), self-reported walking in an office setting (Priebe & Spink, 2015), actual effort in a plank-holding task for Pilates members (Priebe & Spink, 2014), and fewer people using the elevator versus the stairs (Burger & Shelton, 2011).

Injunctive norms, on the other hand, refers to a member's perception of the approval/disapproval of a specified behavior. According to Cialdini and colleagues (1990), these norms involve cognitive processing of what others perceive to be appropriate behavior. They indicate what "ought to be done" and influence behavior through possible social approval or disapproval. As a member of the three Musketeers entourage, I shout, "All for one!" going into battle because it is a battle cry likely to receive two thumbs up from my two teammates.

Similar to descriptive norms, results indicate that injunctive norms impact physical activity behavior. In the sports setting, volleyball players reported greater effort after receiving an injunctive norm message (Crozier & Spink, 2017b). The results of an exercise study revealed that the combined use of injunctive and descriptive norms increased the steps taken by young adults over an 8-day period (Wally & Cameron, 2017). Although descriptive and injunctive norms act simultaneously in many situations (e.g., what is approved of, is often what is done), it is worth noting that they are distinct, and both should be examined (Cialdini et al., 1990).

The second postulate specifies that members only act on normative information that is salient. Normative information only enters an individual's consciousness when deemed relevant. Your eating behavior is not likely to change when, as a vegan, you notice many of your friends replacing their red meat with chicken, because the new meat-eating behavior you notice is likely not salient to you. How do you increase salience? One tactic involves increasing identification with the norm referent group. Some referent groups will be more meaningful than others, so salience of those normative messages increases. As empirical examples, perceptions of others' effort on one's team predicted individual effort more than effort of those on other teams (Spink, Crozier, & Robinson, 2013), and perception of friends' physical activity predicted activity more so than that of coworkers or college peers (Priebe & Spink, 2011). Or it also may be possible to heighten salience by strengthening member identity with the group. In a sporting context, it was found that athletes with stronger social team identities were more susceptible to teammate influences (Graupensperger et al., 2018).

It also is possible to increase salience by linking the normative information with a positive outcome expectation (Bandura, 1986). In a study examining physical activity during a final exam period, undergraduate students who received a normative message that many other students were staying active during the exams and were benefiting academically reported higher activity during the exams than those told that only a few others benefited from staying active (Crozier & Spink, 2017a). The idea was that the positive academic performance benefits drew attention to being active during the exam period (i.e., increase salience of the norm information).

While existing studies provide a good starting point, other questions are worth addressing. A key one concerns how to proceed if the desired behavior is counternormative. What happens when you are trying to get people to be active, and the prevailing norm identifies only 20% as active? One possibility emerging from another health behavior is the use of *dynamic norms*, which are changes in a norm over time (Sparkman & Walton, 2017). These authors examined reducing meat consumption. The results from four studies revealed that individuals exposed to a dynamic norm (e.g., 30% of people have changed their eating behavior and now are eating less meat than they otherwise would) indicated less interest in eating meat moving forward and increased the number of people ordering a meatless meal in a cafeteria setting. Research examining the use of dynamic norms in the activity setting (e.g., 30% have changed their behavior and now are being more active) appears prudent given that being active is counter normative (e.g., only 18% of Canadian adults, 40–59 years, are active enough for health benefits; Rhodes, Janssen, Bredin, Warburton, & Bauman, 2017).

Implications for Group Psychotherapy Research

Given the presented evidence, it would be naive to assume that normative social influence does not operate within group psychotherapy settings, that is, participants modifying their attitudes or behavior in response to perceived norms operating with their therapy group. This played out in a study examining disordered eating in young females (Cruwys, Haslam, Fox, & McMahon, 2015). Specifically, members observing their peers argue against the thin ideal came to believe that the norm for a key reference group (their fellow ingroup members) was not to embrace the thin ideal. This belief change flowing from the normative information preceded a reduction in disordered eating among the participants who had a clinical designation for disordered eating. Although this result suggests that normative influences directly influence therapeutic outcomes through mediators, identification by the therapist of norms that indirectly influence the outcome (i.e., member engagement with a therapy group) also warrant attention. As a starter, examination of group norms for factors identified as generating anxiety in group therapy that inhibit member engagement, such as fear of self-disclosure, criticism, or rejection (Shechtman & Kiezel, 2016), come to mind.

Another research direction could involve the leader identifying anti-therapeutic group norms and then changing them to more adaptive ones. As one example, research revealed causal evidence of a link between correlates of disordered eating and fat talk (e.g., degrading one's or others' bodies) in friendship groups (Cruwys, Leverington, & Sheldon, 2016). In terms of interventions, one suggestion might involve examining whether the leader changing the group norm to talk about the body/health relationship from one that reflects fat talk to determine if this group norm change decreases the risk of disordered eating behaviors.

Implications for Group Psychotherapy Practice

As noted previously, psychotherapy groups do not have opponents like sports teams, so the emergence of a common identity is not likely to be as seamless as it is with sports groups. This has implications for practitioners. As one example, consider those working with psychotherapy groups wishing to use social norms within the group to change individual behavior. Given that a common identity may not emerge organically within the group, the leader may need to consider devoting time to creating a common identity in the early stages of group development because identity has been tied to susceptibility to team member influences (Graupensperger et al., 2018).

Because the recognition of group structure by members of a psychotherapy group also is less likely to occur naturally, those leading such groups may want to devote time and energy to solidifying group structure. Given the importance of acceptance of feedback from group members in psychotherapy groups (Yalom & Leszcz, 2005), those leading such groups should allocate time to firming group structure by ensuring that all members understand that accepting feedback from other members is one of the key norms for the group.

Leadership

In its simplest terms, *leadership* refers to the actions of an individual to influence others to work toward set goals (Northouse, 2010). It is one of the most important components of group structure, and few would dispute its importance in the group setting. There are numerous approaches to examining leadership, and the examination of each would consume more than the allocated space. The interested reader can refer to the group leadership chapter in the Carron and Eys (2012) text for an overview of the different conceptual frameworks used in the sports setting.

This section focuses on actions by the leader associated with developing the cohesiveness of the group. Why emphasize cohesion? As noted earlier, cohesion is the most important small group variable (Lott & Lott, 1965). It relates to many important individual and team outcomes that flow from membership in physical activity groups, and a research base highlights the relationship between leaders and cohesion in physical activity settings.

At one level, the leader's style influences cohesion in activity settings. In terms of leadership style, the more democratic the coach, the greater the tendency for cohesion to develop (Jowett & Chaundy, 2004). Conversely, the more coaches (Kim & Cruz, 2016) and team leaders (Burkett, Blom, Razon, & Johnson, 2014) act independently when making decisions within the team (i.e., autocratic style), the lower the cohesion reported. Note the reference to both coaches and team leaders. Sports researchers make the case that leadership transcends the coach. They note that athlete/peer leaders engage in actions that affect the task, social, and externally focused functions of the team and, as such, deserve examination (Loughead, Hardy, & Eys, 2006).

On another level, the coach's behaviors also impact cohesion. One of the current trends is the focus on leader transformational behaviors. These transformational behaviors are those designed to empower, inspire, and challenge group members to enable them to reach full potential (Bass & Riggio, 2006). Emerging research demonstrates a positive relationship between transformational leadership behaviors and team cohesion perceptions in sports settings (Turnnidge & Côté, 2018). Sports team members reported greater team cohesion when coaches (Cronin et al., 2015) and athlete leaders (Callow, Smith, Hardy, Arthur, & Hardy, 2009) engaged in the transformational behaviors of individual consideration, fostering acceptance of group goals and teamwork, and promoting high performance expectations.

In addition to the previously identified relationships between leadership and cohesion, research also exists reporting leaders enhancing cohesion through team building (TB) interventions. In the physical activity setting, TB describes programs using group dynamics principles to enhance cohesion, which leads to more effective group functioning (Spink, 2014).

A four-stage TB model using the leader as the delivery agent exists (Carron & Spink, 1993). Although not the only existing TB model, other researchers acknowledge it as one of the more accepted group-based physical activity conceptual models for TB (Collins & Durand-Bush, 2015; Harden, Burke,

Haile, & Estabrooks, 2015). The first three stages—introduction, conceptual, and practical—occur in a workshop conducted by a TB specialist with coaches or exercise leaders. The final stage—intervention—involves implementation of the TB strategies by the coaches or leaders (Carron & Spink, 1993). The specifics of each stage follow.

In the *introduction stage,* establishing a rationale for the salience of cohesion is the focus. Leaders receive a brief overview of the benefits of cohesion specific to their setting. For instance, coaches of amateur sports teams learn about the positive relationships established between the perceived task cohesiveness of team and the intention of members to return to the team (Spink et al., 2018b), as well as their actual return to the team in the following season (Spink et al., 2010)

The *conceptual stage* provides the leaders with a frame of reference for connecting the introduced constructs, which is accomplished thorough the introduction of a conceptual model outlining how to use group dynamics principles to enhance cohesion. Within the model, cohesion is presented as an output (or product) of conditions that arise from three different categories of group characteristics. Two of these are the group environment and the structure of the group (i.e., inputs), and the other refers to group processes (i.e., throughput). The rationale is that specific elements in the environment and the structure of the group will contribute to enhanced group processes, which in turn, will lead to members' increased perceptions of cohesiveness in the group. In addition, within each of the categories, specific factors emerge that have an established relationship with enhanced group cohesiveness. These factors include group distinctiveness for group environment, fostering group norms and individual positions for group structure, and increasing communication/interaction and individual sacrifices for group processes. To highlight the factor of distinctiveness, for example, leaders learn that when something in the group's environment is somehow made distinctive (e.g., all group members wear the same T-shirt), members develop a stronger sense of "we," can more readily distinguish themselves from nonmembers, and develop enhanced perceptions of cohesiveness. The protocol of presenting the leaders with a research-based rationale for the inclusion of each factor continues until the coverage of all factors occurs.

The third part of the workshop is the *practical stage* in which leaders become active agents in developing practical strategies they will use in their own group settings. They use the conceptual framework to brainstorm as many specific techniques as possible for TB using distinctiveness, norms, positions, sacrifice, and communication/interaction as frames of reference. From the collective lists created, each leader takes the suggestions that he or she feels would work best.

In *intervention,* the final stage, leaders return to their groups to implement the protocols developed at the workshop.

Researchers using this TB model in exercise settings report the intervention significantly enhanced the members' cohesion in classes of youth (Bruner &

Spink, 2011), young adults (Forrest & Bruner, 2017; Spink & Carron, 1993), and older adults (Watson, Martin Ginis, & Spink, 2004). However, no relationship with cohesion emerges when examining TB in a sports setting (Prapavessis, Carron, & Spink, 1996), which was supported in a meta-analysis examining numerous TB models in sports teams (Martin, Carron, & Burke, 2008).

It is not obvious why the strong results found in exercise settings did not materialize in the sports setting. It could be sports teams are more complex than exercise groups. Therefore, the TB intervention may require a different focus (i.e., model) to enhance cohesion. Alternatively, it could be that there was a ceiling effect in the sports teams (i.e., cohesion was already present to some degree, thus minimizing any putative increase following TB) that was not evident in a newly formed exercise class. Regardless, the sports team setting requires more research with respect to developing cohesion through TB.

As noted, leadership in the sports setting includes both coaches and athletes. Given the importance of each, more research needs to examine the influences of both together. As one exemplar, researchers examined the effects of social influence from coaches and teammates on a player's intention to intervene with teammates by providing feedback when a technical mistake occurred (Spink & Fesser, 2018). Two important findings emerged. Players indicated greater intentions for teammate intervention when both the coach supported teammate intervention around technical mistakes and the norm for teammates was to intervene. Second, when influences from the coach and players were misaligned (e.g., coach encouraged members to provide advice to teammates on how to correct mistakes, but more than 90% of members did not intervene when a teammate made a technical mistake), intention to intervene did not differ. If replicated, these findings suggest that a coach should encourage teammate intervention as well as use TB to cultivate a team culture where providing teammate feedback following a technical mistake is the team norm.

Implications for Group Psychotherapy Research

Leaders in other areas such as psychotherapy also might benefit from this complementary approach. Researchers could examine the effectiveness of different methods of enhancing member engagement in psychotherapy groups. As one example, the effectiveness of bridging (i.e., leaders inviting members to react to the interactions occurring in the group [Ormont, 1992]) to enhance member engagement could be compared with the leader encouraging bridging coupled with the leader using TB to create a norm for the members to bridge without need for a leader prompt.

Leadership style and behaviors also receive little attention in the group therapy setting. Leader–client relationships map directly with group outcomes (Burlingame, Whitcomb, & Woodland, 2014). Thus, examining the impact of a leader style such as being democratic with members or a leader using transformational behaviors that empower members on the cohesiveness of the group appears worthwhile. This is a first step done with a view to improving leader–client relationship and ultimately therapeutic outcomes.

Implications for Group Psychotherapy Practice

Given the import of cohesion for therapeutic outcomes (Burlingame & Jensen, 2017), leaders within a therapeutic setting may wish to proactively engage in strategies that serve to enhance cohesion within the group. Those wanting to increase cohesion in a group therapy setting could use the established TB model presented earlier (Carron & Spink, 1993) because it based on established group dynamics principles and has reliable empirical support. Furthermore, this TB model was developed and used successfully to enhance cohesion and group maintenance in exercise settings. As noted previously, these exercise settings are likely to be more aligned with therapeutic settings given that both settings are approximations of minimal groups as outlined by Tajfel and Turner (1979).

CONCLUSION

As social beings, we look to others for information. However, it is ironic that those studying group processes often do not stray very far from their own setting to examine information generated in other group settings. This chapter presented research from physical activity settings examining cohesion, the Köhler effect, social norms, and leadership as well as possible crossover applications. Three main "hopes" arise from the information included. First, I hope it is clear to the reader that group researchers in the physical activity setting spend a considerable amount of time trying to understand the process (i.e., moderators and mediators), and others could learn from this emphasis. Encouragingly, adoption of this approach appears to be gaining traction in other areas, even where practical outcomes appear sacrosanct (e.g., Is technique A more effective than B?) such as group psychotherapy (Greene, 2017). Second, I hope exposure to sports and exercise settings highlights possibilities for future research in other types of settings, such as therapy groups. Third, I hope this information increases the fertilization of ideas across settings so our understanding and use of group processes improve collectively.

SUGGESTED READINGS

Eys, M. A., & Brawley, L. R. (2018). Reflections on cohesion research with sport and exercise groups. *Social and Personality Psychology Compass, 12*, 1–5. http://dx.doi.org/10.1111/spc3.12379

The examination of cohesion in the physical activity setting covers a lot of ground. The information in the Eys and Brawley article touches on additional topics not mentioned in this chapter. In addition, the authors include a section outlining how cohesion research in the physical activity setting converges as well diverges from literature in other areas. The article ends with suggestions for future research.

Eys, M. A., & Spink, K. S. (2018). Forecasts to the future: Group dynamics. In R. Schinke, K. R. McGannon, & B. Smith (Eds.), *Routledge international handbook of sport psychology* (pp. 572–580). London, England: Routledge.

The information in this chapter focuses on making future predictions for group dynamics in sports by answering four questions. What forces bind members to their team? Who will lead and who will follow? How do team members integrate their efforts? How do teams influence members? To provide some context as to where the research stands now in terms of answering these questions, studies included are categorized using Zanna and Fazio's (1982) three generations of research questions framework (i.e., relationships, moderating conditions, and mediators).

REFERENCES

Bandura, A. (1986). *Social foundations of thought and action: A social cognitive theory.* Englewood Cliffs, NJ: Prentice Hall.

Bass, B. M., & Riggio, R. E. (2006). *Transformational leadership* (2nd ed.). New York, NY: Psychology Press. http://dx.doi.org/10.4324/9781410617095

Benson, A. J., Eys, M. A., & Irving, P. G. (2016). Great expectations: How role expectations and role experiences relate to perceptions of group cohesion. *Journal of Sport & Exercise Psychology, 38*, 160–172. http://dx.doi.org/10.1123/jsep.2015-0228

Benson, A. J., Siska, P., Eys, M. R., Priklerova, S., & Slepicka, P. (2016). A prospective multilevel examination of the relationship between cohesion and team performance in elite youth sport. *Psychology of Sport and Exercise, 27*, 39–46. http://dx.doi.org/10.1016/j.psychsport.2016.07.009

Blanton, H., Stuart, A. E., & Van den Eijnden, R. J. J. M. (2001). An introduction to deviance-regulation theory: The effect of behavioral norms on message framing. *Personality and Social Psychology Bulletin, 27*, 848–858. http://dx.doi.org/10.1177/0146167201277007

Bosselut, G., Heuze, J., Castro, O., Fouquereau, E., & Chevalier, S. (2018). Using exploratory structure equation modeling to validate a new measure of cohesion in the university classroom setting: The University Group Environment Questionnaire (UGEQ). *International Journal of Educational Research, 89*, 1–9. http://dx.doi.org/10.1016/j.ijer.2018.03.003

Bruner, M., & Spink, K. S. (2011). Effects of team building on exercise adherence and group task satisfaction in a youth activity setting. *Group Dynamics, 15*, 161–172. http://dx.doi.org/10.1037/a0021257

Burger, J. M., & Shelton, M. (2011). Changing everyday health behaviors through descriptive norm manipulations. *Social Influence, 6*, 69–77. http://dx.doi.org/10.1080/15534510.2010.542305

Burke, S. M., Carron, A. V., Eys, M. A., Ntoumanis, N., & Estabrooks, P. A. (2006). Group versus individual approach? A meta-analysis of the effectiveness of interventions to promote physical activity. *Sport and Exercise Psychology Review, 2*, 19–35.

Burkett, B. M., Blom, G. A., Razon, S., & Johnson, J. E. (2014). Formal and informal athlete leaders: The relationship between athlete leadership behaviors and cohesion. *Journal of Sport Behavior, 3*, 2–29.

Burlingame, G. M., & Jensen, J. L. (2017). Small group process and outcome research highlights: A 25-year perspective. *International Journal of Group Psychotherapy, 67* (Suppl. 1), S194–S218.

Burlingame, G. M., Whitcomb, K., & Woodland, S. (2014). Process and outcome in group counseling and psychotherapy: A perspective. In J. L. DeLucia-Waack,

D. A. Gerrity, C. R. Kalodner, & M. T. Riva (Eds.), *Handbook of group counseling & psychotherapy* (2nd ed., pp. 55–68). Thousand Oaks, CA: Sage. http://dx.doi.org/10.4135/9781544308555.n5

Callow, N., Smith, M. J., Hardy, L., Arthur, C. A., & Hardy, J. (2009). Measurement of transformational leadership and its relationship with team cohesion and performance. *Journal of Applied Sport Psychology, 21,* 395–412. http://dx.doi.org/10.1080/10413200903204754

Carron, A. V., Brawley, L. R., & Widmeyer, W. N. (1998). The measurement of cohesiveness in sport groups. In J. L. Duda (Ed.), *Advancements in sport and exercise psychology measurement* (pp. 213–226). Morgantown, WV: Fitness Information Technology.

Carron, A. V., & Eys, M. A. (2012). *Group dynamics in sport* (4th ed.). Morgantown, WV: Fitness Information Technology.

Carron, A. V., Prapavessis, H., & Grove, J. R. (1994). Group effects and self-handicapping. *Journal of Sport & Exercise Psychology, 16,* 246–257. http://dx.doi.org/10.1123/jsep.16.3.246

Carron, A. V., & Spink, K. S. (1992). Internal consistency of the Group Environment Questionnaire modified for an exercise setting. *Perceptual and Motor Skills, 74,* 304–306. http://dx.doi.org/10.2466/pms.1992.74.1.304

Carron, A. V., & Spink, K. S. (1993). Team building in an exercise setting. *Sport Psychologist, 7,* 8–18. http://dx.doi.org/10.1123/tsp.7.1.8

Carron, A. V., Widmeyer, W. N., & Brawley, L. R. (1985). The development of an instrument to assess cohesion in sport teams: The Group Environment Questionnaire. *Journal of Sport Psychology, 7,* 244–266. http://dx.doi.org/10.1123/jsp.7.3.244

Carron, A. V., Widmeyer, W. N., & Brawley, L. R. (1988). Group cohesion and individual adherence to physical activity. *Journal of Sport & Exercise Psychology, 10,* 127–138. http://dx.doi.org/10.1123/jsep.10.2.127

Casey-Campbell, M., & Martens, M. L. (2009). Sticking it all together: A critical assessment of the group cohesion–performance literature. *International Journal of Management Reviews, 11,* 223–246. http://dx.doi.org/10.1111/j.1468-2370.2008.00239.x

Cialdini, R. B. (2009). *Influence: The psychology of persuasion.* New York, NY: HarperCollins.

Cialdini, R. B., Reno, R. R., & Kallgren, C. A. (1990). A focus theory of normative conduct: Recycling the concept of norms to reduce littering in public places. *Journal of Personality and Social Psychology, 58,* 1015–1026. http://dx.doi.org/10.1037/0022-3514.58.6.1015

Cialdini, R. B., & Trost, M. R. (1998). Social influence: Social norms, conformity, and compliance. In D. T. Gilbert, S. T. Fiske, & G. Lindzey (Eds.), *The handbook of social psychology* (4th ed., pp. 151–192). New York, NY: McGraw-Hill.

Collins, J., & Durand-Bush, N. (2015). Frameworks of team processes in sport: A critical review with implications for practitioners. *International Journal of Human Movement and Sports Sciences, 3,* 46–59. http://dx.doi.org/10.13189/saj.2015.030304

Cronin, L. D., Arthur, C. A., Hardy, J., & Callow, N. (2015). Transformational leadership and task cohesion in sport: The mediating role of inside sacrifice. *Journal of Sport & Exercise Psychology, 37,* 23–36. http://dx.doi.org/10.1123/jsep.2014-0116

Crozier, A. J., Martin, L. J., & Spink, K. S. (in press). Groupness: Providing a roadmap for an emerging construct in physical activity settings. *Kinesiology Review.*

Crozier, A. J., & Spink, K. S. (2017a). Effect of manipulating descriptive norms and positive outcome expectations on physical activity of university students during exams. *Health Communication, 32,* 784–790. http://dx.doi.org/10.1080/10410236.2016.1172295

Crozier, A. J., & Spink, K. S. (2017b). Examining the effects of normative messages on perceived effort in sport. *Sport Psychologist, 31,* 56–64. http://dx.doi.org/10.1123/tsp.2015-0097

Crozier, A. J., & Spink, K. S. (2018). Coach and peer normative perceptions in relation to youth athlete effort. *International Journal of Sport and Exercise Psychology, 18,* 24–32. http://dx.doi.org/10.1080/1612197X.2018.1478870

Crum, A. J., Leibowitz, K. A., & Verghese, A. (2017). Making mindset matter. *BMJ*, *356*, j674. http://dx.doi.org/10.1136/bmj.j674 (Correction published 2017, *BMJ*, *359*, p. j5308)

Cruwys, T., Haslam, S. A., Fox, N. E., & McMahon, H. (2015). "That's not what we do": Evidence that normative change is a mechanism of action in group interventions. *Behaviour Research and Therapy, 65*, 11–17. http://dx.doi.org/10.1016/j.brat.2014.12.003

Cruwys, T., Leverington, C. T., & Sheldon, A. M. (2016). An experimental investigation of the consequences and social functions of fat talk in friendship groups. *International Journal of Eating Disorders, 49*, 84–91. http://dx.doi.org/10.1002/eat.22446

Emich, K. (2014). A social cognitive investigation of intragroup motivation: Transpersonal efficacy, effort allocation, and helping. *Group Dynamics, 18*, 203–221. http://dx.doi.org/10.1037/gdn0000007

Eys, M., Loughead, T., Bray, S. R., & Carron, A. V. (2009). Development of a cohesion questionnaire for youth: The Youth Sport Environment Questionnaire. *Journal of Sport & Exercise Psychology, 31*, 390–408. http://dx.doi.org/10.1123/jsep.31.3.390

Eys, M. A., & Spink, K. S. (2018). Forecasts to the future: Group dynamics. In R. Schinke, K. R. McGannon, & B. Smith (Eds.), *Routledge international handbook of sport psychology* (pp. 572–580). London, England: Routledge.

Filho, E., Dobersek, U., Gershgoren, L., Becker, B., & Tenenbaum, G. (2014). The cohesion-performance relationship in sport: A 10-year retrospective meta-analysis. *Sport Sciences for Health, 10*, 165–177. http://dx.doi.org/10.1007/s11332-014-0188-7

Forrest, C. K., & Bruner, M. W. (2017). Evaluating social media as a platform for delivering a team-building exercise intervention: A pilot study. *International Journal of Sport and Exercise Psychology, 15*, 190–206. http://dx.doi.org/10.1080/1612197X.2015.1069879

Gallagher, M. E., Tasca, G. A., Ritchie, K. I., Balfour, L., & Bissada, H. (2014). Attachment anxiety moderates the relationship between growth in group cohesion and treatment outcomes in group psychodynamic interpersonal psychotherapy for women with binge eating disorder. *Group Dynamics: Theory, Research, and Practice, 18*, 38–52. http://dx.doi.org/10.1037/a0034760

Graupensperger, S. A., Benson, A. J., & Evans, M. B. (2018). Everyone else is doing it: The association between social identity and susceptibility to peer influence in NCAA athletes. *Journal of Sport & Exercise Psychology, 40*, 117–127. http://dx.doi.org/10.1123/jsep.2017-0339

Greene, L. R. (2017). Group psychotherapy research studies that therapists might actually read: My top 10 list. *International Journal of Group Psychotherapy, 67*, 1–26. http://dx.doi.org/10.1080/00207284.2016.1202678

Harden, S. M., Burke, S. M., Haile, A. M., & Estabrooks, P. A. (2015). Generalizing the findings from group dynamics-based physical activity research to practice settings: What do we know? *Evaluation & the Health Professions, 38*, 3–14. http://dx.doi.org/10.1177/0163278713488117

Hertel, G., Nohe, C., Wessolowski, K., Meltz, O., Pape, J. C., Fink, J., & Hüffmeier, J. (2018). Effort gains in occupational teams—The effects of social competition and social indispensability. *Frontiers in Psychology, 9*, 769. http://dx.doi.org/10.3389/fpsyg.2018.00769

Hogg, M. A., & Terry, D. J. (2000). Social identity and self-categorization processes in organizational contexts. *Academy of Management Review, 25*, 121–140. http://dx.doi.org/10.5465/amr.2000.2791606

Høigaard, R., Säfvenbom, R., & Tønnessen, F. E. (2006). The relationship between group cohesion, group norms, and perceived social loafing in soccer teams. *Small Group Research, 37*, 217–232. http://dx.doi.org/10.1177/1046496406287311

Hüffmeier, J., Filusch, M., Mazei, J., Hertel, G., Mojzisch, A., & Krumm, S. (2017). On the boundary conditions of effort losses and effort gains in action teams. *Journal of Applied Psychology, 102,* 1673–1685. http://dx.doi.org/10.1037/apl0000245

Irwin, B. C., & Feltz, D. L. (2018). Motivation gains in sport and exercise groups. In R. Schinke, K. R. McGannon, & B. Smith (Eds.), *Routledge international handbook of sport psychology* (pp. 494–504). London, England: Routledge.

Jowett, S., & Chaundy, V. (2004). An investigation into the impact of coach leadership and coach–athlete relationships on group cohesion. *Group Dynamics, 8,* 302–311. http://dx.doi.org/10.1037/1089-2699.8.4.302

Karau, S. J., & Williams, K. D. (1993). Social loafing: A meta-analytic review and theoretical integration. *Journal of Personality and Social Psychology, 65,* 681–706. http://dx.doi.org/10.1037/0022-3514.65.4.681

Kerr, N. L. (2017). The most neglected moderator in group research. *Group Processes & Intergroup Relations, 20,* 681–692. http://dx.doi.org/10.1177/1368430217712050

Kerr, N. L., & Bruun, S. E. (1983). Dispensability of member effort and group motivation losses: Free-rider effects. *Journal of Personality and Social Psychology, 44,* 78–94. http://dx.doi.org/10.1037/0022-3514.44.1.78

Kerr, N. L., & Hertel, G. (2011). The Köhler group motivation gain: How to motivate the "weak links" in a group. *Social and Personality Psychology Compass, 5,* 43–55. http://dx.doi.org/10.1111/j.1751-9004.2010.00333.x

Kim, H.-D., & Cruz, A. B. (2016). The influence of coaches' leadership styles on athletes' satisfaction and team cohesion: A meta-analytic approach. *International Journal of Sports Science & Coaching, 11,* 900–909. http://dx.doi.org/10.1177%2F1747954116676117

King, M. F., & Bruner, G. C. (2000). Social desirability bias: A neglected aspect of validity testing. *Psychology & Marketing, 17,* 79–103. http://dx.doi.org/10.1002/(SICI)1520-6793(200002)17:2<79::AID-MAR2>3.0.CO;2-0

Köhler, O. (1926). Kraftleistungen bei Einzel- und Gruppenarbeit [Physical performance in individual and group work]. *Industrielle Psychotechnik, 3,* 274–282.

Lott, A. J., & Lott, B. E. (1965). Group cohesiveness as interpersonal attraction: A review of relationships with antecedent and consequent variables. *Psychological Bulletin, 64,* 259–309. http://dx.doi.org/10.1037/h0022386

Loughead, T. M., Hardy, J., & Eys, M. A. (2006). The nature of athlete leadership. *Journal of Sport Behavior, 29,* 142–158.

Martin, L. J., Carron, A. V., & Burke, S. M. (2008). Team building interventions in sport: A meta-analysis. *Sport and Exercise Psychology Review, 5,* 3–18.

Max, E. J., Feltz, D. L., Kerr, N. L., & Wittenbaum, G. M. (2018). Is silence really golden? Effect of encouragement from a partner or trainer on active video game play. *International Journal of Sport and Exercise Psychology, 16,* 261–275. http://dx.doi.org/10.1080/1612197X.2016.1199580

Mudrack, P. E. (1989). Defining group cohesiveness. A legacy of confusion? *Small Group Behavior, 20,* 37–49. http://dx.doi.org/10.1177/104649648902000103

Nolan, J. M., Schultz, P. W., Cialdini, R. B., Goldstein, N. J., & Griskevicius, V. (2008). Normative social influence is underdetected. *Personality and Social Psychology Bulletin, 34,* 913–923. http://dx.doi.org/10.1177/0146167208316691

Northouse, P. G. (2010). *Leadership: Theory and practice* (5th ed.). Thousand Oaks, CA: Sage.

Ormont, L. (1992). *The group therapy experience.* New York, NY: Aronson.

Osborn, K., Irwin, B., Skogsberg, N., & Feltz, D. (2012). The Köhler effect: Motivation gains and losses in real sports groups. *Sport, Exercise, and Performance Psychology, 1,* 242–253. http://dx.doi.org/10.1037/a0026887

Pain, M. A., & Harwood, C. (2007). The performance environment of the England youth soccer teams. *Journal of Sports Sciences, 25,* 1307–1324. http://dx.doi.org/10.1080/02640410601059622

Paquin, J. D., Kivlighan, D. M., Jr., & Drogosz, L. M. (2013). Person–group fit, group climate, and outcomes in a sample of incarcerated women participating in trauma recovery groups. *Group Dynamics: Theory, Research, and Practice, 17*, 95–109. http://dx.doi.org/10.1037/a0032702

Perkins, H. W., & Berkowitz, A. D. (1986). Perceiving the community norms of alcohol use among students: Some research implications for campus alcohol education programming. *International Journal of the Addictions, 21*, 961–976. http://dx.doi.org/10.3109/10826088609077249

Prapavessis, H., Carron, A. V., & Spink, K. S. (1996). Team building in sport. *International Journal of Sport Psychology, 27*, 269–285.

Priebe, C. S., & Spink, K. S. (2011). When in Rome: Descriptive norms and physical activity. *Psychology of Sport and Exercise, 12*, 93–98. http://dx.doi.org/10.1016/j.psychsport.2010.09.001

Priebe, C. S., & Spink, L. S. (2014). Blood, sweat, and the influence of others: The effect of descriptive norms on muscular endurance and task self-efficacy. *Psychology of Sport and Exercise, 15*, 491–497. http://dx.doi.org/10.1016/j.psychsport.2014.04.012

Priebe, C. S., & Spink, K. S. (2015). Less sitting and more moving in the office: Using descriptive norm messages to decrease sedentary behavior and increase light physical activity at work. *Psychology of Sport and Exercise, 19*, 76–84. http://dx.doi.org/10.1016/j.psychsport.2015.02.008

Rhodes, R. E., Janssen, I., Bredin, S. S. D., Warburton, D. E. R., & Bauman, A. (2017). Physical activity: Health impact, prevalence, correlates and interventions. *Psychology & Health, 32*, 942–975. http://dx.doi.org/10.1080/08870446.2017.1325486

Salas, E., Grossman, R., Hughes, A. M., & Coultas, C. W. (2015). Measuring team cohesion: Observations from the science. *Human Factors, 57*, 365–374. http://dx.doi.org/10.1177/0018720815578267

Samendinger, S., Forlenza, S. T., Winn, B., Max, E. J., Kerr, N. L., Pfeiffer, K. A., & Feltz, D. L. (2017). Introductory dialogue and the Köhler effect in software-generated workout partners. *Psychology of Sport and Exercise, 32*, 131–137. http://dx.doi.org/10.1016/j.psychsport.2017.07.001

Schultz, P. W. (1999). Changing behavior with normative feedback interventions: A field experiment on curbside recycling. *Basic and Applied Social Psychology, 21*, 25–36. http://dx.doi.org/10.1207/s15324834basp2101_3

Schutz, R. W., Eom, H. J., Smoll, F. L., & Smith, R. E. (1994). Examination of the factorial validity of the Group Environment Questionnaire. *Research Quarterly for Exercise and Sport, 65*, 226–236. http://dx.doi.org/10.1080/02701367.1994.10607623

Shaw, M. E. (1981). *Group dynamics: The psychology of small group behavior* (3rd ed.). New York, NY: McGraw-Hill.

Shechtman, Z., & Kiezel, A. (2016). Why do people prefer individual therapy over group therapy? *International Journal of Group Psychotherapy, 66*, 571–591. http://dx.doi.org/10.1080/00207284.2016.1180042

Sparkman, G., & Walton, G. M. (2017). Dynamic norms promote sustainable behavior, even if it is counternormative. *Psychological Science, 28*, 1663–1674. http://dx.doi.org/10.1177/0956797617719950

Spink, K. S. (2014). Team building. In R. C. Eklund & G. Tenenbaum (Eds.), *Encyclopedia of sport and exercise psychology* (Vol. 19, pp. 741–744). Thousand Oaks, CA: Sage.

Spink, K. S., & Carron, A. V. (1993). The effects of team building on the adherence patterns of female exercise participants. *Journal of Sport & Exercise Psychology, 15*, 39–49. http://dx.doi.org/10.1123/jsep.15.1.39

Spink, K. S., & Carron, A. V. (1994). Group cohesion effects in exercise classes. *Small Group Research, 25*, 26–42. http://dx.doi.org/10.1177/1046496494251003

Spink, K. S., Crozier, A. J., & Robinson, B. (2013). Examining the relationship between descriptive norms and perceived effort in adolescent athletes: Effects of different reference groups. *Psychology of Sport and Exercise, 14*, 813–818. http://dx.doi.org/10.1016/j.psychsport.2013.06.006

Spink, K. S., & Fesser, K. (2018). Correcting player mistakes: Effects of coach and player social influence on increasing player intention to intervene with teammates. *International Sport Coaching Journal, 5*, 116–123. http://dx.doi.org/10.1123/iscj.2017-0054

Spink, K. S., McLaren, C. M., & Ulvick, J. D. (2018a). Cues to informing perceived task cohesion in the sport setting: The case for teammate effort. *International Journal of Sport Psychology, 49*, 165–177.

Spink, K. S., McLaren, C. M., & Ulvick, J. D. (2018b). Groupness, cohesion, and intention to return to sport: A study of intact youth teams. *International Journal of Sports Science & Coaching, 13*, 545–551. http://dx.doi.org/10.1177/1747954117732725

Spink, K. S., Ulvick, J. D., Crozier, A. J., & Wilson, K. S. (2014). Group cohesion and adherence in unstructured exercise groups. *Psychology of Sport and Exercise, 15*, 293–298. http://dx.doi.org/10.1016/j.psychsport.2013.11.008

Spink, K. S., Ulvick, J. D., McLaren, C. D., Crozier, A. J., & Fesser, K. (2015). Effects of groupness and cohesion on intention to return in sport. *Sport, Exercise, and Performance Psychology, 4*, 293–302.

Spink, K. S., Wilson, K., & Odnokon, P. (2010). Examining the relationship between cohesion and return to team in elite athletes. *Psychology of Sport and Exercise, 11*, 6–11. http://dx.doi.org/10.1016/j.psychsport.2009.06.002

Steiner, I. D. (1972). *Group process and productivity*. New York, NY: Academic Press.

Tajfel, H., & Turner, J. (1979). An integrative theory of intergroup conflict. In W. G. Austin & S. Worchel (Eds.), *The social psychology of intergroup relations* (pp. 33–47). Belmont, CA: Wadsworth.

Triplett, N. (1898). The dynamogenic factors in pacemaking and competition. *American Journal of Psychology, 9*, 507–533. http://dx.doi.org/10.2307/1412188

Turnnidge, J., & Côté, J. (2018). Applying transformational leadership theory to coaching research in youth sport: A systematic literature review. *International Journal of Sport and Exercise Psychology, 16*, 327–342. http://dx.doi.org/10.1080/1612197X.2016.1189948

von Treuer, K., McLeod, J., Fuller-Tyszkiewicz, M., & Scott, G. (2018). Determining the components of cohesion using the repertory grid technique. *Group Dynamics: Theory, Research, and Practice, 22*, 108–128. http://dx.doi.org/10.1037/gdn0000085

Wally, C. M., & Cameron, L. D. (2017). A randomized-controlled trial of social norm interventions to increase physical activity. *Annals of Behavioral Medicine, 51*, 642–651. http://dx.doi.org/10.1007/s12160-017-9887-z

Watson, J. D., Martin Ginis, K. A., & Spink, K. S. (2004). Team building in an exercise class for the elderly. *Activities, Adaptation & Aging, 28*, 35–47. http://dx.doi.org/10.1300/J016v28n03_03

Weber, B., & Hertel, G. (2007). Motivation gains of inferior group members: A meta-analytical review. *Journal of Personality and Social Psychology, 93*, 973–993. http://dx.doi.org/10.1037/0022-3514.93.6.973

Whitton, S., & Fletcher, R. (2014). The Group Environment Questionnaire: A multilevel confirmatory factor analysis. *Small Group Research, 45*, 68–88. http://dx.doi.org/10.1177/1046496413511121

Wolf, S. A., Eys, M. A., Sadler, P., & Kleinert, J. (2015). Appraisal in a team context: Perceptions of cohesion predict competition importance and prospects for coping. *Journal of Sport & Exercise Psychology, 37*, 489–499. http://dx.doi.org/10.1123/jsep.2014-0276

Yalom, I. D., & Leszcz, M. (2005). *The theory and practice of group psychotherapy* (5th ed.). New York, NY: Basic Books.

Zanna, M. P., & Fazio, R. H. (1982). The attitude-behavior relation: Moving toward a third generation of research. In M. P. Zanna, E. T. Higgins, & C. P. Herman (Eds.), *Consistency in social behavior: The Ontario symposium* (Vol. 2, pp. 283–301). Hillsdale, NJ: Erlbaum.

II

GROUP PSYCHOTHERAPY RESEARCH: IMPLICATIONS FOR GROUP PSYCHOLOGY

8

Attachment and Group Psychotherapy

Applications to Work Groups and Teams

Giorgio A. Tasca and Hilary Maxwell

Attachment theory has emerged over the past 50 years as one of the most important theories of human behavior touching on diverse functions like interpersonal relations and affect regulation. Attachment theory has its roots in infant development (Ainsworth, 1969; Bowlby, 1969, 1973, 1980) and was later adapted to the study of adult functioning (Main, 2000). Two lines of attachment theory have evolved over the years, one in the area of human development and clinical phenomena (e.g., Main, 2000), and the other in social psychology (e.g., Mikulincer & Shaver, 2007). The first line has addressed the impact of attachment insecurity on psychopathology and problems in living (e.g., Fonagy, 2001), whereas the clinical phenomena line has focused on diverse areas like romantic attachment, social interactions, and styles of coping (Mikulincer & Shaver, 2007; Mikulincer, Shaver, & Pereg, 2003). As a result, differences have emerged in terms of language to define the concepts and also in terms of measurement methods. One main issue that has arisen from this dual line of evolution of this theory is whether to describe—as the developmental psychologists are prone to do—attachment as represented by a set of distinct categories or whether to consider attachment as represented by dimensional constructs, as the social psychologists prefer.

In this chapter, we review attachment theory and its implications for group psychology, and group psychotherapy research and practice. In particular, we examine the research on attachment and group psychotherapy, and we evaluate if this research can inform knowledge and practice in organizations,

http://dx.doi.org/10.1037/0000201-009
The Psychology of Groups: The Intersection of Social Psychology and Psychotherapy Research,
C. D. Parks and G. A. Tasca (Editors)

teams, and other group psychology contexts. At times in this chapter, we may refer to types or categories, but we prefer to think of attachment dimensionally because this approach has stronger psychometric support (Fraley, Waller, & Brennan, 2000).

OVERVIEW OF ATTACHMENT THEORY

Human infants engage in attachment behaviors (e.g., reaching, crawling, crying, smiling, gazing) as a means of gaining proximity to adult caregivers, which provides evolutionary advantages to those infants who successfully attract caregiving. That is, infant attachment behaviors result in caregiver proximity, which confers a greater probability of the child's surviving and prospering. These infant attachment behaviors and caregiver responses create numerous repeated interactions between children and caregivers on a moment-to-moment and day-to-day basis. These interactions and the resulting expectations of caregiver responses are encoded in the implicit memory system and lead to the development of internal working models of the self and of others (Ainsworth, 1969; Bowlby, 1969, 1973, 1980). Internal working models provide implicit rules and expectations about how one's self and others will behave and interact. If the infant's attachment figure/caregiver responds to signals for proximity mostly in reliable and predictable ways that create a sense of security, then the infant will develop an internal working model of the self as acceptable and worthwhile and of others as predictable and safe (Bowlby, 1973, 1980; Pietromonaco & Barrett, 2000). Such an internal working model is indicative of a *secure attachment* system. If the attachment figure is mostly inconsistent or unresponsive when the infant signals proximity and contact, then the infant will develop a view of self as unacceptable and unworthy, and will view others as unpredictable and unsafe (Bowlby, 1973, 1980). In this case, the infant will engage in secondary attachment strategies as a way to try to most effectively interact with an unpredictable or unresponsive attachment figure. These might include hyperactivating or deactivating their attachment system by overly maintaining contact or overly avoiding contact, respectively (Bowlby, 1973, 1980; Pietromonaco & Barrett, 2000). As such, the infant will likely develop an organized but *insecure attachment* system characterized by anxious (preoccupied) or avoidant (dismissing) attachment internal working models.

Attachment style or attachment states of mind in adulthood are a reflection of the individual's most accessible internal working models (Mikulincer & Shaver, 2007). Attachment behaviors and internal working models are particularly activated during times of stress, threat, or uncertainty. That is, attachment behaviors are the individual's best possible solution at the time to gaining proximity to an attachment figure, particularly when the individual feels threatened in some way. One can consider attachment anxiety and attachment avoidance as two key dimensions of the attachment system.

Individuals with a secure attachment state of mind are low on both attach-ment anxiety and avoidance dimensions. Those with greater attachment security provide succinct, clear, and complete (i.e., coherent) responses when describing childhood attachment memories (Main, Goldwyn, & Hesse, 2002). They are able to self-soothe and feel worthy, which allows them more easily to empathize and care for others during times of distress. Individuals with greater attachment security maintain a positive view of the self and positive expectations about others' availability in times of distress. They are able to express and share emotions, and, importantly, they use adaptive ways of regulating their emotions (Mikulincer & Shaver, 2007; Mikulincer et al., 2003). Adaptive emotion regulation and coping strategies allow these indi-viduals to engage in supportive, healthy interpersonal interactions.

Individuals with a preoccupied or *anxious attachment* state of mind tend to be high on the attachment anxiety dimension and low on the attach-ment avoidance dimension. These individuals generally struggle to provide succinct, relevant, or clear responses when discussing attachment memories (Main et al., 2002). They tend to exaggerate their perception of threats and also their inability to cope to gain proximity to attachment figures (e.g., parents, romantic partners). They may blame themselves when others are not respon-sive to their needs and are highly preoccupied with the possibility of losing a relationship or with the quality of a relationship. These hyperactivating strat-egies are driven by a negative view of self and a positive view of others. They interfere with these individuals' ability to understand the mental states and needs of others, thereby impeding their ability to genuinely express concern and caring for others. They also hyperactivate their emotional system so that they tend to exaggerate negative feelings and easily recall past hurts and losses, which results in less adaptive coping with stressful situations.

Individuals with a dismissing or *avoidant attachment* state of mind generally are high on the attachment avoidance dimension and low on the attachment anxiety dimension. These individuals provide succinct, relevant, and clear descriptions of attachment memories, but their descriptions are impover-ished and characterized by few or no examples. They may idealize or be derogatory of attachment figures even in the absence of anecdotal evidence (Main et al., 2002). These individuals tend to use deactivating strategies (e.g., deny their needs, avoid emotional states, avoid expression emotions) to maintain emotional distance from attachment figures (Mikulincer & Shaver, 2007). Despite their low-key appearance, they may experience heightened physiological responses in stressful contexts (Dozier & Kobak, 1992). They maintain a positive view of self and a negative view of others. Deactivating strategies interfere with the ability to appreciate mental states in others, which reduces these individuals' ability to empathize and understand others' motives, and to use relationships as a means of coping and soothing.

Those with a disorganized or *fearful attachment* state of mind likely experi-enced trauma, abuse, or severe neglect in a way that was not optimally resolved. They tend to be high on both attachment anxiety and avoidance dimensions. Such individuals might experience confusion when discussing the trauma, disruption in the flow of the narrative (e.g., losing track of their narrative during a response, dissociating), and disorientation with respect to time (Main et al., 2002). Their coping style tends to be inconsistent by excessively approaching and avoiding relationships and emotions, which in turn causes confusion and disorientation when discussing the trauma.

Attachment classifications are remarkably stable across the life span such that 70% of individuals tend to maintain their classification of securely or insecurely attached from childhood to young adulthood (Pinquart, Feußner, & Ahnert, 2013; Waters, Weinfield, & Hamilton, 2000). Attachment insecurity is associated with higher levels of psychopathology and functional impairment in adults. In particular, individuals with disorganized or high fearful attachment display high levels of psychopathology including posttraumatic stress disorder and borderline personality disorder (Bakermans-Kranenburg & van IJzendoorn, 2009).

Some evidence suggests significant cross-cultural consistency of attachment patterns, although researchers believe that contexts affect the rates of attachment security in a society (van IJzendoorn & Sagi-Schwartz, 2008). It is quite possible that collectivist versus individualist cultures may provide different contexts for the development of attachment security or insecurity. For example, avoidant attachment may be less common in Japan, a more collectivist cultural context, than in Europe (van IJzendoorn & Sagi-Schwartz, 2008). Attachment theory views an individual's sense of felt security as developing from an innate drive in infants to connect to others. However, some have argued that concepts like attachment security privilege autonomous functioning, which may be particularly salient in Western cultures (Morelli & Henry, 2013). This argument has implications for the role of attachment in group contexts in which outcomes might be achieved by an individualistic versus a cooperative approach to a performing task.

REFLECTIVE FUNCTIONING

A newer and important development in the attachment literature is assessment and research on reflective functioning, also known as mentalizing. *Reflective functioning* is "the mental process by which an individual implicitly and explicitly interprets the actions of himself and others as meaningful on the basis of intentional mental states such as personal desires, needs, feelings, beliefs, and reasons" (Bateman & Fonagy, 2004, p. 21). Reflective functioning develops in a child from the capacity of attachment figures to have a mental representation of the child as having feelings, intentions, and desires, and from the attachment figure's capacity to respond to internal states of the child appropriately. Such a capacity is indicative of the attachment figure's attachment security. The child's experience of his or her attachment figure as responsive to moment-to-moment changes in the child's experiences are the foundation for the child to develop mentalizing capacities of his or her own (Slade, 2005).

Reflective functioning is an empirically grounded framework for assessing a person's capacity to mentalize (i.e., "the capacity to perceive and understand oneself and others in terms of mental states"; Fonagy, Target, Steele, & Steele, 1998, p. 7). A person demonstrates reflective functioning when he or she has an awareness of the nature of mental states (e.g., that others' mental states are not entirely knowable), makes an effort to understand mental states underlying behavior (e.g., taking into account one's own mental state in interpreting others' behavior), recognizes the developmental aspects of mental states (e.g., taking an intergenerational perspective or making links across generations), or identifies mental states in relation to the person with whom they are speaking (e.g., emotionally attuned with the interviewer; Fonagy et al., 1998), or a combination of these. Deficits in reflective functioning might occur during states of heightened and dampened arousal. Deficits are indicated by nonmentalizing states that include *teleological mode,* in which expectations of others are made on purely observable terms in which only actions matter; *pretend mode,* in which one disconnects internal from external reality by intellectualization or in the extreme case, dissociation; and *psychic equivalence,* in which mental reality is considered equal to external reality (e.g., "I think, therefore it is").

Reflective functioning or mentalizing enhances interpersonal communication and the ability to understanding one's own and others' actions (Fonagy et al., 1998). Moreover, greater reflective functioning is related to having a secure attachment state of mind and plays a protective role in fostering adaptive affect regulation and secure interpersonal environments (Fonagy et al., 1998; Mikulincer & Shaver, 2007). Perhaps because reflective functioning allows individuals to perceive, label, and reflect about emotions (Fonagy & Target, 2002), it is associated with important psychological abilities related to attachment security, including distress tolerance and better emotion regulation (Morel & Papouchis, 2015; Schultheis, Mayes, & Rutherford, 2019). Reflective functioning may protect the individual from negative views of the self that could result from traumatic experiences (e.g., the ability to separate one's view of self from one's negative view of the perpetrator of trauma; Fonagy et al., 1998). With regard to relationships, the ability to mentalize allows one to appreciate another's perspective, which forms the basis for empathy.

ATTACHMENT THEORY AND GROUP THERAPY RESEARCH

There is a growing and substantial research on attachment theory and group therapy. Marmarosh, Markin, and Spiegel (2013) published a clinically oriented textbook on group therapy informed by attachment theory and research, and Marmarosh and Wallace (2016) published a comprehensive review of the research literature of attachment and psychotherapy, including groups. In this chapter, we focus on research that we believe has direct implications for teams and organizations; therefore, our focus is on reflective functioning or mentalizing as a potentially new line of inquiry.

In a chapter on individual psychotherapy, Bowlby (1988) described how attachment theory might inform the treatment context. In particular, he wrote that psychotherapy might help individuals to reevaluate their internal working models of self and others. In attachment-informed therapy, the therapist provides a secure base from which patients may explore new ways of being, encourages patients to examine relationship patterns, helps patients to examine their relationship with the therapist in the context of attachment internal working models, encourages patients to see current working models of self and relationships as based on past attachment relationships, and enables patients to recognize that their internal working models may be inappropriate in the current contexts. Although Bowlby (1988) wrote primarily about individual therapy, one could easily apply these principles to the therapy group. Indeed, one could argue, as did Yalom and Leszcz (2005), that the therapy group represents a recapitulation of the family of origin group, and, as such, attachment working models may be more easily primed in group therapy. This argument represents both a challenge and an opportunity to the therapist and patient. That is, the attachment system may be more easily triggered by a group context, initially resulting in greater attachment insecurity behaviors. However, as the group matures, patients have the opportunity to recognize and change these maladaptive interpersonal patterns within the group context. In particular, if the therapy group becomes a secure base for the individual, then the patient may be able to explore new ways of viewing the self and others within that context, thus providing a corrective emotional experience for the impact of problematic early family interactions.

Attachment to the Therapy Group

Attachment to groups is a relatively new construct within attachment theory that is analogous to attachment to individuals. Group attachments are mental representations of groups that are based on early experiences and influence expectations about new groups within which one might find oneself (Markin & Marmarosh, 2010). Smith, Murphy, and Coats (1999) proposed that individuals can be anxious, avoidant, and secure toward groups as well as toward individuals. They suggested that general group attachment orientations shape expectations about new groups. Individuals with secure group attachment patterns may believe they are worthy as group members, view groups as valuable, and expect groups to accept them. Individuals higher in group attachment anxiety may view themselves as unworthy group members and be concerned about being accepted by the group. Individuals higher in group attachment avoidance may experience closeness to the group as overwhelming and may avoid dependence on the group.

In a rare study to assess this phenomenon in therapy groups, Keating et al. (2014) used a measure developed by Smith et al. (1999) to assess change in attachment to a therapy group and its association with change in individual attachment insecurity. Eighty-seven women with binge-eating disorder (BED) received group psychodynamic interpersonal psychotherapy (Tasca, Mikail, &

Hewitt, 2005) and completed a measure of attachment to the therapy group throughout treatment. Group attachment insecurity decreased significantly during therapy. Reductions in group attachment avoidance predicted decreases in individual attachment insecurity at 1-year posttreatment. The results suggested that attachment to the therapy group may change during a group therapy that focuses on group process and that this change may generalize to improved individual attachment 1 year later. This finding lends support to the notion that the group may develop into a secure base over time for individuals and that this process may have an enduring impact on attachment representations in general.

Individual Attachment, Group Processes, and Outcomes

The research literature suggests that higher attachment insecurity at pretreatment is associated with poorer outcomes in psychotherapy in terms of symptom reduction (Levy, Ellison, Scott, & Bernecker, 2011). The research also indicates that attachment insecurity can improve with group treatment. Several studies showed that group therapy can result in positive changes in attachment insecurity from pre- to posttreatment and follow-ups (Maxwell, Compare, et al., 2018; Maxwell, Tasca, et al., 2018; Maxwell, Tasca, Ritchie, Balfour, & Bissada, 2014). In one study, Maxwell et al. (2014) found that long-term stability of improved attachment security following group therapy was associated with significant decreases in other outcomes. This study suggested an adaptive spiral in which greater reduction in attachment avoidance was increasingly associated with improvements in interpersonal problems even well after group treatment was complete.

Key hypotheses one can draw from attachment theory is that attachment style or dimensions will have an impact on how one relates to fellow group members, therapists, and the group as a whole. That is, one might expect individuals high in attachment anxiety to be preoccupied with how the group functions and whether the group is able to maintain increasing proximity. Those with higher attachment avoidance may dismiss the importance of the group or potentially feel intruded upon by the group. Indeed, several studies of group therapy have borne out these predictions. Tasca, Balfour, Ritchie, and Bissada (2006) found that women with BED and greater attachment anxiety had better outcomes if they experienced an increasing engaged group climate. Kirchmann et al. (2009) also found that group climate mediated the association between attachment anxiety and outcomes for psychiatric inpatients. Similarly, those with BED and greater attachment anxiety benefited most in terms of reduced binge eating from a group treatment that focused on interpersonal relationships and affect regulation (Tasca, Ritchie, et al., 2006).

As further evidence of the importance of the experience of interpersonal functioning among group members for those with greater attachment anxiety, Gallagher, Tasca, Ritchie, Balfour, Maxwell, et al. (2014) assessed discrepancies in ratings of cohesion between the individual and the therapy group. Reductions of these discrepancies across sessions, an index of interpersonal learning, was associated with better treatment outcomes for those with higher attachment anxiety. In another study, Gallagher, Tasca, Ritchie, Balfour, and Bissada (2014) found that group cohesion was related to treatment outcome but only for those with higher attachment anxiety. As a whole, this line of research suggests that those with greater attachment anxiety appear to require the group to be increasingly engaged or cohesive over time for them to benefit. Therapist should be aware that the preoccupation with relationships and need for approval of those with high attachment anxiety means that they require an increasingly secure group context for them to function well and productively in a group.

The emerging picture from the group therapy for those with higher attachment avoidance is quite different. In research from two different samples of those with eating disorders, Tasca and colleagues (Tasca, Ritchie, et al., 2006; Tasca, Taylor, Ritchie, & Balfour, 2004) found that greater attachment avoidance was associated with dropping out of group treatment. Furthermore, Tasca, Balfour, Ritchie, and Bissada (2007) reported that higher pretreatment attachment avoidance was associated with a declining group therapeutic alliance in an interpersonally oriented group therapy. Illing, Tasca, Balfour, and Bissada (2011) used an actor–partner interdependence modeling (APIM) approach to look at the impact of the therapy group on the individual. Recall that those with attachment avoidance may appear dismissing of relationships but that they still may be emotionally—or physiologically—activated in interpersonal contexts (Dozier & Kobak, 1992). Illing et al. (2011) found that the positive association between the therapy group's and the individual's reporting of engaged group climate was significant only for those with higher attachment avoidance. In other words, despite appearances of being distant or disengaged, individuals with higher attachment avoidance appeared quite sensitive to the group's climate and to the group's implicit demands for closeness and self-disclosure. This research as a whole indicates that therapists should carefully consider integrating those with attachment avoidance into a group, prepare them for the implicit demands of a group, and only slowly require these members to self-disclose and engage to reduce the probability of dropping out of treatment.

Reflective Functioning and Group Therapy

As we indicated, a newer and important advancement within attachment theory is the concept of mentalization or reflective functioning. Typically, reflective functioning has been assessed by coding Adult Attachment Interviews with the Reflective Functioning Scale (Fonagy et al., 1998), which can be a time- and labor-intensive process. However, more recently, Fonagy et al. (2016) developed the Reflective Functioning Questionnaire (RFQ) partly as a means of making the assessment of mentalizing more accessible to researchers (see also the Mentalization Scale [MentS]; Dimitrijević, Hanak, Altaras Dimitrijević, & Joliić Marjanović, 2018). Because mentalizing underlies key interpersonal and affect regulation capacities including empathy, one could argue that it could be a precondition for patients to make the best use of group therapy. Similarly, mentalizing may have implications for work group and team functioning.

In a recent study, Maxwell, Tasca, et al. (2018) found that higher reflective functioning scores at pregroup psychodynamic treatment for BED were related to greater decreases in binge eating across four time points. In the interpersonal model of binge eating, interpersonal problems can lead to affect dysregulation, which in turn leads to binge eating (Ivanova et al., 2015). Therefore, Maxwell, Tasca, et al. (2018) argued that it was likely that participants with higher reflective functioning scores were able to use the group format to try out new adaptive ways of relating and expressing their emotions within the therapy group, and then to generalize these changes outside of the group. In a separate study, Maxwell, Compare, et al. (2018) found that reflective functioning improved following emotionally focused group therapy for BED. Furthermore, the quadratic growth in the therapeutic alliance during emotionally focused group therapy was associated with this improved reflective functioning. The study suggested that nonlinear growth in the alliance, which may indicate an alliance rupture and repair process (Safran, Muran, & Eubanks-Carter, 2011), was a corrective therapeutic process that allowed patients to appreciate the role of their own and others' mental states in moderating emotions and binge eating. Research on mentalizing is relatively new and points to potential implications for affect regulation capacities and the role of interpersonal skills like empathy on the effective functioning of groups.

ATTACHMENT AND RESEARCH ON WORK GROUPS AND TEAMS

There is also a concurrent and growing body of research on attachment in organizational contexts (see Yip, Ehrhardt, Black, & Walker, 2018, for a review). Much of that research has focused on how attachment affects individuals' work relationships and organizations' outcomes, such as ethical decision making (Chugh, Kern, Zhu, & Lee, 2014), negotiating behavior (Lee & Thompson, 2011), creative problem solving (Mikulincer, Shaver, & Rom, 2011), leader effectiveness, trust, and job attitudes (Harms, 2011). However, few studies in the organizational context have examined the effects of attachment on group dynamics. Such research in the organizational context may be informed by existing research and methods in the group therapy context.

Lavy, Bareli, and Ein-Dor (2015) found that heterogeneity in attachment styles among student group members completing a project on 52 teams was positively associated with team instrumental functioning when there was high team cohesion. In other words, in the context of higher team cohesion, insecurely attached team members might contribute to better team performance. The issue of heterogeneity and group composition has been more extensively researched in group therapy using methods like APIM. In APIM, one can disaggregate individual from aggregated group attachment scores, and individual from aggregated group cohesion or climate scores. For example, the work of Kivlighan, Lo Coco, and Gullo (2012) found that in therapy group contexts, the aggregated attachment insecurity of other group members was negatively related to an individual member's assessment of group engagement and positively related to an individual member's assessment of group conflict. In other words, the attachment context of a group affected an individual's perception of the group climate. Such research might have implications for the organizational context. For example, one can imagine that the attachment composition of a work team or group might affect the work climate or cohesion, which in turn might affect team and individual performance. Similarly, Parks (2018) discussed the need to examine both level of and dispersion of a personality trait within a group when examining the trait's effect on group functioning.

Rom and Mikulincer (2003) reported a moderating effect of group cohesion among military personnel completing missions in small groups. Those with greater attachment anxiety performed better in the context of higher group cohesion, whereas those with greater attachment avoidance performed worse in the context of higher group cohesion. Research in the group therapy context have approached these individual attachment-to-group cohesion questions somewhat differently. As indicated, using an APIM methodology, Illing et al. (2011) found that the level of cohesion in the therapy group had a specific impact on those with attachment avoidance who tended to be particularly sensitive to the implicit demands to experience group cohesion. In a work group context, this finding may suggest the need to specifically evaluate the level of an individual's attachment avoidance and to monitor and moderate the level of cohesion in the group to achieve the best performance for the individual and group. As just reported and consistent with Rom and Mikulincer (2003), individuals with attachment anxiety required their therapy group to have an increasing alliance and engagement for these individual to benefit (Tasca, Balfour, et al., 2006; Tasca et al., 2007). These studies in the military and therapy group contexts indicate the importance of increasing group cohesion for those with attachment anxiety. Such individuals are highly sensitive to potential relationship loss, and to perform optimally, they need a high level of approval and cohesion.

Although there have been theoretical discussions of organizations as attachment figures (Albert, Allen, Biggane, & Ma, 2015; Grady & Grady, 2013), little research has taken place to test these assumptions. Research by Smith et al. (1999) on group attachment within small groups of undergraduate students speaks to this issue indirectly. Recall that Smith et al. conceptualized attachment to the group as analogous to attachment to individuals, that attachment to the group might parallel one's experiences in early family relations, and attachment to groups are key evolution-based factors to ensure productivity and survival of the group. Smith and colleagues found that those high in group attachment anxiety tended to accommodate to the group and held negative views of themselves as group members, whereas those high in attachment avoidance were less likely to accommodate to the group and identify less with the group. As reported earlier, Keating and colleagues (2014) found that patients showed a decline in group attachment insecurity as a result of therapy, and that this change resulted in improved individual attachment security up to 1-year posttreatment. Despite the limited research in this area in both organizational and group therapy contexts, the concept of attachment to the group and its impact on organizational functioning and outcomes are intriguing. For example, one could predict that greater attachment anxiety to the organization or work group might lead to better productivity for these individuals if they experienced the group as highly cohesive or engaged. Similarly, one could hypothesize that higher attachment avoidance to the group might require a more moderated approach so that the individual does not feel overwhelmed by the implicit demands to be cohesive and to self-disclose. Certainly, greater attachment security toward the group would likely predict greater group cohesion and also greater job satisfaction and employee performance.

The concepts of attachment to the organization and employee loyalty might overlap in that loyal employees tend to adhere to moral principles in pursuit of individual and organizational goals (Coughlan, 2005). Loyalty between an individual and organizations may be symmetrical or asymmetrical with regard to reciprocal obligations (Hart & Thompson, 2007). One can imagine anxiously attached or securely attached individuals as loyal employees with regard to their adherence to and obligations to an organization but whose loyalty might be expressed or held differently. An anxiously attached individual may be loyal to the organization largely as a means of maintaining their own self-worth and to manage their own anxiety; hence, their loyalty, satisfaction, and performance may depend on their own needs for security and thus be tenuous. On the other hand, someone who is securely attached and loyal may be truly committed to advancing the organization's goals and mission because these goals are congruent with their own moral values; hence, their loyalty, satisfaction, and performance may be more stable.

Reflective Functioning and Group Research

One concept that remains unstudied in the organizational or work team research context is the role of mentalization or reflective functioning (Fonagy et al., 1998, 2016). As discussed, reflective functioning refers to an individual's ability to identify his or her own and others' behaviors in terms of mental states, to place oneself in another's state of mind, and to appreciate the opaqueness and developmental nature of mental states. These functions are critical to empathy, effective interpersonal relationships, and emotion regulation in times of stress. Mentalizing is conceptually similar to emotional intelligence, and research indicates a small to moderate correlation between measures of these two constructs ($r = .21–.44$; Dimitrijević et al., 2018). However, mentalizing goes beyond perceiving and understanding emotions, and requires self-reflection as a means of interpreting manifest behaviors in oneself and others. Hence, mentalizing is a key skill for managers and employees to maintain to be productive and to have effective and productive teams. Mentalizing is related to positive outcomes in group therapy and to a growing working alliance (Maxwell, Compare, et al., 2018; Maxwell, Tasca, et al., 2018). There is no research yet on the relative levels of and heterogeneity of reflective functioning within therapy groups or work teams. But one might predict that individuals with lower levels of reflective functioning might perform better if their team or group as a whole had higher levels of mentalizing. Aggregate levels of mentalizing could buffer a team and its individuals from workplace stress, conflict, organizational change, and perhaps even leader–member difficulties. Recent developments in the assessment of mentalizing has resulted in potentially useful self-report scales: the RFQ (Fonagy et al., 2016) and the MentS (Dimitrijević et al., 2018). Items on the RFQ indicate certainty or uncertainty about mental states, whereas the MentS has three scales measuring Mentalizing Self, Mentalizing Others, and Mentalizing Motivation.

Measurement of Attachment in the Organizational or Team Contexts

As indicated at the beginning of this chapter, the development of attachment theory has followed two distinct traditions: the developmental/clinical line or the social psychological line. Developmental/clinical researchers have conceived attachment typically using a typological or categorical approach (e.g., securely attached, insecurely attached), and assessments rely mainly on observational or interview techniques. The emphasis in this line of research has been on deficits within the individual that lead to psychopathology or other clinical states. On the other hand, social psychological researchers have conceived attachment dimensionally rather than categorically such that attachment is defined by relative amounts of attachment anxiety or attachment avoidance. Some have argued that dimensional approaches are more appropriate to capture the degree to which people vary on each dimension (Fraley & Waller, 1998). Dimensional assessments of attachment insecurity have typically relied on self-report measures, and researchers have used the constructs in research on romantic attachment, coping style, emotion-regulation style, and interpersonal effectiveness (Mikulincer et al., 2003).

One of the challenges in using existing attachment measures in the organizational, work, or team context is that typically researchers did not develop the measures with work groups or teams in mind. For example, one of the most commonly used self-report measures for adult attachment is the Experiences in Close Relationships Scale (ECRS; Brennan, Clark, & Shaver, 1998). The ECRS has demonstrated high levels of internal consistency, test–retest reliability, and criterion-related validity. The two dimensions are largely orthogonal, which supports the underlying structure of two independent constructs of attachment anxiety and attachment avoidance. However, the ECRS was developed for romantic attachment contexts and so may be limited when applied to the workplace. A researcher could change the wording of the ECRS (from "my partner" to "others") as was done by Mikulincer and Shaver (2007), to measure attachment in different contexts. Similarly, as indicated earlier, Fonagy et al. (2016) developed a self-report measure of reflective functioning.

However, items of the RFQ are worded such that they do not need to be rephrased for different contexts, and the scale is available in a number of languages (see "The Reflective Functioning Questionnaire (RFQ)," n.d.). Fonagy et al. (2016) recommended using the 8-item version for screening purposes. However, one should note that they developed the scale primarily for clinical samples, so researchers should evaluate its psychometric properties (e.g., internal consistency, concurrent validity) and appropriateness in non-clinical contexts (see also the MentS by Dimitrijević et al., 2018).

RECOMMENDATIONS FOR PRACTITIONERS IN NONTHERAPY CONTEXTS

Research literature and practice literature in group therapy point to a number of applications of attachment theory for coaches, managers, and other team leaders. Those team members with higher attachment anxiety may require a greater sense of team cohesion and a greater sense of belongingness to the collective to perform better. Conversely, team members with higher levels of attachment avoidance may require further distance from the team, less personal and interpersonal demands on the self, and a heightened sense of autonomy to achieve optimal performance. Team leaders should also consider team composition in those situations in which they can select team members and in which team and not necessarily individual performances are primary. Certainly, a higher composition of team members with greater attachment security and higher levels of reflective functioning will be key to collective team performance and team cohesion. Those with greater reflective functioning may be more attuned to other team members and more likely to put aside their own ambitions for the good of the collective. If possible, one could assign those with greater attachment insecurity to teams primarily comprising securely attached individuals so that the insecurely attached individual may perform to the best of his or her abilities. In selecting team leaders, managers may do well to consider capacities to mentalize (being able to consider the intentions, feelings, desires of team members) and attachment security (the ability to regulate one's emotions in stressful contexts) in addition to the specific skills in or knowledge of a particular performance context or task.

DIRECTIONS FOR FUTURE RESEARCH

We have offered a number of hypotheses or predictions based on attachment theory and from our review of group therapy have generated research that might apply to the organizational or work group/team contexts. Such research questions or predictions might include:

- Individuals with greater attachment anxiety may require higher levels of team cohesion or growth in team cohesion to enhance theirs and the team's performance.

- Conversely, individuals with greater attachment avoidance may need to experience attenuated demands for disclosure and cohesion to perform better.

- Using APIM, researchers in organizational contexts may examine the effects of the attachment contexts of work groups on the individual and vice versa. That is, one might expect that someone with higher attachment insecurity (anxious or avoidant) might perform better or experience more cohesion if the aggregated attachments of their work group were more secure.

- In a similar vein, one might need to be concerned with whether the mean level of a trait in the group is important or whether one should also attend to the variance of the trait in the group (Parks, 2018). For example, one could hypothesize that a group with lower mean levels of attachment security might not perform as well as a group with higher mean attachment security. However, if the group with a lower mean level of attachment security also had several members with greater attachment security (i.e., the group had greater dispersion in level of attachment security), then it may perform as well as a group only made up of those with high attachment security.

- Higher individual attachment anxiety to the organization or work group might lead to better productivity if these individuals experienced the group as highly cohesive or engaged.

- Greater attachment security toward the group might predict greater group cohesion and also greater job satisfaction and employee performance.

- Individuals with lower levels of reflective functioning/mentalizing might perform better and experience greater cohesion if their team or group as a whole had higher levels of mentalizing.

- Aggregated higher levels of mentalizing could buffer a team and its individuals from workplace stress, conflict, organizational change, and perhaps even leader–member difficulties.

CONCLUSION

Attachment theory represents an important model of human relationships and affect regulation. As such, it has been applied in clinical contexts and in social psychology to understand the relational aspects of therapy and factors such as coping style, relationship style, and the functioning of groups. Although researchers have used attachment theory to conceptualize group dynamics in organizations and work teams, there is relatively little research in this area (Yip et al., 2018). By contrast, there is a growing literature in the practice and research of group therapy from an attachment perspective (Marmarosh & Wallace, 2016) that may inform future directions in organizational or team dynamics research. Attachment dimensions of individuals have an impact on group functioning, including cohesion, engagement, and working alliance. In addition, research on therapy groups indicates that the aggregate levels of attachment avoidance or anxiety of the therapy group may affect how the individual perceives the group's cohesion, which ultimately affects the individual's outcomes (Illing et al., 2011; Kivlighan et al., 2012). One can easily see how these research findings may generate hypotheses for research on teams and work groups.

We reviewed clinical research on the effects of reflective functioning or mentalizing on therapy groups. Mentalizing of the individual or aggregate mentalizing in groups has not been researched in teams or work groups so represents a potentially fruitful area for understanding how groups function and what leads to their success. A significant challenge to translating attachment concepts to the workplace is that measurement of attachment dimensions was developed with romantic or clinical contexts in mind. Rewording and then reevaluating the psychometrics of attachment scales and mentalizing scales will be a key first step for organizational or team-based researchers.

SUGGESTED READINGS

Marmarosh, C. L., Markin, R. D., & Spiegel, E. B. (2013). *Attachment in group psychotherapy.* Washington, DC: American Psychological Association. http://dx.doi.org/10.1037/14186-000

Although this book is geared toward the clinician, Marmarosh et al. review much of the research on attachment and group psychotherapy up to the date of publication.

Marmarosh, C. L., & Wallace, M. (2016). Attachment as moderator variable in counseling and psychotherapy. In S. Maltzman (Ed.), *The Oxford handbook of treatment processes and outcomes in psychology: A multidisciplinary, biopsychosocial approach* (pp. 206–240). New York, NY: Oxford University Press.

This is a comprehensive review of the empirical research of attachment in psychotherapy, particularly how client attachment affects processes and outcomes. One section of the chapter focuses specifically on group therapy research.

Yip, J., Ehrhardt, K., Black, H., & Walker, D. O. (2018). Attachment theory at work: A review and directions for future research. *Journal of Organizational Behavior, 39,* 185–198. http://dx.doi.org/10.1002/job.2204

This is a comprehensive review of attachment theory as it applies to organizational behavior in general. It briefly reviews issues related to group dynamics and attachment to groups. Yip et al. provide interesting commentary about the role of attachment theory in understanding individuals in organizational contexts.

REFERENCES

Ainsworth, M. D. S. (1969). Object relations, dependency, and attachment: A theoretical review of the infant–mother relationship. *Child Development, 40,* 969–1025. http://dx.doi.org/10.2307/1127008

Albert, L. S., Allen, D. G., Biggane, J. E., & Ma, Q. (2015). Attachment and responses to employment dissolution. *Human Resource Management Review, 25,* 94–106. http://dx.doi.org/10.1016/j.hrmr.2014.06.004

Bakermans-Kranenburg, M. J., & van IJzendoorn, M. H. (2009). The first 10,000 Adult Attachment Interviews: Distributions of adult attachment representations in clinical and non-clinical groups. *Attachment & Human Development, 11*, 223–263. http://dx.doi.org/10.1080/14616730902814762

Bateman, A. W., & Fonagy, P. (2004). *Psychotherapy for borderline personality disorder: Mentalization based treatment.* New York, NY: Oxford University Press. http://dx.doi.org/10.1093/med:psych/9780198527664.001.0001

Bowlby, J. (1969). *Attachment and loss: Vol. 1. Attachment.* New York, NY: Basic Books.

Bowlby, J. (1973). *Attachment and loss: Vol. 2. Separation.* New York, NY: Basic Books.

Bowlby, J. (1980). *Attachment and loss: Vol. 3. Sadness and depression.* New York, NY: Basic Books.

Bowlby, J. (1988). *A secure base.* New York, NY: Basic Books.

Brennan, K. A., Clark, C. L., & Shaver, P. R. (1998). Self-report measurement of adult attachment: An integrative overview. In J. A. Simpson & W. S. Rholes (Eds.), *Attachment theory and close relationships* (pp. 46–76). New York, NY: Guilford Press.

Chugh, D., Kern, M. C., Zhu, Z., & Lee, S. (2014). Withstanding moral disengagement: Attachment security as ethical intervention. *Journal of Experimental Social Psychology, 51*, 88–93. http://dx.doi.org/10.1016/j.jesp.2013.11.005

Coughlan, R. (2005). Employee loyalty as adherence to shared moral values. *Journal of Managerial Issues, 17*, 43–57.

Dimitrijević, A., Hanak, N., Altaras Dimitrijević, A., & Joliić Marjanović, Z. (2018). The Mentalization Scale (MentS): A self-report measure for the assessment of mentalizing capacity. *Journal of Personality Assessment, 100*, 268–280. http://dx.doi.org/10.1080/00223891.2017.1310730

Dozier, M., & Kobak, R. R. (1992). Psychophysiology in attachment interviews: Converging evidence for deactivating strategies. *Child Development, 63*, 1473–1480. http://dx.doi.org/10.2307/1131569

Fonagy, P. (2001). *Attachment theory and psychoanalysis.* London, England: Other Press.

Fonagy, P., Luyten, P., Moulton-Perkins, A., Lee, Y.-W., Warren, F., Howard, S., . . . Lowyck, B. (2016). Development and validation of a self-report measure of mentalizing: The Reflective Functioning Questionnaire. *PLoS ONE, 11*, e0158678. http://dx.doi.org/10.1371/journal.pone.0158678

Fonagy, P., & Target, M. (2002). Early intervention and the development of self-regulation. *Psychoanalytic Inquiry, 22*, 307–335. http://dx.doi.org/10.1080/07351692209348990

Fonagy, P., Target, M., Steele, H., & Steele, M. (1998). *Reflective functioning manual: Version 5.* London, England: University College London.

Fraley, R. C., & Waller, N. G. (1998). Adult attachment patterns: A test of the typological model. In J. A. Simpson & W. S. Rholes (Eds.), *Attachment theory and close relationships* (pp. 77–114). New York, NY: Guilford Press.

Fraley, R. C., Waller, N. G., & Brennan, K. A. (2000). An item response theory analysis of self-report measures of adult attachment. *Journal of Personality and Social Psychology, 78*, 350–365. http://dx.doi.org/10.1037/0022-3514.78.2.350

Gallagher, M. E., Tasca, G. A., Ritchie, K., Balfour, L., & Bissada, H. (2014). Attachment anxiety moderates the relationship between growth in group cohesion and treatment outcomes in group psychodynamic interpersonal psychotherapy for women with binge eating disorder. *Group Dynamics, 18*, 38–52. http://dx.doi.org/10.1037/a0034760

Gallagher, M. E., Tasca, G. A., Ritchie, K., Balfour, L., Maxwell, H., & Bissada, H. (2014). Interpersonal learning is associated with improved self-esteem in group psychotherapy for women with binge eating disorder. *Psychotherapy, 51*, 66–77. http://dx.doi.org/10.1037/a0031098

Grady, V. M., & Grady, J. D., III. (2013). The relationship of Bowlby's attachment theory to the persistent failure of organizational change initiatives. *Journal of Change Management, 13*, 206–222. http://dx.doi.org/10.1080/14697017.2012.728534

Harms, P. D. (2011). Adult attachment styles in the workplace. *Human Resource Management Review, 21*, 285–296. http://dx.doi.org/10.1016/j.hrmr.2010.10.006

Hart, D. W., & Thompson, J. A. (2007). Untangling employee loyalty: A psychological contract perspective. *Business Ethics Quarterly, 17*, 297–323. http://dx.doi.org/10.5840/beq200717233

Illing, V., Tasca, G. A., Balfour, L., & Bissada, H. (2011). Attachment dimensions and group climate growth in a sample of women seeking treatment for eating disorders. *Psychiatry: Interpersonal and Biological Processes, 74*, 255–269. http://dx.doi.org/10.1521/psyc.2011.74.3.255

Ivanova, I. V., Tasca, G. A., Hammond, N., Balfour, L., Ritchie, K., Koszycki, D., & Bissada, H. (2015). Negative affect mediates the relationship between interpersonal problems and binge-eating disorder symptoms and psychopathology in a clinical sample: A test of the interpersonal model. *European Eating Disorders Review, 23*, 133–138. http://dx.doi.org/10.1002/erv.2344

Keating, L., Tasca, G. A., Gick, M., Ritchie, K., Balfour, L., & Bissada, H. (2014). Change in attachment to the therapy group generalizes to change in individual attachment among women with binge eating disorder. *Psychotherapy, 51*, 78–87. http://dx.doi.org/10.1037/a0031099

Kirchmann, H., Mestel, R., Schreiber-Willnow, K., Mattke, D., Seidler, K.-P., Daudert, E., . . . Strauss, B. (2009). Associations among attachment characteristics, patients' assessment of therapeutic factors, and treatment outcome following inpatient psychodynamic group psychotherapy. *Psychotherapy Research, 19*, 234–248. http://dx.doi.org/10.1080/10503300902798367

Kivlighan, D. M., Jr., Lo Coco, G., & Gullo, S. (2012). Attachment anxiety and avoidance and perceptions of group climate: An actor-partner interdependence analysis. *Journal of Counseling Psychology, 59*, 518–527. http://dx.doi.org/10.1037/a0030173

Lavy, S., Bareli, Y., & Ein-Dor, T. (2015). The effects of attachment heterogeneity and team cohesion on team functioning. *Small Group Research, 46*, 27–49. http://dx.doi.org/10.1177/1046496414553854

Lee, S., & Thompson, L. (2011). Do agents negotiate for the best (or worst) interest of principals? Secure, anxious and avoidant principal–agent attachment. *Journal of Experimental Social Psychology, 47*, 681–684. http://dx.doi.org/10.1016/j.jesp.2010.12.023

Levy, K. N., Ellison, W. D., Scott, L. N., & Bernecker, S. L. (2011). Attachment style. *Journal of Clinical Psychology, 67*, 193–203. http://dx.doi.org/10.1002/jclp.20756

Main, M. (2000). Attachment theory. In A. E. Kazdin (Ed.), *Encyclopedia of psychology* (Vol. 1, pp. 289–293). Washington, DC: American Psychological Association.

Main, M., Goldwyn, R., & Hesse, E. (2002). *Adult attachment scoring and classification systems.* Unpublished manuscript, Department of Psychology, University of California at Berkeley.

Markin, R. D., & Marmarosh, C. (2010). Application of adult attachment theory to group member transference and the group therapy process. *Psychotherapy: Theory, Research, Practice, Training, 47*, 111–121. http://dx.doi.org/10.1037/a0018840

Marmarosh, C. L., Markin, R. D., & Spiegel, E. B. (2013). *Attachment in group psychotherapy.* Washington, DC: American Psychological Association. http://dx.doi.org/10.1037/14186-000

Marmarosh, C. L., & Wallace, M. (2016). Attachment as moderator variable in counseling and psychotherapy with adults. In S. Maltzman (Ed.), *The Oxford handbook of treatment processes and outcomes in psychology: A multidisciplinary, biopsychosocial approach* (pp. 206–240). New York, NY: Oxford University Press.

Maxwell, H., Compare, A., Brugnera, A., Zarbo, C., Rabboni, M., Dalle Grave, R., & Tasca, G. A. (2018). Reflective functioning and growth in therapeutic alliance during emotionally focused group therapy for binge-eating disorder. *Group Dynamics, 22*, 32–44. http://dx.doi.org/10.1037/gdn0000078

Maxwell, H., Tasca, G. A., Grenon, R., Faye, M., Ritchie, K., Bissada, H., & Balfour, L. (2018). Change in attachment dimensions in women with binge-eating disorder following group psychodynamic interpersonal psychotherapy. *Psychotherapy Research, 28,* 887–901. http://dx.doi.org/10.1080/10503307.2017.1278804

Maxwell, H., Tasca, G. A., Ritchie, K., Balfour, L., & Bissada, H. (2014). Change in attachment insecurity is related to improved outcomes 1-year post group therapy in women with binge eating disorder. *Psychotherapy, 51,* 57–65. http://dx.doi.org/10.1037/a0031100

Mikulincer, M., & Shaver, P. R. (2007). *Attachment in adulthood: Structure, dynamics, and change.* New York, NY: Guilford Press.

Mikulincer, M., Shaver, P. R., & Pereg, D. (2003). Attachment theory and affect regulation: The dynamics, development, and cognitive consequences of attachment-related strategies. *Motivation and Emotion, 27,* 77–102. http://dx.doi.org/10.1023/A:1024515519160

Mikulincer, M., Shaver, P. R., & Rom, E. (2011). The effects of implicit and explicit security priming on creative problem solving. *Cognition and Emotion, 25,* 519–531. http://dx.doi.org/10.1080/02699931.2010.540110

Morel, K., & Papouchis, N. (2015). The Role of Attachment and Reflective Functioning in Emotion Regulation. *Journal of the American Psychoanalytic Association, 63,* NP15–NP20. http://dx.doi.org/10.1177/0003065115602447

Morelli, G. A., & Henry, P. I. (2013). Afterword: Cross-cultural challenges to attachment theory. In N. Quinn & J. M. Mageo (Eds.), *Attachment reconsidered. Culture, mind, and society* (pp. 241–249). New York, NY: Palgrave Macmillan. http://dx.doi.org/10.1057/9781137386724_10

Parks, C. D. (2018). Personality influences on group processes: The past, present, and future. In K. Deaux & M. Snyder (Eds.), *The Oxford handbook of personality and social psychology* (2nd ed., pp. 593–620). New York, NY: Oxford University Press.

Pietromonaco, P. R., & Barrett, L. F. (2000). The internal working models concept: What do we really know about the self in relation to others? *Review of General Psychology, 4,* 155–175. http://dx.doi.org/10.1037/1089-2680.4.2.155

Pinquart, M., Feußner, C., & Ahnert, L. (2013). Meta-analytic evidence for stability in attachments from infancy to early adulthood. *Attachment & Human Development, 15,* 189–218. http://dx.doi.org/10.1080/14616734.2013.746257

The Reflective Functioning Questionnaire (RFQ). (n.d.) Retrieved from http://www.ucl.ac.uk/psychoanalysis/research/rfq

Rom, E., & Mikulincer, M. (2003). Attachment theory and group processes: The association between attachment style and group-related representations, goals, memories, and functioning. *Journal of Personality and Social Psychology, 84,* 1220–1235. http://dx.doi.org/10.1037/0022-3514.84.6.1220

Safran, J. D., Muran, J. C., & Eubanks-Carter, C. (2011). Repairing alliance ruptures. In J. C. Norcross (Ed.), *Psychotherapy relationships that work* (pp. 224–238). New York, NY: Oxford University Press. http://dx.doi.org/10.1093/acprof:oso/9780199737208.003.0011

Schultheis, A. M., Mayes, L. C., & Rutherford, H. J. V. (2019). Associations between emotion regulation and parental reflective functioning. *Journal of Child and Family Studies, 28,* 1094–1104. http://dx.doi.org/10.1007/s10826-018-01326-z

Slade, A. (2005). Parental reflective functioning: An introduction. *Attachment & Human Development, 7,* 269–281. http://dx.doi.org/10.1080/14616730500245906

Smith, E. R., Murphy, J., & Coats, S. (1999). Attachment to groups: Theory and measurement. *Journal of Personality and Social Psychology, 77,* 94–110. http://dx.doi.org/10.1037/0022-3514.77.1.94

Tasca, G., Balfour, L., Ritchie, K., & Bissada, H. (2006). Developmental changes in group climate in two types of group therapy for binge eating disorder: A growth curve analysis. *Psychotherapy Research, 16,* 499–514. http://dx.doi.org/10.1080/10503300600593359

Tasca, G. A., Balfour, L., Ritchie, K., & Bissada, H. (2007). The relationship between attachment scales and group therapy alliance growth differs by treatment type for women with binge-eating disorder. *Group Dynamics, 11,* 1–14. http://dx.doi.org/10.1037/1089-2699.11.1.1

Tasca, G. A., Mikail, S. F., & Hewitt, P. L. (2005). Group psychodynamic interpersonal psychotherapy: Summary of a treatment model and outcomes for depressive symptoms. In M. E. Abelian (Ed.), *Focus on psychotherapy research* (pp. 159–188). New York, NY: Nova Science.

Tasca, G. A., Ritchie, K., Conrad, G., Balfour, L., Gayton, J., Lybanon, V., & Bissada, H. (2006). Attachment scales predict outcome in a randomized controlled trial of two group therapies for binge eating disorder: An aptitude by treatment interaction. *Psychotherapy Research, 16,* 106–121. http://dx.doi.org/10.1080/10503300500090928

Tasca, G. A., Taylor, D., Ritchie, K., & Balfour, L. (2004). Attachment predicts treatment completion in an eating disorders partial hospital program among women with anorexia nervosa. *Journal of Personality Assessment, 83,* 201–212. http://dx.doi.org/10.1207/s15327752jpa8303_04

van IJzendoorn, M. H., & Sagi-Schwartz, A. (2008). Cross-cultural patterns of attachment: Universal and contextual dimensions. In J. Cassidy & P. R. Shaver (Eds.), *Handbook of attachment: Theory, research, and clinical applications* (pp. 880–905). New York, NY: Guilford Press.

Waters, E., Weinfield, N. S., & Hamilton, C. E. (2000). The stability of attachment security from infancy to adolescence and early adulthood: General discussion. *Child Development, 71,* 703–706. http://dx.doi.org/10.1111/1467-8624.00179

Yalom, I. D., & Leszcz, M. (2005). *The theory and practice of group psychotherapy* (5th ed.). New York, NY: Basic Books.

Yip, J., Ehrhardt, K., Black, H., & Walker, D. O. (2018). Attachment theory at work: A review directions for future research. *Journal of Organizational Behavior, 39,* 185–198. http://dx.doi.org/10.1002/job.2204

9

Group Cohesion

Empirical Evidence From Group Psychotherapy for Those Studying Other Areas of Group Work

Cheri L. Marmarosh and Amy Sproul

Group cohesion not only facilitates group therapy, but it also is a key component of all groups—including groups that function to serve the country, achieve a business goal, or participate in a sport. This chapter explores how we define and measure group cohesion, how cohesion relates to group process and outcome, how member factors influence cohesion, and how leaders can foster or hinder cohesion. Most important, we consider how this research can apply to other areas of group work, particularly social, organizational, health, military, and sport psychology groups.

DEFINING COHESION

Defining cohesion is a challenge within the many fields examining group dynamics, including both clinical and social psychology. Although commonly understood experientially, cohesion has remained difficult to put into words in ways that encapsulate a multifaceted experience felt within a member (Yalom & Leszcz, 2005). Definitions of the construct have ranged from the very general (e.g., a force that keeps members connected to the group; Dion, 2000) to the more precise (e.g., alliance, interpersonal liking, tolerance for space; Burlingame, McClendon, & Alonso, 2011; Yalom & Leszcz, 2005). Research examining cohesion has also endured criticism for its construct variability between different research studies (for a review, see Marmarosh & Van Horn, 2011).

http://dx.doi.org/10.1037/0000201-010
The Psychology of Groups: The Intersection of Social Psychology and Psychotherapy Research,
C. D. Parks and G. A. Tasca (Editors)

Over the years, however, narrow definitions of cohesion have been discarded for more complex and multidimensional conceptions, essentially transitioning cohesion from a "single-celled" organism to a paradigm reflecting a "multi-celled" experience (Marmarosh & Van Horn, 2011). In essence, researchers began to conceive of cohesion as a phenomenon arising from many distinct parts.

Group Cohesion: A Unidimensional Construct

Originally, group psychotherapists borrowed a definition for cohesion from social psychologists and group dynamics researchers (Festinger, Schachter, & Back, 1950; Hogg, 1992; Lewin, 1947). This conception of group-cohesion centered on a mechanism or force that holds group members together, keeping them connected to the group (Dion, 2000). Group therapists described it as an experience of connectedness, as "we-ness," or as being part of a whole (Yalom & Leszcz, 2005). In this sense, cohesion is a collaborative force, constructed through shared dedication to the group's pursuit of common goals (Budman et al., 1989). Other group clinicians emphasized the bond between group members and the attraction group members feel toward the group and to its leader(s) (Evans & Jarvis, 1980; Joyce, Piper, & Ogrodniczuk, 2007; Piper, Marrache, Lacroix, Richardsen, & Jones, 1983). These bonds create systems of relationships, forming a structure from which cohesion can emerge. This begins to illustrate the most common view of cohesion used in group therapy research today, in which cohesion represents the main component of the therapeutic relationship within group psychotherapy. Under this definition, cohesion facilitates a sense of unity, belonging, and safety, even during times of within-group stress and conflict (Marmarosh & Van Horn, 2011).

Group Cohesion: A Multidimensional Construct

One way to understand cohesion is to examine the different relationships that contribute to it. Bliese and Halverson (1996) were two of the first researchers to differentiate between vertical and horizontal cohesion in work groups. They defined *vertical* relationships as those between group member and leader and horizontal relationships as those between members. Burlingame et al. (2011) elaborated on this theory and applied it to group therapy, believing that research most firmly supported two implicit dimensions of cohesion: relationship structure and relationship quality. This concept of "structure" referred to the direction and function of relationships within a group, whereas "quality" referred to the alliance, climate, and level of belonging within these relationships (Burlingame, MacKenzie, & Strauss, 2004). Within this paradigm, two types of cohesion exist: *task cohesion*, which reflects a group's adherence to accomplishing a common goal; and *affective cohesion*, reflecting a group's experience of emotional safety due to the affective support provided by the group (Dion, 2000; Marmarosh & Van Horn, 2011). Burlingame et al. (2011) also understood the multiple relationships within the therapy group and noted that each member perceives cohesion through three structural components: member to member, member to group, and member to leader. The group leader's perspective included two more structural components: leader to group and leader to coleader.

The overlap between constructs describing group alliance, group identity, group engagement, and group climate may lead one to conflate these constructs, and many studies have attempted to explore the relationship among these overlapping factors to prevent inappropriate conceptual fusion (Marmarosh & Van Horn, 2011). In general, *cohesion* is the sense of unity and attachment to the group, whereas group climate is the overall perception of the group environment (Marmarosh & Van Horn, 2011). Both of these constructs mediate the likelihood of members engaging with the group and facilitate the emergence of a group identity.

EMPIRICALLY IDENTIFYING FACTORS CONTRIBUTING TO COHESION

The pursuit of understanding cohesion's many dimensions drew clinical researchers to compare the concept to potential, overlapping constructs that are often essential in group therapy (Johnson, Burlingame, Olsen, Davies, & Gleave, 2005). For example, both alliance and cohesion are highly correlated, and both address the quality of the relationship between patient and therapist (Gillaspy, Wright, Campbell, Stokes, & Adinoff, 2002; Johnson et al., 2005; Joyce et al., 2007; Marziali, Munroe-Blum, & McCleary, 1997; Yalom & Leszcz, 2005). Although a body of research has established that the constructs of alliance and cohesion are correlated and distinct (Bakali, Baldwin, & Lorentzen, 2009; Johnson et al., 2005; Taft, Murphy, King, Musser, & DeDeyn, 2003), there is a growing consensus that group alliance and cohesion are overlapping constructs that both relate to the system of relationships within the group (Marmarosh & Van Horn, 2011).

In order to understand the complex relationship among group therapy factors and cohesion, Johnson et al. (2005) administered measures of cohesion, group climate, working alliance, and empathy to 662 group members from 111 counseling centers; they found that the correlation between factors was high enough to indicate that they were measuring overlapping constructs. However, after further analysis, Johnson and colleagues found that the factors did not load into one singular group factor but instead to three separate factors: positive bond, positive work, and negative relationship (Burlingame et al., 2011; Johnson et al., 2005). These three factors explain how group members perceived the quality of relationships in groups, which then influenced the perception of constructs, such as alliance, climate, and cohesion (Burlingame et al., 2011; Johnson et al., 2005). Positive bond described the affective relationship members experienced among each other, as well as between themselves and the leader (Johnson et al., 2005), whereas the factor of positive work captured shared tasks and goals of the group. The negative relationship factor captured conflict and the leaders' empathic failures. This discovery indicated that cohesion, engagement, and leader empathy were important aspects of positive relationships within groups, but that task-oriented aspects of the relationship were distinct constructs.

Perhaps most important, Johnson et al. (2005) found that a lack of empathy by leaders or members related to perceived negative relationships within the group. Unlike prior studies that focused on clients ranking curative factors facilitating change, this study shed light on lack of empathy as a factor that hinders a group from becoming a positive force for change. Leader empathy is an important contribution that has the potential to influence all types of groups, not just psychotherapy groups.

GROUP COHESION: TREATMENT PROCESS AND OUTCOME

A meta-analysis of 40 studies examining the relationship between cohesion and treatment outcome indicated that cohesion significantly relates to outcome in both inpatient and outpatient settings (Burlingame, McClendon, & Yang, 2018). Several studies have indicated that cohesion positively correlates with an elevation in member self-esteem, reduced symptoms across diagnoses, and higher rates of goal attainment (Braaten, 1989; Budman et al., 1989; Tschuschke & Dies, 1994).

Group cohesion is not only critical in interpersonal process groups, it is also related to treatment outcome in groups designed to address specific problems, such as smoking cessation (Etringer, Gregory, & Lando, 1984) and men in treatment for domestic violence (Taft et al., 2003). For example, Taft et al. (2003) found that member-rated group cohesion, rated early and late in treatment, was related to less physical and emotional abuse for men who were in group therapy for domestic violence.

Some studies stand out because they empirically examine the difference between treatment as usual, where leaders run the groups without focusing specifically on developing cohesion, and cohesion-enhanced treatment, where leaders emphasize cohesion in addition to the standard treatment. For example, Hand, Lamontagne, and Marks (1974) found that members with agoraphobia in cognitive behavioral therapy groups where cohesiveness was emphasized (i.e., the group leader used interventions to increase and foster group members' connection to one another) felt more helped by the groups compared to those in groups where the treatment focused only on symptom reduction. Those members who were in the cohesion-focused groups continued to improve even after treatment ended, whereas the members in groups that did not receive the cohesion intervention began to relapse after termination. Similar findings were reported in group treatment for smoking cessation (Etringer et al., 1984). In Chapter 7 of this volume, we see similar findings with cohesion relating to outcomes in team performance.

Explaining the Variability in Findings

Variability in the strength of the relationship between group therapy cohesion and group process and outcome indicates that the benefits of cohesion depend on many factors. Burlingame et al. (2018) found a number of moderator variables that significantly predicted the magnitude of the correlation between cohesion and outcome. For instance, interpersonally oriented therapies showed the highest cohesion to outcome relationship, whereas other types of therapy (e.g., cognitive–behavioral, psychodynamic, supportive) showed significant, but lower, associations between cohesion and outcome. In fact, any group therapy that focused greater attention on group process or that facilitated interactions among members was associated with higher correlations between cohesion and outcome. The size of the group also affected the relationship between cohesion and patient improvement; groups containing from five to nine members posted the largest correlation, and groups with more than nine members showed the smallest correlation (Burlingame et al., 2018). In addition, the number of group sessions also affected this relationship between group cohesion and outcome; groups lasting 20 or more sessions demonstrated a stronger relationship between cohesion and outcomes, followed by groups lasting 13 to 19 sessions, and then by groups lasting fewer than 13 sessions (Burlingame et al., 2011). This finding suggests that the effects of cohesion may increase over time and, the longer the group, the more cohesion relates to achieving treatment goals.

There are several, additional, hypotheses as to why the relationship between cohesion and outcomes can be so variable between groups. Kipnes, Piper, and Joyce (2002) proposed that cohesion might mediate other group factors, creating an environment where positive change more easily manifests within the group (Alonso, 2011). For example, there is evidence suggesting that cohesion increases: (a) member attendance (Ogrodniczuk, Piper, & Joyce, 2006), (b) decisions to stay in the group (Hand et al., 1974), (c) participation in the group (Budman et al., 1993), (d) tolerance of conflict (Alonso, 2011), and (e) the quality of member listening and empathy (Alonso, 2011). Thus, group cohesion creates a group environment that is conducive to improving psychological symptoms and increasing positive outcomes overall.

Member Interpersonal Styles and Cohesion

Although member mental-health diagnosis does not always influence the strength of the relationship between cohesion and positive outcomes in a group (Burlingame et al., 2011), the characteristics and disorders of group members can influence group cohesion (Woody & Adessky, 2002). For instance, members with longstanding interpersonal difficulties can bring maladapted patterns into the group and struggle with developing a sense of closeness and positive alliance to both group members and leaders (Marmarosh & Van Horn, 2011). Behaviorally, members can exhibit difficulty coping with emotions or inappropriate reactions to group processes (Hilbert et al., 2007). These group members often perceive less cohesion than their healthier peers. However, despite trouble participating in the therapy groups, lower-functioning group members in inpatient hospital settings reported perceived group cohesion to be one of the curative factors in their treatment (Butler & Fuhriman, 1983).

One of the most important findings in the clinical arena is that group cohesion is not helpful to the therapeutic outcomes for all individuals who attend group therapy. German researchers investigating how member inter-personal styles moderate the correlation between cohesion and patient outcomes in depressed patients found that patients who were perceived as "too friendly" improved more when their experience of cohesion decreased during group therapy. Inversely, in the same study, patients perceived as cold or hostile improved most when their experience of cohesion increased during group (Schauenburg, Sammet, Rabung, & Strack, 2001).

In essence, there may be a false sense of cohesion both for those members who are trying too hard to fit in and belong in the group and for those who are detached and avoidant of intimacy. Group therapists often try to understand what individual factors contribute to successful group processes (see Burlingame, Fuhriman, & Johnson, 2001, 2002), and one theory that links both these friendly and detached behaviors in the group is attachment theory.

Member Attachment and Group Cohesion

Member attachment styles (i.e., internal working model of relationships based on their lifelong relational experiences) influence group cohesion and how group cohesion relates to treatment process and outcome (Marmarosh, Markin, & Spiegel, 2013). Shechtman and Dvir (2006) found that adolescents with avoidant attachment styles, those who avoided intimacy, also avoided self-disclosure and devalued disclosures by others more than their peers devalued such disclosures. Chen and Mallinckrodt (2002) studied attachment styles within group therapy in a graduate school environment and found that, members who were high in attachment anxiety, evidenced by their fearfulness of being abandoned or rejected, displayed problematic behaviors in the group (e.g., passivity, vindictiveness, intrusiveness). They also found that avoidant attachment negatively correlated with measures of group working alliance (e.g., group attraction) within group treatment. Other researchers have also found that members with greater attachment avoidance have greater rates of dropping out of group therapy (Tasca et al., 2006; Tasca, Taylor, Ritchie, & Balfour, 2004) and are more likely repelled by the pressures to be more intimate in the group (Illing, Tasca, Balfour, & Bissada, 2011).

There is also some evidence that individuals who exhibit patterns of avoidant or anxious attachment styles have the most to gain from cohesion in psychotherapy. In Gallagher, Tasca, Ritchie, Balfour, and Bissada's (2014) research on group therapy and binge-eating disorder, they found that attachment anxiety at study baseline moderated the relationship between growth in group cohesion and change in symptoms of binge eating. An increase in cohesion was associated with better outcomes, but only for those who were high in attachment anxiety at the beginning of the study.

Kivlighan, Lo Coco, and Gullo (2012) examined the interactions of attachment styles within the group as they related to group climate (which is related to cohesion). Using actor–partner interdependence modeling, they found that aggregated anxiety and avoidance, summing all the attachment of all of the members in the group, related to individual members' perceptions of group conflict and group climate. In essence, members created a unique attachment within the group that influenced how each individual member perceived the group. Insecure groups, groups with more members who were anxious or avoidant, had members with less cohesion and more perceived conflict. These findings are important for leaders who are considering the composition of the group and how the members will influence each other over time. In Chapter 8 of this book, the authors review how attachment mediates the relationship between cohesion and outcome in group treatment. Future research is needed to determine how attachment in group therapy is similar or different for groups that are shorter in length or for members with different mental health diagnoses. There is a large literature linking attachment insecurity to addictive disorders, eating disorders, mood and anxiety disorders, and personality disorders (see Mikulincer & Shaver, 2016).

Member Diversity and Group Cohesion

Group therapists value the impact of race, culture, ethnicity, gender, religion, and economic status on group process and outcome (Delucia-Waack, 2011). We know that the group is a social microcosm, and that hatred, microaggressions, prejudice, and stereotypes are likely to become a part of the group process. Leaders who are not able to help the group examine and resolve conflicts around diversity will have members experience discrimination and hatred in the group that is likely to erode group cohesion. In Chapter 3, the authors review how factors relate to group cohesion in nonclinical groups. For example, researchers have found that diversity can facilitate or impede cohesion during the initial stages of group formation (Kozlowski & Chao, 2012).

Researchers within the field of organizational psychology indicate that diversity is most likely to impede cohesion during the initial stages of group formation (Kozlowski & Chao, 2012). Kozlowski and Chao (2012) suggested that first impressions serve as the initial feedback for other group members to adapt and respond to each other as the group relationship evolves. These initial interactions are more likely to be based on surface-level identities, such as race, age, and gender (Harrison, Price, Gavin, & Florey, 2002; Kozlowski & Chao, 2012). Kozlowski and Chao hypothesized that when a group is homogeneous, surface level attributes form a foundation for member attraction towards the group. However, in heterogeneous groups, the authors posited that surface-level differences cause fault lines that initially fracture groups, reducing feelings of unity (Kozlowski & Chao, 2012; Lau & Murnighan, 1998). As interactions continue, however, group members become less aware of superficial differences, and a matrix of cohesion emerges through transcending commonalities that connect individual members into nets of belonging (Kozlowski & Chao, 2012). This hypothesis suggests that, although diversity within the group impacts levels of cohesion early in the group process, the impact is less as surface level bonds are replaced with deeper understandings of one another.

Research on social integration also reflects this conclusion. *Social integration*, as defined by social and organizational psychologists, is the extent to which individuals from different backgrounds are able to become psychologically linked in the pursuit of a common task or objective (Harrison, Price, & Bell, 1998; Harrison et al., 2002; O'Reilly, Caldwell, & Barnett, 1989). Within this research, cohesion is described as the "primary affective dimension" of social integration, connecting individual members through affective bonds (Harrison et al., 1998, p. 96). Research by Harrison and colleagues (1998) examined the relationship between surface-level diversity (i.e., differences defined by physical characteristics, such as age, sex, and race) and deep-level diversity (i.e., differences based on psychological characteristics, values, and beliefs) and found that negative forces on cohesiveness due to surface-level differences dissipated over time and were replaced by connections based on deep-level similarity. This suggests that, for groups interacting regularly over time, intergroup differences in deep-level characteristics may be more harmful to cohesion than surface-level diversity (Harrison et al., 1998).

IMMATURE AND MATURE COHESION

Group therapists would agree that true cohesion deepens over time and that the immediate liking and agreeableness found within a group form the beginnings of cohesion (see Burlingame et al., 2001, 2002). Yalom and Leszcz (2005) argued that group therapy cohesion does not just happen but is the result of resolved conflict and risk taking. They argued that "it would be a mistake to equate cohesiveness with comfort" (p. 63). If this is true, then measuring cohesion at the very beginning of group can be misleading.

Miles (1953) described how immediate cohesion can be a mixed blessing, because immediately cohesive groups can foster dependence and reduce the likelihood that members will engage in constructive conflict. An overemphasis on group solidarity can inhibit the importance of risk taking, conflict, and true intimacy in the group. Hartmann (1981) not only addressed the negative side effects of cohesion but also described pathological cohesion in groups, where the pressure to belong within the group causes members to regress. During this regression, members lose their sense of self and are unable to engage in the group process. Fears of group cohesion are not surprising and parallel the fears of groups documented in social psychology. "Groupthink," social loafing, conformity, and deindividuation are all negative phenomena attributed to groups.

However, Karau and Hart (1998) studied the impact of cohesiveness on social loafing and found that group cohesion actually eliminated social loafing (i.e., group members doing less in the group or slacking off). They stated that group members who are in cohesive groups and have the opportunity to make positive contributions to group outcomes engage in less social loafing. They suggested that building cohesion and focusing on common goals can reduce social loafing in groups.

Robbins (2003) argued that not all cohesion is the same, and that there are specific populations in which early cohesion may inhibit growth and positive outcome. Roether and Peters (1972) studied the relationship between cohesion in groups for male sex offenders. They found not only that cohesion was not significantly related to positive outcome but also that sex offenders' ratings of cohesion were related to their tendency to reoffend. The greater the member rated group cohesion, the greater he rated the likelihood to engage in sexual offenses in the future. Robbins (2003) argued that certain populations, such as sex offenders, are more likely to be at risk for immature cohesion and have more difficulty moving to mature cohesion. The group situation (e.g., a prison setting) where members are in mandated treatment, have leaders who are part of the system, are concerned about being evaluated, and are already mistrustful of the establishment does not facilitate or encourage honest disclosure. He argued that the combination of these factors with greater character pathology and externalizing defenses commonly seen among sex offenders can lead to members developing rapid solidarity in their group without encouraging risk taking, painful disclosure, conflict, or true intimacy. According to Robbins (2003), the assessment of cohesion early in treatment in these groups is more indicative of playing it safe and bolstering the self than engaging in therapeutic change.

The research shows us that there are developmental levels of cohesion: (a) immature cohesion, based on anxiety and perceived compatibility and similarity; and (b) mature cohesion, based on intimacy that occurs when members expose vulnerability, take risks, and truly know each other. For groups to be cohesive, the leader has a lot to do to make the group safe and move the members from immature connections to more mature relationships within the group.

LEADER FACTORS THAT LEAD TO MATURE GROUP COHESION

Researchers have shown that leaders who promote interpersonal interaction, regardless of their theoretical orientations, facilitate a stronger relationship between cohesion and outcomes within groups than leaders who do not focus on the interpersonal process (Burlingame et al., 2018). In addition, leaders who actively prioritize the cultivation of cohesion have a stronger relationship between cohesion and outcomes within their groups (Burlingame et al., 2018).

Leaders' Orientation

The theoretical orientation of the group leader often indicates how likely it is for a leader to emphasize interpersonal interaction (Burlingame et al., 2018). Burlingame et al. (2018) showed that leaders with an interpersonal orientation had groups that showed the highest correlation between cohesion and outcomes in their groups, whereas psychodynamic and cognitive–behavioral orientations showed weaker, although still significant, correlations. This makes sense because the interpersonal orientation often emphasizes interactions within the group over didactic and linking present to past interventions.

Meta-analyses indicate that cohesion to outcome correlations are significantly higher in groups where cohesion is prioritized when compared with groups where it is not prioritized (see Burlingame et al., 2018). Conversely, group cohesion is hindered when group leaders lack the skill to model appropriate self-disclosure as well as other interpersonal skills that facilitate growth and healthy group dynamics. Cohesion also suffers when leaders inhibit group members from expressing negative feelings towards other group members or the group leader, preventing the group from metabolizing conflict (Marmarosh & Van Horn, 2011; Yalom & Leszcz, 2005).

Leaders' Ability to Facilitate Safety

One of the most inhibiting leadership factors in the development of cohesion is the leader's inability to tolerate emotional reactions (Mikulincer & Shaver, 2007). Failure to be able to express or accept caring, to address conflict, or to explore client's avoidant behaviors (e.g., missed sessions/tardy behavior) will almost always negatively influence the development of cohesion within a group (Yalom & Leszcz, 2005).

Smokowski, Rose, Todar, and Reardon (1999) demonstrated that dropout increases when group members feel that the group leaders are not adequately supporting or protecting them within the group environment. This indicates that a feeling of safety within the group is vital to establishing group cohesion. MacNair-Semands (2002) stated that one way to support members is to provide pregroup screening to help set the stage for the upcoming group process. This is empirically associated with both higher rates of attendance and decreased rates of premature termination, which is important because preventing turnover in groups enables group members to feel a sense of commitment to the group.

Social psychologists have studied the impact of military leaders' capacity to support group members through the lens of attachment theory, and they found that the attachment style of the leader relates to group processes

(Berson, Dan, & Yammarino, 2006; Rom & Mikulincer, 2003). For instance, research indicates that the more a leader engages in avoidant behaviors, such as dismissing vulnerability/avoiding members' needs, the less group members rated cohesion (Davidovitz, Mikulincer, Shaver, Izsak, & Popper, 2007). More important, even soldiers with secure attachments were negatively impacted by dismissing group leaders who were not able to support them during the stress of basic training.

Leadership Behaviors That Facilitate Cohesion

Because group therapists are aware of the leader's powerful impact on group outcomes, they often emphasize the training of leaders. Burlingame et al. (2001, 2002) developed a list of empirically based, leader behaviors that engender cohesive groups. These behaviors are captured empirically based principles that focus on group leader factors that contribute and foster group cohesion. These principles address how the leader can foster cohesion via planning/pregroup preparation, verbal interactions that offer structure, and facilitation of emotional intimacy in the group. Leaders should model real-time observations and guide interpersonal interactions with a moderate amount of authority and control to facilitate safety. Burlingame et al. (2001) described how group leaders need to manage their own struggles to remain present within the group in the service of engagement and to help group members express their feelings and find a shared meaning.

It is no small task to foster a cohesive group; it is one that requires specialized training in group work. When beginning a group, leaders need to engage in behaviors so that members feel safe, choose to participate, and remain in the group. Lack of these leadership behaviors is often due to insufficient education in group dynamics and group therapy. A group facilitated by a leader with limited training, expertise, and knowledge is more likely to struggle to model appropriate self-disclosure, feedback, and communication skills to members (Bernard et al., 2008). Group members who seek the group experience because they lack these skills are less likely to be able to connect or interact with other members in a positive way without leader support and modeling. A leader who does not demonstrate empathy and engage in here and now feedback will have group members who likely to continue to struggle and reenact their problematic interpersonal interactions in the group.

GROUP PSYCHOTHERAPY: METHODS USED TO ASSESS COHESION

Because cohesion is such an important construct within group therapy, researchers have developed many measures of and ways to assess cohesion (for review, see Marmarosh & Van Horn, 2011). In this chapter, we mainly focus on trends that are more recent and methods that may be useful to those wanting to measure cohesion in their groups.

Measures of Group Cohesion

Burlingame et al. (2018) identified nine most studied measures of cohesion and assessed each measure for the structural and affective/task components of cohesion. Although all of the measures assessed the relationship between members and the group, fewer than half focused on the relationship between group members and the leader. The affective bond, or the emotional connection, between members in the group was assessed by all of the cohesion measures. However, cocommitment to a task, which was characterized by agreeing on what needs to happen within the group, was assessed by only a third of the measures. Burlingame and colleagues concluded that the measure one uses is critical when examining the relationship between cohesion and outcome because one can tap into different aspects of cohesion via different measures.

Based on their research, Burlingame and colleagues (2018) described their new measure, the Group Questionnaire (GQ), which taps into two main aspects of cohesion: structure and quality. *Structure* refers to how the member views the group leader's competence and warmth and their view of other members in the group. *Quality* is more complex and taps into (a) the member's sense of belonging within the group and (b) the working aspect of the group, such as the alliance and the group climate. We reviewed the items on the GQ and found that many of the items would be applicable to non-therapy groups. For example, similar to the working alliance items, there are items that assess the bond between the member and the leader, the agreement on group goals, and the sense that the leader is helping the member do the tasks needed to be successful in the group. Other items assess how the member feels about conflict within the group meeting, how withdrawn members are during a meeting, and how well members cooperate during the meeting. All of these items could apply to an organizational group, an athletic team, or to military groups.

The American Group Psychotherapy Association published a guide for group therapists, called the CORE Battery-Revised (see Burlingame et al., 2006), that lists measures that are useful when assessing group members at different points in treatment. The battery describes empirically supported measures, including the GQ (see Burlingame et al., 2016) and Lese and MacNair-Semands's (2000) Therapeutic Factors Inventory, which assesses group members' perceptions of important curative mechanisms within the group (e.g., cohesion). Many of these measures could be applied to other group settings and help leaders understand how the group is functioning and how to intervene in a way that facilitates group cohesion and outcome. There are similar measures developed to assess sport team cohesion (e.g., Group Environment Questionnaire, Team Cohesion Questionnaire; see Carron, Widmeyer, & Brawley, 1985); however, these measures are much older and have less empirical support. One of the challenges across disciplines when studying cohesion is the number of measures that are out there and the lack of research using and validating them. It appears that people who study groups like to develop new measures of cohesion instead of using them in ongoing studies to understand how cohesion influences the process and outcome of different groups. The group therapy literature provides newer reliable and valid measures based on strong psychometrics.

Feedback Monitoring: Assessing Group Member Cohesion After Sessions

Burlingame and his colleagues (2016) focused on how collecting feedback from group members after each therapy session can positively affect group members and help leaders facilitate the group process. He and his colleagues developed a tracking system that allows group leaders to monitor each member and alerts leaders to members who were struggling regarding their perceptions of cohesion and engagement. After a session, a group leader can have a visual display of how each group member is doing when compared with the rest of the group and how that member was doing during prior sessions (Burlingame et al., 2016; Janis, Burlingame, & Olsen, 2018). The group leader receives a notice indicating that there has been reliable deterioration in the quality of the member's relationship to the group. This is an excellent way to detect cohesion ruptures in the group and to track the repair of those ruptures over time.

APPLICATIONS TO OTHER AREAS OF GROUP WORK

The work of group psychotherapists and researchers on cohesion in therapy groups may have useful applications to other group areas, such as sport psychology, social psychology, organizational psychology, and even health psychology. The May 2018 issue of *American Psychologist* was devoted to the science of teamwork, such as in military health care, but only one article out of 22 mentioned cohesion as an important component of teams (Goodwin, Blacksmith, & Coats, 2018). In that article, Goodwin, Blacksmith, and Coats (2018) described how group cohesion is often overlooked but influences how well teammates perform on a task.

We hope that this chapter is useful to anyone working with groups in organizations, sports, and other areas, because the findings are relevant to leaders who want to promote a well-functioning group. Below are recommendations gleaned from the group therapy literature that could inform group practice and research in other areas of group work.

Group leaders can best instill group cohesion when they plan ahead for their groups/teams. They can foster cohesion even before the group/team begins by screening members who may not be ready to participate in the group, preparing members regarding the group process, discussing boundaries and explaining how they will be valuable members, and providing appropriate information about group structure and goals. The CORE Battery-Revised (Burlingame et al., 2006) offers multiple measures that can be used to screen and prepare group/team members for a group experience. Leaders can decide what factors are important to examine for their particular group. For example, military groups have screened soldiers for posttraumatic stress disorder and trauma and found that it does have an impact on group cohesion with some soldiers needing more support before returning to the group after deployment (Whealin et al., 2007). Studies could continue to explore how cohesion moderates group members' traumatic experience, not only in war but also for emergency response teams, police officers, and firefighters. Are there ways that being in a secure group can provide some resilience to the impact of traumatic events?

In addition, group therapists have relied on sophisticated statistical analyses that allow them to examine the impact of individuals on one another (i.e., actor–partner interdependence modeling). Using these data analytic techniques, researchers have learned that the way in which an individual group member compares with other members on a specific attitude or quality can make them more or less at risk for being dissatisfied with the group process. For example, Kivlighan et al. (2012) found that a member who was significantly more avoidantly attached compared with other group members made him/her more likely to perceive a more negative group climate. Leaders of all groups may want to pay attention to a group member being an outlier or too different from the rest of the group, as this may negatively influence cohesion. These sophisticated analyses could easily be applied to other types of groups, such as work groups, military groups, or teams.

Group leaders need to be aware that cohesion based on a false sense of unity, without the ability to tolerate healthy disagreement and honesty, may inhibit individual growth and the successful functioning of groups. Group leaders have the responsibility to provide the safety needed so that group members can be most productive. For example, Greene-Shortridge and colleagues (2007) recommended that military leaders model openness to mental health issues, so that soldiers will reveal more vulnerability and seek out mental health care when needed. Studies need to measure both groupthink, leader style, and cohesion at the same time, so that we can examine the influence of conformity on cohesion and see how it influences the work environment. It would be interesting to see how "false cohesion"—cohesion based on fear and conformity—relates to turnover, productivity, and work satisfaction. On the other side, it would be important to see what types of interventions facilitate more secure attachment in settings where "false cohesion" is likely to occur. For example, in prison settings, is it better to have a leader who is not part of the prison system nor evaluating the prisoners to reduce the "false cohesion" often found. Does reducing "false cohesion" provide better outcomes for these group members?

Group leaders can educate themselves as to the impact of race, ethnicity, and culture, and they can explore how this impact influences group members' needs in the group and the group's sense of safety within the group (DeLucia-Waack, 2011). Leaders who are not able to help the group examine and resolve conflicts around diversity will have members experience discrimination and hatred in the group that is likely to erode group cohesion. It is important for leaders to remember that Puck, Neyer, and Dennerlein (2010) found that the organizational context in which teams are operating influences the diversity–conflict relationship, and that organizational supportiveness and openness influence the diversity–conflict relationship. Over time, group members become less aware of superficial differences, and surface level bonds are replaced with deeper understandings of one another. Training group leaders to expect conflict and facilitate open dialogues about differences can help groups be more productive and foster more cohesion based on less superficial similarities.

Researchers can study the impact of diversity training for group leaders to see how it facilitates both group process and group outcomes in a variety of settings.

Group leaders need to address behaviors in individual members that discourage group cohesion, such as avoidance, lateness, missed sessions, dropouts, lack of disclosure, and risk taking (see Yalom & Leszcz, 2005). One way leaders can identify at-risk members is to monitor how members in their group are doing. Collecting member feedback over time can be extremely useful for leaders who may be able to identify members who are struggling and then intervene to facilitate group cohesion and enhance group performance. For example, a member may miss sessions because she is dissatisfied with the group. She may not say anything during the group session, but she might be willing to disclose her unhappiness if she is asked to rate cohesion after the sessions. Burlingame and colleagues (2016) described the impact of feedback monitoring on therapy groups, but we could not find similar research on process or outcome monitoring in military groups, organizational groups, or sport teams. For example, researchers could examine how tracking members of military groups leads to early detection of depression and reduces suicide attempts in soldiers.

Group leaders can facilitate better outcome when they are sensitive to the importance of relationship factors in group (e.g., the alliance, group climate, cohesion). The perception of safety and trust members have within the group/team can hinder or facilitate performance. Even in groups where it is not apparent that cohesion/group climate is influencing the group (e.g., sport teams, doctors and nurses collaborating in the intensive care unit), cohesion does play a role. For example, research on emergency medical technicians found that job stress is alleviated if more attention was given to the work environment (Revicki & Gershon, 1996). Revicki and Gershon (1996) found that decreasing work stress decreases psychological stress, and they recommended interventions that foster group cohesion in medical settings. Studies have also shown that, for team sports, group cohesion relates positively to self-reported performance (Brawley, Carron, & Widmeyer, 1987). Researchers can continue to study how facilitating cohesion in their groups and work settings relates to satisfaction and outcome.

Group leadership requires specialized training in the area of group dynamics and group treatment. One cannot assume leaders have the skills to run a successful group based on their experience with individuals alone. We have seen how the lack of leader empathy can hinder group therapy (Johnson et al., 2005), and how military leaders with a dismissing style can erode well-being in soldiers (Davidovitz et al., 2007). Within organizations, leader sensitivity has been linked to employee well-being (Kuoppala, Lamminpää, Liira, & Vainio, 2008; Skakon, Nielsen, Borg, & Guzman, 2010), with unhealthy leadership linked to increased stress and anxiety, less satisfaction, and less involvement in work (Hudson, 2013). Barlow (2013) described the training that is needed for group leaders, such as a basic understanding of group dynamics, leadership theory, a capacity to regulate emotions, and an ability to facilitate intimate interactions including conflict resolution. The ability of the leader to be sensitive to the group members' needs and facilitate safety appears to be a common thread across diverse groups. We need research that identifies the best ways to train leaders (didactic vs. experiential learning), what qualities can one easily develop (set group agendas), and which ones are more challenging to teach (empathizing with group members). Studies are needed that examine the impact of training group leaders in diverse settings, such as the military, health fields, and organizations.

SUGGESTED READINGS

Barlow, S. (2013). *Specialty competencies in group psychology*. New York, NY: Oxford University Press.

This important book describes group therapy as a specialty and reviews why groups are distinct from individual work. It also describes the unique training required of group leaders.

Burlingame, G. M., McClendon, D. T., & Yang, C. (2018). Cohesion in group therapy: A meta-analysis. *Psychotherapy, 55*, 384–398. http://dx.doi.org/10.1037/pst0000173

This is an excellent review of the group therapy cohesion literature.

Marmarosh, C. L., Markin, R., & Spiegel, E. (2013). *Attachment in group psychotherapy*. Washington, DC: American Psychological Association.

This book reviews attachment theory and the ways in which group leader and group member personalities influence group cohesion, group process, and outcome.

REFERENCES

Alonso, J. T. (2011). *Cohesion's relationship to outcome in group psychotherapy: A meta-analytic review of empirical research* (Doctoral dissertation). Brigham Young University, Provo, UT.

Bakali, J. V., Baldwin, S. A., & Lorentzen, S. (2009). Modeling group process constructs at three stages in group psychotherapy. *Psychotherapy Research, 19*, 332–343. http://dx.doi.org/10.1080/10503300902894430

Barlow, S. (2013). *Specialty competencies in group psychology.* New York, NY: Oxford University Press.

Bernard, H., Burlingame, G., Flores, P., Greene, L., Joyce, A., Kobos, J. C., . . . Feirman, D. (2008). Clinical practice guidelines for group psychotherapy. *International Journal of Group Psychotherapy, 58*, 455–542. http://dx.doi.org/10.1521/ijgp.2008.58.4.455

Berson, Y., Dan, O., & Yammarino, F. J. (2006). Attachment style and individual differences in leadership perceptions and emergence. *The Journal of Social Psychology, 146*, 165–182. http://dx.doi.org/10.3200/SOCP.146.2.165-182

Bliese, P. D., & Halverson, R. R. (1996). Individual and nomothetic models of job stress: An examination of work hours, cohesion, and well-being. *Journal of Applied Social Psychology, 26*, 1171–1189. http://dx.doi.org/10.1111/j.1559-1816.1996.tb02291.x

Braaten, L. J. (1989). Predicting positive goal attainment and symptom reduction from early group climate dimensions. *International Journal of Group Psychotherapy, 39*, 377–387.

Brawley, L. R., Carron, A. V., & Widmeyer, W. N. (1987). Assessing the cohesion of teams: Validity of the Group Environment Questionnaire. *Journal of Sport Psychology, 9*, 275–294. http://dx.doi.org/10.1123/jsp.9.3.275

Budman, S. H., Soldz, S., Demby, A., Davis, M., & Merry, J. (1993). What is cohesiveness? An empirical examination. *Small Group Research, 24*, 199–216. http://dx.doi.org/10.1177/1046496493242003

Budman, S. H., Soldz, S., Demby, A., Feldstein, M., Springer, T., & Davis, M. S. (1989). Cohesion, alliance and outcome in group psychotherapy. *Psychiatry: Interpersonal and Biological Processes, 52*, 339–350. http://dx.doi.org/10.1080/00332747.1989.11024456

Burlingame, G. M., Fuhriman, A., & Johnson, J. (2001). Cohesion in group psychotherapy. *Psychotherapy, 38*, 373–379. http://dx.doi.org/10.1037/0033-3204.38.4.373

Burlingame, G. M., Fuhriman, A., & Johnson, J. (2002). Cohesion in group psychotherapy. In J. C. Norcross (Ed.), *Psychotherapy relationships that work* (pp. 71–88). New York, NY: Oxford University Press.

Burlingame, G. M., Gleave, R., Beecher, M., Griner, D., Hansen, K., & Jensen, J. (2016). *Administration and scoring manual for the Group Questionnaire—GQ.* Salt Lake City, UT: OQ Measures, Group Relationship Monitoring System LLC.

Burlingame, G. M., MacKenzie, K. R., & Strauss, B. (2004). Small group treatment: Evidence for effectiveness and mechanisms of change. In M. J. Lambert (Ed.), *Bergin and Garfield's handbook of psychotherapy and behavior change* (5th ed., pp. 647–696). New York, NY: Wiley.

Burlingame, G. M., McClendon, D. T., & Alonso, J. (2011). Cohesion in group therapy. *Psychotherapy, 48*, 34–42. http://dx.doi.org/10.1037/a0022063

Burlingame, G. M., McClendon, D. T., & Yang, C. (2018). Cohesion in group therapy: A meta-analysis. *Psychotherapy, 55*, 384–398. http://dx.doi.org/10.1037/pst0000173

Burlingame, G. M., Strauss, B., Joyce, A., MacNair-Semands, R., MacKenzie, K. R., Ogrodniczuk, J., & Taylor, S. (2006). *CORE-Battery-Revised: An assessment tool kit for promoting optimal group selection, process, and outcome.* New York, NY: American Group Psychotherapy Association.

Butler, T., & Fuhriman, A. (1983). Level of functioning and length of time in treatment variables influencing patients' therapeutic experience in group psychotherapy. *International Journal of Group Psychotherapy, 33*, 489–505. http://dx.doi.org/10.1080/00207284.1983.11491347

Carron, A. V., Widmeyer, W. N., & Brawley, L. R. (1985). The development of an instrument to assess cohesion in sport teams: The Group Environment Questionnaire. *Journal of Sport Psychology, 7*, 244–266. http://dx.doi.org/10.1123/jsp.7.3.244

Chen, E. C., & Mallinckrodt, B. (2002). Attachment, group attraction and self-other agreement in interpersonal circumplex problems and perceptions of group members. *Group Dynamics: Theory, Research, and Practice, 6,* 311–324. http://dx.doi.org/10.1037/1089-2699.6.4.311

Davidovitz, R., Mikulincer, M., Shaver, P. R., Izsak, R., & Popper, M. (2007). Leaders as attachment figures: Leaders' attachment orientations predict leadership-related mental representations and followers' performance and mental health. *Journal of Personality and Social Psychology, 93,* 632–650. http://dx.doi.org/10.1037/0022-3514.93.4.632

DeLucia-Waack, J. (2011). Diversity in groups. In R. K. Conyne (Ed.), *The Oxford handbook of group counseling* (pp. 83–101). New York, NY: Oxford University Press. 10.1093/oxfordhb/9780195394450.013.0006

Dion, K. L. (2000). Group cohesion: From "field of forces" to multidimensional construct. *Group Dynamics: Theory, Research, and Practice, 4,* 7–26. http://dx.doi.org/10.1037/1089-2699.4.1.7

Etringer, B. D., Gregory, V. R., & Lando, H. A. (1984). Influence of group cohesion on the behavioral treatment of smoking. *Journal of Consulting and Clinical Psychology, 52,* 1080–1086. http://dx.doi.org/10.1037/0022-006X.52.6.1080

Evans, N. J., & Jarvis, P. A. (1980). Group cohesion. *Small Group Behavior, 11,* 359–370. http://dx.doi.org/10.1177/104649648001100401

Festinger, L., Schachter, S., & Back, K. (1950). *Social pressures in informal groups.* New York, NY: Hayes. http://dx.doi.org/10.2307/3707362

Gallagher, M. E., Tasca, G. A., Ritchie, K., Balfour, L., & Bissada, H. (2014). Attachment anxiety moderates the relationship between growth in group cohesion and treatment outcomes in Group Psychodynamic Interpersonal Psychotherapy for women with binge eating disorder. *Group Dynamics: Theory, Research, and Practice, 18,* 38–52. http://dx.doi.org/10.1037/a0034760

Gillaspy, J., Wright, A., Campbell, C., Stokes, S., & Adinoff, B. (2002). Group alliance and cohesion as predictors of drug and alcohol abuse treatment outcomes. *Psychotherapy Research, 12,* 213–229. http://dx.doi.org/10.1093/ptr/12.2.213

Goodwin, G. F., Blacksmith, N., & Coats, M. R. (2018). The science of teams in the military: Contributions from over 60 years of research. *American Psychologist, 73,* 322–333. http://dx.doi.org/10.1037/amp0000259

Greene-Shortridge, T. M., Britt, T. W., & Castro, C. A. (2007). The stigma of mental health problems in the military. *Military Medicine, 172,* 157–161. http://dx.doi.org/10.7205/MILMED.172.2.157

Hand, I., Lamontagne, Y., & Marks, I. M. (1974). Group exposure (flooding) in vivo for agoraphobics. *The British Journal of Psychiatry, 124,* 588–602. http://dx.doi.org/10.1192/bjp.124.6.588

Harrison, D. A., Price, K. H., & Bell, M. P. (1998). Beyond relational demography: Time and the effects of surface- and deep-level diversity on work group cohesion. *Academy of Management Journal, 41,* 96–107. http://dx.doi.org/10.5465/256901

Harrison, D. A., Price, K. H., Gavin, J. H., & Florey, A. T. (2002). Time, teams, and task performance: Changing effects of surface and deep-level diversity on group functioning. *Academy of Management Journal, 45,* 1029–1045. http://dx.doi.org/10.5465/3069328

Hartmann, J. (1981). Group cohesion and the regulation of self-esteem. In H. Kellerman (Ed.), *Group cohesion: Theoretical and clinical perspectives* (pp. 255–267). New York, NY: Grune & Stratton.

Hilbert, A., Saelens, B. E., Stein, R. I., Mockus, D. S., Welch, R. R., Matt, G. E., & Wilfley, D. E. (2007). Pretreatment and process predictors of outcome in interpersonal and cognitive behavioral psychotherapy for binge eating disorder. *Journal of Consulting and Clinical Psychology, 75,* 645–651. http://dx.doi.org/10.1037/0022-006X.75.4.645

Hogg, M. A. (1992). *The social psychology of group cohesiveness: From attraction to social identity.* New York, NY: New York University Press.

Hudson, D. L. (2013). Attachment theory and leader–follower relationships. *The Psychologist-Manager Journal, 16,* 147–159. http://dx.doi.org/10.1037/mgr0000003

Illing, V., Tasca, G. A., Balfour, L., & Bissada, H. (2011). Attachment dimensions and group climate growth in a sample of women seeking treatment for eating disorders. *Psychiatry: Interpersonal and Biological Processes, 74,* 255–269. http://dx.doi.org/10.1521/psyc.2011.74.3.255

Janis, R. A., Burlingame, G. M., & Olsen, J. A. (2018). Developing a therapeutic relationship monitoring system for group treatment. *Psychotherapy, 55,* 105–115. http://dx.doi.org/10.1037/pst0000139

Johnson, J. E., Burlingame, G. M., Olsen, J. A., Davies, D. R., & Gleave, R. L. (2005). Group climate, cohesion, alliance, and empathy in group psychotherapy: Multilevel structural equation models. *Journal of Counseling Psychology, 52,* 310–321. http://dx.doi.org/10.1037/0022-0167.52.3.310

Joyce, A. S., Piper, W. E., & Ogrodniczuk, J. S. (2007). Therapeutic alliance and cohesion variables as predictors of outcome in short-term group psychotherapy. *International Journal of Group Psychotherapy, 57,* 269–296. http://dx.doi.org/10.1521/ijgp.2007.57.3.269

Karau, S. J., & Hart, J. W. (1998). Group cohesiveness and social loafing: Effects of a social interaction manipulation on individual motivation within groups. *Group Dynamics: Theory, Research, and Practice, 2,* 185–191. http://dx.doi.org/10.1037/1089-2699.2.3.185

Kipnes, D. R., Piper, W. E., & Joyce, A. S. (2002). Cohesion and outcome in short-term psychodynamic groups for complicated grief. *International Journal of Group Psychotherapy, 52,* 483–509. http://dx.doi.org/10.1521/ijgp.52.4.483.45525

Kivlighan, D. M., Jr., Lo Coco, G., & Gullo, S. (2012). Attachment anxiety and avoidance and perceptions of group climate: An actor–partner interdependence analysis. *Journal of Counseling Psychology, 59,* 518–527. http://dx.doi.org/10.1037/a0030173

Kozlowski, S. W. J., & Chao, G. T. (2012). The Dynamics of emergence: Cognition and cohesion in work teams. *Managerial and Decision Economics, 33,* 335–354. http://dx.doi.org/10.1002/mde.2552

Kuoppala, J., Lamminpää, A., Liira, J., & Vainio, H. (2008). Leadership, job well-being, and health effects—A systematic review and a meta-analysis. *Journal of Occupational and Environmental Medicine, 50,* 904–915. http://dx.doi.org/10.1097/JOM.0b013e31817e918d

Lau, D. C., & Murnighan, J. K. (1998). Demographic diversity and faultlines: The compositional dynamics of organizational groups. *Academy of Management Review, 23,* 325–340. http://dx.doi.org/10.5465/amr.1998.533229

Lese, K. P., & MacNair-Semands, R. (2000). The Therapeutic Factors Inventory: Development of a scale. *Group, 24,* 303–317. http://dx.doi.org/10.1023/A:1026616626780

Lewin, K. (1947). Frontiers in group dynamics: Concept, method, and reality in social science, social equilibria and social changes. *Human Relations, 1,* 5–41. http://dx.doi.org/10.1177/001872674700100103

MacNair-Semands, R. R. (2002). Predicting attendance and expectations for group therapy. *Group Dynamics, 6,* 219–228. http://dx.doi.org/10.1037/1089-2699.6.3.219

Marmarosh, C. L., Markin, R., & Spiegel, E. (2013). *Attachment in group psychotherapy.* Washington, DC: American Psychological Association. http://dx.doi.org/10.1037/14186-000

Marmarosh, C. L., & Van Horn, S. M. (2011). Cohesion in counseling and psychotherapy groups. In R. K. Conyne (Ed.), *The Oxford handbook of group counseling* (pp. 137–163). New York, NY: Oxford University Press. http://dx.doi.org/10.1093/oxfordhb/9780195394450.013.0009

Marziali, E., Munroe-Blum, H., & McCleary, L. (1997). The contribution of group cohesion and group alliance to the outcome of group psychotherapy. *International Journal of Group Psychotherapy, 47*, 475–497. http://dx.doi.org/10.1080/00207284. 1997.11490846

Mikulincer, M., & Shaver, P. R. (2007). *Attachment in adulthood: Structure, dynamics, and change.* New York, NY: Guilford Press.

Mikulincer, M., & Shaver, P. R. (2016). *Attachment in adulthood: Structure, dynamics, and change* (2nd ed.). New York, NY: Guilford Press.

Miles, M. (1953). Human relations training: How a group grows. *Teachers College Record, 55*, 90–96.

Ogrodniczuk, J. S., Piper, W. E., & Joyce, A. S. (2006). Treatment compliance among patients with personality disorders receiving group psychotherapy: What are the roles of interpersonal distress and cohesion? *Psychiatry: Interpersonal and Biological Processes, 69*, 249–261. http://dx.doi.org/10.1521/psyc.2006.69.3.249

O'Reilly, C. A., III, Caldwell, D. F., & Barnett, W. P. (1989). Work group demography, social integration, and turnover. *Administrative Science Quarterly, 34*, 21–37. http://dx.doi.org/10.2307/2392984

Piper, W. E., Marrache, M., Lacroix, R., Richardsen, A. M., & Jones, B. D. (1983). Cohesion as a basic bond in groups. *Human Relations, 36*, 93–108. http://dx.doi.org/10.1177/001872678303600201

Puck, J. F., Neyer, A. K., & Dennerlein, T. (2010). Diversity and conflict in teams: A contingency perspective. *European Journal of International Management, 4*, 417–439. http://dx.doi.org/10.1504/EJIM.2010.033610

Revicki, D. A., & Gershon, R. R. M. (1996). Work-related stress and psychological distress in emergency medical technicians. *Journal of Occupational Health Psychology, 1*, 391–396. http://dx.doi.org/10.1037/1076-8998.1.4.391

Robbins, R. N. (2003). Developing cohesion in court-mandated group treatment of male spouse abusers. *International Journal of Group Psychotherapy, 53*, 261–284. http://dx.doi.org/10.1521/ijgp.53.3.261.42827

Roether, H. A., & Peters, J. J. (1972). Cohesiveness and hostility in group psychotherapy. *The American Journal of Psychiatry, 128*, 1014–1017. http://dx.doi.org/10.1176/ajp.128.8.1014

Rom, E., & Mikulincer, M. (2003). Attachment theory and group processes: The association between attachment style and group-related representations, goals, memories, and functioning. *Journal of Personality and Social Psychology, 84*, 1220–1235. http://dx.doi.org/10.1037/0022-3514.84.6.1220

Schauenburg, H., Sammet, I., Rabung, S., & Strack, M. (2001). Zur differentiellen bedeutung des gruppenerlebens in der stationaren psychotherapie depressiver patienten [On the differential importance of group experience in inpatient psychotherapy of depressive patients]. *Gruppenpsychotherapie und Gruppendynamik, 37*, 349–364.

Shechtman, Z., & Dvir, V. (2006). Attachment style as a predictor of behavior in group counseling with preadolescents. *Group Dynamics, 10*, 29–42. http://dx.doi.org/10.1037/1089-2699.10.1.29

Skakon, J., Nielsen, K., Borg, V., & Guzman, J. (2010). Are leaders' well-being, behaviours and style associated with the affective well-being of their employees? A systematic review of three decades of research. *Work & Stress, 24*, 107–139. http://dx.doi.org/10.1080/02678373.2010.495262

Smokowski, P. R., Rose, S., Todar, K., & Reardon, K. (1999). Postgroup-casualty status, group events, and leader behavior: An early look into the dynamics of damaging group experiences. *Research on Social Work Practice, 9*, 555–574. http://dx.doi.org/10.1177/104973159900900503

Taft, C. T., Murphy, C. M., King, D. W., Musser, P. H., & DeDeyn, J. M. (2003). Process and treatment adherence factors in group cognitive-behavioral therapy for partner violent men. *Journal of Consulting and Clinical Psychology, 71,* 812–820. http://dx.doi.org/10.1037/0022-006X.71.4.812

Tasca, G. A., Ritchie, K., Conrad, G., Balfour, L., Gayton, J., Lybanon, V., & Bissada, H. (2006). Attachment scales predict outcome in a randomized controlled trial of two group therapies for binge eating disorder: An aptitude by treatment interaction. *Psychotherapy Research, 16,* 106–121. http://dx.doi.org/10.1080/10503300500090928

Tasca, G. A., Taylor, D., Ritchie, K., & Balfour, L. (2004). Attachment predicts treatment completion in an eating disorders partial hospital program among women with anorexia nervosa. *Journal of Personality Assessment, 83,* 201–212. http://dx.doi.org/10.1207/s15327752jpa8303_04

Tschuschke, V., & Dies, R. R. (1994). Intensive analysis of therapeutic factors and outcome in long-term inpatient groups. *International Journal of Group Psychotherapy, 44,* 185–208. http://dx.doi.org/10.1080/00207284.1994.11490742

Whealin, J. M., Batzer, W. B., Morgan, C. A., III, Detwiler, H. F., Jr., Schnurr, P. P., & Friedman, M. J. (2007). Cohesion, burnout, and past trauma in tri-service medical and support personnel. *Military Medicine, 172,* 266–272. http://dx.doi.org/10.7205/MILMED.172.3.266

Woody, S. R., & Adessky, R. S. (2002). Therapeutic alliance, group cohesion, and homework compliance during cognitive-behavioral group treatment of social phobia. *Behavior Therapy, 33,* 5–27. http://dx.doi.org/10.1016/S0005-7894(02)80003-X

Yalom, I. D., & Leszcz, M. (2005). *The theory and practice of group psychotherapy* (5th ed.). New York, NY: Basic Books.

10

Mutual Influence in Group Psychotherapy

A Review and Application to Group Psychology

D. Martin Kivlighan, III, and Rayna C. Narvaez

The mutual influence of group members has long been theorized to be an important phenomenon in group therapy (Yalom & Leszcz, 2005). Indeed, Yalom and Leszcz (2005) posited that "it is the *group* that is the agent of change" (p. 120; emphasis added) and explicitly noted the importance of group members influencing one another. Other scholars have similarly noted the importance of mutual influence in effective group treatments (Kenny & Judd, 1986; Kenny, Mannetti, Pierro, Livi, & Kashy, 2002). Conceptually, several therapeutic factors, such as vicarious learning, installation of hope, and cohesion, inherently involve mutual influence. Additional processes in group therapy, such as maladaptive and adaptive spirals, are also achieved through the mutual influence of group members. Given theoretical and conceptual writings of the importance of mutual influence in group therapy, it is not surprising that group therapy researchers have sought to understand the complex ways in which group members influence one another. These efforts have led to important findings regarding the influence of the group on individual members and advancements in the field of group psychotherapy. Not unlike the group therapy literature, the group psychology literature notes the importance of mutual influence, and many theories of communication, participation, decision making, and others rest on the notion of mutual influence; however, with some notable exceptions (see Ervin & Bonito, 2014), there has been less attention paid to mutual influence in experimental group research.

http://dx.doi.org/10.1037/0000201-011
The Psychology of Groups: The Intersection of Social Psychology and Psychotherapy Research,
C. D. Parks and G. A. Tasca (Editors)

In this chapter, we define the phenomenon of mutual influence in group therapy, review the extant literature that has tested the mutual influence of group members in therapy groups, and extend this research to the group psychology literature. Specifically, we review group psychotherapy studies that apply Kashy and Kenny's (2000) actor–partner interdependence model (APIM) to test the mutual influence of group therapy members, identify limitations and future directions for studying mutual influence, and provide direction and practical examples for the application of mutual influence theory and research methods within the field of group psychology.

MUTUAL INFLUENCE DEFINED

The dynamic interplay between members of therapy groups is often referred to as group-to-individual or individual-to-group influence, hereafter referred to as mutual influence, and has been shown to be an important factor in group treatment outcomes (Kivlighan III, Paquin, Hsu, & Wang, 2016; Lo Coco, Gullo, Oieni, et al., 2016; Paquin, Kivlighan, & Drogosz, 2013). Kenny (1996) defined *mutual influence* as reciprocal causation between individuals of a dyad or group. Moreover, Kenny et al. (2002) delineated two dimensions of mutual influence: direct and indirect. *Direct* influence occurs when an individual influences the same aspect within another individual. For example, an individual group member self-disclosing may positively influence the other members to self-disclose. *Indirect* influence occurs when an aspect of one member affects a different aspect in another member. As an example, an individual member's sense of group cohesion may be negatively influenced by the other member's frequent absences.

There are both conceptual and statistical issues regarding the mutual influence of group members. Conceptually, interpersonal group theory suggests that group treatments are effective to the degree to which members positively and mutually influence the perceptions, behaviors, and ultimately the outcomes of one another. As noted earlier, Yalom and Leszcz (2005) proposed several therapeutic factors that inherently involve the mutual influence of therapy group members. For example, vicarious learning can only occur in the presence of others, whereas installation of hope is commonly activated when a group member witnesses other group members improving. For instance, Yalom and Leszcz (2005) noted: "[We] have often heard clients remark at the end of their group therapy how important it was for them to have observed the improvement of others [in their own group]" (p. 5).

Probably the best evidence of the other group members' effect on a group member's outcome comes from meta-analyses of the relationship between group cohesion and outcome. Group cohesion inherently involves both the group member and the other group members. In one of the most comprehensive meta-analyses of the cohesion–outcome relationship in group therapy, Burlingame, McClendon, and Yang (2018) found a robust relationship between cohesion and treatment outcome ($r = 0.25$).

Maladaptive and adaptive spirals, based on Yalom and Leszcz's (2005) interpersonal theory, similarly occur through the phenomenon of mutual influence in therapy groups. A maladaptive spiral entails the maintenance of psychological symptoms through interpersonal distortions about the self and others. It is theorized that group members are likely to be ensnared in some type of maladaptive spiral at the time of seeking help (Yalom & Leszcz, 2005). Therefore, fostering a group member's engagement in an adaptive spiral is either an implicit or explicit goal of most group therapies. In an adaptive spiral, a group member's "interpersonal distortions diminish and her or his ability to form rewarding relationships is enhanced. Social anxiety decreases; self-esteem rises; the need for self-concealment decreases" (Yalom & Leszcz, 2005, p. 49). Furthermore, it is posited that "others respond positively to this behavior and show more approval and acceptance of the patient, which further increases self-esteem and encourages further change" (Yalom & Leszcz, 2005, p. 49). Therefore, the therapeutic progress of the other members of a group influences an individual group member's own progress and vice versa. Together, it makes sense that if group members mutually influence one another to engage in desirable behaviors and processes, therapy groups will prove effective.

In addition to the conceptual and theoretical importance of mutual influence, there are several statistical issues to consider when studying mutual influence. Primarily, data from small groups are interdependent. Kenny et al. (2002) defined interdependence of observations in groups as the positive or negative correlation between group member observations; it represents the extent to which members within a group are more similar or dissimilar in comparison with members within other groups. Nonindependence violates the assumption of many statistical models (e.g., analysis of variance and regression), which, if unaccounted for, results in biased standard errors and estimates (Baldwin, Murray, & Shadish, 2005; Kenny et al., 2002). Although an in-depth discussion of the statistical analysis of nonindependent data is beyond the scope of this chapter, it is important to note that mutual influence is a common source of nonindependence (Kenny & Judd, 1986) and, as such, specific methods are needed for analyzing the mutual influence of group therapy members. Given the conceptual importance of mutual influence in group therapy and the statistical problems inherent to analyzing nonindependent data from therapy groups, researchers have suggested several appropriate methods for analyzing mutual influence processes. One such method is Kashy and Kenny's (2000) APIM.

ACTOR–PARTNER INTERDEPENDENCE MODEL

Although there are a variety of methods to study mutual influence (e.g., social relations model [SRM], intraclass correlation coefficient, the APIM), we focus on the APIM, as this method provides insight into how to model simultaneous mutual influence; additionally, it is the most commonly applied method to study mutual influence in group psychotherapy research. Although this chapter focuses on the application of the APIM in a group therapy context, it should be noted that this method was originally developed and applied to basic group research outside of a clinical context. However, we believe that the advances made within the group therapy literature regarding the modeling of mutual influence provide insights into mutual influence theory and research for basic group researchers.

Kashy and Kenny (2000) originally developed the APIM to examine the effects of partners in a dyadic relationship (e.g., parent and child, intimate partners). In addition to dyadic data, Kashy and Kenny propose the use of the APIM for small group data to model the effect of both the individual group member (i.e., actor effect) and the other group members (i.e., partner effect) on an individual group member. Conceptually, an actor effect represents the association between various cognitive, affective, and/or behavioral phenomena within an individual. In contrast, a partner effect represents changes in an individual's cognitions, affect, and/or behaviors as a function of the other members of their group.

The APIM addresses methodological and statistical concerns inherent in analyzing dependent small group data. Commonly, multilevel approaches are used to analyze mutual influence. Multilevel modeling is a complex form of ordinary least squares regression that models relationships within and between hierarchical data (Woltman, Feldstain, MacKay, & Rocchi, 2012). Typically, small group data consist of two-level nested data, wherein group members at Level 1 are nested within therapy groups at Level 2. One method for modeling mutual influence is to enter the group mean at Level 2 to predict individual scores at Level 1 (Bryk & Raudenbush, 1992). In an APIM, however, rather than using the group-as-a-whole mean as a Level 2 predictor, partner scores, which represent the group mean excluding the focal individual group member, are entered for each participant at Level 1. This modified group mean (which is unique to each individual) is then entered as a Level 1 predictor (i.e., partner effect) in a multilevel model (Kenny et al., 2002). The APIM is a more appropriate method for examining mutual influence because, in this method, the focal group member is not accounted for twice, resulting in a method that more accurately accounts for the dependency of small group data when calculating group-level variables.

APPLICATION OF THE APIM TO STUDY MUTUAL INFLUENCE

Given the conceptual and statistical strengths of the APIM, group therapy researchers have utilized this method to study the mutual influence of group members. To date, 15 studies have applied the APIM to examine actor and partner effects across a variety of variables, such as the alliance (Gullo et al., 2014), absences (Kivlighan Jr., Kivlighan, & Cole, 2012; Kivlighan Jr., Paquin, & Hsu, 2014; Paquin, Miles, & Kivlighan, 2011), treatment outcomes (Kivlighan III et al., 2016; Paquin et al., 2013), intimate behaviors (Kivlighan Jr. & Paquin, 2014; Miles, Paquin, & Kivlighan, 2011), attachment styles

(Kivlighan Jr., Lo Coco, & Gullo, 2012; Kivlighan Jr. et al., 2017; Lo Coco, Gullo, Oieni, et al., 2016), therapeutic factors (Kivlighan Jr., 2011), group relationships (Lo Coco, Gullo, Di Fratello, Giordano, & Kivlighan, 2016), and group climate (Kivlighan Jr. & Paquin, 2014; Lo Coco, Gullo, Lo Verso, & Kivlighan, 2013). Within this body of research, the APIM has been applied to group therapy data to assess reciprocal actor–partner effects, actor–partner interaction effects, and actor–partner effects longitudinally.

Applying Kenny et al.'s (2002) APIM to assess reciprocal actor–partner effects in group therapy, Kivlighan Jr., Lo Coco, and Gullo (2012) examined the association between group member attachment anxiety and avoidance and perceptions of group climate (i.e., group engagement and group conflict). Specifically, Kivlighan Jr., Lo Coco, and Gullo (2012) administered the Attachment Style Questionnaire pretreatment and the Group Climate Questionnaire (GCQ) following the third group session for 110 Italian graduate students participating in six interpersonal growth groups. The GCQ is a frequently used group psychotherapy process measure that assesses group member's perceptions of the therapeutic environment (Johnson, Burlingame, Olsen, Davies, & Gleave, 2005; Johnson et al., 2006). The GCQ is the most commonly used measure of group climate and consists of three subscales: engagement, conflict, and avoidance. Moreover, studies have found a significant association between members' perceptions of the group's climate and treatment outcome (Johnson et al., 2005; Johnson et al., 2006). Kivlighan Jr., Lo Coco, and Gullo (2012) used the APIM to model an individual group member's attachment dimension, the aggregated other group members' attachment dimension, an individual group member's perception of the group climate, and the aggregated other group members' perceptions of the group climate (Kivlighan Jr., Lo Coco, & Gullo, 2012). Specifically, path analysis was used to test the association between an individual group member's attachment dimension, the aggregated other group members' attachment dimension, an individual group member's perception of group climate, and the aggregated other group members' perceptions of group climate (Kivlighan Jr., Lo Coco, & Gullo, 2012).

Results indicated that an individual group member's attachment anxiety and avoidance were not significantly related to their perceptions of group engagement or conflict (Kivlighan Jr., Lo Coco, and Gullo, 2012). In other words, there was a nonsignificant actor effect, which means the individual group member's attachment anxiety did not have a significant impact on their perception of the group engagement or conflict. However, Kivlighan Jr., Lo Coco, and Gullo (2012) found significant actor–partner effects, such that the aggregated other group members' attachment anxiety was negatively associated with an individual group member's perception of group engagement. In other words, a group member's perceptions of the group's engagement was related to the other member's attachment anxiety. Moreover, results indicated that the aggregated other group members' attachment anxiety was positively associated with an individual group member's perception of group conflict; when other members' aggregated attachment anxiety was higher, the individual focal member (i.e., actor) endorsed higher group conflict. Lastly, Kivlighan Jr., Lo Coco, and Gullo found that the aggregated other group members' attachment avoidance was positively associated with an individual group member's perception of group conflict. Put simply, there were significant actor–partner effects, suggesting that the other group members' attachment significantly influenced an individual's perception of group climate. When other group members' aggregated attachment anxiety was high, the individual focal member perceived higher group conflict and lower group engagement (see Chapter 8, this volume, for more on attachment and group therapy). These results suggest that the behaviors and perceptions of the other group members can significantly impact individual members.

Group therapy researchers have also applied the APIM to assess actor–partner interaction effects. For example, Kivlighan Jr., Kivlighan, and Cole (2012) used Kenny et al.'s (2002) APIM to assess the effect of previous group absences on the probability of a group member being absent in the subsequent session. Specifically, Kivlighan Jr., Kivlighan, and Cole modeled time as a time-varying covariate to assess the relationship between an individual group member's previous absences (actor effect), the other group members' previous absences (partner effect), and the interaction between an individual group member's previous absences and the other group members' previous absences (actor–partner interaction effect) on the probability of an individual group member being absent in the following session. In other words, Kivlighan Jr., Kivlighan, and Cole (2012) tested the effect of both an individual member's absence history and the absence history of the other group members on the likelihood of the individual group member being absent in the subsequent session. As hypothesized, a group member's probability of attending the next session was significantly predicted by the group member's own previous absences (actor effect), the other group members' previous absences (partner effect), and the interaction between an individual group member's commitment to the group (i.e., the individual group member's previous absences) and the absence norms of the group (i.e., the other group members' previous absences). Despite previous research that assumes a uniform influence of group norms on an individual, Kivlighan Jr., Kivlighan, and Cole (2012) found a significant interaction, which suggests that group absence norms differentially affect an individual based on their commitment to the group. Therefore, rather than all members being equally influenced by absence norms, these results showed evidence of differential impact on individual group members based on their own individual behaviors. This study suggests that, not only are individuals influenced by the behaviors of the group, but that this influence can vary as a function of the individual's own behavior. In this example, an individual's history of absences interacted with the group's absence norms to predict whether the individual member would be absent in the following session.

Lastly, a handful of studies have used the APIM to test mutual influence over time. For example, Gullo et al. (2014) used a time-lagged APIM to examine the relationship between the other group members' perceptions of the working alliance to the group as a whole in a previous session, as well as an individual group member's perception of the alliance to the group as a whole in a subsequent session. This time-lagged design examined the relationship between early ratings of the working alliance, in this case, and alliance to the group in later sessions. Gullo et al. analyzed data from 73 patients diagnosed as overweight or obese who participated in 10 short-term, therapeutic weight-management groups. As hypothesized, the other group members' (partner) earlier perceptions of the alliance to the group were positively and significantly related to an individual group member's (actor) perception of the alliance to the group in a later session. Moreover, this relationship was stronger for group members who experienced more change, as measured by the Outcome Questionnaire-45, and nonsignificant for members who experienced more posttreatment symptoms (Gullo et al., 2014). In other words, the other group members' perceptions of the alliance in early sessions were related to an individual's perceptions of the alliance at later sessions, and this group-to-individual influence was stronger for members who experienced more change. These results suggest that individual group member's perceptions of the alliance to the group is influenced by the other group members, and that this group-to-individual influence may be important for members to benefit from the group. This study illustrates how group researchers can use a time-lagged APIM to empirically test predictive actor–partner relationships and provides evidence of the importance of group member influence in effective therapy groups.

KEY UNRESOLVED QUESTIONS AND FUTURE DIRECTIONS

As illustrated above, the APIM is an effective method for assessing mutual influence in group therapy. A primary finding across the majority of studies in this body of literature is the significant impact of the other group members on an individual member. Despite the conceptual and statistical advantages of the APIM to study mutual influence, there are several key unresolved issues to consider. Primarily, issues regarding the assumption of equal influence, dynamic versus static influence, and congruent and discrepant actor–partner effects need further attention.

One primary assumption of Kashy and Kenny's (2000) APIM is the notion that all members are equally influential, yet as Kenny et al. (2002) noted, "not all members of groups are created equal" (p. 135). Some group members may have higher status within the group and, therefore, they may be more influential on the group. In the same vein, there may also be individual differences in how easily influenced some people are. Kenny et al. provided guidance and formulas for calculating a weighted average based on member status in order to operationalize member influence. Unfortunately, none of the aforementioned APIM studies in our review considered weighting member status or individual differences in the analysis of mutual influence. Moving forward, researchers should further consider these individual differences when studying actor and partner effects.

In addition to the methods proposed by Kenny et al. (2002) for conceptualizing status and influence, researchers could utilize round robin designs and apply social network theory to formally operationalize members' influence and prestige. Social network theory conceptualizes individuals' prestige and influence within a network as in-degree centrality and out-degree centrality, respectively. When data are collected on every member of a group from every member's perspective, members' influence (i.e., out-degree centrality) and prestige (i.e., in-degree centrality) can be calculated and used to weight actor and partner effects. Utilizing the methods proposed by Kenny et al. or applying social network concepts to APIMs of mutual influence will allow researchers to further understand the nuanced ways in which individual-to-group and group-to-individual influence occur. Moreover, social network analysis allows researchers to create visual representations of the connections and influence between members of a group, which represents a unique and innovative aspect of this analytic method. Unfortunately, since the introduction of social network analysis as a viable method in counseling research (Koehly & Shivy, 1998), to our knowledge no study has utilized this approach to study the mutual influence or social network within therapy groups.

A second limitation of the aforementioned APIM literature is the lack of attention to mutual influence as a dynamic phenomenon. Although the majority of APIM studies either assessed actor and partner effects at the session level (Kivlighan Jr., 2011; Kivlighan Jr. & Paquin, 2014; Kivlighan Jr., Paquin, & Hsu, 2014; Miles, Paquin, & Kivlighan, 2011) or applied a time-lagged design (Gullo et al., 2014; Kivlighan Jr., Kivlighan, & Cole, 2012; Paquin, Miles, & Kivlighan, 2011), only two studies considered mutual influence over the course of group development (Lo Coco, Gullo, Di Fratello, et al., 2016; Lo Coco, Gullo, Oieni, et al., 2016). Specifically, Lo Coco, Gullo, Di Fratello, et al. (2016) and Lo Coco, Gullo, Oieni, et al. (2016) examined actor and partner effects early and late in group and provide evidence that the mutual influence of the group significantly varies across stages of group development. For example, Lo Coco, Gullo, Oieni, and colleagues (2016) found that the relationship between an individual group member's attachment and their perceptions of the group climate was stable across time, however, the relationship between the other group members' attachment and perceptions of group climate significantly changed over time. Although the APIM does not directly specify time, we recommend researchers assess actor and partner effects longitudinally, including a time covariate as well as an interaction between the actor and partner terms and the time-covariate variable in models of mutual influence. In this way, researchers are able to move beyond cross-sectional analyses of mutual influence and are better able to understand how mutual influence may change over time. For example, it may be that the other group member's self-disclosure may differentially impact an individual member's perception of group cohesion over the course of the group. Given developmental theories that suggest different processes are more or less important given stages of group development, it makes conceptual sense that the group may be more or less influential at various stages of group development.

Third, the majority of APIM studies examining mutual influence in group therapy have only considered actor and partner main effects, as opposed to the interaction between actor and partner effects. Utilizing polynomial regression and response surface analysis (RSA) would allow researchers to move beyond examining actor–partner main effects, and further understand how the congruence or discrepancy in actor–partner effects influence members' outcomes. Recently, Kivlighan Jr. et al. (2017) applied multilevel polynomial regression and RSA to an APIM of group members' attachment styles and group relationships. Specifically, Kivlighan Jr. and colleagues examined the effect of an individual member's attachment anxiety and avoidance (i.e., actor effect) and the other group members' aggregated attachment anxiety and avoidance (i.e., partner effect) on an individual member's perceptions of positive bonding, positive working relationships, and negative working relationships within therapy groups. They utilized polynomial regression and RSA to test the congruence and discrepancy between an individual's attachment anxiety and avoidance and the other group members' attachment anxiety and avoidance on members' perceptions of group relationships. In other words, they were interested in examining the effect of congruent and high levels, congruent and low levels, and discrepant high–low and low–high levels of an individual's attachment and the other group members' attachment on an individual's perceptions of group relationships. Results indicated that the congruence and discrepancy in actor and partner effects matters, and that relatively congruent and discrepant levels of actor and partner effects are related to various dimensions of group relationships. For example, when an individual member's attachment anxiety was low and the other group member's attachment anxiety was high, that individual group member reported low negative and high positive bonding relationships. As opposed to testing the relative importance of either an actor or partner effect, polynomial regression and RSA allows researchers to examine the interaction between actor and partner effects.

Although the APIM is an effective method for assessing mutual influence in small groups, the aforementioned limitations should be considered in order to advance research on mutual influence. Examining individual differences in APIM studies, mutual influence over the life of groups and the congruence and discrepancy in actor–partner effects may prove beneficial in further understanding the nuanced and complex ways in which group members undoubtedly influence one another.

IMPLICATIONS FOR GROUP PSYCHOLOGY RESEARCH

Whereas group psychotherapy researchers have used the APIM to study mutual influence within therapy groups, group psychologists may similarly benefit from the application of the APIM to study mutual influence within experimental groups. Many social and organizational psychology theories directly involve the mutual influence of group members, such as conformity, motivation, social contagion, social loafing, conflict management, and others. The APIM is an effective method to test and refine such theories of mutual influence within the field of group psychology. In fact, a recent review of partner effects outside the group psychotherapy literature (Ervin & Bonito, 2014) identified four studies that utilized the APIM to operationalize group effects and test mutual influence within experimental groups. For example, Pierro, Presaghi, Higgins, Klein, and Kruglanski (2012) applied the APIM to study the effect of team members' goal pursuit on work performance. Specifically, Pierro et al. tested the effect of an individual team member's and the other team members' goal pursuits on an individual member's work performance and found evidence of both actor and partner effects; both the individual's and the other group members' goal pursuit was related to an individual's work performance. In another study, Kenny and Garcia (2012) applied the APIM to test the effect of an individual group member's gender and the gender composition of the other group members on an individual member's identification with the group. Results indicated that a group member identified least with the group when he or she was different in gender from the other group members and those other members were all of the same gender (Kenny & Garcia, 2012). Similar to the group psychotherapy literature, these studies suggest the importance of the other group members on an individual member or, in other words, the importance of mutual influence in nonclinical groups.

Ervin and Bonito (2014) noted that, in general, the APIM has been applied to small decision-making and student groups, and the majority of these studies, conducted by Bonito and colleagues (Bonito, 2001, 2002, 2003, 2004; Bonito, DeCamp, Coffman, & Fleming, 2006; Bonito & Lambert, 2005), examined various aspects of participation. Moreover, it should be noted that these studies were conducted within the field of communication, which further highlights the interdisciplinary application of the APIM and importance of studying mutual influence across diverse fields and content area.

In addition to research on decision-making groups, the APIM can be utilized to test theories of mutual influence across a variety of settings, such as military groups, sports/performance groups, educational groups, intergroup dialogues. As an example, within the self-efficacy literature, it is commonly known that self-efficacy and performance are positively correlated; however, few studies have examined collective self-efficacy within classroom settings on individual students' performance. Researchers interested in understanding the relationship between a student's self-efficacy and their academic performance, as well as the effect of the other student's self-efficacy on an individual student's performance, could apply the APIM to model both actor and partner effects of self-efficacy and academic performance. In a recent and similar study, O'Neal (2018) examined individual student's grit and peer grit within classrooms and found that peer grit, not the student's individual grit, was significantly associated with the individual student's literacy achievement. This study provides meaningful insights beyond the intrapersonal implications of actor effects, highlighting the importance of group-to-individual influence in educational group settings.

The APIM could similarly be applied to military groups. Presently, there is a growing body of research that has used the APIM to study actor–partner effects within military couples (Marini, Wadsworth, Christ, & Franks, 2017; Monk & Nelson Goff, 2014; O'Neal, Lucier-Greer, Mancini, Ferraro, & Ross, 2016); however, few military group studies have utilized the APIM. In one study examining the effect of trauma symptoms on military couples' satisfaction, higher levels of trauma symptoms were related to both the individual's relationship quality (i.e., actor effect), as well as their partner's relationship quality (i.e., partner effect; Monk & Nelson Goff, 2014). Additional studies have found actor–partner effects across a variety of variables that significantly impact relationship aspects for military couples (Marini et al., 2017; O'Neal et al., 2016). Applying the APIM to military groups, researchers could similarly examine the effect of military team environments on aspects of individual's romantic relationships.

Lastly, the APIM has been applied to study dyadic processes between both athletes and coaches (Carr & Fitzpatrick, 2011; Jackson, Beauchamp, & Knapp, 2007; Nicholls & Perry, 2016); however, few studies have examined actor–partner effects in sports teams. Carr and Fitzpatrick (2011) examined athletes' attachment characteristics and the quality of dyadic sporting friendships; they found that both an individual's attachment characteristics and the attachment characteristics of their best friend significantly impacted their perception of friendship quality. In addition to this study, sports psychologists could apply the APIM to larger sports teams to understand how the behaviors and perceptions of the other team members significantly impact an individual team member. Sports psychologists could apply the APIM to test actor–partner effects for cohesion, team climate, goal orientation, and other processes, as well as individual and team outcomes.

Additionally, group psychologists could utilize the APIM to answer meaningful questions about mutual influence, such as the following:

- How might the mutual influence of motivation impact the cohesion, decision making, and performance of military units?

- How might members of organizational teams influence one another to reduce social loafing?

- What is the relationship between self- and other-disclosures on outcomes of intergroup dialogues?

- How might the attendance of the employees on a work team affect the attendance of an individual employee?

IMPLICATIONS FOR GROUP PSYCHOLOGY PRACTICE

In addition to research implications, mutual influence theory and APIM research provide meaningful implications for group psychology practice as well. Mutual influence may occur across diverse small group contexts, such as sports/performance teams, educational settings, military units. Broadly, nonclinical group leaders should be cognizant of ways in which group members influence one another in both negative and positive ways. As referenced earlier, O'Neal's (2018) study informs both individual- and group-level interventions to enhance student performance within an educational context. Given the finding that peer grit significantly influenced individual student performance, teachers should be cognizant of the potential positive effect of the class on individual student's performance. For example, findings regarding peer effects in classroom settings have direct implications for classroom composition. Teachers and administrators may want to consider the composition of classrooms regarding peer grit and other constructs at the classroom level (e.g., self-efficacy, motivation). If peer-to-individual influence occurs in classroom settings, attention to classroom composition may be important to enhance individual student performance. These considerations regarding group composition may similarly prove helpful in other small group contexts, such as performance teams and military units.

Additionally, small group leaders should work to enhance positive mutual influence between members. Leaders may benefit from identifying when mutual influence is occurring and use group interventions, such as enhancing member to member interactions to further positive mutual influence processes. Conversely, small group leaders across diverse contexts should attempt to disrupt negative peer influence when present. Group leaders may use functional subgrouping to this end and to disrupt negative influence processes as they emerge. Group leaders may also intervene at the individual level to disrupt negative mutual influence processes. For example, military unit leaders may attempt to alter negative perceptions of climate through explicitly noting influential members' positive perceptions of unit climate and positioning these members in a way that they can have more influence on the other members of the unit. Ultimately, group leaders can intervene at both the group and individual level to enhance positive mutual influence processes and disrupt negative influence.

CONCLUSION

Individual-to-group and group-to-individual influence, also referred to as mutual influence, is an underlying phenomenon of several theories within the group psychotherapy and group psychology literature. Mutual influence as a construct and the APIM as a method of statistical analysis have strong implications for the domain of experimental group psychology. Applying the APIM to group psychology may prove beneficial for researchers seeking to understand the complex ways in which members of groups influence one another. Small group researchers in social, organizational, and experimental psychology can benefit from the exploration of mutual influence with the APIM.

SUGGESTED READINGS

Ervin, J., & Bonito, J. A. (2014). A review and critique of partner effect research in small groups. *Small Group Research, 45*, 603–632. http://dx.doi.org/10.1177/1046496414551027

This article serves as a review of group effects research within group psychology. Ervin and Bonito provide an overview of group effects and define this construct for readers. The authors review three methods for analyzing group effects: (a) the SRM, (b) the APIM, and (c) a variation of the APIM (i.e., the group actor–partner interdependence model [GAPIM]); they then identify differences between these statistical approaches. The authors review studies that have applied the SRM, APIM, and GAPIM and encourage readers to utilize these methods to further test group effects within the group psychology literature.

Kenny, D. A., Mannetti, L., Pierro, A., Livi, S., & Kashy, D. A. (2002). The statistical analysis of data from small groups. *Journal of Personality and Social Psychology, 83*, 126–137. http://dx.doi.org/10.1037/0022-3514.83.1.126

This article provides a brief, but illustrative, discussion of mutual influence and the issue of nonindependence in small group research. The article also details several commonly used methods of analysis of small group data and the limitations related to those approaches. The authors recommend the APIM as an effective method for addressing the issues of nonindependence in small groups as well as provide noteworthy limitations of this method. This article provides an overview of the mathematical properties of the APIM and provides several recommendations for the application of the APIM to small group data.

REFERENCES

Baldwin, S. A., Murray, D. M., & Shadish, W. R. (2005). Empirically supported treatments or type I errors? Problems with the analysis of data from group-administered treatments. *Journal of Consulting and Clinical Psychology, 73*, 924–935. http://dx.doi.org/10.1037/0022-006X.73.5.924

Bonito, J. A. (2001). An information-processing approach to participation in small groups. *Communication Research, 28*, 275–303. http://dx.doi.org/10.1177/009365001028003002

Bonito, J. A. (2002). The analysis of participation in small groups: Methodological and conceptual issues related to interdependence. *Small Group Research, 33*, 412–438. http://dx.doi.org/10.1177/104649640203300402

Bonito, J. A. (2003). A social relations analysis of participation in small groups. *Communication Monographs, 70*, 83–97. http://dx.doi.org/10.1080/0363775032000133755

Bonito, J. A. (2004). Shared cognition and participation in small groups: Similarity of member prototypes. *Communication Research, 31,* 704–730. http://dx.doi.org/10.1177/0093650204269406

Bonito, J. A., DeCamp, M. H., Coffman, M., & Fleming, S. (2006). Participation, information, and control in small groups: An actor–partner interdependence model. *Group Dynamics: Theory, Research, and Practice, 10,* 16–28. http://dx.doi.org/10.1037/1089-2699.10.1.16

Bonito, J. A., & Lambert, B. L. (2005). Information similarity as a moderator of the effect of gender on participation in small groups: A multilevel analysis. *Small Group Research, 36,* 139–165. http://dx.doi.org/10.1177/1046496404266164

Bryk, A. S., & Raudenbush, S. W. (1992). *Hierarchical linear models.* Newbury Park, CA: Sage.

Burlingame, G. M., McClendon, D. T., & Yang, C. (2018). Cohesion in group therapy: A meta-analysis. *Psychotherapy, 55,* 384–398. http://dx.doi.org/10.1037/pst0000173

Carr, S., & Fitzpatrick, N. (2011). Experiences of dyadic sport friendships as a function of self and partner attachment characteristics. *Psychology of Sport and Exercise, 12,* 383–391. http://dx.doi.org/10.1016/j.psychsport.2011.03.003

Ervin, J., & Bonito, J. A. (2014). A review and critique of partner effect research in small groups. *Small Group Research, 45,* 603–632. http://dx.doi.org/10.1177/1046496414551027

Gullo, S., Lo Coco, G., Pazzagli, C., Piana, N., De Feo, P., Mazzeschi, C., & Kivlighan, D. M., Jr. (2014). A time-lagged, actor–partner interdependence analysis of alliance to the group as a whole and group member outcome in overweight and obesity treatment groups. *Journal of Counseling Psychology, 61,* 306–313. http://dx.doi.org/10.1037/a0036084

Jackson, B., Beauchamp, M. R., & Knapp, P. (2007). Relational efficacy beliefs in athlete dyads: An investigation using actor–partner interdependence models. *Journal of Sport & Exercise Psychology, 29,* 170–189. http://dx.doi.org/10.1123/jsep.29.2.170

Johnson, J. E., Burlingame, G. M., Olsen, J. A., Davies, D. R., & Gleave, R. L. (2005). Group climate, cohesion, alliance, and empathy in group psychotherapy: Multilevel structural equation models. *Journal of Counseling Psychology, 52,* 310–321. http://dx.doi.org/10.1037/0022-0167.52.3.310

Johnson, J. E., Pulsipher, D., Ferrin, S. L., Burlingame, G. M., Davies, D. R., & Gleave, R. (2006). Measuring group processes: A comparison of the GCQ and CCI. *Group Dynamics: Theory, Research, and Practice, 10,* 136–145. http://dx.doi.org/10.1037/1089-2699.10.2.136

Kashy, D. A., & Kenny, D. A. (2000). The analysis of data from dyads and groups. In H. T, Reis & C. M. Judd (Eds.), *Handbook of research methods in social and personality psychology* (pp. 451–477). New York, NY: Cambridge University Press.

Kenny, D. A. (1996). Models of non-independence in dyadic research. *Journal of Social and Personal Relationships, 13,* 279–294. http://dx.doi.org/10.1177/0265407596132007

Kenny, D. A., & Garcia, R. L. (2012). Using the actor–partner interdependence model to study the effects of group composition. *Small Group Research, 43,* 468–496. http://dx.doi.org/10.1177/1046496412441626

Kenny, D. A., & Judd, C. M. (1986). Consequences of violating the independence assumption in analysis of variance. *Psychological Bulletin, 99,* 422–431. http://dx.doi.org/10.1037/0033-2909.99.3.422

Kenny, D. A., Mannetti, L., Pierro, A., Livi, S., & Kashy, D. A. (2002). The statistical analysis of data from small groups. *Journal of Personality and Social Psychology, 83,* 126–137. http://dx.doi.org/10.1037/0022-3514.83.1.126

Kivlighan, D. M., Jr. (2011). Individual and group perceptions of therapeutic factors and session evaluation: An actor–partner interdependence analysis. *Group Dynamics, 15,* 147–160. http://dx.doi.org/10.1037/a0022397

Kivlighan, D. M., Jr., Kivlighan, D. M., III, & Cole, O. D. (2012). The group's absence norm and commitment to the group as predictors of group member absence in the next session: An actor–partner analysis. *Journal of Counseling Psychology, 59,* 41–49. http://dx.doi.org/10.1037/a0025506

Kivlighan, D. M., Jr., Lo Coco, G., & Gullo, S. (2012). Attachment anxiety and avoidance and perceptions of group climate: An actor–partner interdependence analysis. *Journal of Counseling Psychology, 59,* 518–527. http://dx.doi.org/10.1037/a0030173

Kivlighan, D. M., Jr., Lo Coco, G., Oieni, V., Gullo, S., Pazzagli, C., & Mazzeschi, C. (2017). All bonds are not the same: A response surface analysis of the perceptions of positive bonding relationships in therapy groups. *Group Dynamics: Theory, Research, and Practice, 21,* 159–177. http://dx.doi.org/10.1037/gdn0000071

Kivlighan, D. M., Jr., & Paquin, J. D. (2014). Whose perceptions matter more: Mine or my group's? An actor–partner interdependence analysis disaggregating between-person and between-session effects of group climate perceptions on intimate behaviors. *Journal of Counseling Psychology, 61,* 333–339. http://dx.doi.org/10.1037/cou0000025

Kivlighan, D. M., Jr., Paquin, J. D., & Hsu, Y. K. K. (2014). Is it the unexpected experience that keeps them coming back? Group climate and session attendance examined between groups, between members, and between sessions. *Journal of Counseling Psychology, 61,* 325–332. http://dx.doi.org/10.1037/cou0000022

Kivlighan, D. M., III, Paquin, J. D., Hsu, Y. K. K., & Wang, L. F. (2016). The mutual influence of therapy group members' hope and depressive symptoms. *Small Group Research, 47,* 58–76. http://dx.doi.org/10.1177/1046496415605638

Koehly, L. M., & Shivy, V. A. (1998). Social network analysis: A new methodology for counseling research. *Journal of Counseling Psychology, 45,* 3–17. http://dx.doi.org/10.1037/0022-0167.45.1.3

Lo Coco, G., Gullo, S., Di Fratello, C., Giordano, C., & Kivlighan, D. M., Jr. (2016). Group relationships in early and late sessions and improvement in interpersonal problems. *Journal of Counseling Psychology, 63,* 419–428. http://dx.doi.org/10.1037/cou0000153

Lo Coco, G., Gullo, S., Lo Verso, G., & Kivlighan, D. M., Jr. (2013). Sex composition and group climate: A group actor–partner interdependence analysis. *Group Dynamics: Theory, Research, and Practice, 17,* 270–280. http://dx.doi.org/10.1037/a0034112

Lo Coco, G., Gullo, S., Oieni, V., Giannone, F., Di Blasi, M., & Kivlighan, D. M., Jr. (2016). The relationship between attachment dimensions and perceptions of group relationships over time: An actor–partner interdependence analysis. *Group Dynamics, 20,* 276–293. http://dx.doi.org/10.1037/gdn0000056

Marini, C. M., Wadsworth, S. M., Christ, S. L., & Franks, M. M. (2017). Emotion expression, avoidance and psychological health during reintegration: A dyadic analysis of actor and partner associations within a sample of military couples. *Journal of Social and Personal Relationships, 34,* 69–90. http://dx.doi.org/10.1177/0265407515621180

Miles, J. R., Paquin, J. D., & Kivlighan, D. M., Jr. (2011). Amount and consistency, two components of group norms: An actor partner interdependence analysis of intimate behaviors in groups. *Group Dynamics, 15,* 326–342. http://dx.doi.org/10.1037/a0024676

Monk, J. K., & Nelson Goff, B. S. (2014). Military couples' trauma disclosure: Moderating between trauma symptoms and relationship quality. *Psychological Trauma: Theory, Research, Practice, and Policy, 6,* 537–545. http://dx.doi.org/10.1037/a0036788

Nicholls, A. R., & Perry, J. L. (2016). Perceptions of coach–athlete relationship are more important to coaches than athletes in predicting dyadic coping and stress appraisals: An actor–partner independence mediation model. *Frontiers in Psychology, 7,* 447. http://dx.doi.org/10.3389/fpsyg.2016.00447

O'Neal, C. R. (2018). Individual versus peer grit: Influence on later individual literacy achievement of dual language learners. *School Psychology Quarterly, 33,* 112–119. http://dx.doi.org/10.1037/spq0000212

O'Neal, C. W., Lucier-Greer, M., Mancini, J. A., Ferraro, A. J., & Ross, D. B. (2016). Family relational health, psychological resources, and health behaviors: A dyadic study of military couples. *Military Medicine, 181*, 152–160. http://dx.doi.org/10.7205/ MILMED-D-14-00740

Paquin, J. D., Kivlighan, D. M., III, & Drogosz, L. M. (2013). If you get better, will I? An actor–partner analysis of the mutual influence of group therapy outcomes. *Journal of Counseling Psychology, 60*, 171–179. http://dx.doi.org/10.1037/a0031904

Paquin, J. D., Miles, J. R., & Kivlighan, D. M. (2011). Predicting group attendance using in-session behaviors. *Small Group Research, 42*, 177–198. http://dx.doi.org/ 10.1177/1046496410389493

Pierro, A., Presaghi, F., Higgins, E. T., Klein, K. M., & Kruglanski, A. W. (2012). Frogs and ponds: A multilevel analysis of the regulatory mode complementarity hypothesis. *Personality and Social Psychology Bulletin, 38*, 269–279. http://dx.doi.org/10.1177/ 0146167211424418

Woltman, H., Feldstain, A., MacKay, J. C., & Rocchi, M. (2012). An introduction to hierarchical linear modeling. *Tutorials in Quantitative Methods for Psychology, 8*, 52–69. http://dx.doi.org/10.20982/tqmp.08.1.p052

Yalom, I. D., & Leszcz, M. (2005). *The theory and practice of group psychotherapy* (5th ed.). New York, NY: Basic Books.

11

Forgiveness and Group Therapy

Current Research and Implications for Group Psychology Research and Practice

Nathaniel G. Wade and Meredith V. Tittler

In his novel *The Schopenhauer Cure*, Yalom (2005) illustrated group psychotherapy with a fictional account that embodies much of his clinical experience. At one point in the life of the group, the fictional group therapist, Julius, sees a moment for "forgiveness" in his group. He then takes a momentary mental detour:

> Julius almost flinched when the buzzword *forgiveness* passed through his mind. Of all the recent movements swirling around the field of therapy, the hullabaloo around "forgiveness" annoyed him the most. He, like every experienced therapist, . . . had always used a wide variety of methods to help his patients "forgive"—that is, detach from their anger and resentment. (Yalom, 2005, p.179)

This likely represents the thoughts of many therapists, group or otherwise, who have also worked with scores of clients and patients struggling to let go of past hurts. So, then, is forgiveness nothing more than helping clients to "detach from their anger and resentment?" Is the "hullabaloo" around psychotherapeutic attempts to promote forgiveness unwarranted? The considerable research that has been done on forgiveness would suggest otherwise.

Although group therapists have addressed the negative experiences and pain of their group members for as long as group therapy has been conducted, explicitly helping clients to forgive their offenders has only more recently been a focus of treatment. Group treatments to explicitly promote forgiveness have been developed and tested over the last 25 years. Research has shown that these interventions are viable and effective options for individuals who

http://dx.doi.org/10.1037/0000201-012
The Psychology of Groups: The Intersection of Social Psychology and Psychotherapy Research,
C. D. Parks and G. A. Tasca (Editors)

have been hurt by others (Wade, Hoyt, Kidwell, & Worthington, 2014). In this chapter, we provide an overview of forgiveness interventions and their uses, as well as potential applications in group settings. On the basis of our review, we explore the possibility of integrating forgiveness interventions into other therapeutic and nontherapeutic group contexts.

FORGIVENESS DEFINED

Forgiveness has been defined variously in different research literatures that span from brain imaging (e.g., Ricciardi et al., 2013), to primate studies (e.g., de Waal & Pokorny, 2005), to survivors of genocide (e.g., Staub, Pearlman, Gubin, & Hagengimana, 2005). With such a broad area of investigation, forgiveness has been defined in a wide spectrum of ways. However, within the field of psychotherapy, researchers have mostly gained consensus on a working definition that goes beyond simple detachment from anger and resentment. In a meta-analysis on forgiveness and therapy, Wade, Hoyt, et al. (2014) summarized a two-part definition of forgiveness that includes "(a) the reduction in vengeful and angry thoughts, feelings, and motives [and], (b) an increase in some form of positive thoughts, feelings, and motives toward the offending person" (p. 1). Put another way, forgiveness is the process of "replacing the bitter, angry feelings of vengefulness often resulting from a hurt, with positive feelings of goodwill toward the offender" (Wade, Bailey, & Shaffer, 2005, p. 634). Other intervention researchers have provided similar definitions. For example, Enright and Fitzgibbons (2000) described forgiveness in the following way:

> People . . . forgive when they willfully abandon resentment and related responses (to which they have a right) and endeavor to respond to the wrongdoer based on the moral principle of beneficence, which may include compassion, unconditional worth, generosity, and moral love. (p. 24)

The other area of agreement that has emerged across different researchers' definitions of forgiveness is the clarification of what forgiveness expressly is *not*. Most current researchers agree that forgiveness is *not* forgetting, condoning, pardoning, or excusing the wrongdoing (Wade, Tucker, & Cornish, 2014). These researchers also assert that forgiveness is different from reconciliation. Although the two often accompany one another, and in many cases are both desired, someone might forgive without reconciling or reconcile to some degree without forgiving. Thus, the focus of this chapter is on forgiveness as an intrapersonal process that occurs following a significant hurt or offense in an interpersonal context. In this internal process people reduce their negative feelings towards offenders and experience love, compassion, or positive regard for the offending person in a capacity similar to what they may have felt prior to the offense. In addition, we will explore the interpersonal implications of such forgiveness, particularly in and through a group therapy setting.

THE REACH OF FORGIVENESS RESEARCH

Although in this chapter we focus on forgiveness research as it is applied primarily in psychotherapeutic group settings, it is important to provide an overview of the broader reach of forgiveness research. Since the 1990s, research on forgiveness has expanded dramatically. For instance, a PsycINFO search of journal articles with "forgiv*" in the title returned 36 results between the years 1890 and 1989. When that same search was performed for articles published between 1990 and 2019, it produced 1,556 results. There is virtually no subfield within psychology that has not addressed forgiveness. Research has been conducted from social, cognitive, neuropsychological, developmental, cultural, organizational, and evolutionary perspectives, in addition to applied, psychotherapeutic perspectives.

Social, organizational, and close-relationship researchers have contributed a significant amount to our understanding of forgiveness. In a widely cited meta-analysis of forgiveness research, Fehr, Gelfand, and Nag (2010) reported findings from many of these studies. For example, they reported on the association between forgiveness and relationship (a) closeness, (b) commitment, and (c) satisfaction, showing that each of these relationship factors are positively correlated with greater forgiveness for a specific offense. The current research in this area has been conducted using correlational, experimental, longitudinal, naturalistic, and randomized clinical trial designs.

Although a full accounting of the results of this research is beyond the scope of this chapter, in general, researchers have reported that forgiveness tends to be beneficial (although not always; e.g., Gordon, Burton, & Porter, 2004) for both the person doing the forgiving and for the relationship within which the offense occurred, if ongoing. Specifically, forgiveness appears to benefit physical health (e.g., Witvliet & McCullough, 2007; Worthington & Scherer, 2004), psychological well-being (e.g., Bono, McCullough, & Root, 2008), and relationship stability (e.g., Berry & Worthington, 2001). Forgiveness may be one way to increase work-team success through reducing counteractive meeting behaviors (e.g., blaming others, terminating discussions; Schulte, Lehmann-Willenbrock, & Kauffeld, 2013) and might reduce workplace burnout, particularly in human service jobs (e.g., Booth et al., 2018). Forgiveness is broadly relevant, particularly in relational and group psychological research, and there is a strong foundation upon which to build. In fact, one of the most thoroughly investigated areas of forgiveness research is psychological group interventions to promote forgiveness.

CURRENT LITERATURE ON FORGIVENESS IN GROUP THERAPY

Forgiveness, as a focus of clinical intervention, emerged in the literature in the late 1970s and mid-1980s and became more widespread in the 1990s and into the 2000s (Witvliet, 2014). Much of this work specifically addressed the development and testing of interventions designed to help people forgive others for specific offenses.

Limitations and Cautions Regarding Forgiveness in Therapy

Before exploring this research in detail, however, it is important to explore the limitations to and cautions against promoting forgiveness in a psychotherapeutic setting. Forgiveness has often been categorized as a virtue, which might help explain some of the hesitancy to research forgiveness that psychologists exhibited prior to 1990. With the rise of "positive psychology" and a renewed focus on human values and virtues, forgiveness as a research topic became more relevant. However, because forgiveness can be seen as a value that people may or may not hold, any broad statements that extol the benefits of forgiveness without a strong empirical foundation and a recognition of the ambiguities of human relationships should be viewed with skepticism. This is particularly true in any psychotherapeutic contexts, within which participants/clients/patients are often emotionally, psychologically, and even physically vulnerable. Forgiveness is certainly not universally beneficial and should never be seen as a panacea. For example, empirical evidence suggests that women in abusive romantic relationships who are more forgiving of their abusive partners have greater intentions to return to that relationship (Gordon et al., 2004) and tend to minimize the aggression more (Gilbert & Gordon, 2017). In addition, others have argued that forgiveness might undermine the energy or motivation to seek social justice among people who are marginalized or oppressed in a society (Tittler & Wade, 2019). Thus, although much of the research on forgiveness indicates that forgiveness tends to be helpful for people on a variety of outcomes, it is important to keep in mind that there may be limitations to its therapeutic utility. As a result of the potential for harm and misunderstanding, clinicians and applied researchers follow general guidelines when researching and providing forgiveness interventions.

One broad guideline that serves to protect vulnerable individuals grows out of the ethical principle of participant/client autonomy (American Psychological Association, 2017). Participant autonomy is supported in forgiveness intervention research by the practice of providing sufficient information about the intervention to participants up front to allow participants informed consent. For those who are not interested, alternative options to forgiveness are provided (e.g., coping skills, assertiveness training). Thus, clients engaging in forgiveness interventions are volunteering to participate, have specifically identified an offense they want to forgive, and are interested in achieving forgiveness or at least exploring the option. Thus, the results based on the research in the following sections should be understood within that context.

Another important guideline in this area is to highlight the differences between forgiveness, which is most often viewed as an internal process in psychotherapeutic settings, and reconciliation, which is viewed as an interpersonal process. Clients are encouraged to make the decision to forgive independent of their decision to restore the relationship with that person. For example, in situations in which a person has been hurt by an unrepentant and potentially abusive person, forgiveness as an internal process to release resentment and achieve peace might still be warranted, whereas reconciliation, or a restoration of the relationship, might not be. A third important guideline is helping people to understand the full process of forgiveness, which includes (often as the foundational step) an exploration of the emotional, relational, and other consequences of the offense. This is an accounting, and often recounting, of the harm suffered. Forgiveness is not about forgetting, condoning, or minimizing the offense and its consequences (Freedman & Enright, 1996). In fact, forgiveness can occur while still holding offenders responsible for their actions. One way of conceptualizing this has been to describe true forgiveness as a process that includes a full accounting of the harm versus pseudo-forgiveness which involves moving too quickly toward resolution (Enright, 2001; Wade, Tucker, et al., 2014). With these general understandings of forgiveness and guidelines for intervention, professionals in this area seek to protect vulnerable people while still providing opportunities for them to seek healing and growth through forgiveness.

Existing Efficacy Research: Are Group Interventions Useful?

Two main research groups have emerged as the leaders in empirical studies on forgiveness interventions. Each group developed a treatment model that can be used to facilitate forgiveness within a therapeutic setting. Enright (2001) and his colleagues developed an intervention based on four main phases consisting of multiple steps. These four phases include *Uncovering, Decision, Work,* and *Deepening.* Through these phases, therapists help clients to explore the hurt and its impact on their lives (uncovering); decide whether they want to truly work toward forgiveness (decision); engage in therapeutic activities that develop empathy for the offending person and resolve their anger and bitterness (work); and integrate their decision and resolution to forgive the offending person to make further growth in their lives (deepening).

The other leading research group is based on a model that was developed by Worthington (2006) and his colleagues, known as the REACH Forgiveness model. The name is an acronym, with each letter referring to a step in the forgiveness intervention. Recalling (R) the offense is the first step in which clients share and process the events and ramifications of the offense. They then engage in therapeutic activities designed to develop empathy (E) for the offending person. This is supported by interventions to help the clients acknowledge (A) their own failings and need for forgiveness in the past. Clients then work to make a commitment (C) to forgiveness and to hold (H) onto the forgiveness that they have achieved. Both intervention models conceptualize forgiveness as an intrapersonal process in which the individual's internal experience and feelings toward their transgressor change. Both groups specify that forgiving does not imply or require that one reconcile with the person who has transgressed against them and thus does not necessarily involve a focus on an interpersonal process.

Group Interventions to Explicitly Promote Forgiveness

Most forgiveness interventions have been implemented in a group format, with some interventions implemented individually (e.g., Freedman & Enright, 1996) and in a couples' format (e.g., Greenberg, Warwar, & Malcolm, 2010; see Wade, Hoyt, et al., 2014, for a review). The group formats are mostly psychoeducational, with some variation in how much the group focuses on education versus therapeutic interaction. There is one meta-analysis of explicit forgiveness interventions focused only on a group format (Wade, Worthington, & Meyer, 2005). Based on an analysis of 27 intervention studies, the authors reported that group interventions to promote forgiveness demonstrated clinical efficacy over no treatment and alternative treatments (i.e., groups that are not intended to explicitly promote forgiveness, such as those focused on conflict resolution or stress reduction). Furthermore, the authors reported that time spent on specific interventions was correlated with outcome. That is, in treatments intending to promote forgiveness, greater time spent helping the client build empathy for the offending person and making a commitment to forgiveness was related to greater forgiveness for a particular offense.

This meta-analysis was followed by another that updated the literature and included any forgiveness intervention regardless of modality (individual, group, or couple; Wade, Hoyt, et al., 2014). In their analyses of 54 intervention studies, the authors confirmed earlier findings that forgiveness interventions help clients to become more forgiving of those who had hurt them when compared with alternative treatments or in no treatment at all. In addition, the clients in the forgiveness treatments had a greater reduction in depression and anxiety and a greater increase in hope for the future than clients in the other conditions.

To assess the size or clinical significance of the effect, we can evaluate the reported effect sizes of forgiveness as an outcome in relation to the average duration of the treatments. In 2005, Wade and colleagues found that the average duration of the groups explicitly designed to promote forgiveness was about 9 hours ($M = 542$ minutes) and the average effect size (Cohen's d) of theoretically grounded forgiveness treatment compared with no treatment was .57, 95% CI [.51, .63], a medium effect. In 2014, Wade and colleagues found that the average duration of groups was 10 hours and the average effect size (Becker's delta) was .56, 95% CI [.43, .68], a medium effect. Furthermore, Wade, Hoyt, and colleagues (2014) reported the results of a single moderator regression analysis that provided a more specific estimate of the effect for each hour of intervention based on the intercept and slope of the analysis. Specifically, the predicted effect size was equal to 0.102 (estimate of the intercept) plus .047 (estimate of the slope) times the number of hours intervening. These two findings lead to a similar conclusion: about 18 to

20 hours of intervention (or 12–13 ninety-minute group sessions) are needed for approximately one standard deviation (*SD*) of change in forgiveness. In other words, a client receiving a 12-session forgiveness group will achieve more forgiveness than about 84% of comparable people not participating in such a group.

Individual Versus Group Therapy to Explicitly Promote Forgiveness

There is really no doubt that forgiveness interventions help people to develop greater forgiveness toward specific people who have hurt them. It also appears that these interventions help people to reduce symptoms of depression, anxiety, and even increase hope for the future. In an exploration of moderators in addition to treatment duration, Wade, Hoyt, and colleagues (2014) assessed treatment model (i.e., Enright, Worthington, or other), the severity of the offense that was the target of forgiveness, and treatment modality (i.e., group, individual, or couples). After controlling for treatment duration, treatment model and offense severity were not significant predictors of outcome. That is, all treatment theories, regardless of offense severity, produced equivalent outcomes.

In contrast, treatment modality was a significant predictor of outcome. Individual interventions were significantly more effective than group, even after controlling for treatment model, duration of treatment (individual treatments were considerably longer than group), and offense severity (individual treatments tended to address more severe offenses). However, this finding only held true when comparing forgiveness treatments with no treatment. When the forgiveness treatment was compared with an alternative treatment (i.e., an attention control or nonforgiveness specific treatment), there was no significant difference between individual and group modalities. In both comparisons, couples' treatments were equivalent to group and individual modalities.

The finding that hour-for-hour an individual modality might be more effective than a group modality is intriguing. However, none of the studies assessed in the meta-analysis conducted a direct comparison of these modalities (i.e., they focused solely on group, individual, or couples). Thus, any differences in modality observed in the meta-analysis are from cross-study comparisons, which introduces significant sources of bias that cannot be fully controlled. As Burlingame et al. (2016) pointed out in their meta-analysis of individual and group treatments of psychological disorders, when group and individual treatments are compared within the same study, there are no differences in outcome. Differential effects only emerged when studies were compared in which either an individual or group modality was used (i.e., indirect comparisons between modalities). Thus, differences between the modalities treating psychological disorders may be a result of methodological differences across those studies (e.g., fundamental differences in therapists, settings, and diagnoses; Burlingame et al., 2016). For example, although the analyses of forgiveness treatment modality controlled for severity of the offense that participants were trying to forgive, this covariate is difficult to quantify accurately across studies and may still have had an impact on the results. Studies of individual treatment modality tended to address much more severe offenses (e.g., childhood incest, spousal emotional abuse) than the group interventions (e.g., friendship betrayal, parental neglect). If the coded severity variable did not accurately capture the magnitude of difference between offense types, then severity of offense may not be adequately controlled leading individual therapy to appear more effective than group therapy (i.e., because participants with more severe offenses have greater room to change). Therefore, the observed differences between individual and group therapy may be a methodological artifact. Still, it can be informative to consider implications of such a finding, should an individual modality truly be more effective, hour-for-hour, than a group modality.

First, as we described earlier, forgiveness intervention researchers have emphasized the intrapersonal versus interpersonal process of forgiveness, claiming that forgiveness is the internal process and reconciliation is the interpersonal process. One apparent reason for the explicit differentiation between forgiveness and reconciliation is to protect against clients' returning to potentially abusive and dangerous relationships (Wade, Johnson, & Meyer, 2008). Although many hurts may occur within relationships that are healthy and stable, there are many interpersonal relationships that are not healthy for an individual and, in some instances, are dangerous (e.g., in the case of physically abusive relationships). An individual intervention might provide greater individualized support, greater ease of disclosure of painful past hurts, and more opportunities for the client to discuss their experiences and concerns. This could lead clients in individual contexts to develop more forgiveness in the same amount of time as clients in a group context.

Second, should true differences exist between individual and group modalities, this might be explained by the way in which the forgiveness groups were provided. Most of the group forgiveness interventions do not leverage group dynamics or interpersonal process to improve their efficacy. As noted earlier, most of the group interventions are psychoeducational in nature. This allows for more people to receive help than an individual modality, but it often ignores the group dynamics as a healing agent. A group process focus, which is promoted by many group experts (e.g., Corey, Corey, & Corey, 2018; Yalom & Leszcz, 2005), includes not only the content of what is shared in group but also the ways in which the members interact and how that might be leveraged for learning, healing, and growth.

What might be the effectiveness of forgiveness interventions that leverage group processes? In two studies of group forgiveness interventions, we compared general process techniques with a psychoeducational treatment (Wade et al., 2018; Wade & Meyer, 2009). In the first study, participants in the process group reported equivalent outcomes to those in the explicit forgiveness group. However, as a pilot project, the study did not have enough power to detect small or large effect size differences between treatments. In the second study, which had adequate power to find medium effects, we showed that, in general, the process group was equivalent to the forgiveness intervention, with some caveats (e.g., those with avoidant attachment tended to do better in the explicit forgiveness condition; Wade et al., 2018). Thus, focusing on the group process within a general treatment context of moving toward forgiveness provided equivalent outcomes to an explicit treatment. However, the process-oriented groups did not make use of standard forgiveness interventions or protocols. What might be the effect of integrating the best of the forgiveness interventions with the best of process group interventions? Would it be possible to integrate the structured processes of the forgiveness interventions with the more spontaneous interpersonal dynamics of a process group to aid members in forgiving others? There is no direct research on this question, but it is possible that even more effective group interventions could be developed to promote forgiveness.

Finally, the comparison between group and individual treatment becomes more nuanced when one shifts perspective from serving a single client to providing care for a group of clients or a community. In the latter case, providing individual care to individual clients is not as efficient as offering care to a group of clients (Cuijpers, van Straten, & Warmerdam, 2008). Only one person is receiving care in individual treatment compared to the six, eight, or even 10 clients who are reached at one time in group treatment. In their meta-analysis, Wade, Hoyt, et al. (2014) estimated that individual modalities produce one *SD* of change in about 10 hours of treatment. Group modalities, on the other hand, produce one *SD* of change in about 20 hours. (This relationship is not linear; instead, the dose–response association for individual and group converges at higher amount of change, such that to produce two *SDs* of change individual treatment would take about 40 hours of intervention, whereas similar change in group therapy would take about 50 hours.) Thus, in 20 hours of total intervention, an individual therapist might help two clients reach one *SD* of change, whereas the group therapist might help 5 to 10 clients reach that same level of improvement.

Working with clients in a group setting to help them forgive others is an effective way to reduce anger and bitterness, promote forgiveness, and even address psychological symptoms, such as depression and anxiety. The current forgiveness intervention literature relevant to groups focuses almost exclusively on treatment packages that are explicitly designed to help people forgive others in their personal lives. However, there are other possible applications of forgiveness in a group setting. An example of one such application would be in the integration of forgiveness interventions with a process group. Could the application of the forgiveness literature to therapy process groups help group counselors understand and intervene when members of a therapy group have conflict and hurt one another?

Forgiveness, Interpersonal Conflict, and Anger Among Members in a Therapy Group

Clinical researchers have described forgiveness as an intrapersonal process that occurs in an interpersonal context (e.g., Rotter, 2001). Given the interpersonal dimension of forgiveness, the question arises of whether forgiveness interventions could be adapted and used within traditional group psychotherapy to help members deal with conflict and repair ingroup relationship ruptures. The obvious type of group that would support an interpersonally oriented, forgiveness intervention would be an interpersonal-process group (Yalom & Leszcz, 2005), although intervening to explore and perhaps promote forgiveness could be useful in almost any treatment group.

Conflict is central to most groups of people, including any treatment groups that last longer than a few sessions. In fact,

> conflict is so inevitable . . . that its absence suggests some impairment of the developmental sequence. Furthermore, conflict can be exceedingly valuable to the course of therapy. . . . Learning how to deal effectively with conflict . . . contributes to individual maturation and emotional resilience. (Yalom & Leszcz, 2005, p. 364)

Conflict is so central an experience to small groups that stage theories make conflict a central aspect of group development. In the classic description of small group development (i.e., forming, storming, norming, and performing; Tuckman, 1965), conflict has a central role. In the *storming* stage, members outwardly express hostility towards one another as a way to assert their independence and resist the group structures and norms (Tuckman, 1965). Yalom and Leszcz's (2005) description of group evolution is similar, with the movement toward or away from conflict being a central process that marks the second and third stages of development. Only after conflict has been successfully navigated can the "rich and complex working-through process begin" (Yalom & Leszcz, 2005, p. 345).

Given the prevailing view that conflict is central to group process, a group leader's ability to guide members in effectively managing and processing conflict would appear to be a basic, foundational skill that all group therapists should have. Because conflict is helpful as long as its "intensity does not exceed the members' tolerance" (Yalom & Leszcz, 2005, p. 364), one of the leader's tasks is to manage the level of conflict in the group and titrate it to a level that members can manage. This means that there are times when a leader should highlight and encourage the open discussion of conflict and times when a leader should reduce conflict. Unger (1990) stated that in the early stages of a group, members assess how safe a group is for conflict and how effectively the leader creates a safe environment. The presence of conflict in a group is largely dependent on the perception of the leader as someone who can manage and tolerate the conflict.

One way group leaders can manage conflict is through a two-step process (Yalom & Leszcz, 2005). The first step is to encourage the members involved in the conflict to *experience* or affectively express their emotional experience. The second step is *reflection* and processing of the first step. The level of conflict can be controlled by moving from the first step to the second step. When members' emotions begin to increase beyond what the group can tolerate at that time, the leader can direct the members to the second step and begin to reflect on the conflict and each members' contributing role in it.

Another basic strategy for dealing with conflict, or any anxiety-provoking situation in group, is to add structure (Bednar, Melnick, & Kaul, 1974). Adding structure to a group helps clients feel safer and may allow them to take more risks, such as increasing self-disclosures and providing interpersonal feedback (Crews & Melnick, 1976; Lee & Bednar, 1977). This does not mean that leaders should shut down conflict or restrict it in the group. Instead, effective therapists create structures that allow conflict and its resolution to proceed. For example, such structure can come in the form of explicit group rules (e.g., express your emotions with words not actions), shared group contracts (e.g., all members commit to sticking to the discussion until everyone has felt understood), or guided exercises.

FUTURE DIRECTIONS FOR GROUP PSYCHOTHERAPY AND GROUP PSYCHOLOGY

This brief review of forgiveness in psychotherapeutic settings provides a foundation from which to explore unresolved issues and possible future directions for research. In the this section, we outline specific issues about forgiveness that have not been adequately resolved in the group therapy literature and then pose important questions that might be asked by group researchers not focused on therapeutic groups.

Individual Interventions Versus Group Interventions for Promoting Forgiveness

As we discussed previously, the most recent and extensive meta-analysis of treatments to promote forgiveness (Wade et al., 2018) suggests that hour-for-hour individual treatments might be more effective than group treatments. However, we also presented various issues with those data that might temper such a conclusion, such as the limitations of indirect comparisons between modalities across studies and the fact that group may still be more efficient because it reaches more people per hour. Thus, this individual versus group intervention issue remains mostly unresolved. The next step for research in this area is to conduct studies that directly compare these two modalities while holding important treatment characteristics—such as offense severity, treatment duration, therapist training and allegiance, and client population—constant.

The Necessity of Explicit Forgiveness Interventions

This is an important issue with relevance to professional practice, client well-being, and the expenditure of resources on intervention development, training, and implementation. It also reflects the broader debate within psychotherapy outcome research: how much of client outcomes are attributable to specific interventions versus factors that all treatments have in common (Wampold & Imel, 2015). In the general psychotherapy literature, there is strong evidence to suggest that the factors common to treatments are much more important for client outcomes than the specific interventions that a therapist provides. Thus, we might expect that forgiveness interventions would follow this same pattern. This is supported by the finding we discussed previously—that treatment model (Enright vs. Worthington vs. other) did not significantly predict forgiveness outcomes after controlling for covariates. However, these models share so much in common that even their specific interventions (e.g., helping clients develop empathy for the offending person) are similar. The more difficult, and perhaps more interesting, test is whether more general psychotherapy treatments would provide equivalent outcomes. This research is mixed, with some outcome studies showing greater effectiveness of an explicit forgiveness intervention (e.g., Reed & Enright, 2006) and others showing no difference (e.g., Wade et al., 2018). This remains an important and unresolved issue that could be fruitfully explored in future research.

The Natural Course of Forgiveness Among Therapy Group Members

We are not aware of any research studies of forgiveness explicitly in a therapy group. There is a solid body of research on the normal course of forgiveness among people in relationships, however (e.g., Kato, 2016; Tsang, McCullough, & Fincham, 2006). Much of the findings from this work could be applied to make hypotheses about the ways that group members might experience offenses and deal with those in the group setting. Thus, there is a considerable amount of research that could be conducted to understand how forgiveness works within a therapy group. The findings from such work could inform clinical group therapy practice and suggest important applications to other group settings.

Benefits of Forgiveness Following a Group Conflict

In addition to understanding the normal course of offenses and forgiveness in a therapy group setting, understanding the role that forgiveness plays specifically with helping clients benefit from group therapy may also be valuable. Of course, there is worth in developing knowledge about the process of forgiveness generally in such a setting. However, most therapists (and other stakeholders) would also be interested in knowing how those processes affect outcomes. In other words, are there certain aspects to the development or achievement of forgiveness among group members that leads members to benefit more (or less) from group? For example, conflict and its resolution is considered a crucial group process. What about this process helps people to truly benefit from group? Perhaps it is the foundational development of trust. Perhaps, instead, there is an intimacy that is developed when members work through their conflict and forgive each other. This process then might help members to share even more vulnerable information, leading to greater psychological change. Research on therapeutic ruptures (i.e., a breakdown in the collaborative relationship between therapists and clients) and their repair in individual therapy shows that repairs to therapeutic ruptures predict client outcomes (Safran, Muran, & Eubanks-Carter, 2011). Perhaps similar results would be found in member-to-member conflict resolution in group therapy. Furthermore, is forgiveness central to the usefulness of conflict? Do clients need to experience an internal shift in their feelings from bitterness to compassion to reap the benefits of conflict in group? What happens for group members who hold a grudge against another group member; do they benefit from group to the same degree?

Therapist Intervention to Promote Forgiveness Among General Group Members

Finally, to the degree that forgiveness is useful within the context of a therapy group, group leaders should have tools to help their members forgive each other (or the group) when necessary. Research is needed to understand the ways that leaders could most effectively promote member forgiveness. Of course, this would likely begin with the research on existing forgiveness interventions. However, this literature might be limited because, most of the time, it addresses helping people who were hurt by someone that is not present. In a therapy group, the offended and offender(s) are present. Thus, interventions to address forgiveness might also need to address reconciliation. How can therapists help clients navigate hurts, develop an internal experience of forgiveness, and then reconcile with those members who hurt them? There is a considerable amount of work that still needs to be done in this area.

Effective Interventions for Helping People to Forgive Others in Nontherapeutic Groups

In work and sports teams, family groups, hobby or activity groups, and religious groups, there are often leaders, official or not, who might intervene to help people manage conflict and restore relationships. Naturalistic research could be conducted to see what works, when, and for whom. These could be done on exemplar groups (e.g., groups nominated for their ability to deal with conflict through forgiveness) or on more typical groups. For example, how do coaches or team captains deal with conflict among sports team members to facilitate forgiveness, and which of these behaviors are the most effective? Would training coaches or team captains the tenets of forgiveness interventions help them promote forgiveness among team members, as well as help foster conflict resolution between team members and coaches when ruptures occur? Also, does increased forgiveness within the team lead to better outcomes (e.g., more victories)? Alternatively, intervention research could be conducted to assess the effectiveness of specific forgiveness techniques in different group settings. This could lead to theoretically-driven and empirically-supported interventions to help with a wide range of groups.

One research design issue that is important to consider is the need to include comparison groups. Research in forgiveness group therapy shows that intervening is generally effective. Thus, one can expect that doing something regarding forgiveness also will be effective in nontherapy groups. However, more consequential findings will emerge from comparisons of different interventions. Researchers should seek to incorporate multiple intervention conditions and not simply compare to no-treatment or waitlist conditions.

The Role of Forgiveness in Work Settings and Among Work Teams

This broad issue reflects the many specific research projects that could be done to understand forgiveness in the workplace. This would include the great variety of workplace settings. For example, how does forgiveness play out for those in work settings that are hierarchical with highly-centralized leadership versus settings with flatter organizational structures and decentralized leadership? Also, is forgiveness even a concept that people generally accept as relevant for work relationships? If so, how and when do people employ forgiveness and toward what ends (e.g., to feel better, to have a higher quality of life at work, or to get the job done more effectively)? There is some work to build on in this area (see Aquino et al., 2003). For example, in a study of work team meetings, forgiveness was correlated with less complaining during meetings, especially for older team members (Schulte et al., 2013). This research could be followed with explorations of other ways that forgiveness might reduce unwanted behaviors at work or ways to increase forgiveness to improve work meeting effectiveness.

An important research design issue relevant to this issue is the measurement of forgiveness. As we argued above, the target of forgiveness should be clearly identified. This allows for accurate measurement of forgiveness (i.e., measuring the participant's forgiveness of another person, themselves, or a group). However, researchers should also pay attention to the level of forgiveness being measured. Both trait (e.g., Berry, Worthington, O'Connor, Parrott, & Wade, 2005) and state (e.g., Enright, Rique, & Coyle, 2000) measures of forgiveness have been developed and both might be relevant to the workplace. Finally, with attention to one's definition of forgiveness, one can more accurately match the measurement of forgiveness with a specific conceptualization.

Effect of Group Dynamics in the Development of Self-Forgiveness After One Member or Group Offends Another

This is a very broad issue that could lead to many research questions. For example, in the context of offenses that were organized and perpetrated by the member's group, how does an individual who was a part of the group and participated in the perpetration of the offense address self-forgiveness when the wrong is acknowledged? Does this lead to disassociation from the group or can the individual forgive themselves and remain in the group? What moderates this outcome (e.g., being a group leader, time in the group, centrality of group membership to one's identity)? Alternatively, researchers might explore how groups unrelated to an offense help people to overcome them. Religious or spiritual groups might be a prime example of this (Wuthnow, 2000). When an individual has remorse for past actions, are there specific group-level actions or experiences (e.g., confession, rituals, social support) that help the person to forgive themselves? Another layer of this question might address intergroup conflict, and group self-forgiveness (in which a group seeks forgiveness for harms that it has perpetrated). Finally, although there is some work on forgiveness within the justice system (Exline et al., 2003), many research questions are left unanswered about the ways group psychology might help us to understand how both victims and offenders navigate the experiences and aftermath of different types of crimes and their punishment.

CONSIDERATIONS AND CONCERNS FOR GROUP PSYCHOLOGY RESEARCH AND PRACTICE ON FORGIVENESS

In any situation that brings people together for a common task (e.g., work groups, teams) or in contexts in which people share some affiliation (e.g., neighborhoods, congregations), groups are formed. And where groups are formed, interpersonal conflict and offenses are likely to be present. In the following section, we outline some broader considerations for researchers and others expanding the application of forgiveness research to nontherapy groups, for both research and practice.

Integrating Research Across Group Psychology Domains

One basic step in the integration of group psychology domains is the application of findings from one domain to the other. Specifically, there are several important applications from the forgiveness group therapy literature that could benefit group psychology research and practice.

Clearly Define Forgiveness

We opened this chapter with a discussion of forgiveness definitions because this has been a difficult topic in this research area. Given varying understandings of forgiveness from scholarly and popular perspectives (Exline et al., 2003), a clear understanding of what is being studied or promoted is essential. Researchers and practitioners interested in applying developments from forgiveness group therapy to other types of groups should start by explicitly defining what they mean by forgiveness. This would include identifying the pros and cons of a particular definition. For example, if forgiveness is defined as an intrapersonal process (as we have in this chapter), then one pro is that people can move toward forgiveness without necessarily achieving reconciliation, which is very useful in situations in which the person cannot or does not want to reestablish a relationship with the offending person. However, one con is that many people understand forgiveness to include an interpersonal component and, in the context of groups in which members continue to function together (e.g., work groups, teams), reconciliation may be a crucial aspect to include. In the case of an intergroup dialogue, for example, a goal of a forgiveness intervention would likely involve reaching a point of interpersonal forgiveness, where members of a marginalized nonprivileged identity group might work toward forgiveness that would include some degree of reconciliation and maintained contact with members of a privileged identity group.

Engage People in the Forgiveness Process

Forgiveness efforts seem to be helpful, and many different paths to forgiveness probably exist for people. Engagement in the process generally may be more important than the specific techniques used to promote forgiveness. Still, little is known about what might be done to intervene in nontherapy groups to help people to forgive others. Exploring both general and specific factors that contribute to intervention or outreach efforts in nontherapeutic settings may be very useful. At this point, the evidence suggests that helping people develop empathy for offenders, providing support as they work through the process (Wade, Worthington, et al., 2005), and intervening to help others can be done in various ways that best fit the situation and people involved. For example, applying these specific factors to an intergroup dialogue of members from both privileged and marginalized identity groups may mean adjusting the process of forgiveness depending on a group members' identity status. That is, when working with members from the marginalized identity group, the facilitator may approach the idea of forgiveness from a more tentative standpoint to ensure the decision to forgive comes from the group member's own volition. This may ensure that the act of forgiveness is not just accepted as a prescribed step by the facilitator, thus potentially reenacting harmful social dynamics, especially if the facilitator holds a majority identity status. Spending more time in the processing-of-anger stage with members from the marginalized identity group may be necessary to ensure that the member is ready to move toward forgiveness. In some cases, the facilitator may discourage forgiveness if it appears premature and if it risks hurting the marginalized member. For those looking for more specific intervention ideas, resources exist (e.g., Enright, 2001; Worthington, 2006).

Understand the Target of Forgiveness

Although the group therapy literature on forgiveness focuses almost exclusively on forgiving one specific offender, the broader forgiveness research indicates that the focus of forgiveness can be varied. For example, there is a growing body of work on self-forgiveness (Woodyatt, Worthington, Wenzel,

& Griffin, 2017). Outside of therapy groups, there are important applications of groups to self-forgiveness. In research, this is an almost entirely unexplored area. How might group dynamics, such as membership, power, or identification, impact self-forgiveness? Specifically, this question could be explored in a range of settings, from cultural groups that historically have perpetrated harm against individuals of other cultural groups, to individuals who have broken the law or harmed others within the context of a small group (e.g., gangs). In addition to other and self-forgiveness, there is intergroup forgiveness as well. Understanding and paying careful attention to the different targets of forgiveness will help to properly direct the research and provide important research questions.

Consider the Context in Which Forgiveness Might Be Sought

One of the important implications of the group therapy literature on forgiveness is to consider in what contexts forgiveness might be more effectively achieved. Certainly, there is real benefit to working through anger toward forgiveness with a group of people, whether that offense occurred within that group or not. In the context of an intergroup dialogue, hearing others' stories of personal and systemic injustice at the hands of one identity group as well as witnessing others' process of working towards forgiveness could conceivably help an individual in that same journey. However, there might be group settings that create barriers to people developing forgiveness. Perhaps, giving space and time for people to work individually on forgiveness might prove more effective in some situations. Researchers could certainly explore the different variables that might be related to effective forgiveness-promoting contexts.

Understand the Importance of and Distinction Between Forgiveness and Reconciliation

We close this section with a prime implication from the forgiveness group therapy literature. Understanding the difference between forgiveness and reconciliation has been one of the most foundational issues emerging from this area. In practice, separating the process of forgiveness from the process of reconciliation has freed countless clients from being stuck in bitterness because they do not want to reconcile. Giving clients permission to set boundaries with hurtful people in their lives without having to hold on to grudges and bitterness has ended unnecessary suffering and enriched lives. This distinction has multiple applications to group psychology research and practice. First, it is an important conceptual distinction to have in mind when researching and working with nontherapy groups, for the reasons just stated. Second, despite the importance of this differentiation for psychotherapy clients (many of whom have been hurt repeatedly in some very dramatic ways), the differentiation may not be the same for nontherapy clients in everyday, work, team, or professional relationships. These nonclinical situations might prove that the distinction between forgiveness and reconciliation is much less important, if at all distinguishable. For example, in task groups, like work or sports teams, forgiving typical and more minor offenses among team members might be tantamount to reconciling. In other words, if members forgive, they might necessarily reconcile as well.

So far in this section we have addressed more intervention-oriented applications of the group therapy forgiveness literature. However, the research on groups and forgiveness might lead to fruitful work from a basic research perspective as well. In fact, there is a strong foundation from which group researchers might build in this area. For example, research on ingroup and outgroup membership has been done related to forgiveness. In one set of studies, researchers showed that people might apply a double standard for their ingroup leaders, such that under certain conditions (e.g., seeing the leader as serving the group's interests), they are more likely to forgive ingroup leaders than they are other ingroup members (or outgroup leaders; Abrams, Randsley de Moura, & Travaglino, 2013). This finding has been supported with political groups as well (e.g., Eisinger, 2000).

Another area upon which researchers might build is the intergroup contact hypothesis. One of the more recent developments in this area is to understand the role of forgiveness between groups that have had historical conflict. In a large meta-analysis of research on the contact hypothesis, Pettigrew, Tropp, Wagner, and Christ (2011) reported that not only do the conditions proposed by Allport (1954; e.g., equal group status, common goals, support of authorities) help with reducing prejudice, they also appear to help with building trust and encouraging greater forgiveness for past injuries. A more recent follow-up to these ideas explored the notion that a belief in the ability of groups to change would moderate the relationship between a group apology and forgiveness (Wohl et al., 2015). Across varying groups (e.g., Israelis, university students, corporate employees), the researchers found that group apologies predicted forgiveness for the offending group (e.g., Palestinian leaders, rival university) for those who generally saw the offending groups as more able to change.

Another area that appears to be ripe for attention is the impact that being a marginalized member of a social group might have on forgiveness. Typically, marginalized members have less power and influence to respond to offenses from other group members. When this occurs, what is the role of forgiveness for such people? When does forgiveness in these situations lead to positive outcomes for the individual and group and when does it not? Do findings from marginalized members of smaller groups (e.g., specific work teams) generalize to members of marginalized groups within societies (e.g., racial minority groups)? There is considerable work that could be done to understand how group dynamics, in all their variations, might affect forgiveness in these and many other situations.

Implications for Group Practitioners

In general, forgiveness is likely to be helpful in many group settings, from classrooms to sports teams, from cultural groups to work groups. Coaches, managers, educators, clergy, and other group leaders can benefit from a clear understanding of forgiveness and how it might be applied in various contexts. For example, a clear understanding of what forgiveness is and is not could arm leaders with useful information for helping advise members of their groups or working with them to build forgiveness. Forgiveness, as we define it, can be encouraged but should not be forced. It is often an issue of personal or group values and might be important to some and not to others. Likewise, in some situations, reconciliation might be a very useful by-product of forgiveness when offenses occur within the group itself (among members) or with other groups. However, reconciliation is not a necessary component of forgiveness; such an understanding can free people to work toward forgiveness without the extra burden of reconciling. Even a basic understanding of forgiveness can be useful in many different groups. Leaders of such groups could use this information in various ways to help navigate some of the difficulties or nuances of forgiveness (e.g., allowing or facilitating a full accounting of the wrong and its consequences, not using forgiveness as a way to short-circuit anger or conflict).

Forgiveness and the research on it might be particularly helpful for diversity professionals and those who facilitate intergroup dialogues. In an intergroup dialogue setting, the reality of needing to continue to interact with members from different identity groups in society may make it so that forgiveness and some form of reconciliation is the ultimate, if not necessary, goal. However, being mindful about how this is achieved and what messages are communicated—especially if a facilitator holds privileged identities—is very important. These situations may call for an individual to practice holding anger at ongoing injustices in a useful and constructive way, while releasing resentments from a past injustice that becomes personally burdensome and gets in the way of daily functioning. This is complex. It is further complicated by the power differentials that often exist between different identity groups. Navigating forgiveness, justice, reconciliation, as well as personal growth and healing in such contexts is challenging and yet so important.

Finally, in practice, understanding the different targets of forgiveness is also important. In the group therapy literature on forgiveness, clients are encouraged to focus on a single individual and even a single offense. For many people who have been hurt, they have experienced multiple offenses over time and often from various people. Attempting to facilitate forgiveness for all of these could quickly become overwhelming, even in a therapy setting. Thus, those who work in nontherapy settings might also attend to this by helping people to circumscribe the targets of their forgiveness. In some group situations, the target may be obvious or already established based on the context. In the case of an intergroup dialogue, the target of forgiveness for members of the marginalized identity group may be individuals from the privileged identity group. For members of the privileged group, the target may be the self. The intervention may be that of helping members of the privileged group work towards self-forgiveness for the harmful societal dynamics in which they knowingly or unknowingly participated. In the context of a work environment or a sports team, the application of forgiveness interventions would likely arise in the instance of specific hurts or tension between members of the group.

CONCLUSION

Forgiveness is a topic that is ripe for interdisciplinary collaboration between group psychotherapy and group psychology. Research on therapeutic forgiveness interventions has shown that it is a viable and effective treatment option for individuals who have endured an interpersonal hurt or offense (Wade, Hoyt, et al., 2014). Understanding how that might play out with nontherapeutic groups in work, organizations, teams, and intergroup dialogues is an important and practical next step. Furthermore, findings from group psychology might be more thoroughly integrated into forgiveness group interventions. This integration and collaboration call for continuing work on how groups might be used to help people to develop forgiveness.

SUGGESTED READINGS

Noor, M. (2016). Suffering need not beget suffering: Why we forgive. *Current Opinion in Psychology, 11,* 100–104. http://dx.doi.org/10.1016/j.copsyc.2016.06.013

Masi Noor offers a review of intergroup forgiveness in this article. He focuses on developing a clearer definition of forgiveness for this area of inquiry, reviewing the evidence for social psychological interventions, and providing a warning for the ways that forgiveness might reduce the motivation to seek justice when warranted. For group researchers and practitioners interested in larger social/identity groups and culture, this is a foundational article to understanding the application of forgiveness research to this area.

Wade, N. G., Hoyt, W., Kidwell, J. E. M., & Worthington, E. L., Jr. (2014). Efficacy of psychotherapeutic interventions to promote forgiveness: A meta-analysis. *Journal of Consulting and Clinical Psychology, 82,* 154–170. http://dx.doi.org/10.1037/a0035268

In this meta-analysis of studies testing the efficacy of forgiveness interventions, Wade et al. provide compelling evidence that forgiveness interventions are efficacious. These treatments not only help people struggling with interpersonal offenses to forgive the offending person but also help to reduce depression and anxiety and increase hope. The majority of these interventions were offered in a group context, with most offered through a psychoeducational format. Group researchers and practitioners can use this information as a foundation for intervening (and researching such interventions) in various other contexts described in this chapter.

Worthington, E. L., Jr., & Wade, N. G. (Eds.). (2020). *Handbook of forgiveness* (2nd ed.). New York, NY: Routledge.

In this second edition of the *Handbook of Forgiveness*, Worthington and Wade compile state-of-the-science reviews of forgiveness research. Many of the chapters have significant implications for group research and practice. Several chapters are devoted to research on forgiveness across cultural groups, including African, Asian, and Latin American populations. Chapters reviewing research on forgiveness in organizational settings, families, and across cultural groups are also included. This handbook provides excellent, up-to-date coverage of research on forgiveness that group researchers and practitioners can use to inform and inspire their work.

REFERENCES

Abrams, D., Randsley de Moura, G., & Travaglino, G. A. (2013). A double standard when group members behave badly: Transgression credit to ingroup leaders. *Journal of Personality and Social Psychology, 105*, 799–815. http://dx.doi.org/10.1037/a0033600

Allport, G. W. (1954). *The nature of prejudice*. Reading, MA: Addison Wesley.

American Psychological Association. (2017). *Ethical principles of psychologists and code of conduct* (2002, Amended June 1, 2010, and January 1, 2017). Retrieved from http://www.apa.org/ethics/code/index.aspx

Aquino, K., Grover, S., Goldman, B., & Folger, R. (2003). When push doesn't come to shove: The role of interpersonal forgiveness in organizations. *Journal of Management Inquiry, 12*, 209–216. http://dx.doi.org/10.1177/1056492603256337

Bednar, R., Melnick, J., & Kaul, T. (1974). Risk, responsibility and structure: A conceptual framework for initiating group counseling and psychotherapy. *Journal of Counseling Psychology, 21*, 31–37. http://dx.doi.org/10.1037/h0036057

Berry, J. W., & Worthington, E. L., Jr. (2001). Forgiveness, relationship quality, stress while imagining relationship events, and physical and mental health. *Journal of Counseling Psychology, 48*, 447–455. http://dx.doi.org/10.1037/0022-0167.48.4.447

Berry, J. W., Worthington, E. L., Jr., O'Connor, L. E., Parrott, L., III, & Wade, N. G. (2005). Forgivingness, vengeful rumination, and affective traits. *Journal of Personality, 73*, 183–225. http://dx.doi.org/10.1111/j.1467-6494.2004.00308.x

Bono, G., McCullough, M. E., & Root, L. M. (2008). Forgiveness, feeling connected to others, and well-being: Two longitudinal studies. *Personality and Social Psychology Bulletin, 34*, 182–195. http://dx.doi.org/10.1177/0146167207310025

Booth, J. E., Park, T., Zhu, L., Beauregard, T. A., Gu, F., & Emery, C. (2018). Prosocial response to client-instigated victimization: The roles of forgiveness and workgroup conflict. *Journal of Applied Psychology, 103*, 513–536. http://dx.doi.org.proxy.lib.iastate.edu/10.1037/apl0000286

Burlingame, G. M., Seebeck, J. D., Janis, R. A., Whitcomb, K. E., Barkowski, S., Rosendahl, J., & Strauss, B. (2016). Outcome differences between individual and group formats when identical and nonidentical treatments, patients, and doses are compared: A 25-year meta-analytic perspective. *Psychotherapy, 53*, 446–461. http://dx.doi.org/10.1037/pst0000090

Corey, M. S., Corey, J., & Corey, C. (2018). *Groups: Process and practice* (10th ed.). Boston, MA: Cengage Learning.

Crews, C., & Melnick, J. (1976). Use of initial and delayed structure in facilitating group development. *Journal of Counseling Psychology, 23*, 92–98. http://dx.doi.org/10.1037/0022-0167.23.2.92

Cuijpers, P., van Straten, A., & Warmerdam, L. (2008). Are individual and group treatments equally effective in the treatment of depression in adults? A meta-analysis. *The European Journal of Psychiatry, 22*, 38–51. http://dx.doi.org/10.4321/S0213-61632008000100005

de Waal, F. B. M., & Pokorny, J. J. (2005). Primate conflict and its relation to human forgiveness. In E. L. Worthington, Jr., (Ed.), *Handbook of forgiveness* (pp. 17–32). New York, NY: Routledge.

Eisinger, R. M. (2000). Partisan absolution? Exploring the depths of forgiving. *International Journal of Public Opinion Research, 12*, 254–258. http://dx.doi.org/10.1093/ijpor/12.3.254

Enright, R. D. (2001). *Forgiveness is a choice: A step-by-step process for resolving anger and restoring hope.* Washington, DC: American Psychological Association.

Enright, R. D., & Fitzgibbons, R. P. (2000). *Helping clients forgive: An empirical guide for resolving anger and restoring hope.* Washington, DC: American Psychological Association.

Enright, R. D., Rique, J., & Coyle, C. T. (2000). *The Enright Forgiveness Inventory user's manual.* Madison, WI: The International Forgiveness Institute.

Exline, J. J., Worthington, E. L., Jr., Hill, P., & McCullough, M. E. (2003). Forgiveness and justice: A research agenda for social and personality psychology. *Personality and Social Psychology Review, 7*, 337–348. http://dx.doi.org/10.1207/S15327957PSPR0704_06

Fehr, R., Gelfand, M. J., & Nag, M. (2010). The road to forgiveness: A meta-analytic synthesis of its situational and dispositional correlates. *Psychological Bulletin, 136*, 894–914. http://dx.doi.org/10.1037/a0019993

Freedman, S. R., & Enright, R. D. (1996). Forgiveness as an intervention goal with incest survivors. *Journal of Consulting and Clinical Psychology, 64*, 983–992. http://dx.doi.org/10.1037/0022-006X.64.5.983

Gilbert, S. E., & Gordon, K. C. (2017). Predicting forgiveness in women experiencing intimate partner violence. *Violence Against Women, 23*, 452–468. http://dx.doi.org.proxy.lib.iastate.edu/10.1177/1077801216644071

Gordon, K. C., Burton, S., & Porter, L. (2004). Predicting the intentions of women in domestic violence shelters to return to partners: Does forgiveness play a role? *Journal of Family Psychology, 18*, 331–338. http://dx.doi.org.proxy.lib.iastate.edu/10.1037/0893-3200.18.2.331

Greenberg, L., Warwar, S., & Malcolm, W. (2010). Emotion-focused couples therapy and the facilitation of forgiveness. *Journal of Marital and Family Therapy, 36*, 28–42. http://dx.doi.org/10.1111/j.1752-0606.2009.00185.x

Kato, T. (2016). Effects of partner forgiveness on romantic break-ups in dating relationships: A longitudinal study. *Personality and Individual Differences, 95*, 185–189. http://dx.doi.org/10.1016/j.paid.2016.02.050

Lee, F., & Bednar, R. (1977). Effects of group structure and risk-taking disposition on group behavior, attitudes, and atmosphere. *Journal of Counseling Psychology, 24*, 191–199. http://dx.doi.org/10.1037/0022-0167.24.3.191

Pettigrew, T. F., Tropp, L. R., Wagner, U., & Christ, O. (2011). Recent advances in intergroup contact theory. *International Journal of Intercultural Relations, 35*, 271–280. http://dx.doi.org/10.1016/j.ijintrel.2011.03.001

Reed, G. L., & Enright, R. D. (2006). The effects of forgiveness therapy on depression, anxiety, and posttraumatic stress for women after spousal emotional abuse. *Journal of Consulting and Clinical Psychology, 74*, 920–929. http://dx.doi.org/10.1037/0022-006X.74.5.920

Ricciardi, E., Rota, G., Sani, L., Gentili, C., Gaglianese, A., Guazzelli, M., & Pietrini, P. (2013). How the brain heals emotional wounds: The functional neuroanatomy of forgiveness. *Frontiers in Human Neuroscience, 7*, 839. http://dx.doi.org/10.3389/fnhum.2013.00839

Rotter, J. C. (2001). Letting go: Forgiveness in counseling. *The Family Journal, 9*, 174–177. http://dx.doi.org/10.1177/1066480701092012

Safran, J. D., Muran, J. C., & Eubanks-Carter, C. (2011). Repairing alliance ruptures. In J. C. Norcross (Ed.), *Psychotherapy relationships that work: Evidence-based responsiveness* (2nd ed., pp. 234–238). New York, NY: Oxford University Press. http://dx.doi.org/10.1093/acprof:oso/9780199737208.003.0011

Schulte, E. M., Lehmann-Willenbrock, N., & Kauffeld, S. (2013). Age, forgiveness, and meeting behavior: A multilevel study. *Journal of Managerial Psychology, 28*, 928–949. http://dx.doi.org/10.1108/JMP-06-2013-0193

Staub, E., Pearlman, L. A., Gubin, A., & Hagengimana, A. (2005). Healing, reconciliation, forgiving and the prevention of violence after genocide or mass killing: An intervention and it's experimental evaluation in Rwanda. *Journal of Social and Clinical Psychology, 24*, 297–334. http://dx.doi.org/10.1521/jscp.24.3.297.65617

Tittler, M. V., & Wade, N. G. (2019). Forgiveness interventions from a multicultural perspective: Potential applications and concerns. In L. E. Van Zyl & S. Rothmann, Sr. (Eds.), *Theoretical approaches to multi-cultural positive psychological interventions* (pp. 179–199). Switzerland: Springer. http://dx.doi.org/10.1007/978-3-030-20583-6_8

Tsang, J., McCullough, M. E., & Fincham, F. (2006). The longitudinal association between forgiveness and relationship closeness and commitment. *Journal of Social and Clinical Psychology, 25*, 448–472. http://dx.doi.org/10.1521/jscp.2006.25.4.448

Tuckman, B. W. (1965). Developmental sequence in small groups. *Psychological Bulletin, 63*, 384–399. http://dx.doi.org/10.1037/h0022100

Unger, R. (1990). Conflict management in group psychotherapy. *Small Group Research, 21*, 349–359. http://dx.doi.org/10.1177/1046496490213004

Wade, N. G., Bailey, D. C., & Shaffer, P. (2005). Helping clients heal: Does forgiveness make a difference? *Professional Psychology: Research and Practice, 36*, 634–641. http://dx.doi.org/10.1037/0735-7028.36.6.634

Wade, N. G., Cornish, M. A., Tucker, J. R., Worthington, E. L., Jr., Sandage, S. J., & Rye, M. S. (2018). Promoting forgiveness: Characteristics of the treatment, the clients, and their interaction. *Journal of Counseling Psychology, 65*, 358–371. http://dx.doi.org/10.1037/cou0000260

Wade, N. G., Hoyt, W. T., Kidwell, J. E. M., & Worthington, E. L., Jr. (2014). Efficacy of psychotherapeutic interventions to promote forgiveness: A meta-analysis. *Journal of Consulting and Clinical Psychology, 82*, 154–170. http://dx.doi.org/10.1037/a0035268

Wade, N. G., Johnson, C. V., & Meyer, J. E. (2008). Understanding the concerns about interventions to promote forgiveness: A review of the literature. *Psychotherapy: Theory, Research, Practice, Training, 45*, 88–102. http://dx.doi.org/10.1037/0033-3204.45.1.88

Wade, N. G., & Meyer, J. E. (2009). Comparison of brief group interventions to promote forgiveness: A pilot outcome study. *International Journal of Group Psychotherapy, 59*, 199–220. http://dx.doi.org/10.1521/ijgp.2009.59.2.199

Wade, N. G., Tucker, J. R., & Cornish, M. A. (2014). Forgiveness interventions and the promotion of resilience following interpersonal stress and trauma. In M. Kent, M. C. Davis, & J. W. Reich (Eds.), *The resilience handbook: Approaches to stress and trauma* (pp. 256–269). New York, NY: Routledge.

Wade, N. G., Worthington, E. L., Jr., & Meyer, J. E. (2005). But do they work? A meta-analysis of group interventions to promote forgiveness. In E. L. Worthington, Jr., (Ed.), *Handbook of forgiveness* (pp. 423–440). New York, NY: Routledge.

Wampold, B. E., & Imel, Z. E. (2015). *The great psychotherapy debate: the research evidence for what works in psychotherapy* (2nd ed.). New York, NY: Routledge. http://dx.doi.org/10.4324/9780203582015

Witvliet, C. V. O. (2014, September 16). Forgiveness rising [Blog post.] Retrieved from http://fetzer.org/blog/forgiveness-rising

Witvliet, C. V. O., & McCullough, M. E. (2007). Forgiveness and health: A review and theoretical exploration of emotion pathways. In S. G. Post (Ed.), *Altruism and health: Perspectives from empirical research* (pp. 259–276). Oxford, England: Oxford University Press. http://dx.doi.org/10.1093/acprof:oso/9780195182910.003.0017

Wohl, M. J. A., Cohen-Chen, S., Halperin, E., Caouette, J., Hayes, N., & Hornsey, M. J. (2015). Belief in the malleability of groups strengthens the tenuous link between a collective apology and intergroup forgiveness. *Personality and Social Psychology Bulletin, 41*, 714–725. http://dx.doi.org/10.1177/0146167215576721

Woodyatt, L., Worthington, E. L., Jr., Wenzel, M., & Griffin, B. G. (Eds.). (2017). *Handbook of the psychology of self-forgiveness*. New York, NY: Springer. http://dx.doi.org/10.1007/978-3-319-60573-9

Worthington, E. L., Jr. (2006). *Forgiveness and reconciliation: Theory and application*. New York, NY: Routledge.

Worthington, E. L., Jr., & Scherer, M. (2004). Forgiveness is an emotion-focused coping strategy that can reduce health risks and promote health resilience: Theory, review, and hypotheses. *Psychology & Health, 19*, 385–405. http://dx.doi.org/10.1080/0887044042000196674

Wuthnow, R. (2000). How religious groups promote forgiving: A national study. *Journal for the Scientific Study of Religion, 39*, 125–139. http://dx.doi.org/10.1111/0021-8294.00011

Yalom, I. (2005). *The Schopenhauer cure: A novel*. New York, NY: Harper Collins.

Yalom, I., & Leszcz, M. (2005). *Theory and practice of group psychotherapy* (5th ed.). New York, NY: Basic Books.

12

Group Therapy Development

Implications for Nontherapy Groups

John S. Ogrodniczuk, Joanna Cheek, and David Kealy

Groups are multifaceted systems with many moving parts. Each group houses a unique and dynamic interplay of the intrapsychic worlds of each individual, the interpersonal exchanges between individuals, and the process of the group as a whole, all influenced by the larger world playing an active role in the background (von Bertalanffy, 1966). Although the focus of psychotherapy theory largely favors the intrapersonal and interpersonal fields, we also must consider how the group develops as a whole. As Bion (1961) stated in his seminal paper on groups, echoing Aristotle's ideas, humans are not just individuals but also social and political beings. Group development considers these sociopolitical forces at play.

Group development refers to a process whereby a collection of individuals with loose ties to one another develops into a unified entity with an identity, structure, behavioral norms, and roles for members (Brower, 1996; Lewis, Beck, Dugo, & Eng, 2000). Groups are believed to develop along predictable paths but with particular detours, shortcuts, and speed bumps unique to each group (Arrow, Poole, Henry, Wheelan, & Moreland, 2004). For example, a group's specific path may be guided by factors externally imposed on the group, such as whether the group is open or closed and time limited or open ended, session frequency and duration, group size and makeup, leadership style, and the task that the group is asked to perform (American Group Psychotherapy Association, Science to Service Task Force, 2007). As Yalom and Leszcz (2005) described, "Each group is, at the same time, like all groups, like some groups and like no other group!" (p. 323).

http://dx.doi.org/10.1037/0000201-013
The Psychology of Groups: The Intersection of Social Psychology and Psychotherapy Research,
C. D. Parks and G. A. Tasca (Editors)

In this chapter we provide a brief, introductory overview of the group development literature as it pertains to psychotherapy groups. A short synopsis of group development models is followed by a selective review of empirical investigations in three areas: (a) stage changes in group development, (b) factors that are related to group development, and (c) the association between group development and treatment outcome. Next, we consider important issues for future research on group development, concluding with reflections on the relevance of the literature on group development in psychotherapy to group contexts outside of treatment settings.

GROUP DEVELOPMENT MODELS

Authors from different theoretical perspectives have delineated phases of group development that are believed to be common to all groups, such as Bennis and Shepard's (1956) and Bion's (1961) two-stage models, Schutz's (1958) three-stage model, Beck's (1974) nine-stage model, Worchel's (1994) six-stage model, Tuckman's (1965; Tuckman & Jensen, 1977) five-stage model, and Agazarian and Gantt's (2003) integrative model. As Paquin (2017) described, these theories attempt to elucidate how a group moves from a room full of individuals in the same place at the same time to become a working whole with a sense of shared identity, interconnection, and unity that is able to negotiate individual versus group needs, resolve differences, and provide therapeutic benefit to its members (Forsyth, 2011). As a complement to one's theoretical orientation or specific treatment protocol, these models can provide a helpful framework for the group leader trying to understand and contextualize group-level phenomena as they unfold over the course of therapy.

Group development models typically include a beginning phase of interaction as group members come together: a phase of uncertainty about participation, objectives, and competing needs; a phase of cooperation and cohesiveness, during which some of the most important work gets accomplished; and a termination phase, in which the group disbands or adjusts to the loss of a member (Kieffer, 2001). There is considerable variability across the numerous models of group development, yet many propose some version of Tuckman's (1965) basic stages, referred to as *forming, storming, norming, performing,* and *adjourning.*

The first stage, *forming,* involves the introduction of members to the group, their consideration of acceptable group behavior, and the evolution of an identity for the group (Tuckman, 1965). Group members often experience a variety of emotions during this stage, including pride in being selected for the group, anticipation, and anxiety not only about the tasks of the group and how these will be accomplished but also about the potential for shame and being hurt by a group of strangers. The second stage, *storming.* tends to be the most difficult period for a group. Individual members often have strong opinions as to how the group should function and thus bring personal agendas to the group. They are confronted with the realization that the tasks to be undertaken are different and sometimes more difficult than they had anticipated and that compromise is necessary for the group to move forward. The tendency toward arguments, defensiveness, and competition within the group gives way to more productive behaviors during the third stage, *norming*. The group becomes more unified as members recognize and adhere to group-developed norms and rules and assume the roles and responsibilities required of members. This norming process results in a decrease in conflict and competition within the group, opening the way to the *performing* stage of group development, which is characterized by the group's increased capacity for problem solving and implementation of changes that lead to task accomplishment. The relationships within the group during the performing stage tend to be stable, as group members focus on the work of the group; this stage involves the understanding and acceptance of one another's strengths and weaknesses. The group is able to work through barriers that might arise— including within the group itself—and members exhibit a close sense of identification with the group. The last stage, *adjourning*, brings closure to the group. Group members may feel relatively satisfied that an achievement has been made, and most have strong feelings about the group experience, whether negative or positive. Reflecting on their time together, group members are able to see what they have accomplished, although it is common for some group members to experience a sense of loss.

MacKenzie's (1997) group development model is arguably the most well known and studied in the group therapy field. He emphasized that the psychotherapy group, like any group, is a social system that develops in stages with related interactional tasks. In the first developmental stage, *engagement*, the group members' task is to engage in therapy and in the relationships with the other members of the group. This is a time to carefully share thoughts and feelings with others and to develop an awareness of and appreciation that the group members have important issues in common to work on. The first stage of therapy tends to establish a sense of togetherness in the group. As this occurs, the leader's role is critical to the viability of the group, instilling a sense of hope and serving as the architect for change. The *differentiation* stage is the second phase, and during it group members more easily feel their own distinctness in the group. Group members' heightened experience of themselves as individuals—separate from one another and from the group leader—during this phase renders the group more susceptible to conflict. Thus, integration of the diversity within the group must be acknowledged and balanced with the group's need for structure and norms for relating within the group. In the third developmental stage, *individuation*, the group shifts its focus from interpersonal differentiation and conflict to each member's issues. This shift in the group's attention contributes to strengthened cohesion in the group, resulting in mutual responsibility, active participation, warmth, empathy, and trust between group members. In later stages of the group's development, interpersonal themes are more flexibly interwoven into the work of the group; hence, subsequent stages are less distinct as the group members often discuss topics introduced in earlier stages in more sophisticated ways. The *termination* stage is a time for mourning the loss of the group and for reorienting toward the outside world.

MOVING THROUGH STAGES OF GROUP DEVELOPMENT

Group development models tend to share similar conceptions of what constitutes a more developed state. Bushe and Coetzer (2007) described four common themes identified in mature groups: (a) a greater awareness of itself—the group can talk to itself about itself; (b) a shift from emotional, reactive behaviors to rational, goal-directed behaviors; (c) an improved ability to actualize its potential; and (d) a greater sense of identity and a greater openness to changing that identity.

Although there is general agreement that groups develop progressively over time, the field of psychology lacks a consensus regarding the precise nature of how groups develop. Gersick (1988) suggested that groups develop through short periods of instability with dramatic change in the context of long periods of minimal change, that is, by punctuated equilibrium, similar to models describing biological evolution. Other authors (e.g., Wheelan & Kaeser, 1997) have similarly rejected the notion of smooth developmental progress through a series of stages, emphasizing how groups become absorbed in the same issues, only temporarily resolving them before cycling back to address them again. Perhaps these different perspectives are complementary given that specific characteristics of group processes—such as cohesion and relatedness—may progress linearly (MacKenzie, 1994), whereas other characteristics, such as conflict and resolution, may cycle back and forth (American Group Psychotherapy Association, Science to Service Task Force, 2007; Worchel, 1994).

As a consequence of these conflicting viewpoints, group development is understood as a complex interplay of different characteristics of the group—such as cohesion, conflict, engagement, and avoidance—each changing in specific ways. According to MacKenzie's (1997) group development model, engagement in a therapy group is initially expected to be high (engagement stage), but then drop after a few weeks (because of conflict in the differentiation stage), before rising throughout treatment (individuation stage and later). Conflict is expected to chart a course from an initial low level (engagement stage), followed by a rise after a few weeks (differentiation stage), and then decreasing throughout the remainder of treatment. MacKenzie did not view engagement and conflict as necessarily being linked negatively with each other, suggesting that the group may be simultaneously engaged and in conflict. However, in terms of developmental stages, the dimensions are expected to develop in opposite directions. Avoidance is initially expected to be high, diminishing over the course of treatment. Nevertheless, increasing levels of anxiety as group conflict emerges are expected to lead to group avoidance in the differentiation stage. The impending termination is also expected to increase group avoidance in the termination stage; otherwise, group avoidance is generally expected to decrease, but with fluctuations throughout the course of treatment.

Not all groups achieve mature stages of development that reflect optimal functioning. For some groups, various factors may impede or reverse progress in their developmental path; such factors are generally referred to as *antigroup forces*. According to Nitsun (1996), common antigroup forces include fear of merging, fear of losing one's independence, fear of the loss of one's fantasy of specialness, and fear of rejection. As a consequence, participants may act out their anxieties about group membership with the use of distancing behaviors, devaluing the group rather than risk being rejected, controlled, or engulfed by it (Yalom & Leszcz, 2005). Bion (1961) outlined antigroup forces that can undermine the functioning group: *dependence*—relying on an idealized leader or member; *fight–flight*—attacking or fleeing from challenges; and *pairing*—two idealized members pairing off while the others passively watch and wait for them to produce something of value in the future, while no work is being done in the present. Antigroup forces may affect the group at many levels of the group system: individual, subgroup, or the group as a whole. For example, individuals' rejection sensitivity may be shared among group members to produce a stilted group atmosphere. At the group-as-a-whole level, the group may enact antigroup forces through the projection of disavowed fears onto an individual (or subgroup), as in the scapegoating phenomenon, which involves disowned or unwanted aspects of the self or the group (Nitsun, 1996). Although antigroup forces can have destructive qualities, they also create the potential for growth and transformation, in that the group may develop confidence as a secure system that can contain and overcome challenges to its viability (Nitsun, 1996).

RESEARCH RELATED TO GROUP DEVELOPMENT

A growing body of research in the group therapy literature has given new perspective to the various issues related to group development. The most comprehensive review of much of this work can be found in Brabender and Fallon's (2009) book, with summaries of more recent studies appearing in Kivlighan and Kivlighan's (2013) and Bakali, Wilberg, Klungsøyr, and Lorentzen's (2013) article. In this chapter, we provide a selective review that focus on three areas characterizing much of the research on group development in therapy groups: (a) stage changes in group development, (b) factors that are related to group development, and (c) the association between group development and treatment outcome.

Stages

The earliest and most typical investigations of group development focused on examining changes in group development over time. Several reviews support the existence of stages of group development in therapy groups (Brabender, 2010; Brabender & Fallon, 2009; Wheelan, 1997), although a consensus regarding how the stages unfold remains elusive. Much of the research on stage changes is oriented around MacKenzie's model of group development and uses his Group Climate Questionnaire (MacKenzie, 1983). Bakali et al. (2013) succinctly summarized this work, characterizing the early group atmosphere as avoidant of therapeutic tasks and relatively free of within-group conflicts, with avoidance decreasing and conflict increasing as the group progresses (Joyce, Azim, & Morin, 1988; Kivlighan & Goldfine, 1991; MacKenzie, 1983, 1997). Study findings diverge in regard to whether engagement starts out relatively low (Tasca, Balfour, Ritchie, & Bissada, 2006) or high (Kivlighan & Goldfine, 1991) and whether it has an increasing (Joyce et al., 1988) or decreasing trend (MacKenzie, 1983) toward the next stage. Consistent patterns across time have been difficult to identify. For instance, Kivlighan and Goldfine (1991) found that the third stage was characterized by high cohesiveness combined with low conflict and avoidance, as predicted by MacKenzie's theory. However, some studies have reported high levels of conflict during later stages of group development (Brossart, Patton, & Wood, 1998), whereas others (e.g., Restek-Petrović et al., 2016) have failed to find clear indicators of developmental phases. These studies challenge the presumption of a uniform pattern of development that is valid for all groups. Indeed, as Bakali and colleagues pointed out, there has been criticism of group developmental research for its overemphasis on discovering a specific sequence of development that is applicable to most groups when instead the particular sequence of phases for any one group appears to depend more on environmental, structural, and personality factors that influence inter-member behavior.

Influencing Factors

Recognizing that myriad factors shape the unique developmental paths of each therapy group, researchers have investigated different variables that may underlie the diverging patterns of group development noted above; for example, a handful of studies have examined theoretical orientation of treatment as an influencing factor. Tasca et al. (2006) observed different developmental patterns of group climate in psychodynamic-oriented groups compared to cognitive behavioral groups for binge eating disorder. In observations of group engagement in this study, the psychodynamic groups showed a developmental pattern similar to what would be expected on the basis of MacKenzie's (1997) model, whereas the cognitive behavioral groups demonstrated a linear increase in engagement over time, contrasting starkly with the expected development. Another study that compared the development of group climate in cognitive behavioral therapy versus interpersonal group therapy for people with social phobia reported opposite patterns of engagement in the two types of therapy, neither of which corresponded to the pattern as predicted by MacKenzie's model (Bonsaksen, Lerdal, Borge, Sexton, & Hoffart, 2011). In a recent study that explored the development of group climate in two brief group therapies, cognitive behavioral group therapy and interpersonally oriented group psychotherapy for people with social anxiety disorder, the authors reported a general trend of increasing engagement, decreasing avoidance, and overall low conflict that did not significantly differ between the two treatments (Thorgeirsdottir, Bjornsson, & Arnkelsson, 2015). The authors did not find support for MacKenzie's four-stage developmental model, instead indicating that the groups remained in the engagement stage because of their brevity.

Most models of group development do not specify how the length of group therapy influences the progress of stages; thus, whether short-term groups move through developmental sequences differently from long-term groups remains unclear (Bakali et al., 2013). The few studies that have attempted to investigate this issue have produced inconsistent results. Joyce and colleagues (1988) reported a significantly stronger increase in engagement and decrease in conflict during an eight-session brief group psychotherapy compared with the patterns observed in the first eight sessions of long-term groups. Another study found that the levels of avoidance and conflict were lower in short-term groups than in the first 26 sessions of long-term groups (Kanas, Stewart, Deri, Ketter, & Haney, 1989). A recent study compared group climate development in short- (20 sessions) and long-term (80 sessions) group psychotherapy for outpatients with mixed diagnoses (Bakali et al., 2013). The authors found no appreciable difference between the two formats early in treatment, but avoidance and conflict decreased in the short-term treatment while increasing in the long-term treatment between Sessions 10 and 18. However, when sessions were divided into early, middle, and late stages of therapy a similar trend emerged: Engagement increased, and conflict and avoidance followed a low-high-low pattern. The authors interpreted their findings as reflecting an accelerated progress of development within short-term groups and a delayed but strengthened process in long-term groups.

Clinicians have long been aware that the interpersonal fit among group members can have an important effect on the developmental processes of the group (Yalom & Leszcz, 2005), and researchers have recently begun to examine this issue. The findings from a series of studies conducted by Paquin and her colleagues (Paquin & Kivlighan, 2016; Paquin, Kivlighan, & Drogosz, 2013; Paquin, Miles, & Kivlighan, 2011) have indicated that a group member who does not "match" her or his group in terms of in-session behaviors or perceptions of the group's climate (or both) may be at risk for poor attendance or early dropout. For example, the authors found that, when compared with the group as a whole, if a member was engaging in more or less intimate behaviors than the other group members during a session (signifying her as an outlier), that person was more likely to be absent from the next group session (Paquin et al., 2011). As Paquin (2017) described, it was not only the individual's behavior that was predictive of absence; it was the individual's behavior in the context of the whole group's behavior that mattered. A more recent study by Paquin and Kivlighan (2016) examined the relationship between group member absence and perceptions of the group climate by attending members, during earlier and later sessions in a group's development.

The authors reported that the group responded to absences during early sessions with higher levels of engagement and lower levels of avoidance (i.e., a more productive group atmosphere), whereas absences during later sessions related to the group demonstrating lower levels of engagement and higher levels of avoidance. As Paquin and Kivlighan suggested, the findings imply that absences may have a different impact depending on the point at which in a group's development they occur. It appears that for group members attending early sessions, the absence of other members may stimulate an increased sense of cohesion among those in attendance, yet during later sessions absences may have an eroding effect on cohesion for others in the group (Paquin & Kivlighan, 2016).

Outcome

Clinicians ultimately want to know whether a group's developmental processes have an impact on group members' outcomes. On the basis of their review of the literature regarding this issue, Brabender and Fallon (2009) concluded that the existing evidence falls short of unequivocally demonstrating that a specific developmental sequence influences group members' outcome. However, some findings have emerged to suggest that certain aspects of the group development process may contribute to positive outcomes. For example, Castonguay, Pincus, Agras, and Hines (1998) found that people's experiences of positive affect in the beginning of a cognitive behavioral therapy group and the perception of a negative group climate in the middle of treatment predicted favorable treatment response. Similar observations have been reported in other studies (Bonsaksen, Borge, & Hoffart, 2013; Bonsaksen, Lerdal, Borge, Sexton, & Hoffart, 2011), which found that higher levels of engagement in the group had a positive impact on group member outcomes.

Although most investigations of the relationship between group developmental phenomena and treatment outcome have focused on static assessments of group processes, some studies have used more sophisticated approaches to examine how changes or patterns in group processes affect outcome. For instance, Kivlighan and Lilly (1997) found that groups with a high level of cohesion and a low level of avoidance at mid-treatment had more favorable outcomes and that a low–high–low pattern of conflict across the course of treatment was associated with greater benefit. Tasca and colleagues (2006) reported that a linear increase in engagement partially mediated the relationship between attachment anxiety and outcome for people in psychodynamically oriented groups but not for those in cognitive behavioral therapy groups.

A notable study by Lo Coco and colleagues (Lo Coco, Gullo, Di Fratello, Giordano, & Kivlighan, 2016) examined how the perceptions of individual group members and other group members regarding fundamental relationship aspects (positive bonding, positive working, and negative relationships) related to group members' change in interpersonal problems. The authors reported that early positive bonding and late positive working, both for individual group members and the other members of the group, related to improved interpersonal problems. Furthermore, late positive bonding and early positive working, for both individual group members and the other members of the group, related negatively to improvement in interpersonal problems. Most significantly, Lo Coco et al. (2016) also found that an individual group member's perceptions of positive bonding related to his or her improvement in interpersonal problems only in the context of high perceptions of positive bonding by other group members. The significant interaction suggests that other group members' perceptions have a synergistic effect on the individual member's perceptions. These findings are similar to those of Lo Coco, Gullo, and Kivlighan (2012) and Paquin et al. (2013), which indicated that when individual members agreed with others in the group that relationships were positive, the individual members had better outcomes. As Lo Coco and colleagues (2016) suggested, perceptual "fit with the group" (agreement in perceptions) appears to be related to better group outcomes across types of groups and group settings.

UNRESOLVED ISSUES IN GROUP DEVELOPMENT RESEARCH

Although research has advanced our understanding of group development in the past several decades, several important issues still need addressing. Many of these issues have been carefully summarized and discussed by Kivlighan and Kivlighan (2013), Johnson (2013), and Brabender (2010). For example, Brabender concluded that little is known about how factors such as session length, treatment duration, group size, and group composition affect group development. Regarding composition, the work of Burlingame and colleagues (Burlingame, Cox, Davies, Layne, & Gleave, 2011) may provide some impetus for researchers to consider how member selection affects group development. Through their work in developing the Group Selection Questionnaire (GSQ), Burlingame et al. reported that individuals who described themselves as less interpersonally open endorsed group-generated insight as less helpful and showed less improvement than those with an open, participatory style. However, individuals who initially reported a nonparticipatory style at intake ended up reporting cohesion as more helpful than those with a more open, participatory style; this finding emerged only in latter stages of group treatment. As Burlingame and colleagues speculated, these findings suggest that people with less experience and skill in interpersonal settings eventually find greater appreciation for group processes such as cohesion when they have been sufficiently exposed to its effects. These intriguing findings certainly give cause for further investigations into group member selection and its influence on group development. For example, do individuals who are identified as potentially poor group candidates respond to interventions designed to improve their capacity to contribute to—and benefit from—positive group developmental processes?

Regarding the possible positive impact of such pregroup interventions, Wheelan (1997) argued that in order to actively promote favorable group development, group members need the knowledge and skills necessary to be effective group participants. She argued that this could occur in a pregroup preparation session held before the start of group therapy, providing potential group participants with the opportunity to discuss their goals and expectations, and establishing group guidelines. The positive influence of pregroup sessions might be enhanced if leaders provide education about group development, including both the leader and member roles in facilitating group development and how it relates to achieving goals. Then, together, the leader and the members could facilitate positive group processes that are likely to contribute to achieving both group and individual goals. Although pregroup preparation has been advocated in the group therapy literature (Ogrodniczuk, Joyce, & Piper, 2005) and is frequently used and studied in industry settings (Wheelan, 1997), researchers in the group therapy field have not yet investigated the potential impact of pregroup preparation on group development.

In addition to the influence of group members' characteristics and preparedness, group leaders almost certainly play a role in the developmental processes of the group (for a thorough review of leadership in groups research, see Chapter 7, this volume). Many authors (e.g., Brabender & Fallon, 2009; Johnson, 2013; MacKenzie, 1997; Paquin, 2017) have offered guidelines for group therapists that are believed to facilitate favorable developmental processes in groups, on the basis of the premise that members are likely to benefit from group participation to the extent that the therapist can assist the group in moving through these processes. However, such guidelines are based largely on the authors' clinical experiences, as research on the effect of leader behaviors on group developmental processes is virtually nonexistent. As such, many questions regarding leader behaviors remain unexplored. For example, Moffett, Kharrazi, and Vaught (2016) discussed the potential implications of leader behavior on group processes in the specific context of novice group leaders and coleaders of group therapy. They argued that novice therapists often struggle with understanding the kind of norms and resulting social climate that would be optimal for a particular group. Without fully appreciating beneficial group norms, including leader behaviors, a novice group therapist risks floundering when faced with the need to establish positive developmental processes for a given group. When uncertain, a group leader may impose expectations and resultant processes on the group to moderate his or her own anxieties rather than facilitating processes that are optimal for the group's developmental trajectory. Equally important, cotherapists may have conflicting beliefs about the types of group processes that are most suitable for a given group. As a consequence, they can behave in ways that reinforce contradictory norms, thereby potentially confusing the group members and delaying the development of a cohesive group atmosphere. On the basis of the equivocal findings generated by investigations with nontherapy groups, some authors have cautioned about the limited return of research inquiring about the effect of leader behaviors on group development (Wheelan, 1997). However, we believe that the circumstances of group therapy are sufficiently different to merit study on this topic.

In regard to group leader behaviors, Paquin and Kivlighan (2016) discussed the need to investigate what the therapist should do when a member or members of the group are absent, a void in the literature that they refer to as a "black hole" (p. 522). Although research indicates that absences can be disruptive for the group, many questions regarding the impact of such absences on group processes remain, including what role the therapist plays. Does the group leader address the absence in the group and, if so, how? How does the process of addressing an absence influence the developmental processes of the group? Are there specific group processes, either facilitated by the leader or by the other group members that minimize the occurrence of absences? Given the ubiquity of absences in group therapy, investigations of such issues would certainly have broad relevance.

IMPLICATIONS OF GROUP DEVELOPMENT FOR NONTHERAPY GROUPS

To the extent that the phase of development influences the work a group can do, and to the extent that managing the factors that shape a group's development potentiates its productivity, knowledge about group development dynamics is important for leaders who work with a variety of groups outside of treatment settings.

The work of Paquin and her colleagues regarding person–group fit, as *fit* relates to the extent to which a person feels that he fits into a group, is relevant to consider for nontherapy groups, such as task groups. From a group developmental perspective, groups formed to accomplish specific tasks in relatively short time frames may not have to grapple with membership and fit issues that are typically addressed in the forming or engagement phase of a group if members can accomplish the task without needing to feel a part of the group. It is likely that the clearer and more accepted the task is, and the less negotiation that is required to clarify members' roles and the power relations in the group, the less likely it becomes that a person's sense of fit with the group is relevant to group performance. When groups exist for longer periods of time; where there is more uncertainty regarding roles; and where they have to deal with conceptual, creative, or less clearly defined tasks, the developmental phase of membership is more likely to require consideration of participants' sense of belonging and fit with the group. In this case, the extent to which members feel they fit with the group and come to psychologically join the group becomes more important. Future research on task groups could thus consider not only the relevance of person–group fit for task group performance but also factors, such as time frame, goal clarity, and member roles, that may mediate the possible impact of person–group fit on task group outcomes.

Paquin's (e.g., Paquin et al., 2013) work on person–group fit also highlights the importance of considering individual group member's perceptions of the group in the context of how others in the group perceive it. It is generally regarded that group members "being on the same page" is conducive to cohesion and goal accomplishment, and thus it is reasonable to presume that a mismatch between a member and the rest of her group could interfere with group development. The following example, provided by Kivlighan and Kivlighan (2013), illustrates the relevance of considering the group context. Imagine two groups. In one group, Bob rates engagement on MacKenzie's (1983) Group Climate Questionnaire as 4.5 (out of 7) and the aggregated engagement ratings of the other group members is 4.4. In the other group, Sally rates engagement as 4.5, but the rest of the group rates it as 6.8. Although Bob and Sally rate engagement exactly the same, their ratings have different meanings considering how others in each of their groups perceived engagement. Future research with task groups could investigate whether "fit" contextualized on the basis of other members' perceptions of the group environment affects performance and goal achievement.

The issue of person–group fit naturally brings up the topic of group composition and the potential relevance of the work of Burlingame and colleagues regarding group member selection. Their GSQ (Burlingame et al., 2011) considers three fundamental factors that are believed to influence a person's sense of belonging to, engagement with, and contribution to a group: Expectancy, Participation, and Domineering. *Expectancy* reflects a person's expectations about the benefits of joining a group (e.g., "I think that working in a group will really help me"). *Participation* represent the person's willingness to participate and level of comfort in groups (e.g., "I like to share my feelings with others"). Finally, *Domineering* reflects the extent to which a person engages in behaviors such as dominating, competing, and inappropriate disclosing (e.g., "I argue for argument's sake" and "I am the life of a party"). Although the GSQ was developed specifically for the purpose of selecting people for therapy groups, one can imagine that, with slight modification, it could be used for selecting participants for other types of groups, such as task groups. For example, a potential task group member whose GSQ scores reflect low expectations for benefiting from being in the group, an unwillingness to participate in the group, and challenging/difficult behavioral tendencies is unlikely to contribute positively to task group goals. Consideration of the use of the GSQ when composing task groups fits with the long history of research on compositional factors and group performance in the field of organizational psychology. For example, Harrison and colleagues (Harrison & Klein, 2007; Harrison, Price, Gavin, & Florey, 2002) have examined whether compositional effects change over the life of task groups and, building from this work, it would be interesting to consider how such changes themselves are affected by the use of a selection tool to compose different types of groups (e.g., ad hoc and continuing groups).

Understanding the behaviors of individual group members and of the group as a whole in the context of a group's phase of development provides an important perspective for leaders. When behaviors are understood through a group development lens, leaders can encourage the group to focus on developmentally appropriate tasks instead of focusing the group on tasks or issues that it is not yet ready or able to address. Group leaders can address the various factors that facilitate or restrain developmental progress, thereby creating the context for effective and efficient group functioning. For example, early developmental phases of a group often focus on clarifying norms, structure, and roles, which undoubtedly includes attention to issues of trust among group members. In task groups, trust issues may be approached in more covert ways (e.g., joking, teasing, or testing) rather than more overtly, as in therapy groups. Thus, leaders of task groups not only need to be mindful of facilitating behaviors that align with the developmental phase of the group (e.g., helping group members clarify the purpose of the group, expected roles of members, and norms for engagement before focusing on the work of the group), but they should also be attentive to how group members negotiate the developmental tasks of the different group phases (e.g., does Henry's comment about "just following what Amanda does" reflect the group's impression of Amanda being the de facto group leader, or a lack of clarity about what the other members can contribute to the group?).

The concept of antigroup phenomena (Nitsun, 1996, 2011), described earlier in this chapter, may also be usefully translated to nontherapy work groups. Antigroup phenomena—such as rivalry, envy, lack of commitment, weak leadership, and fear of being exposed or attacked—encapsulate negative and disruptive aspects of a group that potentially undermine its goal or task. For example, rivalry may play out in a group of young, highly ambitious software developers, programmers, and graphic artists who are part of a project group tasked with designing a new video game. In such a group, rivalry may be expressed between the programmers, who perceive their role as critical to the success of the new game, and the graphic artists, who believe that their work with the visuals of the game will make or break its success. For much of the project, the rivalry may be containable, but as time goes on, and without a strong leader to harmonize the members' collective efforts, it becomes fiercer and nastier, contributing to the ultimate failure of the group (see Nitsun, 1996, 2011, for excellent examples of antigroup forces). These phenomena refer to a process rather than a concrete entity, and they vary from group to group; in some groups it hardly exists, whereas in others the whole group is suffused with negativity. Antigroup phenomena play out at several levels—individual, subgroup, and group as a whole. Recognizing antigroup forces is necessary in order to contain negativism and potential destructiveness and to open the way for constructive group relationships. As leaders contemplate the developmental phase and tasks of the group, an awareness of the potential for anxieties related to group membership may help mitigate the emergence of destructive forces that are likely not exclusive to therapeutic groups. Group leaders in organizational contexts might introduce the idea to members that groups present unique opportunities for the evocation of common concerns surrounding group-based work. Identifying and normalizing anxieties pertaining to autonomy, uniqueness, belongingness, and dependence—themes that frequently emerge in therapy groups—may help members of organizational groups feel more open to contemplating such feelings in themselves and within the group at large. Group members may thus be enlisted to collectively watch for behaviors, such as losing task focus, that at a group level may reflect the enactment of antigroup anxieties. Empirical research concerning antigroup phenomena could benefit group work in both therapeutic and organizational contexts, potentially clarifying strategies that group leaders could use to reduce the impact of forces that threaten optimal group development.

CONCLUSION

As Yalom and Leszcz (2005) argued, there are advantages to group leaders possessing at least some broad schema of group development sequences as it enables them to "chart the voyage" (p. 323) of the group and be tuned in to its ebbs and flows, yet they caution that group development models are essentially heuristic constructs that "exist for the group leaders' semantic and conceptual convenience" (p. 320) and should not be taken as concrete templates for the unfolding of group processes. Approaching group development models in too literal a manner risks minimizing the realness and authenticity of how people interact in groups.

SELECTED READINGS

Agazarian, Y., & Gantt, S. (2003). Phases of group development: Systems-centered hypotheses and their implications for research and practice. *Group Dynamics, 7,* 238–252.

This article conceptualizes phases of group development using Agazarian and Gantt's theory of living human systems and discusses four models that build the bridges from the theoretical understanding of phases of system development to being able to research the assumption that systems do indeed develop through predictable phases. These models provide a way of organizing and collecting research data so that the systems-centered hypothesis about phase development and group dynamics can be tested.

Brabender, V., & Fallon, A. (2009). *Group development in practice: Guidance for clinicians and researchers on stages and dynamics of change.* Washington, DC: American Psychological Association.

This book is the most comprehensive volume available that is specifically dedicated to the topic of group development, integrating theory, research, and clinical examples. It is an essential resource for anyone interested in learning about group development.

Kivlighan, D. M., Jr., & Kivlighan, D. M., III (2013). Group climate research: Where do we go from here? *International Journal of Group Psychotherapy, 63,* 419–431.

This commentary not only provides thoughtful discussion of specific empirical investigations of group development by Bakali et al. (2013) and Bonsaksen et al. (2013) but also considers several important issues that are sure to shape the evolution of group development research in years to come. These issues include the implementation of new statistical techniques that describe patterns in how group climate changes across time, and the use of the actor–partner interdependence model as a way to account for multiple perspectives and influences in a group.

Yalom, I. D., & Leszcz, M. (2005). *The theory and practice of group psychotherapy* (5th ed.). New York, NY: Basic Books.

This quintessential book in the field of group therapy considers various issues related to group development from an applied perspective. The authors, who are abundantly pragmatic and skillful writers, provide a compelling discussion of developmental processes in group therapy, informed by decades of clinical experience.

REFERENCES

Agazarian, Y., & Gantt, S. (2003). Phases of group development: Systems-centered hypotheses and their implications for research and practice. *Group Dynamics, 7*, 238–252. http://dx.doi.org/10.1037/1089-2699.7.3.238

American Group Psychotherapy Association, Science to Service Task Force. (2007). *Practice guidelines for group psychotherapy*. Retrieved from http://www.agpa.org/home/practice-resources/practice-guidelines-for-group-psychotherapy

Arrow, H., Poole, M. S., Henry, K. B., Wheelan, S., & Moreland, R. (2004). Time, change, and development: The temporal perspective on groups. *Small Group Research, 35*, 73–105. http://dx.doi.org/10.1177/1046496403259757

Bakali, J. V., Wilberg, T., Klungsøyr, O., & Lorentzen, S. (2013). Development of group climate in short- and long-term psychodynamic group psychotherapy. *International Journal of Group Psychotherapy, 63*, 366–393. http://dx.doi.org/10.1521/ijgp.2013.63.3.366

Beck, A. (1974). Phases in the development of structure in therapy and encounter groups. In D. Wexler & Rice (Eds.), *Innovations in client-centered therapy* (pp. 421–463). New York, NY: Wiley.

Bennis, W. G., & Shepard, H. A. (1956). A theory of group development. *Human Relations, 9*, 415–437. http://dx.doi.org/10.1177/001872675600900403

Bion, W. R. (1961). *Experiences in groups*. New York, NY: Basic Books.

Bonsaksen, T., Borge, F. M., & Hoffart, A. (2013). Group climate as predictor of short- and long-term outcome in group therapy for social phobia. *International Journal of Group Psychotherapy, 63*, 394–417. http://dx.doi.org/10.1521/ijgp.2013.63.3.394

Bonsaksen, T., Lerdal, A., Borge, F. M., Sexton, H., & Hoffart, A. (2011). Group climate development in cognitive and interpersonal group therapy for social phobia. *Group Dynamics, 15*, 32–48. http://dx.doi.org/10.1037/a0020257

Brabender, V. (2010). Group development. In R. K. Conyne (Ed.), *The Oxford handbook of group counseling* (pp. 182–204). New York, NY: Oxford University Press.

Brabender, V., & Fallon, A. (2009). *Group development in practice: Guidance for clinicians and researchers on stages and dynamics of change*. Washington, DC: American Psychological Association. http://dx.doi.org/10.1037/11858-000

Brossart, D. F., Patton, M. J., & Wood, P. K. (1998). Assessing group process: An illustration using Tuckerized growth curves. *Group Dynamics, 2*, 3–17. http://dx.doi.org/10.1037/1089-2699.2.1.3

Brower, A. (1996). Group development as constructed social reality revisited: The constructivism of small groups. *Families in Society, 77,* 336–344. http://dx.doi.org/10.1606/1044-3894.931

Burlingame, G. M., Cox, J. C., Davies, D. R., Layne, C. M., & Gleave, R. (2011). The Group Selection Questionnaire: Further refinements in group member selection. *Group Dynamics, 15,* 60–74. http://dx.doi.org/10.1037/a0020220

Bushe, G. R., & Coetzer, G. H. (2007). Group development and team effectiveness: Using cognitive representations to measure group development and predict task performance and group viability. *The Journal of Applied Behavioral Science, 43,* 184–212. http://dx.doi.org/10.1177/0021886306298892

Castonguay, L. G., Pincus, A. L., Agras, W. S., & Hines, C. E. (1998). The role of emotion in group cognitive-behavioral therapy for binge eating disorder: When things have to feel worse before they get better. *Psychotherapy Research, 8,* 225–238. http://dx.doi.org/10.1080/10503309812331332327

Forsyth, D. R. (2011). The nature and significance of groups. In R. K. Conyne (Ed.), *The Oxford handbook of group counseling* (pp. 19–35). New York, NY: Oxford University Press.

Gersick, C. J. G. (1988). Time and transition in work teams: Toward a new model of group development. *Academy of Management Journal, 31,* 9–41.

Harrison, D. A., & Klein, K. J. (2007). What's the difference? Diversity constructs as separation, variety, or disparity in organizations. *Academy of Management Review, 32,* 1199–1228. http://dx.doi.org/10.5465/amr.2007.26586096

Harrison, D. A., Price, K. H., Gavin, J. H., & Florey, A. T. (2002). Time, teams, and task performance: Changing effects of surface- and deep-level diversity on group functioning. *Academy of Management Journal, 45,* 1029–1045. http://dx.doi.org/10.5465/3069328

Johnson, J. E. (2013). Beware of storming: Research implications for interpreting group climate questionnaire scores over time. *International Journal of Group Psychotherapy, 63,* 433–446. http://dx.doi.org/10.1521/ijgp.2013.63.3.433

Joyce, A. S., Azim, H. F. A., & Morin, H. (1988). Brief crisis group psychotherapy versus the initial sessions of long-term group psychotherapy: An exploratory comparison. *Group, 12,* 3–19. http://dx.doi.org/10.1007/BF01419848

Kanas, N., Stewart, P., Deri, J., Ketter, T., & Haney, K. (1989). Group process in short-term outpatient therapy groups for schizophrenics. *Group, 13,* 67–73. http://dx.doi.org/10.1007/BF01586435

Kieffer, C. C. (2001). Phases of group development: A view from self psychology. *Group, 25,* 91–105. http://dx.doi.org/10.1023/A:1011076825221

Kivlighan, D. M., Jr., & Goldfine, D. C. (1991). Endorsement of therapeutic factors as a function of stage of group development and participant interpersonal attitudes. *Journal of Counseling Psychology, 38,* 150–158. http://dx.doi.org/10.1037/0022-0167.38.2.150

Kivlighan, D. M., Jr., & Kivlighan, D. M., III. (2013). Group climate research: Where do we go from here? *International Journal of Group Psychotherapy, 63,* 419–431. http://dx.doi.org/10.1521/ijgp.2013.63.3.419

Kivlighan, D. M., Jr., & Lilly, R. L. (1997). Developmental changes in group climate as they relate to therapeutic gain. *Group Dynamics, 1,* 208–221. http://dx.doi.org/10.1037/1089-2699.1.3.208

Lewis, C. M., Beck, A. P., Dugo, J. M., & Eng, A. M. (2000). The group development process analysis measures. In A. P. Beck & C. M. Lewis (Eds.), *The process of group psychotherapy: Systems for analyzing change* (pp. 221–261). Washington, DC: American Psychological Association. http://dx.doi.org/10.1037/10378-009

Lo Coco, G., Gullo, S., Di Fratello, C., Giordano, C., & Kivlighan, D. M. (2016). Group relationships in early and late sessions and improvement in interpersonal problems. *Journal of Counseling Psychology, 63,* 419–428. http://dx.doi.org/10.1037/cou0000153

Lo Coco, G., Gullo, S., & Kivlighan, D. M., Jr. (2012). Examining patients' and other group members' agreement about their alliance to the group as a whole and changes in patient symptoms using response surface analysis. *Journal of Counseling Psychology*, 59, 197–207. http://dx.doi.org/10.1037/a0027560

MacKenzie, K. R. (1983). The clinical application of a group climate measure. In R. R. Dies & K. R. MacKenzie (Eds.), *Advances in group psychotherapy: Integrating research and practice* (pp. 159–170). Madison, CT: International Universities Press.

MacKenzie, K. R. (1994). Group development. In A. Fuhriman & G. Burlingame (Eds.), *Handbook of group psychotherapy* (pp. 223–268). New York, NY: Wiley.

MacKenzie, K. R. (1997). Clinical application of group development ideas. *Group Dynamics*, 1, 275–287. http://dx.doi.org/10.1037/1089-2699.1.4.275

Moffett, L. A., Kharrazi, N., & Vaught, A. (2016). Using clinicians' ideal social climate ratings in group therapy training: Staff development, supervision, and teaching. *International Journal of Group Psychotherapy*, 66, 34–55. http://dx.doi.org/10.1080/00207284.2015.1089686

Nitsun, M. (1996). *The anti-group: Destructive forces in the group and their creative potential*. London, England: Routledge. http://dx.doi.org/10.4324/9780203424926

Nitsun, M. (2011). Uses and abuses of theory: A group analytic perspective. *European Journal of Psychotherapy & Counselling*, 13, 115–127. http://dx.doi.org/10.1080/13642537.2011.570014

Ogrodniczuk, J. S., Joyce, A. S., & Piper, W. E. (2005). Strategies for reducing patient-initiated premature termination of psychotherapy. *Harvard Review of Psychiatry*, 13, 57–70. http://dx.doi.org/10.1080/10673220590956429

Paquin, J. D. (2017). Delivering the treatment so that the therapy occurs: Enhancing the effectiveness of time-limited, manualized group treatments. *International Journal of Group Psychotherapy*, 67(Suppl. 1), S141–S153.

Paquin, J. D., & Kivlighan, D. M., Jr. (2016). All absences are not the same: What happens to the group climate when someone is absent from group? *International Journal of Group Psychotherapy*, 66, 506–525. http://dx.doi.org/10.1080/00207284.2016.1176490

Paquin, J. D., Kivlighan, D. M., Jr., & Drogosz, L. M. (2013). Person–group fit, group climate, and outcomes in a sample of incarcerated women participating in trauma recovery groups. *Group Dynamics*, 17, 95–109. http://dx.doi.org/10.1037/a0032702

Paquin, J. D., Miles, J. R., & Kivlighan, D. M., Jr. (2011). Predicting group attendance using in-session behaviors. *Small Group Research*, 42, 177–198. http://dx.doi.org/10.1177/1046496410389493

Restek-Petrović, B., Gregurek, R., Petrović, R., Orešković-Krezler, N., Mihanović, M., & Ivezić, E. (2016). Characteristics of the group process in long-term psychodynamic group psychotherapy for patients with psychosis. *International Journal of Group Psychotherapy*, 66, 132–143. http://dx.doi.org/10.1080/00207284.2015.1096104

Schutz, W. C. (1958). *FIRO: A three dimensional theory of interpersonal behavior*. New York, NY: Holt, Rinehart & Winston.

Tasca, G. A., Balfour, L., Ritchie, K., & Bissada, H. (2006). Developmental changes in group climate in two types of group therapy for binge-eating disorder: A growth curve analysis. *Psychotherapy Research*, 16, 499–514. http://dx.doi.org/10.1080/10503300600593359

Thorgeirsdottir, M. T., Bjornsson, A. S., & Arnkelsson, G. B. (2015). Group climate development in brief group therapies: A comparison between cognitive-behavioral group therapy and group psychotherapy for social anxiety disorder. *Group Dynamics*, 19, 200–209. http://dx.doi.org/10.1037/gdn0000029

Tuckman, B. W. (1965). Developmental sequence in small groups. *Psychological Bulletin*, 63, 384–399. http://dx.doi.org/10.1037/h0022100

Tuckman, B. W., & Jensen, M. A. (1977). Stages of small-group development revisited. *Group & Organization Management, 2,* 419–427. http://dx.doi.org/10.1177/105960117700200404

von Bertalanffy, L. (1966). General system theory and psychology. In S. Arieti (Ed.), *American handbook of psychiatry* (Vol. III, pp. 705–720). New York, NY: Basic Books.

Wheelan, S. A. (1997). Group development and the practice of group psychotherapy. *Group Dynamics, 1,* 288–293. http://dx.doi.org/10.1037/1089-2699.1.4.288

Wheelan, S. A., & Kaeser, R. M. (1997). The influence of task type and designated leaders on developmental patterns in groups. *Small Group Research, 28,* 94–121. http://dx.doi.org/10.1177/1046496497281004

Worchel, S. (1994). You can go home again: Returning group research to the group context with an eye on developmental issues. *Small Group Research, 25,* 205–223. http://dx.doi.org/10.1177/1046496494252004

Yalom, I. D., & Leszcz, M. (2005). *The theory and practice of group psychotherapy* (5th ed.). New York, NY: Basic Books.

13

Change Processes of Interpersonal Functioning in Group Therapy

Implications for Team Functioning

Martyn Whittingham

Interpersonal theory offers considerable insight into how individuals function within specific group dynamics and how change processes can either be facilitated or blocked. In particular, examining interpersonal behavior with the interpersonal circumplex allows one to promote change in individuals participating in a team or group. This chapter explores how interpersonal theory informs therapy and sports and military teams, using the lens of interpersonal functioning in relation to larger group change processes. The specific question posed in this chapter is, how does change occur in groups and individuals, and how can this be explained by interpersonal theory? I also discuss the implications of research in group psychotherapy and interpersonal theory for team functioning and performance. However, before discussing interpersonal theory, there is a need to locate the theory within broader constructs surrounding the notion of change in individuals and groups.

PSYCHOTHERAPY AND THE VARIANCE-EXPLAINED MODEL

The general psychotherapy literature has vigorously debated which constructs are implicated in client change. Lambert and Barley's (2001) *variance explained model* looked at the percentages of total outcome variance explained by factors related to psychotherapy. It attributed the percentages accordingly, from largest to smallest: unexplained variance (factors such as statistical "noise"

http://dx.doi.org/10.1037/0000201-014
The Psychology of Groups: The Intersection of Social Psychology and Psychotherapy Research,
C. D. Parks and G. A. Tasca (Editors)

in the study and factors in the client's life that are not related to psychotherapy; 40%); client contribution (factors such as initial severity, coping style, resistance; 30%); therapy relationship (the working alliance between client and therapist;12%); treatment method (the specific theory and interventions used by the therapist; 8%); individual therapist (differences in outcomes between therapists; 7%) and other factors (3%). These proportions provide an important counternarrative to the notion that outcome can be attributed solely to a specific, empirically supported therapy. In fact, Wampold and Imel (2015), in a wide-ranging review, challenged the notion that differences between specific theoretical approaches were really meaningful. They posited that instead, factors common to all psychotherapies accounted for more change in psychotherapy than the specific techniques within a specific theory. As Norcross and Wampold (2011) stated in their review of meta-analyses, these common factors include therapist alliance, repairing alliance ruptures, therapist empathy, managing countertransference, client factors, and progress monitoring. This research, which spans more than 50 years, suggests that factors outside of the specific therapy method or techniques have a significant impact on outcomes. Furthermore, DeRubeis, Gelfand, German, Fournier, and Forand (2014) suggested that the interrelationship between these factors can affect change considerably, citing as an example how variance in client responsiveness to change combines with quality of therapy to determine outcome.

This more nuanced and interrelated description of change is more complex when we consider group therapy. In their seminal summary of the field, Burlingame, Strauss, and Joyce (2013) outlined the domains and types of change for group therapy. They described five categories related to therapeutic outcomes of group treatment: (a) client, (b) structural factors, (c) small-group processes, (d) formal change theory, and (e) the leader.

Client Factors in Group Therapy

Burlingame and colleagues described client factors in terms of considerations such as initial severity of the presenting issue as well as in terms of group-related factors. The relationship between attachment style and group treatment, as outlined elsewhere in this book (see Chapter 8, this volume) appear to affect both the process and outcome of therapy groups. For example, greater skill at mentalizing (the ability to understand one's own and others' behaviors and intentions in term of mental states) is related to better group therapy outcomes. Client interpersonal style and specific domains of interpersonal distress have also been used in a group treatment model to focus group treatment, prevent dropout, prophylactically address problems, and generate interpersonal flexibility (Whittingham, 2018). Whittingham (2018) identified specific treatment goals based on a client's placement around the interpersonal circle; that is, interpersonal treatment goals are more achievable if the clients are encouraged to shift only moderately (and not extremely) their interpersonal behaviors to a more adaptive interpersonal position. Thus, client factors can be not only related to outcome but also directly tied to treatment by means of goal attainment and process–outcome variables.

Structural Factors

Structural factors include constructs such as treatment dose (how many sessions and what length), setting for the group (hospital, college counseling center), and factors related to culture and diversity. Built into this is the concept of culture and context. For example, Cloud and Granfield (2004, 2008) have discussed the concept of the impact of marginalization on treatment. They described the concept of *recovery capital*—how factors such as unemployment, prior incarceration, monetary resources, and social networks influence one's ability to access and benefit from treatment.

Small-Group Processes

Principles of small-group process outline how therapy groups provide their own independent mechanism of change, separate from individual group process. In other words, how does being in a *group* affect individual change? This idea is one that is well validated in the scientific literature, with the field of social psychology in particular addressing how individuals are profoundly impacted by their presence in groups through constructs such as group conformity, ingroup and outgroup behavior, and ostracism, among other concepts (Forsyth, 2018). In the group therapy literature, *group cohesion*, or the sense of belonging and experienced value of the group, represents a key group process related to positive outcomes (Burlingame, McClendon, & Yang, 2018).

Formal Change Theory

Formal change theory relates to how a specific theory outlines its mechanism of change on the basis of empirical evidence. For example, what is the impact of the psychoeducational technique on a group for people with schizophrenia? This type of effectiveness or efficacy study is what much of the research literature in psychotherapy focuses on. As in individual therapy, the group therapy literature indicates that, in cases in which there is sufficient evidence, there is little to suggest that specific theoretically oriented techniques result in differential group treatment outcomes (Burlingame et al., 2016). However, as indicated, there is good evidence to indicate that specific group-related concepts, such as cohesion, are related to positive outcomes (Burlingame et al., 2018).

The Group Leader

Burlingame and colleagues (2013) indicated that the therapeutic skill set of the group leader is crucial in combining the previously described therapeutic factors. This skill set can range from treatment selection to implementation of specific group therapy techniques. However, group leadership has also been related to a wide number of process and outcome variables, such as the ability to establish and maintain the working alliance and group cohesion (see Chapter 9, this volume). Such factors are related to the functioning of all groups, albeit with considerable difference in emphasis depending on the group.

Relative Importance of Factors

Piper (1994) argued that of Burlingame et al.'s (2013) five factors, client variables are the most important. This was echoed by Lambert and Barley's (2001) variance-explained model that estimated client contribution and the therapy relationship as explaining 30% and 12% of treatment variance, respectively. Compared with the 8% attributed to differences between specific theoretical approaches to therapy, client factors explain a considerable amount of the outcome variance. The concept of evidence-based relationships (Norcross & Wampold, 2011) suggests that individual client factors (attachment style, coping, resistance, cultural factors, gender, sexuality) and therapists' responsiveness to these factors are core components of treatment. Therefore, one could argue that client variables account for the most significant amount of variance in treatment. Although many factors affect client functioning, my discussion will focus on just one factor: interpersonal functioning as explained by interpersonal theory (Horowitz & Strack, 2011).

INTERPERSONAL THEORY

As Tasca and Maxwell outline in Chapter 8 of this volume, attachment style is a key variable to understanding engagement in, and outcomes of, group therapy. Another lens through which to consider variables in client change in group is interpersonal theory. Whereas attachment style measures clients' underlying motivation, interpersonal style measures the overt behaviors (Whittingham, 2018). For example, the goal of the anxious/avoidant attachment style may be to avoid argument, dismiss the importance of relationships, and downplay emotions. The interpersonal behaviors that emanate from such an attachment style include behaving in submissive ways (Holtforth, Thomas, & Caspar, 2011), such as by being silent or outwardly agreeing to everything dominant people say.

The interpersonal circumplex model is the most used and well-validated measure of interpersonal functioning. Interpersonal theory that underlies the circumplex model dates back to the work of Stack Sullivan (1940). Later, Leary (1957) formalized interpersonal theory into a circumplex, and now interpersonal psychology has been informed by the accumulation of several thousand studies (Horowitz & Strack, 2011). The interpersonal circumplex was constructed by organizing elements of interpersonal functioning around a circle. There are two axes to the circle: (a) *agency* (sometimes referred to as *power* or *dominance*) on the vertical dimension, represented by dominance at one end and submission at the opposite end, and (b) *affiliation* (sometimes referred to as *love*) on the horizontal dimension, represented by warmth at one end and coldness/distance at the opposite end. The theory posits that agency and affiliation represent basic human drives that define how one positions oneself relative to others and how one connects with others. These two dimensions are uncorrelated, and their orthogonal relationship results in a circular representation of the constructs around a two-dimensional space (see Figure 13.1). The circle, or circumplex, may be divided into octants, with all points around the circle theoretically construed as a relative combination of the two main axes. For example, the social inhibition octant is a combination of submissiveness and coldness. As a result of this circular structure, closely linked and highly positively correlated constructs, such as submission and social inhibition appear next to each other on the circumplex. Distally related constructs such as dominance versus submission appear directly across from each other on the circumplex and are negatively correlated (see Figure 13.1). In terms of measurement, self-report and observer rating scales have been developed, at times with overall scores representing interpersonal distress and subscale scores representing each of the octants around the circle (see Alden, Wiggins, & Pincus, 1990).

The concept of *complementarity* is also key to circumplex theory. This well-researched construct suggests that each axis carries with it an invitation and a desired response. For example, dominance invites submission, and

FIGURE 13.1. The Interpersonal Circumplex

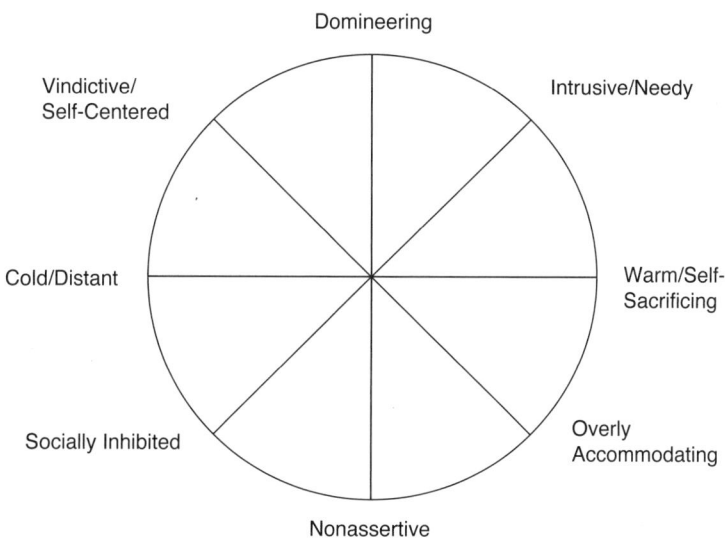

Copyright 2000 by L. M. Horowitz. Adapted with permission.

submission invites dominance. However, warmth invites more warmth, and coldness invites more coldness. In combination, these invitations invite more complex complementary responses. For example, warm submission (overly accommodating) invites its complement of warm dominance. As an example, an overly accommodating person continually makes him- or herself available as a shoulder to cry on, perhaps to avoid expected rejection. A person with a complementary style that is warm and dominant (intrusive/needy) takes advantage of this shoulder to cry on while seldom reciprocating. The overly accommodating person continues with the behavior but begins to resent it and may feel taken advantage of. However, both parties are familiar with this pattern, even if one of them is unhappy with it. The pattern of interaction is likely to continue because complementary interactions are self-reinforcing and tend to reduce anxiety. However, if the overly accommodating person in this example confronts the situation (which is highly unlikely if the style is rigid and extreme), he or she risks the relationship ending, or the pattern might change. If the relationship ends, the pattern of needing to avoid confrontation and continue to be overly accommodating is reinforced because the expected rejection has occurred; therefore, reinforcing that to change style is highly risky.

In other cases, styles can be anticomplementary (both dimensions are not complementary) or noncomplementary (one dimension is not complementary). For example, a dominant and warm invitation ("Can I help you carry that?") followed by a dominant and cold reply ("No, get away from me!") would be anticomplementary because neither invitation is reciprocated. Complementarity can be restored if one party modifies their stance, for example, if the first person replies with cold submission ("OK, then. I will leave you to it!").

CHANGE AND INTERPERSONAL THEORY

The implications of this model for psychotherapy are wide ranging. One main use of the theory has been to measure outcomes for general therapy approaches. McFarquhar, Luyten, and Fonagy's (2018) meta-analytic review of studies showed some clear, strong findings along with some degree of variability in its results. They found that most well-designed studies showed some improvement in total interpersonal distress as a result of psychotherapy. These findings translate to a range of treatment settings. Liebherz and Rabung (2014) found an impact on interpersonal distress in hospital settings, Fjeldstad, Høglend, and Lorentzen (2017) found one in short- and long-term outpatient settings, and Rotsinger-Stemen and Whittingham (2013) found one in a university counseling center. Moreover, for the studies that used subscales as a measure, treatment impact was predominately positive, with seven of nine studies finding change on all subscales. When the highest subscale scores are specifically targeted for change, as in focused brief group therapy (Whittingham, 2018), specific subscale scores were found not only to improve but also to provide a diffuse effect on other, connected subscales (Allison, 2015).

McFarquhar et al.'s (2018) findings also showed clear differences on the impact of treatment on different subscales, suggesting that treatment pathways may be different depending on one's interpersonal style. For example, Burlingame, Cox, Davies, Layne, and Gleave (2011) noted that differences in interpersonal style were related to likelihood of successful completion of group therapy. They found that clients with an aggressive interpersonal demeanor did poorly at the beginning of therapy but often improved by midpoint. Using the Inventory of Interpersonal Problems–32 (IIP-32; Horowitz, Alden, Wiggins, & Pincus, 2000), Whittingham (2018) found a similar pattern of difficulties with clients with high scores on Scales 1 (Domineering), 2 (Vindictive/Self-Centered), and 8 (Intrusive/Needy; see Figure 13.1). These clients tended to prematurely and overly self-disclose, leading to ruptures in cohesion early in the life of groups. This suggests that people with different interpersonal styles have different needs in therapy that might affect their likelihood of dropping out or their predicted final outcomes of therapy. Thus, treatment must be responsive to these interpersonal issues.

INTERACTIONS BETWEEN GROUP THERAPY FACTORS

It is important to note that Burlingame and colleagues (2013) also outlined the complexity of change that occurs when group therapy factors interact. For example, small-group processes can interact with structural group properties, such as when being in a larger group may make formation of a close connection between individual members problematic. Similarly, Dinger and Schauenburg (2010) looked at how cohesion and interpersonal style correlated in inpatient treatment and found that clients high in interpersonal distance experienced more cohesion over time but that clients too high in interpersonal warmth experienced less cohesion. These findings suggest a need to consider the process–outcome relationship in which interpersonal style may interact with key aspects of the mechanism of change like cohesion.

A group therapist might consider interaction effects that include more variables and therefore greater levels of complexity. For example, Whittingham (2018) used the technique of inoculation to prevent members with specific interpersonal subscale profiles from sabotaging their treatment. By preassessing interpersonal style and nonjudgmentally helping clients understand how they might self-sabotage (a client factor), therapists can take into account interactions among a complex host of factors, such as structural dynamics (focused brief group therapy is based on an eight-session model in which early problems can result in group dissolution), leader variables (the possibility that inexperienced leaders may not be able to effectively intervene to build cohesion), formal change theory (focused brief group therapy [Whittingham, 2018] is built on the idea of rapid movement toward insight, leading to behavioral activation), and small-group processes (the group climate is protected and cohesion maintained, thereby promoting the conditions for change to take place).

INTERPERSONAL CHANGE PROCESSES

The typical pathway to change conceptualized in interpersonal theory considers that interpersonal behaviors become personally problematic when they are rigid, extreme, or marked by duplicitous communication (e.g., passive-aggressiveness). Interpersonal behavior is also problematic when there is a distinct discrepancy between one's self-evaluation and that of others (e.g., seeing yourself as warm while others perceive you as domineering and cold) or by swinging between extremes of behavior (Kiesler, 1996). This pathway is based on the notion that people who are not well adjusted tend not to adapt well to situational demands. This has also been linked to difficulties with perceptions of others and situations. Such individuals often respond in ways that are situationally inappropriate.

Another aspect of interpersonal theory suggests that cross-situational variability also influences adjustment. Consider, for example, a highly domineering individual who becomes CEO of a company known for its competitiveness and hierarchical decision making. She cohabits with a partner who is submissive, and so the CEO may experience little distress because the two situations match well with her interpersonal style. However, if this person enters into situations in which encouragement, empathy, and compassion are required, feedback from others may indicate that all is not well, potentially leading to some felt distress.

Paulhus and Martin (1987, 1988) introduced the idea of *situational flexibility,* which posits that a key to rigidity is the inability to access behaviors to meet the needs of specific situations. Moskowitz and Zuroff (2004) updated these concepts with the notions of flux and spin. *Flux* describes the extent to which someone behaves consistently across situations, and *spin* refers to the extent to which the person's behaviors vary within the same situation. A high-flux person will behave dominantly in some situations and submissively in others, whereas a low-flux person will behave consistently (always dominant or always submissive) across situations. Similarly, a high-spin person will change strategies within the same situations (from appeasing and submissive one moment to angry and rejecting the next), and a low-spin person will use just one strategy for the duration of the situation. Moskowitz and Zuroff found both flux, in submissive behavior, and spin in general, to be positively correlated with neuroticism. High-neurotic individuals showed the greatest degree of cross-situational variability in submissiveness and the greatest degree of within-situation behavior change. This reduced ability to modulate behavior may contribute to the interpersonal problems experienced by people high in neuroticism. Erickson, Newman, and Pincus (2009) extended these ideas to the perception of other group members, arguing that there can be flux and spin in perception as well as behavior. Their study found that internal perceptions of others were more consistently related to higher distress. They recommended training in discriminative social perception (mindfulness; expansion of views; and increasing understanding of others' behaviors, motivations, and states) as a means of potentially broadening perceptions of others and thereby reducing distress. The impact of spin and flux on interpersonal functioning may well be a question of degree. To be effective in a wide range of interpersonal situations, it is important to be flexible in interaction style. However, too much spin and flux in interpersonal behaviors leads to perceptions of the self as being unstable; that is, others may perceive the individual as unpredictable, making it then harder to establish homeostatic relationships based on predictable patterns of interaction. Therefore, spin and flux are functional when the range is small, but if variation becomes too large, spin and flux can become a source of instability in intra- and interpersonal functioning.

Given that interpersonal distress is amenable to change and that many factors are implicated in interpersonal change (spin, flux, situational flexibility, rigidity), it is also possible that distress patterns may be more complex, suggesting more than one pathway to change. In other words, each individual brings with them a complex pattern of interpersonal distress based on multiple, interrelated factors. These factors may relate to the person, the situation, roles, identity, and culture, to name but a few.

THEORIES OF CHANGE AND INTERPERSONAL PSYCHOTHERAPIES

Meta-analytic findings (McFarquhar et al., 2018) indicate stronger effects on interpersonal distress for approaches that included some emotional/relational focus. Research indicates that dynamic, process-based therapies, interpersonal psychotherapy, and short-term dynamic therapies have larger effects on interpersonal distress than behavioral or cognitive approaches (McFarquhar et al., 2018). This is notable because it suggests that emotional and relational approaches to treatment may be more successful in addressing interpersonal problems.

Although research suggests a larger overall effect for emotionally focused types of therapy on interpersonal problems, some research indicates that individuals with specific interpersonal styles may struggle with emotional closeness and cohesion in groups. For example, in a study of group therapy, Kivlighan, Li, and Gillis (2015) found that someone with a distant interpersonal style may find a cohesive group particularly difficult to experience. This is consistent with Kiesler's (1996) suggestion that change on the circumplex should be at a 90° angle on the circumplex to the starting point. For example, someone with an initial problem with being too dominant may need to change in the direction of becoming warmer rather than attempting a 180° change to become more submissive (see Figure 13.1). Perhaps an interpersonally distant or cold person finds techniques related to advice giving and active listening (90° turns on the circumplex) more appropriate than warm, empathic responses that elicit closeness (which are at 180° to the subtype). Another approach with clients of an interpersonally distant subtype may be to engage them with cognitive and behavioral approaches for general therapy, unless they are specifically attempting to work on being less distant.

TREATMENT APPROACHES

There are several individual treatment approaches that attempt to influence interpersonal distress. Interpersonal approaches developed by Benjamin (2018) and Kiesler (1996), as well as interpersonal therapy (Weissman, Markowitz, & Klerman, 2018), all use interpersonal theory to a greater or lesser degree in individual treatment. Moreover, the relationship between treatment and interpersonal theory is echoed in the field of group and attachment theory, with approaches described by Marmarosh, Markin, and Spiegel (2013) and Tasca, Balfour, Ritchie, and Bissada (2007) representing close corollaries of interpersonal theory–based approaches. Lorentzen (2014) and Whittingham (2018) have more overtly used the interpersonal circumplex in group treatments of differing length.

Focused brief group therapy (Whittingham, 2018), a brief, integrative, process-based approach, uses the interpersonal circumplex to focus treatment around a client's highest interpersonal distress on the IIP-32. The treatment requires the therapist to first understand his or her own interpersonal style so he or she can make adjustments to better meet the needs of each client. After administering the IIP-32 to the client, the group leader builds a working alliance by nonjudgmentally exploring the client's interpersonal distress while also incorporating their self-identified cultural data. From this, a strong working alliance is built that promotes attendance, task accomplishment, goal agreement, and bond. This in turn promotes greater group cohesion. Then group members are invited to read aloud their goals, based on their highest score on the interpersonal circumplex, and then to work on the goals together in the emotionally involving arena of the therapy group. Within this model group cohesion, the working alliance, client interpersonal style, group culture, leader interpersonal style, group dynamics, treatment parameters (the model was developed to work in eight sessions or less), and routine outcome measurement all inform the therapy. Research has shown strong effects at termination for all interpersonal problem subscales of the IIP-32 (Allison, 2015) and significant changes in depression, social anxiety, hostility, and overall interpersonal distress (Rotsinger-Stemen & Whittingham, 2013). Thus, the need to understand and use interpersonal theory can be seen as central to, but not the only determinant of, treatment outcomes.

In fact, outcomes were informed by a careful balancing of the group factors outlined by Burlingame and colleagues (2013). These include interpersonal style (of the clients, leader, and group dynamic), structural factors (eight-session outpatient treatment), small-group processes (interpersonal styles interacting through complementarity), formal change theory (a step-by-step guide on how to implement mechanisms of change), and the leader (interpersonal style, building the working alliance, facilitating change).

APPLYING INTERPERSONAL THEORY TO SPORTS TEAMS

Consideration of these interpersonal elements as illustrated by the circumplex model also translates into team functioning and performance. For team performance, some anecdotal accounts of successful managers describe an ability to determine which players require which type of management style to promote change. Sir Alex Ferguson, the legendary manager of the highly successful English soccer team Manchester United, is well known for his ability to adjust his interpersonal style to meet the styles of different players (Guardian staff, 2012). His method of adjusting his interpersonal style to address players' emotional needs and their resistance to change and corrective feedback are akin to the group leader's need to manage cohesion and climate while facilitating change. An effective leadership style must manage cohesion and promote change while maintaining a working alliance with players, in the same way that therapy group leaders are constantly balancing those same forces. Ferguson acknowledged that he adapted his style to manage generational cohort shifts in players' ego strengths, shifting toward a slightly softer, more encouraging style in line with his perception that players were becoming more emotionally fragile over generations. This is also in line with Burlingame et al.'s (2013) assertion that context and structural factors matter when considering how to promote change.

Understanding that soccer culture had changed (a structural factor related to cohort effects) led Ferguson to adapt his style (a leader factor) and to become more encouraging of younger players (a client factor), using principles of warmth and dominance to promote change rather than the cold dominance he had used with previous cohorts. He described in the interview that he was typically very decisive and would at times be ruthless in dealing with behaviors he deemed counter to the identity and functioning of the team.

It is also notable in the interview, however, that at times Ferguson used disqualifiers when dropping a player from the team for a game. He reported using the following phrasing to help protect players from the pain of being deselected for a game: "I'm not ever sure what they are thinking, but I tend to say 'Look, I might be making a mistake here,'—I always say that—'but I think this is the best team for today'" (Guardian staff, 2012). This is a classic interpersonal strategy of working with dominant interpersonal styles. Kiesler (1996) proposed that it would be important for therapists to initially match clients on interpersonal style, rather than simply always leading with warmth–submission or warmth with slight dominance. They then suggested moving toward anticomplementary stances as the therapy progresses as a means of challenging clients to move away from familiar patterns.

In this case, a typically dominant leader—Ferguson—flexed his interpersonal style to mitigate damage caused by disqualifying his decision ("I might be making a mistake") as a means of allowing the players to preserve their feelings of dominance and maintain their egos. Despite being famous for his strength, determination, and sometimes harsh criticism of players in private, Ferguson understood the need to flexibly soften a blow at times. His spin and flux are therefore within a smaller range, thus making him predictable to others so they can manage their behavior in relation to his, yet flexible enough to adjust to the needs of different cohorts. He could therefore move back and forth between different interpersonal styles consistent with the needs of the situation; however, he also understood the need to manage the group dynamic, and if the overall functioning of the team was jeopardized by a player's extreme behavior that strongly violated team cultural norms or excessively challenged his leadership role, he could act ruthlessly and would sometimes transfer that player to another team. Thus, the spin and flux have limits. Team members are oriented to the limits of their behavior, and the climate of the group involves both the provision of warmth as well as an understanding of limits and boundaries of acceptable behaviors. This flexibility shows an appreciation of the need to maintain the group climate and cohesion while also modifying one's own interpersonal style at times to manage the changing needs and interpersonal styles of both people, a generational cohort, and a team.

INTERPERSONAL THEORY AND MILITARY SETTINGS

For military units and teams an indicator of a successful outcome is not just the obvious performance of team tasks—for example, winning or being combat ready. More than 20 years ago, Griffith and Vaitkus (1999) reviewed the literature on cohesion and the military and found numerous studies that had explored everything regarding cohesion's link to combat readiness, responsiveness, and trauma. More recently, Jones, Campion, Keeling, and Greenberg (2018) studied the interrelationship between leadership and barriers to treatment and cohesion, suggesting that military studies are also moving further in the direction of methodological complexity as well as establishing a more complex understanding of the interrelatedness among variables. Jones et al.'s study also indicated that a significant barrier to treatment for posttraumatic stress disorder in soldiers was the fear of being perceived as weak by leaders, with the presence of group cohesion also a factor in willingness to seek help. Members of highly cohesive units reported both a desire to help colleagues who were struggling with mental health issues and comfort with approaching colleagues to request such help. Furthermore, members of cohesive units rarely reported thinking less of a colleague who was receiving mental health treatment.

This is a clear example of structural factors (the army and perceptions by soldiers of the need to show strength) interacting with leader variables (whether the leader can also be supportive) and the cohesion of the unit. What Jones et al. (2018) did not measure, but may have proved illuminating, was how interpersonal styles form the underpinning to all these variables. Interpersonal theory may have had explanatory value in understanding the soldiers' willingness to seek help and admit vulnerability: the leaders' interpersonal flexibility in providing support for treatment and the unit's group dynamic and cohesion based on their own combinations of interpersonal style. Consider, for example, a soldier with a nonassertive interpersonal style. This person is likely not going to come forward with personal or mental issues but will nonetheless demonstrate behaviors that are indicative of problems. A noncohesive unit will be unlikely to detect these clues, but a cohesive unit, which is attuned to the normal patterns of behavior among its members, will likely realize that something is not right with this person. If the unit is led by a commander who has a dominating neutral or a warm leadership style, then the person's fellow soldiers might approach the commander and encourage him or her to take action, whereas if the leader's style is dominating but cold and distant, the soldiers might instead take matters into their own hands and work directly with their suffering colleague to get help.

INTERPERSONAL THEORY AND EDUCATIONAL SETTINGS

Interpersonal theory has major implications for educational settings, ranging from elementary to higher education. Attachment style, the previously discussed flip side of interpersonal theory, has been linked to school dropout (Ramsdal, Bergvik, & Wynn, 2015). Given how important social relationships are to children and young adults, it makes sense that insecure attachment styles predict difficulty in connecting to others and developing feelings of belonging. Given that schools are often rife with cliques, and social status and social connection are such important constructs in schools and even universities, interpersonal theory is particularly relevant to these settings. Castro-Schilo, Ferrer, Hernández, and Conger (2016) also noted that attachment is a particularly important predictor of school dropout for Mexican American children. They found longitudinal links to attachment to teachers, aspirations, expectations of schools, and even cognitions regarding the use of substances. University dropout is also predicted by attachment style. Lopez, Mitchell, and Gormley (2002) found that securely attached students were more able to cope with adjustment to college life. They found that such students tended to find it easier to emotionally regulate, manage relationships, maintain a consistent self-view, and manage the transition to college. However, some researchers (Smith, Murphy, & Coats, 1999) have also found that people have a *group* attachment style; that is, people attach differently to groups than they do to individuals, and this predicts a range of outcomes, including likelihood of dropping out of college (Marmarosh, Holtz, & Schottenbauer, 2005). This suggests that there are two sets of interpersonal skills that may need to be considered when contemplating interventions to decrease dropout: (a) what interpersonal skills can be taught that promote attachment to individuals and (b) what interpersonal skills promote attachment to groups.

As can be seen from the literature, schools and universities who care about dropout rates would do well to consider how attachment styles interact with their school climates. More research on how basic interventions at school (ranging from buddy systems to social skills training) might improve interpersonal skills, foster connection, and reduce dropout is needed. More attention should also be paid to particularly vulnerable groups. For example, the way students from racial/ethnic minority groups feel connected to their schools, classmates, and teachers may well predict a wide range of negative and positive outcomes. Last, the relative importance of factors related to dropout needs more research. To quote a recent interaction this author had with a child asking to change schools due to feelings of exclusion, "If I had just *one* friend at school I would feel so different about it." For this child, the presence of one satisfying peer relationship would have been a significant protective factor. More research on the key constructs relating to dropout, and what interventions (relationship/social skills teaching, buddy systems, group therapies) might be effective in promoting school success is needed.

FUTURE DIRECTIONS

With increasing sophistication in methodology, researchers are now able to explore statistical interactions and multilevel data in increasingly complex ways. Interpersonal theory is an important construct that can provide significant explanatory value in understanding change in groups. It allows for finely grained analyses of the role of the group leader, client or team member, structural factors, and small-group processes that together can be potent in creating change or affecting performance.

Each setting must consider the ramifications of interpersonal theory for its milieu, based on relevant outcomes. For example, school dropout, team functioning, and leader effectiveness are all potential outcomes that might be considered; however, they cannot be considered in isolation. The literature makes clear that interpersonal style, although predictive of considerable variance, should be considered in combination with setting variables, group dynamics, and other external factors. It is the combination of effects that provides the most explanatory power and that should be considered in research design. Mixed-method research that uses more sophisticated analytic techniques offers the greatest opportunity for insight into what are complex, fluid combinations.

The application of these theories can be aided by the use of group assessment tools such as the IIP-32 a measure structured around the interpersonal circumplex, and the Group Questionnaire (Jensen & Burlingame, 2018), a tool used to capture group processes at the level of leader, client, and group.

These can be useful tools in process–outcome research and team performance research. The increasing use of ever-more-sophisticated statistical techniques can begin to model the combinations of variables that contribute to positive outcomes. With increasing methodological complexity and a consideration of how interpersonal style interacts with change processes, greater light can be shed on how clinical outcomes and team performance are affected by interactions of interpersonal and group structural variables. This can provide the tools for greater specificity in interventions targeted at all levels of individual, interpersonal, and group change and team performance.

REFERENCES

Alden, L. E., Wiggins, J. S., & Pincus, A. L. (1990). Construction of circumplex scales for the Inventory of Interpersonal Problems. *Journal of Personality Assessment, 55,* 521–536. http://dx.doi.org/10.1207/s15327752jpa5503&4_10

Allison, J. (2015, February). *Focused brief group therapy change scores for interpersonal subtypes: The impact of an eight session model on targeted interpersonal distress.* Presentation given at the national conference of the American Group Psychotherapy Association, San Francisco, CA.

Benjamin, L. S. (2018). *Interpersonal reconstructive therapy for anger, anxiety, and depression: It's about broken hearts, not broken brains.* Washington, DC: American Psychological Association. http://dx.doi.org/10.1037/0000090-000

Burlingame, G. M., Cox, J. C., Davies, D. R., Layne, C. M., & Gleave, R. (2011). The Group Selection Questionnaire: Further refinements in group member selection. *Group Dynamics, 15,* 60–74. http://dx.doi.org/10.1037/a0020220

Burlingame, G. M., McClendon, D. T., & Yang, C. (2018). Cohesion in group therapy: A meta-analysis. *Psychotherapy, 55,* 384–398. http://dx.doi.org/10.1037/pst0000173

Burlingame, G. M., Seebeck, J. D., Janis, R. A., Whitcomb, K. E., Barkowski, S., Rosendahl, J., & Strauss, B. (2016). Outcome differences between individual and group formats when identical and nonidentical treatments, patients, and doses are compared: A 25-year meta-analytic perspective. *Psychotherapy, 53,* 446–461. http://dx.doi.org/10.1037/pst0000090

Burlingame, G. M., Strauss, B., & Joyce, A. (2013). Change mechanisms and effectiveness of small group treatments. In M. J. Lambert (Ed.), *Bergin and Garfield's handbook of psychotherapy and behavior change* (pp. 640–689). Hoboken, NJ: Wiley.

Castro-Schilo, L., Ferrer, E., Hernández, M. M., & Conger, R. D. (2016). Developmental outcomes of school attachment among students of Mexican origin. *Journal of Research on Adolescence, 26,* 753–768. http://dx.doi.org/10.1111/jora.12223

Cloud, W., & Granfield, R. (2004). The social process of exiting addiction: A life course perspective. *Nordic Studies on Alcohol and Drugs, 44,* 185–202.

Cloud, W., & Granfield, R. (2008). Conceptualizing recovery capital: Expansion of a theoretical construct. *Substance Use & Misuse, 43,* 1971–1986. http://dx.doi.org/10.1080/10826080802289762

DeRubeis, R. J., Gelfand, L. A., German, R. E., Fournier, J. C., & Forand, N. R. (2014). Understanding processes of change: How some patients reveal more than others—and some groups of therapists less—about what matters in psychotherapy. *Psychotherapy Research, 24,* 419–428. http://dx.doi.org/10.1080/10503307.2013.838654

Dinger, U., & Schauenburg, H. (2010). Effects of individual cohesion and patient interpersonal style on outcome in psychodynamically oriented inpatient group psychotherapy. *Psychotherapy Research, 20,* 22–29. http://dx.doi.org/10.1080/10503300902855514

Erickson, T. M., Newman, M. G., & Pincus, A. L. (2009). Predicting unpredictability: Do measures of interpersonal rigidity/flexibility and distress predict intraindividual variability in social perceptions and behavior? *Journal of Personality and Social Psychology, 97*, 893–912. http://dx.doi.org/10.1037/a0016515

Fjeldstad, A., Høglend, P., & Lorentzen, S. (2017). Patterns of change in interpersonal problems during and after short-term and long-term psychodynamic group therapy: A randomized clinical trial. *Psychotherapy Research, 27*, 350–361. http://dx.doi.org/10.1080/10503307.2015.1102357

Forsyth, D. R. (2018). *Group dynamics* (7th ed.). Belmont, CA: Cengage Learning.

Griffith, J., & Vaitkus, M. (1999). Relation cohesion to stress, strain, disintegration, and performance: An organizing framework. *Military Psychology, 11*, 27–55. http://dx.doi.org/10.1207/s15327876mp1101_3

Guardian staff. (2012, December 9). Sir Alex Ferguson reveals secrets of his success to Harvard academics. *The Guardian*. Retrieved from https://www.theguardian.com/football/2012/dec/19/alex-ferguson-secrets-harvard-academics

Holtforth, M. G., Thomas, A., & Caspar, F. (2011). Interpersonal motivation. In L. M. Horowitz & S. Strack (Eds.), *Handbook of interpersonal psychology* (pp. 107–122). Hoboken, NJ: Wiley.

Horowitz, L. M., Alden, L. E., Wiggins, J. S., & Pincus, A. L. (2000). *The Inventory of Interpersonal Problems (IIP-32)*. San Antonio, TX: The Psychological Corporation.

Horowitz, L. M., & Strack, S. (Eds.). (2011). *Handbook of interpersonal psychology*. Hoboken, NJ: Wiley.

Jensen, J., & Burlingame, G. (2018). An item reduction analysis of the Group Questionnaire. *Psychotherapy, 55*, 144–150. http://dx.doi.org/10.1037/pst0000145

Jones, N., Campion, B., Keeling, M., & Greenberg, N. (2018). Cohesion, leadership, mental health stigmatisation and perceived barriers to care in UK military personnel. *Journal of Mental Health, 27*, 10–18. http://dx.doi.org/10.3109/09638237.2016.1139063

Kiesler, D. J. (1996). *Contemporary interpersonal theory and research*. New York, NY: Wiley.

Kivlighan, D. M., Jr., Li, X., & Gillis, L. (2015). Do I fit with my group? Within-member and within-group fit with the group in engaged group climate and group members feeling involved and valued. *Group Dynamics, 19*, 106–121. http://dx.doi.org/10.1037/gdn0000025

Lambert, M. J., & Barley, D. E. (2001). Research summary on the therapeutic relationship and psychotherapy outcome. *Psychotherapy, 38*, 357–361. http://dx.doi.org/10.1037/0033-3204.38.4.357

Leary, T. (1957). *Interpersonal diagnosis of personality*. New York, NY: Ronald Press.

Liebherz, S., & Rabung, S. (2014). Do patients' symptoms and interpersonal problems improve in psychotherapeutic hospital treatment in Germany? A systematic review and meta-analysis. *PLoS ONE, 9*, e105329. http://dx.doi.org/10.1371/journal.pone.0105329

Lopez, F. G., Mitchell, P., & Gormley, B. (2002). Adult attachment orientations and college student distress: Test of a mediational model. *Journal of Counseling Psychology, 49*, 460–467. http://dx.doi.org/10.1037/0022-0167.49.4.460

Lorentzen, S. (2014). *Group analytic psychotherapy: Working with affective, anxiety and personality disorders*. New York, NY: Routledge.

Marmarosh, C., Holtz, A., & Schottenbauer, M. (2005). Group cohesiveness, group-derived collective self-esteem, group-derived hope, and the well-being of group therapy members. *Group Dynamics, 9*, 32–44. http://dx.doi.org/10.1037/1089-2699.9.1.32

Marmarosh, C. L., Markin, R. D., & Spiegel, E. B. (2013). *Attachment in group psychotherapy*. Washington, DC: American Psychological Association. http://dx.doi.org/10.1037/14186-000

McFarquhar, T., Luyten, P., & Fonagy, P. (2018). Changes in interpersonal problems in the psychotherapeutic treatment of depression as measured by the Inventory of Interpersonal Problems: A systematic review and meta-analysis. *Journal of Affective Disorders, 226,* 108–123. http://dx.doi.org/10.1016/j.jad.2017.09.036

Moskowitz, D. S., & Zuroff, D. C. (2004). Flux, pulse, and spin: Dynamic additions to the personality lexicon. *Journal of Personality and Social Psychology, 86,* 880–893. http://dx.doi.org/10.1037/0022-3514.86.6.880

Norcross, J. C., & Wampold, B. E. (2011). *Evidence-based therapy relationships: Research conclusions and clinical practices.* New York, NY: Oxford University Press.

Paulhus, D. L., & Martin, C. L. (1987). The structure of personality capabilities. *Journal of Personality and Social Psychology, 52,* 354–365. http://dx.doi.org/10.1037/0022-3514.52.2.354

Paulhus, D. L., & Martin, C. L. (1988). Functional flexibility: A new conception of interpersonal flexibility. *Journal of Personality and Social Psychology, 55,* 88–101. http://dx.doi.org/10.1037/0022-3514.55.1.88

Piper, W. E. (1994). Client variables. In A. Fuhriman & G. M. Burlingame (Eds.), *Handbook of group psychotherapy: An empirical and clinical synthesis* (pp. 83–113). New York, NY: Wiley.

Ramsdal, G., Bergvik, S., & Wynn, R. (2015). Parent–child attachment, academic performance and the process of high-school dropout: A narrative review. *Attachment & Human Development, 17,* 522–545. http://dx.doi.org/10.1080/14616734.2015.1072224

Rotsinger-Stemen, S., & Whittingham, M. (2013, July–August). *Focused brief group therapy: An effectiveness study.* Poster presented at the 121st Annual Convention of the American Psychological Association, Honolulu, Hawaii.

Smith, E. R., Murphy, J., & Coats, S. (1999). Attachment to groups: Theory and management. *Journal of Personality and Social Psychology, 77,* 94–110. http://dx.doi.org/10.1037/0022-3514.77.1.94

Sullivan, H. S. (1940). *Conceptions of modern psychiatry.* New York, NY: Norton.

Tasca, G., Balfour, L., Ritchie, K., & Bissada, H. (2007). Change in attachment anxiety is associated with improved depression among women with binge eating disorder. *Psychotherapy, 44,* 423–433. http://dx.doi.org/10.1037/0033-3204.44.4.423

Wampold, B. E., & Imel, Z. E. (2015). *The great psychotherapy debate: The evidence for what makes psychotherapy work.* New York, NY: Routledge. http://dx.doi.org/10.4324/9780203582015

Weissman, M. M., Markowitz, J. C., & Klerman, G. L. (2018). *The guide to interpersonal psychotherapy* (updated and expanded ed.). New York, NY: Oxford University Press.

Whittingham, M. (2018). Innovations in group assessment: How focused brief group therapy integrates formal measures to enhance treatment preparation, process, and outcomes. *Psychotherapy, 55,* 186–190. http://dx.doi.org/10.1037/pst0000153

Afterword

Conclusions and Ways Forward for Group Psychology and Group Psychotherapy Research

Craig D. Parks and Giorgio A. Tasca

The principal aim of this book was to document common interests among researchers who study group psychology and those who study group psychotherapy. The chapter authors did excellent work, and they have provided an inspiring number of suggestions for how their areas of research can be applied effectively to other types of groups.

In reading across the chapters, we saw a few key constructs emerge— ideas that were generated independently but nonetheless echoed across a number of authors. These represent higher order themes that cut across areas of research from social and organizational contexts to group psychotherapy and may provide fruitful areas of convergence and synergies. In this conclusion to the book, we discuss these broad integrative themes, and we use them to consolidate some thinking in the groups research domain and to generate potentially prolific avenues of inquiry.

COHESION IS CRITICAL

The most commonly recurring theme across the chapters is that cohesion is a central factor in the success of all types of groups. Cohesion as a key process affecting group performance is discussed in Baumann and Deller's chapter on group composition (Chapter 3), Parks's chapter on cooperation (Chapter 4), Forsyth's chapter on group influence (Chapter 5), and Spink's chapter on influence in sports teams (Chapter 7). Similarly, Tasca and Maxwell's discussion

http://dx.doi.org/10.1037/0000201-015
The Psychology of Groups: The Intersection of Social Psychology and Psychotherapy Research,
C. D. Parks and G. A. Tasca (Editors)

of attachment theory (Chapter 8), Marmarosh and Sproul's chapter on cohesion (Chapter 9), and Whittingham's chapter on interpersonal problems (Chapter 13) show how cohesion affects the functioning of a therapy group. Digging more deeply, we see that the chapters by Baumann and Deller, by Spink, and by Marmarosh and Sproul all examine how cohesion is related to the composition of the group. These reviews suggest a complex association among composition and cohesion and performance. What is evident from these chapters is that composition of members in terms of personality and demographics has an impact on cohesion, that heterogeneity in group composition is the norm, and that leaders must take into account this heterogeneity to optimize performance of a work group, team, or therapy group.

In the chapter by Parks on cooperation, the one by Tasca and Maxwell on attachment, the chapter by Marmarosh and Sproul on cohesion, and the one by Whittingham on interpersonal style, the authors discuss how interpersonal and interactive styles relate to cohesion. Generally, an individual's interpersonal coldness, avoidance, and disengagement can have a negative impact on the group's cohesion, but this research is just scratching the surface. That is, the research may be obscuring a tipping point factor such that groups of more than a certain number of individuals with these interpersonal characteristics may be particularly susceptible to lower cohesion. As Kivlighan and Narvaez's chapter on mutual influence (Chapter 10) suggests, useful statistical modeling techniques are now available to address these research questions. The chapters by Forsyth, by Tasca and Maxwell, and by Marmarosh and Sproul each considers how cohesion and attachment to the group itself are related. The key issue here is that people can have attachment representations of groups and not just of individuals, and so individuals' interpersonal needs and reactions to a group can impact their sense of belonging and commitment to the group and, by extension, the group's performance. The research in this area is novel and preliminary but does offer a glimpse into the broader impact of attachment theory to group functioning. Although none of the authors in this book discussed military groups, it is worth noting that cohesion is a major consideration for researchers and practitioners who work with combat units (e.g., Siebold, 2011).

Identification of general principles of cohesion and group-specific aspects of cohesion is thus clearly needed and is a long-term research endeavor. We offer a few examples of potential research questions related to cohesion in groups.

Does the Range of Skill Level Impact Cohesion in the Same Way Regardless of Group Task?

Sports teams, work teams, and military teams will almost always contain some members who are outstanding, some who are very good, and some who have minimal qualification for membership in the group. Similarly, therapy groups may have some members who readily and easily respond to treatment, some for whom the impact of treatment develops more slowly, and some who struggle to benefit from the therapeutic environment. Does cohesion develop in the same way across these different forms of skill? The research on attachment styles reviewed in the chapter by Tasca and Maxwell suggests that cohesion may develop at different rates and may be experienced differently by different members. Although such research could be highly informative to researchers and practitioners, currently little research in group psychology and in group psychotherapy addresses these questions.

Is the Nature of the Group Leader's Influence on Cohesion Consistent Across Group Type?

A group leader behaves quite differently depending on the type of group. The head of a work team may perform the same tasks as the team members but with the added responsibility of personnel coordination; however, a therapy group leader is not concurrently a patient and so has a separate experience from the group members in many ways. A sports team coach quite likely played the sport at some level and thus once had the experiences that the players are currently undergoing, but a military officer may have entered the service in a leadership position having never been involved in frontline activity. Nevertheless, all leaders have an effect on cohesion among their group members. What are the common and unique aspects of how the leader promotes cohesion? Undoubtedly, certain elements are particular to the type of group: The head of a work team can serve as a rallying point and inspiration by taking on difficult and unpleasant tasks, but a football coach is not going to suit up and take a few snaps to boost the morale of the players. Yet, all leaders certainly use some techniques to promote group cohesiveness. Identifying these leadership aspects is critical to promoting well-functioning groups in different contexts.

Is Cohesion Equally Critical for Successful Group Performance Regardless of Group Type?

It may be the case that cohesion is more important for some group tasks than others. One would think that groups operating in extreme circumstances— combat units, firefighting teams, or rescue squads, for example—need strong levels of cohesion. But what about groups existing in more common everyday situations? Is cohesion equally fundamental for successful performance? The sports world provides ready examples of championship teams in which members did not get along well. The Oakland Athletics and New York Yankees baseball teams of the 1970s, the Los Angeles Lakers basketball team in the early 2000s, the Chicago Bears football team in 1986, and Brazil's 1994 World Cup soccer team are just a few examples of teams that won championships despite having some members who actively and publicly disliked each other. (In the case of the Chicago Bears, the enmity was primarily among the coaching staff.) Are these simply unusual cases that are vivid because of their rarity or might it be that cohesion is helpful but unnecessary for groups that are not confronting life-threatening situations? Alternatively, might it be that there is something unique about sports teams that renders lack of cohesion tolerable for them only?

LEADERS HAVE INTRICATE EFFECTS ON THE GROUP

This point is argued persuasively by Platow, Haslam, Reicher, Grace, and Cruwys (Chapter 6), who provide a thorough and ambitious discussion of how experimental research on leadership can inform group psychotherapy and vice versa. However, it is a point worth emphasizing because Ogrodniczuk, Cheek, and Kealy in their chapter on group development (Chapter 12), Spink in his chapter on sports teams, and Whittingham in the chapter on interpersonal style each also introduce leadership into their reviews.

A facet of leadership that we will add to the mix is *leader legitimacy*, or the extent to which the members perceive group leader to be deserving of and qualified for the position. Essential to leader legitimacy is perception of the leader as prototypical of the group. Simply put, at least in the workplace, prototypical leaders tend to be more strongly and broadly supported than leaders who do not seem similar to group members (Ullrich, Christ, & van Dick, 2009). In the psychotherapy context, patients' experience of the therapist and therapy as credible is positively related to patient outcomes (Wampold & Imel, 2015). Whether this phenomenon holds for leaders of other types of groups is an open question. Are therapy group members more likely to commit to a group if the therapist appears similar to the members or who are perceived as credible and capable? Do juries elect chairs who share interests with the greatest number of other members? What barriers exist for assigned leaders who clearly differ, at least at a surface level, from everyone else?

ATTACHMENT IS DISTINCT FROM COHESION

As with leadership, the influence of attachment style on group functioning is directly discussed in the chapters by Tasca and Maxwell, by Marmarosh and Sproul, and by Kivlighan and Narvaez. The reader's immediate reaction might be that the authors are conflating cohesion and attachment, but the two phenomena are quite different. Cohesion describes the overall tenor of relations among group members, whereas attachment addresses how individual members approach interpersonal relationships in general. Hence, these two concepts should have separable effects on group functioning, yet little research has investigated to what extent this is true and whether the two factors operate differently in different types of groups.

An excellent example of the value of such research can be found in Landen and Wang (2010), who tested the separate effects of attachment style and cohesion on the psychological well-being of firefighters, who must work as a group in dangerous and extreme situations. Landen and Wang (2010) found attachment style and cohesion within the firefighting unit to each influence unit member well-being. Furthermore, neither variable mediated the other. It is certainly possible that this pattern is unique to extreme-situation groups, but this is a testable proposition. More to the point, Landen and Wang's (2010) results indicated that there is value in testing for the separate influence of cohesion and leadership on group functioning. In the context of military groups and in therapy groups, individuals with higher attachment anxiety (e.g., need for approval) performed better in more cohesive groups, but those with greater attachment avoidance performed better in groups experiencing lower cohesion (Illing, Tasca, Balfour, & Bissada, 2011; Rom & Mikulincer, 2003). That many of our authors identified one or both of these variables as important for understanding their specific type of group underscores the need for research that examines the interactive effects of attachment and cohesion to explain group performance.

CONCLUSION

For decades, research on group dynamics has been conducted along multiple paths that run mostly parallel to each other: a work path that focuses on groups engaged in a task that will result in some single output representing the efforts of all members, an intervention path that studies groups that are vehicles of change for their members, and a performance path that investigates groups as facilitators of individual performance. Occasionally, the paths intersect, but for the most part, these knowledge bases have grown with little consideration for whether the knowledge gained might apply to groups on the other paths. Besides being an inefficient approach to understanding the "group" as a general entity, this lack of collaboration denies researchers exposure to new ways of thinking about group phenomena and new methodologies that might help them untangle especially puzzling questions in their own area of interest.

There are many such questions in the groups field; indeed, a lengthy chapter could be written on lines of research on groups that ground to a halt because of lack of progress. In the group psychology research domain, two such lines of research include (a) how to encourage members of decision-making groups to take seriously and integrate relevant information that is not already known by all group members (Sohrab, Waller, & Kaplan, 2015), and (b) under what conditions the task group environment will induce motivation gains versus losses in members (Kerr & Hertel, 2011). In the group psychotherapy domain, a number of questions could be informed by group psychology research on teams and organizations. For example, despite early promising research, little progress has been made on the selection and preparation of potential members for optimal processes and outcomes in group therapy (Piper & Perrault, 1989); leadership qualities and skills to determine effective leader behaviors (Kivlighan & Tarrant, 2001); and the effects and nature of group composition based on patient factors in the context of type of group or group focus (Piper, Ogrodniczuk, Joyce, Weideman, & Rosie, 2007; Tasca et al., 2006).

Chapters in this book highlight the potential synergies between group psychology research and group psychotherapy research, and on how research in one domain may inform research and practice in the other. Despite early acknowledgment in the field of how important it is to understand that processes occurring within a task group or social group also happen in a therapy group and vice versa, research in these two areas has diverged over the past decades to the detriment of both domains. Bridging this gap would provide important insight into the nature of group phenomena and would give valuable guidance for practitioners who research and work with groups of all forms. Important advances in both group psychology and group psychotherapy will come from cross-domain collaborations. The chapters in this book provide a blueprint to researchers and practitioners for a collaborative way forward and perhaps for a renaissance in groups research.

REFERENCES

Illing, V., Tasca, G. A., Balfour, L., & Bissada, H. (2011). Attachment dimensions and group climate growth in a sample of women seeking treatment for eating disorders. *Psychiatry: Interpersonal and Biological Processes, 74*, 255–269. http://dx.doi.org/10.1521/psyc.2011.74.3.255

Kerr, N. L., & Hertel, G. (2011). The Köhler group motivation gain: How to motivate the "weak links" in a group. *Social and Personality Psychology Compass, 5*, 43–55. http://dx.doi.org/10.1111/j.1751-9004.2010.00333.x

Kivlighan, D. M., Jr., & Tarrant, J. M. (2001). Does group climate mediate the group leadership–group member outcome relationship? A test of Yalom's hypotheses about leadership priorities. *Group Dynamics, 5*, 220–234. http://dx.doi.org/10.1037/1089-2699.5.3.220

Landen, S. M., & Wang, C.-C. D. C. (2010). Adult attachment, work cohesion, coping, and psychological well-being of firefighters. *Counselling Psychology Quarterly, 23*, 143–162. http://dx.doi.org/10.1080/09515071003776028

Piper, W. E., Ogrodniczuk, J. S., Joyce, A. S., Weideman, R., & Rosie, J. S. (2007). Group composition and group therapy for complicated grief. *Journal of Consulting and Clinical Psychology, 75*, 116–125. http://dx.doi.org/10.1037/0022-006X.75.1.116

Piper, W. E., & Perrault, E. L. (1989). Pretherapy preparation for group members. *International Journal of Group Psychotherapy, 39*, 17–34. http://dx.doi.org/10.1080/00207284.1989.11491146

Rom, E., & Mikulincer, M. (2003). Attachment theory and group processes: The association between attachment style and group-related representations, goals, memories, and functioning. *Journal of Personality and Social Psychology, 84*, 1220–1235. http://dx.doi.org/10.1037/0022-3514.84.6.1220

Siebold, G. L. (2011). Key questions and challenges to the standard model of military group cohesion. *Armed Forces and Society, 37*, 448–468. http://dx.doi.org/10.1177/0095327X11398451

Sohrab, S. G., Waller, M. J., & Kaplan, S. (2015). Exploring the hidden-profile paradigm: A literature review and analysis. *Small Group Research, 46,* 489–535. http://dx.doi.org/10.1177/1046496415599068

Tasca, G. A., Ritchie, K., Conrad, G., Balfour, L., Gayton, J., Lybanon, V., & Bissada, H. (2006). Attachment scales predict outcome in a randomized controlled trial of two group therapies for binge eating disorder: An aptitude by treatment interaction. *Psychotherapy Research, 16,* 106–121. http://dx.doi.org/10.1080/10503300500090928

Ullrich, J., Christ, O., & van Dick, R. (2009). Substitutes for procedural fairness: Prototypical leaders are endorsed whether they are fair or not. *Journal of Applied Psychology, 94,* 235–244. http://dx.doi.org/10.1037/a0012936

Wampold, B. E., & Imel, Z. E. (2015). *The great psychotherapy debate: The evidence for what makes psychotherapy work* (2nd ed.). New York, NY: Routledge. http://dx.doi.org/10.4324/9780203582015

INDEX

ABOUT THE EDITORS

Craig D. Parks, PhD, is vice provost for system innovation and policy and professor of psychology at Washington State University. He is a past president of American Psychological Association (APA) Division 49 (Society of Group Psychology and Group Psychotherapy) and former editor of *Group Dynamics: Theory, Research, and Practice*. His areas of expertise are human cooperation and group decision making, and he is particularly interested in the roles of personal traits, social comparison, and information processing in cooperative choice. Dr. Parks's research has focused specifically on trust and social value orientation, outcomes received from cooperation relative to others, and incomplete information as influences of willingness to cooperate. He has written theoretical and review articles on the role of personality traits in interpersonal cooperation and task group performance. A consistent theme of his work has been the need to integrate findings across different types of groups and across the personality, physiological, and group research domains.

Giorgio A. Tasca, PhD, is a full-time professor in the School of Psychology at the University of Ottawa, Ontario, Canada. He also holds a cross-appointment in the Department of Psychiatry. Dr. Tasca is the founder and director of the Psychotherapy Practice Research Network (https://socialsciences.uottawa.ca/pprnet/), whose mission is to bring together psychotherapists, educators, researchers, students, and policymakers for knowledge translation and practice-based research to improve psychotherapists' effectiveness and patient mental health outcomes. He is a past president of APA Division 49, a fellow of APA Division 29 (Society for the Advancement of Psychotherapy) and Division 49, and editor-in-chief of the journal *Group Dynamics: Theory, Research, and Practice*. Dr. Tasca is a visiting professor at L'Università degli studi di Bergamo (the University of Bergamo), and is the scientific director of la Scuola di Psicoterapia Integrata (the School of Integrated Psychotherapy) in Bergamo, Italy. He has published several randomized controlled trials of group psychotherapy, extensively researched processes and mechanisms of change in therapy groups, and written on the application of advanced statistical modeling for group research. Visit http://www.gtasca.ca and follow him on Twitter (@giorgiotasca).